TRUE STORIES of FALSE MEMORIES

By Eleanor Goldstein and Kevin Farmer

Upton
BOOKS

2 3 4 5 6 7 8 9 0

Library of Congress Cataloging-in-Publication Data

Goldstein, Eleanor C.
    True stories of false memories / by Eleanor Goldstein and Kevin
Farmer.
    p. cm.
    Includes bibliographical references and index.
    ISBN 0-89777-145-1 : $16.95
    1. False memory syndrome — United States — Case studies.
2. Incest victims — United States — Case studies. 3. False memory
syndrome — Patients — United States — Family relationships —
Case studies. 4. Incest victims — United States — Family
relationships — Case studies. I. Farmer, Kevin. II. Title.
RC560.I53G65 1993
616.89'14—dc20   93-29899
                                                                                   CIP

Typesetting and design by Michelle McCulloch

Printed in the United States of America

Published by:

UPTON Books
1100 Holland Drive
Boca Raton, FL 33487
(407) 994-0079 • Fax (407) 994-4704

Acknowledgments

Brothers and sisters of adult children with false memories wrote their stories in order to help others as well as themselves. It was traumatic as well as cathartic to look back in order to recapitulate what had happened to their families to bring them to the brink of disaster. We thank them for their efforts to expose the phenomenon of False Memory Syndrome.

Retractors, who suffered in abusive therapy that almost destroyed their lives, labored over writing their stories. They are heroically moving forward, but they look backward to tell their stories because they want to help expose this national mental health crisis that is running roughshod over peoples' rights and destroying lives in the name of healing.

To the mother who wrote her story. We know your suffering. You described it so well — we appreciate your sharing.

To Dr. Pamela Freyd, Director of FMS Foundation. Her endless days and long nights spent in an effort to help people has brought comfort to thousands as she helps to expose the greatest mental health issue of our times. Her goals are to document and educate and she has accomplished them. Now, people know they are not alone when falsely accused on the basis of repressed memories, and professionals and the media have become aware of False Memory Syndrome due to her efforts and the people she has mobilized around this phenomenon.

In 1992, Eleanor Goldstein and Kevin Farmer co-authored a landmark book on the topic of False Memory Syndrome entitled *Confabulations — Creating False Memories, Destroying Families.*

The book recounts the stories of 20 families, out of more than 4,000 documented cases, ravaged by this epidemic. It also includes interviews with therapists and provides analyses of the origins of the problem.

Comments on Confabulations:

... Goldstein has compiled a highly volatile book .... The book will make you think hard about the rights of the accused in family abuse situations. ...
> — Joanne Kirschner, December 1992,
> *Rapport Magazine*

Confabulations *is one of the very few sources of information available about False Memory Syndrome. ...*
Confabulations *does not deny the reality of sexual abuse. It does claim, however, that False Memory Syndrome is also real and does cause tremendous pain to families.*
Goldstein has tackled many controversial issues in her day, and has received awards from the American Library Association and from the Intellectual Freedom to Read Foundation because of her activities in supporting free access to information. ...
There are many books in the library about sex abuse—it is a major social issue today. However, libraries have an obligation to present all sides of social issues. False Memory Syndrome and false accusations are another facet of this one.

> — Marg Hardie, March 28, 1993,
> Sudbury Public Library, Ontario
> (from a review in the *Sudbury Star*)

Confabulations *chronicles the heavy price being paid by families subjected to this cruel healing process. ...*
The laments in Confabulations *are a sharp contrast to the lurid testimonials that pepper self-serving recovery books.*
> — George Paul Csicsery, October 11, 1992,
> *San Jose Mercury News*

To order *Confabulations* call (407) 994-0079. MasterCard and VISA orders accepted.

iv

Lynn Gondolf ——————

has described her therapy experiences on *Donahue, The Maury Povich Show, Tom Snyder, Night Talk with Jane Whitney* and *Hard Copy*. Magazines and newspapers — *McCall's, Insight, Mother Jones, Issues in Child Abuse Accusations, Rocky Mountain News, Arizona Republic, San Jose Mercury News* and *Toronto Star* — have written about Lynn's experiences. Her story begins on page 367.

Melody Gavigan ——————

publishes a newsletter called *The Retractor*. She has appeared on *The Oprah Winfrey Show, Front Page* and *CNN News*. Her experiences with false memories were recounted in *Psychology Today, American Health, Options, Salt Lake City Tribune* and *San Francisco Examiner*. Her story begins on page 251.

Laura Pasley ——————

was featured in articles in *Philadelphia Inquirer, Boston Globe* and *Sacramento Bee*. She appeared on *Prime Time Live*, which investigated therapists who convince clients to believe in memories which are false. She recently received a settlement as a result of a lawsuit against her therapists. Her story begins on page 347.

FMS or **False Memory Syndrome** — Refers to a condition in which the person's personality and inter-personal relationships are oriented around a memory that is objectively false but strongly believed in to the detriment of the welfare of the person and others involved in the memory.

"While our awareness of childhood sexual abuse has increased enormously in the last decade and the horrors of its consequences should never be minimized, there is another side to this situation, namely that of the consequences of false allegations where whole families are split apart and terrible pain inflicted on everyone concerned. This side of the story needs to be told, for a therapist may, with the best intentions in the world, contribute to enormous family suffering."

November, 1991, Harold Lief, M.D.
Emeritus Professor of Psychiatry,
University of Pennsylvania

For further information about FMS contact:
FMS Foundation
3401 Market Street, Suite 130
Philadelphia, PA 19104
(215) 387-1865
1-800-568-8882

Table of Contents

Introduction 1
Painful Memories, True or False? 5

STORIES OF SIBLINGS ···································· 11

Return to Sender 13
She Used to Call Me "Mai-Mai" 23
The Phone Call 29
My Last Letter to My Sister 33
Susan's Memories 47
Becoming Schizophrenic 53
An Answer for Everything 57
A Sad Reunion 63
Another Family's Tragedy 71
Unanswered Communications 77
Another Sister Lost to Therapy 83
Manipulated By New Age Therapy 87
I Want My Sister Back 93
Recovering from Accusations 107
Jana Never Calls 115
To a Brother-in-Law 129
To My Sister's Therapists 131
Dear Pastor 147

CREATING RAGE ····································· 159

Why Would They Believe Such Things
If They Weren't True? 161
The "Authorities" Emerge 169
A Social Consensus Develops 206

STORIES OF RETRACTORS ····················· 221

Memories Not Mine 223
Who Made Her God? 235

My Recovery from "Recovery" 251
Surviving "Therapy" 285
The Truth Set Me Free 333
Misplaced Trust... 347
Traumatic Therapy.. 367
Diagnosed as MPD 387
Victoria's Husband – His Perspective 407
Victoria's Daughter – "Mom, Where Are You?" 419

The Epidemic Grows 423

A MOTHER'S STORY ················· 427
A Mother's Journey with FMS 429

EMERGING FROM THE DARKNESS ··············· 481
The Parent's Dilemma 483
A Landmark Meeting................................. 490
References... 505
Suggested Readings 509
Index 513

Introduction

Visualizations and dreams, as interpreted and validated by psychotherapists, are now considered sufficient evidence for accusing people of horrendous crimes.

Many thousands of adult children are engaged in "trauma therapy," "regression therapy," or "survivor therapy" in every state of the United States, and in Canada, England, Australia, and New Zealand. In these settings, they are visualizing sexual abuse that they supposedly suffered as children. Whatever has brought them to therapy – depression, a weight problem, troubled relationships – the theory is that the underlying cause of all their problems is abuse as a child. The theory states that a person can "do the work" to recover memories of abuse, utilizing such techniques as hypnosis, body work, trance writing, guided imagery, dream interpretation, psychodrama, and visualization. The work is done under the guidance of a psychotherapist, with the support of a group. Hundreds of books are available that confirm this unscientific method of therapy.

The therapist and group validate the visualizations, no matter how far-fetched, unlikely, even impossible. No corroboration is considered necessary. These memories have been dredged up from the repressed mind, where they supposedly lay dormant for decades in a pristine form, causing all sorts of havoc in the person's life. The memories are considered true. True enough so that the adult child believes them and feels it is necessary to confront the perpetrators of the heinous crimes that have now come forth and have been validated. According to the theory, healing will take years, perhaps a lifetime. Part of the healing process is to identify and expose the perpetrator.

Thousands of parents have been confronted with outrageous claims of recently recovered abuse, including incest and satanic ritual abuse. The parent is considered to be guilty, despite lack of evidence, because why would any person make such claims if they weren't true?

Powerful mind–altering techniques have been unleashed upon an unwary public and are being used by many psychotherapists specializing in recovering memories of childhood sexual abuse. These techniques do not uncover the truth; rather they create confabulations – a mixture of fact and fantasy. In these therapy settings, a person's life script is rewritten and the parents are deemed villains, supporting the underlying theory that the American family is dysfunctional.

The knowledge that scientists have gathered about the way the memory really works is ignored. The concept of "working" to regain a memory is ludicrous. You either remember something or you don't. Everyone forgets many things. If you work to retrieve memories, they will most likely be contaminated by the very suggestion that such memories are repressed in the subconscious mind.

Beliefs that are derived from adult child psychotherapy are permeating society. The idea that it is possible to find "the truth" in therapy without the necessity for corroboration is now widely accepted. The legal arena is currently considered an appropriate place to confront parents for past abuse which is forthcoming from so-called therapeutic settings. It is considered acceptable to accuse parents without allowing them to defend themselves. The legal system is involved in this emotional issue, largely on the side of the repressed memory concept, ignoring parents' rights. Just as "believe the child" has taken hold, believe the "repressed memory" is now considered politically correct.

The time-honored concept in a democratic society of listening to all sides in an open forum is ignored in this type of therapy. The response when the accused asks for communication is, "The perpetrator will never admit guilt, so why even speak to him? He is in denial."

Therapy clients are encouraged to abandon the "family of origin" and create a "family of choice." Thousands of families are being destroyed by the hunt for perpetrators. Thousands of parents have documented their stories of having been falsely accused of horrible acts of torture against their children. All of these stories have common elements. An adult child goes to therapy and eventually comes up with repressed memories of sexual abuse. After identifying the perpetrator the protocol is to expose him or her, demand a confession and, if it is not forthcoming, to cut off all ties with that person and anyone who doesn't believe the accusations. This is the perfect way to destroy a man or a woman. If you would abuse a child you are considered by society to be demented. How can a person defend such a charge? It haunts the family forever. Imagine the humiliation a man or woman feels when confronted with such terrible false accusations. Imagine the frustration at not being able to defend oneself against repressed memories.

Painful Memories, True or False?

A woman in her early thirties wakes up in the middle of the night with uncontrollable shuddering. The next morning, friends will help pack the few remaining possessions in the house; a garage sale the previous week disposed of many non-essentials for a few hundred dollars. Her four-year-old daughter was born in the house. Her six-year-old son was two when they moved in. The house, financed with a mortgage co-signed by her father, is being repossessed. She has separated from her family after spending thousands of dollars in therapy, frequently under hypnosis, where she was convinced she had been sexually abused by her father, grandfather, uncle and countless others. The anger and terror she feels towards her parents has encouraged her to give up all contact, including financial support from them. She can no longer afford the house her parents helped her buy. Friends from her support group are providing temporary shelter. She wonders how her husband can sleep so soundly when their familiar world is being torn apart.

About the same time, this woman's father, a man in his mid-sixties awakes with a start. It takes a few minutes to orient himself. He is in a hospital, the sixth day after lung surgery. The awareness of where he is dismays him. He realizes his future is bleak. He doesn't even want to wake up. Flooding his mind are thoughts even worse than the prognosis of his illness. His daughter is gone from his life; she will no longer speak to him. His life is shattered by a series of accusations that he cannot understand. He received a letter from her claiming that he is a perpetrator of heinous crimes, that he engaged in ritual abuse; he killed babies, raped his daughter and allowed his friends and relatives to do so also. This man, a minister, now lays in pain — physical and spiritual. The physical pain he can cope with, aided by pain-killers. The spiritual pain is worse. He closes his eyes, hoping never to awaken again.

Thousands of adult children and their aging parents are being separated, turned into adversaries by a new type of psychotherapy. They are no longer there for each other to share life's experiences. The adult child is the accuser; the parent the accused. It is called "trauma therapy" or "regression therapy" or "repressed memory therapy" or "survivor therapy." In this therapy, the patient regresses to childhood to gain repressed memories. Bombarded with suggestions of sexual abuse, memories of abuse do occur. Are they real? Are they false? Are they confabulations? We have spoken to hundreds of people who are being affected by this type of therapy.

In 1992 we authored the book *Confabulations* which tells the stories of twenty families, written mostly by parents, affected by what is now recognized as False Memory Syndrome. The stories all have a striking resemblance to one another. The common factors are: 1) accusations of sexual abuse by adult children against parents, sometimes including ritual abuse, 2) all the accusations were revealed in therapy with the aid of hypnosis, body work, trance induction, workbooks, group validation, dream interpretation, and other pseudoscientific techniques, 3) all the memories had been unknown for decades, or repressed, and are called decades–delayed discoveries, 4) all the parents were cut off from normal family contacts with their accusing adult children, and 5) all the accusations are uncorroborated by facts.

We hypothesized about what was happening to these

families from their stories and our own research. We believed that false memories were being created in the minds of vulnerable adult children. We believed that aspects of the radical feminist movement, excesses in the recovery movement and elements of the New Age movement provide a milieu in which false memories can flourish.

Since the publication of *Confabulations* in 1992, we have spoken to hundreds of people on every side of the issue of adult childrens' sexual abuse claims against parents.

We've spoken to accusers, accused parents, siblings, recanters, social workers, psychiatrists, hypnotherapists, incest victims who've never forgotten the abuse, parents of incest victims, lawyers, people suing parents, parents being sued. Every day for nearly two years, this has been the focus of our work because in our opinion it is the most compelling issue we have ever encountered.

We find that an epidemic of false memories is being created in the minds of intelligent, mostly well-educated, adults by sometimes well-meaning, often highly credentialed, professionals. We find techniques of mind control, either knowingly or unwittingly being used to the detriment of thousands of families. We have learned how powerful mind-altering techniques can be used to create memories, and are being used by many so-called professionals. We have seen how lawyers, legislators and judges have come under the influence of therapists who use techniques to gather information that would never be allowed in a court of law. Yet the results of these dangerous information-gathering techniques are permeating the legal system. As a result, many innocent people are being accused of sexual abuse on the basis of repressed memories, and sometimes even sentenced to long terms and imprisoned.

We know of insurance companies paying hundreds of

thousands of dollars for treatments that are dangerous and that destroy families.

The scenario with which this introduction began is being played out in multitudinous variations as families are being torn apart by accusations of horrendous abuse emerging from therapy without any corroboration.

This epidemic is so widespread that it has become institutionalized. Hundreds of books have been written validating anecdotal stories about repressed memories. We now know what goes on in many therapists' offices and groups. Life scripts are being created and treated as truth, disregarding facts and logic. Hundreds of thousands of therapists have gone to seminars which teach pseudoscientific techniques to retrieve repressed memories. No matter how bizarre the retrieved memories may be, therapists are trained in these seminars to believe the memories and validate them. There is a network of therapists who are well-entrenched, who actively help their patients confabulate and then accept those confabulations as truth.

We know the pain suffered by the incest survivor. We have spoken to many of them who have never forgotten the episodes that profoundly affected their lives. These women, betrayed by a parent, recognizing that betrayal of trust, have suffered and they do not want us to minimize their suffering. We wholeheartedly sympathize with them.

We know the anguish of incest survivors who say they repressed their memories for decades and claim new identities sometimes with a diagnosis of Multiple Personality Disorder (MPD). They often confabulated these memories in therapy. They suffer tremendous pain as they cut off relationships with their families, in the name of healing.

We have heard the pain of siblings whose families have been torn asunder, after an adult brother or sister has made an accusation so horrible that it shatters the family. These siblings have little peace in their lives. They are crushed as they are made to choose between a sister or brother and parents.

We know the pain of the parents, who are stunned and feel they will never be happy again. Children they love and who once loved them now believe the most horrendous things about their parents. The adult children have been coached to break off all relationships with their parents, by therapists, books and groups. They sometimes have mock funerals for their parents. They teach their own children to hate and fear grandma and grandpa.

We know the pain of retractors — women who survived a therapy that teaches and preaches hate, supposedly in order to "heal" and be "saved." After years of therapy, they often had to reach bottom. Often hypnotized and drugged, these women somehow came to realize they were victims of sham therapy. They have lost years of productive living and spent tens of thousands of dollars because they trusted the wrong people.

Now we know that False Memory Syndrome is an iatrogenic disease created by therapy gone haywire. We know that false memory syndrome has reached epidemic proportions. Between April 1992 and June 1993, almost 5,000 families contacted the False Memory Syndrome Foundation to tell and document their stories.

We know that this epidemic of false memories, gone unchecked, will destroy hundreds of thousands of lives.

In this book we are publishing stories of siblings because they have a unique perspective — right in the middle of this dreadful situation, poised precariously between parents and a brother or a sister. They struggle with this issue in a most heart-rending fashion.

We also are including the stories of retractors, those women who have overcome the abuse done to them by overzealous therapy. What they went through and how they managed to return to normal lives provides enlightenment about this shocking mental health crisis.

A mother's story is included because she tells, in graphic detail, her torturous journey to find the answers to the greatest mystery ever imagined — how her beloved daughter could turn into a deluded, demented, destroyed personality.

We analyze the origin and evolution of some of the theories behind the search for repressed memories.

We report on some of the findings of world renowned experts on the mind and memory.

We know that true stories are not 100 percent accurate; but a true story reflects a person's beliefs and recollections under circumstances utilizing the normal intelligence and insight that a person possesses when not unduly influenced.

A false memory can be created as a result of hypnosis, drugs, body work or other pseudo-scientific techniques.

The stories in this book reflect the true feelings of people as they confront the phenomenon of false memories.

After reading many professional papers, speaking to hundreds of people and reading dozens of books, we feel that we now understand what is happening to create the greatest mental health issue of our times.

STORIES OF SIBLINGS

Brothers and sisters are in an impossible position. They are being asked to support the charges of sexual abuse, no matter how outrageous, against their parents.

They are tormented with the notion that their sibling is being influenced by unethical treatment. They plead with their siblings' therapists for understanding, but to no avail.

As they tell their stories the pain seeps through on every page.

They still hope for family reconciliation. They desire to protect their identity so that no further harm is done to the tenuous relationships they now have with a brother or sister; therefore, names have been changed to protect identities.

Return to Sender

My sister, Alice, is the middle child of seven girls born in seven years. We were raised Catholic and grew up on the East Coast. My father died in 1986 at the age of 51. My mother is now 55 and remarried. The seven sisters now range in age between 28 and 35.

My father valued education and encouraged us to get degrees in "marketable" areas. My parents saved enough to help pay our way through college. With their support all six of Alice's sisters graduated from college debt-free. Alice, who believed she was in school just to please our parents and didn't know what she wanted for herself, dropped out after completing three years. I think she wanted to prove she could make it her own way without having to conform to the idea that one needs a degree. With that on her mind, a con artist persuaded her to work for him for a summer with promises of lots of money and a great job in Los Angeles. She didn't tell the family the details of what happened, but the episode seemed to be an embarrassment to her. She still moved to L.A. with her boyfriend, but without a job or much of a plan.

Things went downhill fast once she was in L.A. Over the next few years she went through a string of jobs, had severe money problems and several bad relationships with men. The rest of the family remained close both geographically and emotionally. The family maintained regular communication with Alice and she came back to visit about once a year. Several of us went to visit her. From what I gather, Alice was fairly promiscuous at this time in her life and she drank a fair amount, generally only on weekends. While dating someone who was in Alcoholics Anonymous

(AA) she decided she, too, was an alcoholic, and got heavily involved in AA. Her relationship did not last, but she stayed involved in AA and most of her friends were in it. At that point she seemed to be doing much better. She still had problems finding a job she liked and had financial problems. There were no arguments between her and any family members, but the family was worried about her and she resented that. She hated feeling like "the failure" because she couldn't get any kind of a career going.

Alice had been in L.A. for about two years when my father was diagnosed with cancer. That was April of 1984 and he died in March of 1986. During that period the rest of the family became closer than ever. Alice came home to visit and was there when he died, but the experience was very different for her because she hadn't been around very much and felt out of touch. After his death we all had a very difficult time – we loved him very much – but we had each other to help get through it. My mother remarried eight months after my father died. She married an old friend of my parents whose wife died of cancer one month before my dad died. Several months after my dad died, I visited Alice in L.A. She told me she had completely resolved all of her feelings toward my dad, but it would later become apparent that she had not.

Christmas 1986 was nine months after our father died and the family planned to spend it together away from our family home. My mother flew everyone to Florida for a 10-day trip. It was a tough Christmas for all of us. My mother's new husband joined us after Christmas day and stayed through New Year's. My father's death had been very hard on us and we were still deeply grieving his loss. So six of the sisters were in a similar state of mind – but Alice was in a very different state of mind. We could tell she didn't miss my father the way the rest of us did, so we didn't relate to her very well. There were no big arguments, but there was stress and tension when she was around. I think she felt she was being judged negatively around the family. But everyone in the family felt she took things defensively. We were grieving and did not have a lot of energy to watch out for her feelings — but we did try.

Alice kept a little more distant after that Christmas and has not been back to visit the family since. Several of us, including my mother, made trips to L.A. to visit Alice. Those visits were always very pleasant. She seemed much more comfortable in her own territory with a one-on-one type visit than she did around the entire family. The rest of the family continued to heal from my father's death and adjust to the changes in the family. We are a very strong and loving family. We are all close and gain strength and support from our family relationships. We all have our own lives and several of us have started our own families, but we really watch out for each other and enjoy each other. It's sad to think Alice's last image of the family as a unit was that very painful and difficult Christmas.

We later found out that shortly after the Christmas visit to Florida, Alice began to attend Adult Children of Alcoholics (ACOA) meetings. Alice knew neither of our parents was an alcoholic, but a friend suggested she go because she had a lot of the same "issues" as someone who is from a dysfunctional family. It was at those meetings, she says, that for the first time she felt safe to tell of her childhood pain.

In the summer of 1988, after about eight months of attending ACOA meetings, Alice mentioned to a friend from her ACOA group that she was feeling "sexually shut down" in her relationship with her boyfriend. She also said she had been having strange sexual dreams. Her friend thought this implied some kind of sexual abuse had occurred and suggested that Alice contact a therapist she knew who specialized in incest therapy. It is interesting to note how Alice now describes her initial reaction to all of this: "It was as if someone told me I had a horn growing out of the side of my head. I couldn't believe they really thought this could mean I was sexually abused." This friend finally convinced her to call the therapist by saying, "If you can't make the call for yourself, do it for the little girl inside you."

That call started her on the road to recovering what we all believe to be false memories. She says she was sure the therapist would confirm that the reason for the dreams was because she had been listening to many other stories of sexual abuse in the ACOA meetings. But the therapist told her she should meet with her right away. She began seeing the therapist and, with the help of regression techniques, the memories started. Her "recovered memories" of abuse involve her father and grandfather, now both deceased, and a family friend. She "knows for a fact" that not only she, but all six of her sisters as well as the six children of the family friend, were sexually abused. Her memories go back to the age of three months. She believes we were all fondled and forced to touch the accused as well as forced to perform oral sex. She believes she was raped at the age of seven, but she says she has no knowledge of any of the rest of us being raped.

It took her a while to fully believe it all, but over the course of the following year she apparently became convinced. She saw the therapist once or twice a week and slowly worked through what she considers to be her denial that it happened. No one in the family knew anything about it until about a year and a half later. But we did know something was wrong and that there was something she wasn't telling us. She stopped coming home for visits and missed my wedding. This was the first time that any of us had missed a major family event. We are a close family, and I could not imagine any of us missing another's wedding. Alice had had trouble with family relationships for several years at that point, but her decision to not come to the wedding was disappointing and another sign of a problem. At that point no one in the family had any idea that she thought she, and the rest of us, had been sexually abused.

In 1989, approximately one year later, my sister Jane was able to get Alice to reveal what she had uncovered in therapy. Alice asked Jane not to tell anyone from the family, but said she would be there for Jane should she start having memories. Jane realized she couldn't and shouldn't keep this information to herself and she told the family when everyone gathered for Thanksgiving in 1989. The initial reactions were shock and incredulity. We have all talked about this a lot and we have spent many hours trying to understand and absorb it.

Could it be true? It would explain some of Alice's problems. All of the six sisters have given it careful consideration. After all, Alice tells us she had actual, very detailed memories of these events. It seemed more likely that someone could forget something that did happen than remember something that did not. Even looking back as objectively as possible, we can only deduce that it absolutely could not have happened. If her allegations were true, I think in looking at our mother as she is and was, and my father as he was, certain patterns would emerge. The pattern that emerges when I look back is of two people who could never be the people in Alice's memories. Everything I know about my parents, and all the memories I have, even from very early on, make no sense whatsoever when contrasted with Alice's memories. Taking that in combination with the fact that the 12 other "known" victims not only have no memories of any abuse, but are leading healthy, happy lives, leaves no room for any doubt. It could not have happened. All six sisters feel the same about it, even after hours and hours of talking and reminiscing about the past, talking to therapists, reading *The Courage to Heal* and whatever else we could find to read. But to Alice we are simply "in denial."

Alice was unaware that we knew what she was thinking and so none of us talked to her about it. My mother repeatedly asked her what was wrong during telephone conversations, hoping Alice had figured out she was confused. We did not know what to do. In late 1989 Alice moved to Washington state. She had been wanting to get out of L.A. for some time and she was directed to another therapist near Seattle. She says that it is with that therapist that she did most of her work. She used a post office box for mail and had her phone disconnected. She decided to write to my mom with her allegations. My mother, not realizing how deeply Alice was immersed in all of this, was very shocked by the letter. She reacted with a lot of anger in a return letter. It's now easy to see that was not the approach to take, but to be accused of such horrible things and to be told you cannot deny any of it was more than she could take. Alice then wrote to all of her sisters with the same story. She warned all of us that if we did not come out of our denial we were risking the abuse of our own children. She told us that her therapist would screen all of our letters so that no "scapegoat-type messages" would reach her. It was now late 1990. Over the course of the next year several of us tried to communicate with her through letters. She never allowed anyone to discuss why we thought she must be mistaken and any such attempts were met with strong hostility. I successfully maintained communication with her for about year by sounding open-minded and remaining non-confrontational. When she asked me to provide her with the addresses of the family friend she accuses and all six of his children, as well as our other relatives, I told her I didn't want to do that until I was sure about what happened. She immediately completely cut off communication with me. She felt hurt that I seemed more concerned about hurting them than her, and she decided to sever all ties with the family. In a year of letter writing I had been so careful. I felt devastated that my big fear was realized — being completely cut off. She had realized that no one believed her allegations could be true. She found another way to get all the addresses she wanted and contacted the family friend she accuses, the only living person she accused; and all six of his children, as well as our aunts and uncles who "must have known what was going on." She wrote to all of her sisters cutting off all communications. Since then, letters to Alice came back unopened and marked "return to sender."

In the summer of 1992 I moved back to the East Coast after living for three years overseas. I was determined to find Alice and so one of my sisters and I took my infant son and flew to Seattle to find her. I wanted to see that she was okay and to let her know how much I loved her and missed her. We found her and she was willing to see us. I told her that I was aware she only wanted to see family members if they were "out of denial." I explained that I was not yet where she needs me to be but I just couldn't wait to see her. I loved her and missed her too much. I had read a lot

about people who are in mind-control situations and I felt
that insight was invaluable when I finally saw her again.
We talked and worked out a way to maintain comunications.
She told me that her incest therapy is done, but now she is
devoting her life to helping other incest survivors. She
believes her purpose in life is to heal incest on a global
level. She speaks regularly to incest survivor groups and all
of her income is from her incest artwork. She described
how moved everyone is when she speaks. She says they
are all amazed at how well she is doing considering the
extreme abuse she endured. She is planning to start a
publishing company related to sexual abuse issues. How
can she ever come back from this?

It has been a devastating experience for our family. We
ask ourselves how, and why, and the most difficult question of all — what can we do about it?

How can Alice feel so convinced of something that is so
obviously impossible? I remember saying, "This must be
happening to other families. It's probably so new that no
one realizes it's a problem yet." Finally we started seeing
similar stories in the newspaper. Many other families were
being victimized by improper therapeutic techniques used
on vulnerable people.

Looking back I can see several things that made Alice
vulnerable to what has come to be known as False Memory
Syndrome (FMS). Our childhood was good, but there were
some problems. There were seven of us so close in age that
it was very tough to feel all the love and attention that
children need to feel. I think my parents did a remarkable
job, but Alice was the middle child and perhaps it was even
more difficult for her to feel special. The bigger problem
was that my father was not very sensitive and he had a
problem with his temper. Having seven children in seven

years makes for a lot of stress and a lot of work. He did not know how to handle anger and frustration well and we all suffered because of it. He hit us and yelled at us when he was angry over something done wrong. My mother sided with us when he lost his temper and that left him feeling even more frustrated. That is the only thing any of us remember them arguing about.

My dad softened a lot when we were older and he no longer had the stress of living with eight females with whom he didn't always know how to deal. I believe the other six daughters really felt loved by my father and had a peaceful, good relationship with him before his illness and death. Alice, on the other hand, never felt he loved and accepted her. She never had an adult relationship with him. A year after his death, attending ACOA meetings brought a lot of it out. She felt a lot of pain and she knew it was still affecting her life. The fact that the other six sisters were not having problems must have made her feel even more alienated from the family. She had been spending time listening to people describe childhood abuse at her ACOA meetings. She says she felt that something terrible must have happened in order to produce the kind of problems she was having. She was also having sexual problems with her boyfriend. All of this made her vulnerable to FMS. Suddenly there was an explanation for every problem in her life. Alice really seems to feel that either the abuse happened or she must be a defective person. She believes we want to make her out to be crazy to avoid the pain of remembering and healing.

It seems likely to me that anyone who looked at the situation objectively would have to come to the same conclusions that I have. The problem is that there is no mechanism to detect any mistakes. All of her own intuition that she was wrong was discounted as "all survivors feel that way." Therapists advise incest victims not to listen to anyone who suggests you could be wrong and to cut off your "family of origin." Then they support their methods by saying they have never known of anyone who was mistaken — what a surprise! Perhaps their methods are valid for actual victims. If only they knew the impact of these methods on vulnerable people who were NOT sexually abused.

We have been living with this for a few years now, but the pain is still so deep. When I recently saw Alice I told her, "I may not know what is right or wrong, but I feel very strongly that never seeing you again, going through life without knowing whether you are alive or dead, and you not knowing the same about me, is wrong! Things weren't meant to be that way and I will do anything and everything I can to prevent that." My family is doing okay. We can now see that our pain is no match for the pain Alice is living with. She is living her life believing that our father viciously and sadistically molested her, our mother did nothing to protect her, and her own sisters are so deep in denial that they abandon her to heal alone. If only she could see into our hearts — there is so much love and caring there. She should know that.

She Used to Call Me "Mai-Mai"

She told me that it was a Chinese word that roughly translated as "little sister" but really meant so much more than that. The English language limited its true meaning so she tried to explain it to me: Mai-Mai (pronounced May-May) was a special term of endearment, of closeness, of being cherished.

In fact, being sisters, it was rare that she would call me Mai-Mai. I would almost forget her name for me and then, unexpectedly, she would call me Mai-Mai. It made me feel exceptional, strong and worthy.

My sister is 17 months older than I am. She taught me how to walk by myself to our aunt and uncle's house; to love the cottage; to buy a jade ring; she taught me how to write and how to drive, always reminding me that if I could drive on the correct side of the road I'd be an excellent driver; she selected our big dog "Stevie" and she taught me yoga postures.

When we were much older, she told me how important it was for her to take good care of me. She felt I needed her care and I am sure that I did. We each had a soul, but throughout the years we became each other's shadow; a strong presence within grasp of each other.

I cannot say that we did not have problems. Our mother had been an active alcoholic, and at times I would notice that my sister seemed to have mom's behavior. But my sister always seemed to be trying to break free from that through a 12-Step Program. She was aware of it and it scared her.

Even though she had moved and now lived in the east, we still kept in almost daily contact. However, I was near our father and she was alone in another state.

But three years ago we lost my sister. Her name is only important to us, my father and I. I flew out to visit her for my 35th birthday. I went to her therapy appointment with her. And, on my birthday, I lost her. In 1989, our lives began to change when my father inherited over $112,000.

Her therapist started the session by saying my sister had something that she wanted to share with me. Right then I knew that my sister had again gotten caught in her own web of stories that, unbeknownst to either my father or me, had surfaced again in our family – the untruths that had eventually taken the life of our alcoholic mother.

As I sat on her therapist's couch, realizing all this and having a sinking feeling of losing, my sister continued the "therapy session" and said that our aunt had sexually abused her as a child. That our aunt, at age 87 and in a nursing home with her memories gone, had attempted to "take her sweater off and touched her breast." She went on to say that our aunt winked at her and stated, "We had our secrets, didn't we."

Her therapist spoke up again and said that my sister wanted to share her memories with me in case it had happened to me. "No," I said. I refused to be a part of this madness and of this cruelty.

And with that, I lost her.

My sister's stories would eventually culminate into three and a half years of agony and anger. Amazing stories emerged of satanic ritual sexual abuse which grew to include "all the members of my father's family." Eventually my father had to pay a lawyer $30,000 in order to defend his innocence.

We lived through the letters between the lawyers; her deposition, which reads like Nancy Friday's book on women's sexual fantasies, *My Secret Garden*; our father's deposition; and a postponement of our first arbitration.

All the while I, who had lived in the same house with her, was not given a deposition by her lawyer. I, who could contradict all of her stories, those supplied by the multitude of incest survivor books she had read, those that she had simply made up — I never gave my story except to my father's attorney. I, who could have ended this fiasco shortly after the papers were served, was not given a deposition by her lawyer.

Being her "witness," which she stated in her deposition, I was the only one who could truly dispute her stories. Everyone else that my sister accused, except our father, had died and could not defend themselves. I was the only one left who had also resided in the household during the period that my sister claimed to have been abused.

The day before my father and I were to go to arbitration and see her for the first time in two years, she suddenly dropped the suit.

Her contention for dropping the lawsuit, which was actually written in a letter by her lawyer, was that December was too close to the "satanic cult month of October (Halloween)" and that her therapist, one who specialized in cult memories, had said that for her to come to our state during this time might result in my sister harming herself.

I have lost my shadow, a part of my strength. I have reentered therapy to help me decide just what it is I should do about her. What do I need to do and what do I do with it? We had years of struggle, of seeing and then reaching for saneness, of sharing our love of men, our 12-Step Program and our service, of our future together.

Do I want her back? Not if she continues to reside in her stories. Do I miss her? Enough to stop my breath. To cry in the shower and in the darkness, to touch her photo, to wonder what her laughter sounds like, to try and remember how she smelled.

After almost four years I realize that I never allowed myself to cry in front of anyone else. At first, my anger pulled me through. It is only recently that I began to seek comfort, to stop my heart and soul from coming apart and ending up so empty.

And what do I tell people? For those who are willing to listen, the truth. After 13 years in a 12-Step Program it is all that I have and all that I need.

Those individuals who do not listen insist that the "abuse" also happened to me and that "my memories haven't returned yet." I get the impression that these people feel sorry for me and that my "repressed" memories will substantially harm their recovery. It seems useless to look them in the eye and say, "but *I* lived in the household, not you. What of *my* truth?"

Dating, marrying, work, old friends, new friends, tomorrow? – all I can do is maintain my belief and my knowledge in my Higher Power and in my innocence. I have worked very hard to reach my sanity.

The only thing I know to say is that we lost her. . . .

She is naive, trusting, innocent, tells excruciating lies and is very manipulative; but she is my sister, and I love her. Where do I put that love and that touch? Of that soul that walked so well next to me? I reach out to try and touch her and I am startled to remember that we have the same hands.

Does she think of me? Does she wonder what I am doing? Does she hate me? Will she remember me?

I remember her, know her closeness, her knowing of me and my ways, the laughter, the way she accepted that I was her little sister and she was my older sister — willing to put up with my craziness and my teasing her, the way I could talk her into brushing my hair, the way she could help me when I was hurt. The quietness of her.

I have started a "sister" box for her, to show her that I never forgot her. In it I will put items that I believe she would be interested in — the photo of Ella Fitzgerald, the movies "Ping Pong" and "101 Dalmations." The jade ring, articles on the old Motown, cards, dreams, notes on our father and on me, those who she shut out of her life.

I might not ever be able to forgive her, but I know I can't ever forget her.

I wish for her to find her way.

The Phone Call

I remember getting the phone call from my sister. I was working at a job in Fresno, trying to adjust to the summer heat, and to being alone in a strange place. It was on a Sunday afternoon when she called and hit me with the revelation. She said she had a "dream" that our dad had sexually abused her when she was a kid. A dream? What the hell does that mean? I have dreams, but I know they aren't reality. Well, damage done, I was freaked out. She went on and on, in gross, graphic detail. The man she was talking about and the man I knew as my father didn't at all seem to be one and the same. The abuse went on for years according to her. Rape, sodomy, oral sex were the abuses "du jour." But here was the clincher, here is where I became part of the scenario. She insisted that I was not only a witness to these violations on her, but I was a "violatee" myself. Whoooaa! Wait a minute here, dear sister. I have a pretty good memory of my childhood, and much of my time was spent around her. We were only about a year and one-half apart in age, and we shared the same bedroom for many years. None of these attacks took place in the bedroom I slept in.

Of course, in her mind, everything was now falling into place. The reason she couldn't fully function as a productive human being was because of him. She couldn't stay in a relationship, couldn't hold down a job, couldn't pay her credit card bills. COULDN'T COULDN'T COULDN'T . . . Now she had a face and a name to blame her failures on, and a very familiar face at that. Did she ever stop to ask herself, maybe she had the wrong man? Maybe all the hurt and anger she harbored against our father for not being perfect and loving her the way she needed was being severely misdirected? Maybe an uncle, male babysitter, neighbor — it could have been anybody — was the perpetrator (one of her favorite words). I know how she felt about Dad, because I got an earful more than a few times. He favored my little sister and me. He sent me to Europe, he bought her a horse. All *she* got was abuse. So she says. My recollection of our childhood was not all that different from anyone else who grew up in the 1950s and 1960s. All three of us girls went to Catholic school, which, in my opinion, didn't exactly prepare us for the world, but it was all we knew. Sure, the nuns weren't really qualified to nurture and bring out the best in children, but not all of them were monsters. My older sister and I went to the same Catholic high school, did our share of drinking, drugs, and having sex with various boyfriends. But it was the way we lived and it seemed normal to us and our friends.

My dad and sister fought a lot, as I recall, but it seemed the usual rebellious stuff that goes on when you are growing into an adult, still living at home, and can't wait to be on your own. She got married at about 20 or 21. She didn't have a baby until she was 30. She had an adorable son.

What the hell happened to my sister? Up until the day I got the phone call, I thought she was perfectly neurotic, just like everyone else, but not schizophrenic like she seems today. If she has so much hate and resentment for my father and mother why didn't she try to talk to them about it, or at least get some counseling? But to accuse him of having sex with her, and saying my mom was just as guilty by not doing anything about it, well, that's nothing but crazy. I should know, I was there!

Well, I can't say that this "adventure" has been easy on our family. My parents were devastated at first, and so very hurt. Now they are mad. I'm angry at her too, but also feel somewhat sorry for her because she is such a mess. Someone, somehow planted a wicked seed in her vulnerable brain and it not only took root, it has grown into a big, ugly "blame-bush." She now has a cause, a reason for living, a crusade. I no longer have an older sister, at least not the one I knew for 35 years. My parents, younger sister and I are so much closer now. So, you could say this has some advantage, although most days it doesn't feel that way. I pray for my mom and dad, that they have the strength and courage to get through this intact. I pray for my sister, that someday she has another "revelation" called the truth. I'm not counting on that happening, as much as I would like for the five of us to be a family again. So, for the forseeable future, it will be the four of us, growing, learning, loving each other, and getting stronger every day. I hope I see her again; you see, I still love her. As much as I hate what she is doing . . . I still love her.

December 1992

A few months have passed since writing this "story," and things have changed. My sister decided to "settle" out of court for $15,000. Compared to what it would have cost to go to trial it doesn't seem like a lot of money, but when you are retired, it's a hell of a lot. My parents felt like they bought her off, just to get rid of her. But we will never be free of her, although it is unlikely any of us will ever see her again. You just can't exorcise a family member. We'll always think about her, wonder what she's doing, what she looks like, if she's happy or miserable — sometimes hoping she's miserable after what she's done to us.

As for me, most of the anger against her has passed, but a lot still remains for the therapist or group who "helped" her. Some help! She was vulnerable, reaching out, and someone found an incredible weak spot. I doubt if I'll ever really know what happened, or if this whole "incest" issue was someone's fault. It doesn't matter anyway, because the accusation did happen.

Life continues. My family has survived. We still get up each day and have our routines, go to church, watch television, visit our friends, walk the dog, do our jobs. We share more, hug more, and cry more. We have forgiven her. When we think about her, we still hurt. It might be easier if she were dead.

My Last Letter to My Sister

I am 22 years old and the youngest of three children. I have a brother who is 30 years old and my sister is 31 years old. My parents worked very hard to give their children a normal life. I don't doubt there were times when they wondered where their next dollar was coming from, or whether we should eat peanut butter and jelly for dinner. Things were tough at times, but they always provided for us. They have always been there when we needed them, even now that we are grown. Just when they should be enjoying their lives, a tragic event has taken place. They have lost one of their children to one of the cruellest things that could ever happen to a family — untrue accusations of neglect and child sexual abuse!

My sister was one of the nicest people you could meet. She was exceptional. I am not saying that just because she was my sister. She was gifted at writing. A beautiful girl with a great sense of humor and an exceptional interest in caring for others. I can remember one Christmas she received rabbit fur slippers. She asked my mother to return them because an animal had to die in order to make the slippers. She said she couldn't wear them and feel good about it. This may give you an indication of what kind of girl she used to be. She always had friends in school, even though she was overweight for most of her life. You know how kids can be. There was a nice girl underneath, and people saw the life she had in her eyes. She was nice to be around. Very comforting and caring. She always blamed my mother for her weight problem, but we thought it was just another one of those things kids do. People go through stages when they are not fond of their mothers.

My sister went on to college, where she graduated as a

registered nurse. Each summer during the three-year course she would work at a camp for children. She loved her work. Everyone was very proud, especially my parents. Their first-born! They must have thought they were doing something right. A child moving on with her life. Were they wrong! My sister worked at a nearby hospital for about five years. She then decided to take a job several hundred miles away. We were all shocked at the news, but were happy for this move. She was there one year. She wrote, she sent pictures, she phoned at least once a week. She had a lot of duties there, including dealing with suicidal, neglected children and victims of incest. I found out all of this later. I also found out that she had been seeing a therapist before she moved away.

During the time she was away, I put my parents through a trauma of my own. I went to a therapist for a drug dependency, referred by my doctor. I went once a week for one-on-one therapy, and workshops once a week, as well as group meetings. I always knew deep down that I just needed some direction. I knew I didn't need to see a therapist. She did help me with my problems. Then she started to tell me to search for my "inner child" and that "I should get in touch with my feelings." The therapist told me that she suspected I had been abused as a child, and that I should get closer to my feelings. She recommended the famous book, *The Courage to Heal,* among other books. I never read these books, since I knew that they did not apply to me. I too could have fallen into this absurd cult thinking.

When my sister returned, she went with me to see my therapist. The therapist wanted to meet her. My parents also went on different occasions.

Within four or five months came accusations that were

unbelievable. My sister said she had been molested by a neighbor and that she had told my mother, who did not do anything about it. She said that the abuse had started earlier, around the age of one year, but she could not tell us who abused her. She said she had been having "flash-backs." She did not feel comfortable telling us. Her thera-pist told her to cut off all contact with her family. She wrote a form letter to my parents and her friends stating that she would not be having contact with anyone until she could resolve her problems. If we needed to get in touch with her, we should contact her "therapist."

Within a year, she had quit her job where she was making approximately $30,000-35,000 per year and moved nearby, so that she could get closer to her "inner child." My parents have not seen or heard from her in almost two years. I am the only one with her phone num-ber. I gave the number to my parents once and they phoned. She was very cold and callous towards them. She says to me that she is doing this as much for me as she is for herself. She says she is protecting me. From what? She won't tell me, or anyone, anything. She has sold everything she ever worked for except her bed and her car. Her apartment is a mess of Salvation Army furniture and books. All the books refer to sexual abuse as a child. This is part of her therapy. She has sold literally everything that ever meant anything to her. In her bedroom she has a picture of herself when she was a baby. She said that this was her "inner child." She talks to this person all the time. I have seen her do it. It is very eerie. It is like she is crazy. There is a fan in one corner of her room. This is because her inner child is afraid to be alone and the noise of the fan helps her sleep. She has a night light because her inner child is afraid of the dark. I don't know how she survived living the past ten years alone in an apartment if her inner child was afraid to be alone and afraid of the dark. It does not make sense. That was the last time I saw my sister. I don't want to see her; she makes me very upset. I can't believe this is the same woman I have known and loved for the past 22 years of my life.

I have spoken with her only a few times in the past two years. I am the one who phones, not she. She is very bold, cold, arrogant and rude. She has nothing nice to say about anyone. She lives on medical disability. She will never work in the medical field again, not unless she wants to hang a sign on her door saying she is a "therapist." She has had thoughts of doing that. What a scary idea. She has a ruined life. This is not the same woman I knew. She went from a girl who took at least two trips a year, had whatever she wanted, a basically good life to someone who now has absolutely nothing. She has no friends outside of these "groups" she is involved with.

Now you tell me that this is the same person I spoke so highly of earlier. I don't think so. Something has to be done about these absurd people who are walking into our lives and calling themselves therapists, and literally ruining families.

In high school they ask you to look ten years down the road and think about what you will be doing. Every girl's dream at that time was to be married, have a couple of children, a good job and a stable lifestyle. My sister, I am sure, had those same dreams, but by the time she reached 30, they were all fading fast. Who did she turn to, to take away her depression and loneliness? A "therapist." It was the biggest mistake of her life, and she doesn't even know it.

I've been having nightmares about the funeral of my parents, and "she" shows up at the funeral. I need to be physically restrained from ripping her face off.

I often visualize the day of my wedding, standing in the chapel, asking God to watch over my sister, and not let anything happen to her, and I remember the dream I had as a child, of my sister helping me put on my wedding dress, getting ready for the big day. My childhood dream has now been shattered.

I remember when I rode my first two-wheel bicycle, and who the person was standing there watching me ride over the railway tracks, cringing in hope that I didn't fall — my dad. The man who watched over me from the time I was a small child and still does to this day. Only now he, as well as my mother, my grandfather and a neighbour have all been accused of the most horrifying thing imaginable, sexual abuse of a child. They are being put on trial for something that has been brought out in a therapy session. Well I know what happened — nothing of the sort! But how do you prove this when no one wants to listen to you?

I remember following my sister around the house, watching her put on her makeup, baking cakes with her, cooking our favorite meal — Kraft Dinner, crying on her shoulder when our mother was very ill in the hospital. Now I can't even phone her because that is called "not respecting her wishes," or "you are responsible for your own actions and your feelings." I can't even tell her if someone in our family is sick, because I don't know where she lives, or what her phone number is. She changes her phone number all the time because she is afraid that someone will contact her.

These are the stages that I have gone through in the past two-and-a-half years since the death of my sister. I call it a death, because that is the only way to deal with the tragedy that has occurred in my family. I tried to keep in contact with my sister for the first two years, but she didn't want anything to do with me or my family unless we believed what she was saying. I can't believe something that has never happened.

I have examined every moment of my childhood, from the times when I was babysat by someone to graduation night. There is nothing there. She has tried to ruin all the good memories that I have of my childhood and turn them into some sort of a horror story. All she could say when I was trying to explain to her that nothing had happened was, "You are in denial." Who is the one in denial here?

I have made my share of mistakes in my life, but I have always known who was to blame; at least I don't have to blame my parents because I screwed up. That is taking the easy way out. You don't have to deal with real problems if a therapist encourages you to believe that there must be a deep-rooted reason why you are overweight, or why you are a drug addict, or why you are an alcoholic. Ah! the answer — childhood sexual abuse. Your father or your mother molested you as a child, that is why you are over-weight. That takes away all the responsibility, doesn't it? At least now my sister knows what is the matter with her, and now she can blame someone else for her problems. Wrong! She has been brainwashed. This is the only way to describe this phenomenon that is taking over families all over the world, and these therapists are getting rich from the devastation they are causing. It is sick.

It was July 23, 1992 when my "belated" sister finally came to my parents' house, after two years of no contact whatsoever. I was the only one who had spoken with her. She came in the house and my mother went to hug her. She said, "Don't touch me."

That was the start of what was to be the last time they probably will ever see my sister.

She came into the house with her therapist. My mother described him as "the most arrogant, egotistical son of a bitch" she had ever met. He treated them like criminals in their own home. My sister sat down on the couch in her rags. My sister used to be a very well-dressed, clean woman. She read the most horrifying pack of lies and smut I have ever read in my life. She was at the house approximately 20 minutes and she left. My father asked the therapist, "What credentials do you have to be here at my house tonight?" The therapist replied, "I don't carry my credentials in my back pocket." My father also asked the therapist why he was fired from his past position. When my father became visibly angry, the therapist said this is the way people like you react, denial. He left with my sister soon afterward.

Two weeks later I received a copy of the letter she left my parents, as well as a little note, telling me that if I ever had children, not to take my children to my parents. I wrote the following letter in response:

Dear Sara:

I don't really know how to begin to tell you how I feel. Number one, I will tell you that I am writing this letter on my own, that "my" parents had nothing to do with this letter, and that they don't know that I am doing this, or they would be very upset with me. They seem to think that there is still hope for you. Well, that is their problem.

You once told me that shit would hit the fan when all this came out. Well I hope that you are satisfied. I am going to say things in this letter that you will not agree with, but I really don't care, because as you once told me, I am responsible for how I feel and how I say things. This will be the last time we ever have contact whatsoever, so it really doesn't matter what I say.

I heard about what happened the other night with "my" mom and dad. I don't believe a word of it. If that is what you believe, then you really are a sick person. It appalls me that you could think such things. Your grandfather is dead, and thank God he doesn't have to hear such vulgarities. But mark my words, he is watching over you, and one day, I believe, whoever or whatever person or persons put these sickening thoughts in your head will be punished. They are the ones who need psychiatric help.

I firmly believe that you have been the victim of some sort of brainwashing. If you can sit for a sane moment and think of the way your life used to be, you would realize that you have become just what they want you to be, vulnerable. You will believe anything because that will take away the pain that you are feeling. You are too sick now to get "professional" help. You have become their victim. They are preying on you, just like they have preyed on so many others. You are not the first one that they have tried to do this to, and certainly won't be the last. Unless someone can stop them. There are people out there right now, as we speak, that are trying to do just that. I think you will find out some surprising things once their court case is finished. They may not have any qualifications left to do this sort of thing to anyone else. I hope they get the sons of bitches. If you could think for a minute, do you really think they are professional therapists that have been trained to deal with "recurred memories of sexual abuse?" Think again; their credentials consist of C.D.A.C. (Canadian Drug and Alcohol Counsellors). Does this mention anything about sexual abuse therapy? Not one thing. They may think that it is all related, but they are wrong.

They are not doctors or psychiatrists and have no

right to counsel you on anything other than drug- and alcohol- related cases. They have probably read a lot of books and think they know it all. Well they don't, if you could only realize this. I believe they have read the book The Courage to Heal *one too many times. Any person who reads this book would begin to wonder. The people who wrote this book aren't even qualified to give advice. Everything seems to be through personal experience. But some therapists seem to worship the book.*

I can only say that I am sick over this. I know you think you are doing the right thing, but I firmly believe that you have become very sick. You need a psychiatrist, not some unprofessional person who thinks he or she is a therapist. There are places you can go for help, that you wouldn't have to pay for. Can't you see they want your money? What professional therapist would sit and listen to you read a letter to your parents, and at the end of the letter ask for money? Do you think that this is professional? You don't quit a good job, live like a pig, pour every ounce of your energy into healing, and think that this is right. My God, what has happened to you? A professional therapist would not let this happen. Can't you see that? Your family would do whatever it takes to get you "professional" help. Not this kind of help. We would literally do anything to help you. I personally think that you are too far gone now for any kind of help. I can't put into words what kind of an animal you have become. You call this healing? I call this sick.

I am sending you some information that I want you to read. If you have an ounce of sense left in your head, you will read it and try and put your life back together. If you do ever realize the pain that you have caused yourself, I don't think that you could possibly live with yourself. I know it may be too late for you to try and get your life back together in a sane way. You are too far out in space. It is all like a bad dream that won't go away. You always did like "Star Trek," or maybe you would like to accuse Captain Kirk of some subliminal sexual message you received through the T.V. I should watch what I say. They all seem to be coming out of the woodwork. Maybe it will be someone new next week. You know, we had a lot of old neighbors, but most of them are still alive so you can't accuse them of anything yet. Give it a couple of years.

     As you can tell by the tone of this letter, I am really pissed off. Not so much with you, but with the kind of treatment that you have been receiving. I think that you have become very sick over the last two years. Maybe you were always sick and I just didn't see it. You have hurt me badly, deeper than you will ever know. If you think that this happened to me, you are wrong, and I will say that until the day I die. And no, I am not in denial. You know what you can do with your denial. I always thought that you were such a bright girl, not the animal that you have become. I think you were very depressed when you went to get some therapy, and look what has happened. This is not the answer to your problems. I can just hear what you are saying now. That she doesn't know what my problems are. I think I may know them better than you do. You see everyone around you getting on with their lives, getting married, and having babies, and here you don't have all those things. You are very lonely, depressed, and you need someone to blame for all those things. The only thing that this therapy has brought out in you is really how depressed and sick you are. Oh! and also your inner child. She seems like a lovely girl. Well for you, your inner child, or whoever the hell you are, because I really don't know. It is now as if you have died.

My sister died two years ago as far as I am concerned. If you think that this is the way that I want to deal with things, by denying what is going on, you are wrong. I don't want to know this person you have become. She is very sick and needs "professional" help. I am upset that you could not come to me when you thought you were having problems in the first place, and it seems that it is much too late for help for you. I guess good things come out of a death in the family. I have now gained a brother I did not know I had before. You really brought the good side out of him. I guess maybe it took losing a sister to gain a brother. He really is a nice guy. I have never heard him talk so much in all my life. He is very hurt, and we talk a lot about how we feel. We have become very close. Everyone in our family has become much closer. There is a lot of support for what we are going through.

You know, you seem to have had the upper hand through this whole horrible nightmare. Well let me tell you how I feel about this whole mess that you have caused:

May your life be complete to "your" satisfaction, and may God watch over you, and try to guide you in the right direction. When there is no more ink left on this page, this is the end. The end of a relationship that I once thought I was lucky to have with my sister. It has now met its demon. You can now erase my name from your memory "and what a good memory you seem to have." For me, the sister I once had has died, and may you rest in peace.

That was the last time I had any contact with my sister.

I feel partly responsible sometimes for what has happened to my sister. I was the one who introduced my sister to the "therapist." I was involved with a therapist for approximately one-and-a-half years due to a drug addiction. Now that I look back, I can see what the therapist was trying to plant in my head. She tried telling me that I had been sexually molested as a child. When I told her that I had not been abused, she became cold and callous and soon afterward I ceased my visits with her. Not soon enough, she got a hold of my sister. This is where the nightmare began.

Unlike a lot of other families involved, I know the therapist who has done this to my sister. I know the techniques that are used. I have read many articles, and the techniques they described are right on the money. Hypnosis, watching films, support groups. The counseling my sister and I received was covered by health insurance—until the therapists were fired from their jobs. After that, they worked out of their homes. They were fired because the people at the counseling center did not like their therapy techniques, and they were receiving a lot of complaints from families that had children involved with these two people.

It would seem, at least in my case, that these two people somehow wanted to start some sort of a "family" of their own. They wanted to see how many people they could persuade to be in their group, to follow their ethics. I can't really explain what I mean. They preached a different therapy than the rest of the therapists involved. It seemed that they wanted so badly to show that this kind of therapy works. It was like they were trying to prove something. They were trying to get as many people involved in their way of therapy. I have spoken to therapists after these two were fired and no one was sad to see them go. They sued for wrongful dismissal. These people are dangerous. They have covered their tracks very well. They have protected themselves so well by saying "you are responsible for all your actions and feelings." That, right there, is a cover-up. They have brainwashed people into believing this phrase so that they can't be blamed for their clients' actions.

It makes me so angry to think that I know who these people are that have done this to my sister, but I can't do a thing about it. We just have to pray every day and keep hope and faith that one day this will be all over.

It is my mother's birthday today. When I phoned to wish her a happy birthday, she was crying. She tried to put on a front that she was happy to hear from me, but I know what she was crying about. Is this what the 1990's generation of liberated woman is supposed to be like — people who blame others for the problems in their lives? I'm glad I am a woman who knows what I want and won't trample over my family to get it.

My only hope for my sister is that if she ever does come out of this cult she will able to live with the consequences of what she has caused for the past two-and-a-half years.

Susan's Memories

My story begins in December 1988 when my father died after a two-year struggle with cancer. I believe that grief is what drove my older sister to seek therapy a few months later. Susan called me to ask to borrow a tape recorder. When I asked why, she told me she was starting therapy for depression, and that her therapist wanted to hypnotize her and she wanted to record the session. It was the first time she had ever told me she was feeling depressed. Shortly after this, before I was able to give her the recorder, she called and asked to talk to me in person. She revealed to me that she had remembered being raped by my brother when they were children. I was shocked. I didn't know quite how to react, but I gave Susan support and compassion for what she had gone through. I had no idea that this was just the beginning of a long series of allegations that grew more and more bizarre.

Until this time, we had been a close family of mother, father and four children, Hank, Tim, Susan, and me, Janice. Our current ages are 41, 39, 37, and 30. We often socialized as a family, including our respective spouses and children, enjoyed watching football games, playing backyard volleyball, and eating holiday dinners together. Susan and I had been close for all of our adult lives.

By the summer of 1989, Susan had accused both brothers of abuse. She asked me to lunch one day, and told me of her most recent recovered memory, that of being raped and sexually abused by a neighbor. While listening to her, and trying to be compassionate, I was thinking, "Why do these memories continue to get worse and worse? What is next? And how long is it going to be before she accuses

Dad?" But I was giving her the benefit of the doubt and trying to believe her. Every conversation we had was about her past, about the abuse she was so painfully digging for in her memories. I began to dread her phone calls, because she only called me when she had a new revelation to share.

It was sometime that fall when she next asked to get together. This time it was to tell me that she had remembered being sexually abused by my father. I wasn't exactly surprised by this; it seemed logical in a twisted sort of way that if she had been abused by so many men, my father could hardly be left out. Nevertheless, I was shaken by the accusation. This was the first one I felt I could evaluate from personal experience. I couldn't imagine my father doing such a thing. Yet, "Could he have done it?" I wondered. "If he abused Susan, he most likely abused me too. Have I repressed memories of my own abuse?"

The memories Susan gave were non-specific; she never gave me any specific details of her memories. She couldn't pinpoint what age the memory came from, and I never was sure exactly what kind of abuse she remembered. I continued to be supportive of her, while trying to sort out my own feelings. She gave me the book *The Courage to Heal*. I read some of it. I remember the part that said you don't have to have memories, and that some people never recover any memories of their abuse. I guess the book did not strike a chord in me, because I didn't finish reading it. Even though I was trying to believe Susan, I was beginning to doubt her.

After the new year, Susan seemed to focus most of her anger towards my mother. By this time Susan and I were not talking very often. I was still confused about her accusations and I didn't know how to deal with her except to listen. At one point I told her that she seemed to be getting worse, instead of better, as her therapy progressed. She responded in a letter, saying she was getting better, although it appeared to be the opposite. The memories were getting worse, but she felt she was getting stronger and much more able to handle them. The whole situation was really upsetting for me. Sometime in February or March, Susan asked Mom to go to a therapy session with her. Mom agreed. Mom thought the session didn't accomplish much.

Shortly after this, Susan called, and over the phone she told me that although she didn't want to talk about it because it was so disgusting, she felt she had to tell me something. She first made me promise not to discuss it with Mom. I heaved a mental sigh and agreed. She said that after their session with Mom, her therapist had called to make sure she was okay, something he had never done before. She assured him that she was fine. That night she had a dream involving "robes and candles," and in the morning felt she remembered abuse involving an altar. She called her therapist and asked if he thought my mother was capable of satanic abuse. Susan said he definitely thought she was capable, and he was so disturbed by my mother he had felt the need to check on Susan afterwards. She also told me that he called my mom evil.

After this conversation I totally distrusted her therapist, a man with no license and, as far as I know, only some sort of degree in theology. I thought it was totally irresponsible of him to draw any conclusions about anyone after only an hour of talking, and that his label of my mother as "evil" clearly showed his bias. I honored my sister's request not to discuss it with Mom, though I really wanted to.

I didn't hear from Susan for a couple of months and frankly was relieved. Then she called. She told me that her problem was very serious, that she had been diagnosed with multiple personality disorder, that her therapist had referred her to one of the top experts in satanic ritualistic abuse at a local psychiatric hospital, that she had been given the Multiphasic Personality test and that if it were evaluated by a mainstream psychiatrist she would be called schizophrenic. She was close to being hospitalized, but she was working it out so she could do intensive outpatient therapy instead. She was also seeing another therapist who led a group for survivors.

Her next call, about three weeks later, was a call filled with profane, hate-filled, somewhat incoherent diatribe about Mom and our family.

I only spoke to Susan one more time. She spent a half-hour trying to convince me to take her side. By this time I knew something was terribly wrong. My logic kicked in. During the conversation when she had told me she had MPD, I asked her who was in the cult that abused her. When she listed several neighbors, an uncle, and the family doctor, as well as my parents, I knew that a conspiracy this widespread could not possibly be kept secret from me. Since I knew this supposed satanic cult could not possibly exist, I finally realized that all of her other memories must be false as well. I told her that I didn't believe her. I don't remember all of the conversation, but she told me she was in a group of survivors. "Why," she asked me, "if this satanic abuse is not real, do we all have the same memories?" Then, I did not have an answer for her. Now, I know it is because therapists are looking for these "memories," and survivor support groups provide a great feedback system for generating false memories.

These are my thoughts on why Susan succumbed to this phenomenon. She really needed some grief counseling, and got involved with an incompetent therapist. She often spoke of how fast she was uncovering her past and how unusual she was in that regard, and that it had only taken her a few months what it took most people years to do. For a while she said her therapist was going to write a book about her. Later, she herself was going to write the book and she was warning me that all of our family's secrets would be revealed.

She had found a way to get lots of emotional support. She found a group of people in her life whom she could trust, people who knew of her "abuse" and who helped her deal with it.

A caring group of people, they listened with love. They shared her terror and her pain and her grief.

They were working together on the difficult and noble task of healing, gaining strength from one another and cheering each other on.

Susan was at a transition stage in her life. Her father had just died, her sons were of school age, and, an intelligent woman, she was unhappily working part-time. I guess it was sort of an early mid-life crisis time. She had told me before this started that she didn't know what to do next. In therapy, suddenly she was getting strokes for being such an unusually interesting and better than average patient. Going to therapy, recovering memories, writing stories about her pain, going to survivors' groups filled her life. She didn't have to figure out what to do next anymore, she was too busy figuring out her past.

In trying to understand Susan's "memories," I came to the conclusion that her therapists had gotten out of her exactly what they expected, exactly what their specialties made them look for, and that Susan had acted in a way which got her approval and attention. Information from the False Memory Syndrome Foundation has clarified and confirmed the conclusions about Susan's therapy I had come to on my own.

It has been two-and-a-half years since that last telephone conversation with Susan. A few months ago, I wrote her a note that said simply, "I think of you often. I love you and I care about you."

Becoming Schizophrenic

My sister Veronica and I moved to Canada from Latin America when we were young children. We became a blended family with my father and his two sons. We had a fairly average childhood, with good times and bad times and a few adjustment problems, as you might expect. We all went to Catholic school, where Veronica and I quickly learned English. From the very beginning Veronica excelled at everything she did; she was confident and charismatic and very beautiful. Everyone seemed to like her, and she had a great many friends. She was an "A" student and an exceptional athlete, having earned an invitation to the Olympic qualifying tryouts as a middle distance runner. She was also a very accomplished figure skater. It was her plan to study medicine and go to a poor Latin American country as a volunteer doctor.

About the time she graduated from high school, my sister's personality began to change in a very frightening way. She would unexpectedly become very angry for no reason and fly into an uncontrollable rage. At other times she would suddenly start to laugh or cry without any cause. Sometimes she seemed to be talking to people who weren't there. Soon she had cut herself off from all her usual friends and was associating with astrologers, herbalists and "new age healers" who were against science and didn't know anything about it. She physically attacked our parents several times and as a result she had to move into her own place. She didn't go on to university as planned, and stopped caring about her hygiene. She became preoccupied with "healing" and went to all sorts of quacks like "channelers" and "past lives" hypnotists. I can see now that she was very terrified about what was happening to her and desperately trying to find someone who could help her. It was during this period that she started seeing a "counsellor." She had started to abuse drugs and alcohol, and wanted to stop, because this was not really her true nature.

As soon as she started to see the counsellor she became obsessed with finding out about our childhood. She collected every old photograph she could find, and started asking countless questions about our parents, our grandparents and all of our relatives in Latin America. Then one day she came to the house and told us that she had been sexually abused as a child. She was very angry, and accused our parents of concealing information from her. She didn't seem to know who had abused her, but said she was working very hard to remember.

Veronica went downhill very rapidly. She expressed terror that Michael the Archangel was coming to rape her and gouge out her eyes. She climbed to the top of a local mountain in the middle of the night to talk to "star people" and to look for rocks which had baby stars inside. Then, a few days later, an elderly couple brought her to our home, half frozen. She had been hiding in a crack in the rock right next to the ocean for over 24 hours, dressed only in a thin exercise suit. My mother, who is a nurse, was able to warm her up in a lukewarm bath. When Veronica had been revived, she became extremely hysterical. She was convinced that my father had chopped me up and buried me in the back yard, and that he had murdered my mother and replaced her with an android. My parents had to call for help, and an ambulance came with two police cars to take her to the hospital.

At the hospital, the attending psychiatrist had to tell my parents that my sister was very ill, suffering from paranoid schizophrenia. This psychiatrist is a marvelous doctor. He put Veronica on medication, and spent a lot of time with her. She improved rapidly; she became quite relaxed and happy, the way she had been two years before. She started to make plans to get a job planting trees, then resume her education.

At this point, just when things were going so well, her "counsellor" started to visit her in the hospital. We have extremely stupid "human rights" laws in Canada, and you can't stop a patient being visited by anyone she wants. Even worse, you can't make a very ill person take her medication or stay in the hospital. This "counsellor" told my sister that psychiatry was a conspiracy of the "patriarchy" and that its purpose was to take power away from women. She also told her that there was no such thing as schizophrenia, and that all the symptoms were caused by a person's mind trying to blot out memories of sexual abuse. According to her, my parents had put her in the hospital to shut her up. She convinced Veronica that her medication was to take away her will and make her forget, so she stopped taking it.

Before we knew what was happening, Veronica had discharged herself from the hospital. The "counsellor" picked her up and helped her carry her stuff. Veronica started going to "survivors' groups" for two hours every day, where she was told to smash up plates with a baseball bat and to think up fantasies of mutilating our father, castrating him and watching his blood run into the gutter. She came to the house a couple of times to stand on the front lawn and shout about the abuse. Before too long she started to believe that the counsellor had sexually abused her. She thought all the old people in our city were aliens who were torturing her, and that her head had been cut off.

The next thing we knew was that we got a phone call

from one of Veronica's former friends in a town in the Rockies where she had once worked. He said that she was terrorizing people on the street, accusing them of being aliens. Her friends were very worried, and didn't know what to do with her. My mother and I made an emergency trip, and when we arrived we found that my sister had shaved off all her beautiful hair because she thought she was a concentration camp victim. She was living under a tree in the woods, and all the children and teenagers were making fun of her. We spent two days cooped up in a hotel room with Veronica, which were the most difficult two days of my life. She never slept, and kept seeing and hearing monsters and aliens who were coming to harm us all. She accused me of raping her, and told my mother that she had no memories of the sexual abuse, but that Janet (the counsellor) was "helping her to remember." At one point she went out in the snow at 3 o'clock in the morning to cleanse herself in the river.

It turned out that she had gotten some money from Social Services for a place to live, but had used it to buy a plane ticket to one of the maritime provinces at the other end of the country, because she believed that the aliens had followed her from our city to the Rockies. That is where she is now, terrified and alone, and afraid of the only people who can help her.

Our family, like any other family, has its shortcomings, but we have managed to cope with many difficulties. We would have coped with my sister's schizophrenia if the un-qualified "repressed memory counsellor" had kept her nose out of something she knew absolutely nothing about. She has a lot to answer for, and I'm going to see that she does answer for it.

An Answer for Everything

When my sister was seeing a sexual abuse counselor and called to tell me that she thought we may have been sexually abused, I just laughed inside. I figured that she was just on another kick. When my sister called to tell me that we had been satanic ritually abused by my parents and that it was her therapist who told her so, I went into a sort of shock. I knew that she believed this and that when she becomes determined that something is so, there is no way of talking her out of it.

When I received her letter that indicated she could no longer see me, I just shook. During the first month of no contact with her, I felt flat out scared and eerie. I didn't know if this was just a kick, or if this was the end. I just didn't know.

After a month or two, we re-established contact for several months. What I saw in her during this time was someone going blank in the eyes, drawing pictures in a way that seemed strange to me, a change in posture during which time she would stiffen and talk in a tightened voice. I saw her go into trancelike states. I heard stories that seemed based on real events, but were taken out of context and rewoven into events that I certainly think were far- fetched. I listened to stories that twisted some of my favorite times into ugly events. Seeing my sister like this just freaked me out.

My time with her came to an end when I let my parents into my home while her children were visiting, a strict prohibition to which I never agreed, but was told I had. I learned early in the game that to speak my mind was to say good-bye. I was torn to shreds inside watching my parents suffer for beliefs that I felt were incorrect and therapist-induced, and knowing that if my sister got angry at me, I might never see her again. My parents knocked at my door and I knew that I had a choice to make. Did I stand behind my sister who was my best friend and who I loved the most, or did I stand behind what I believe to be the truth? I let my parents in. I love them, too. My sister removed her children's things from my home. My parents received an angry letter that did not tell them what she believed they had done. At this point, I told the whole family what my sister thought, and she then broke contact with me. I sobbed. I begged her not to cut me off. Then, I blasted her verbally with what I really thought – that she was being flat-out cruel. I called friends and sobbed. I'm normally not much of a crier. I went to a class the next day sobbing, stating that my sister had died.

After a week or so, she let her children come back to my house, but remained cut off from me. I live in the same neighborhood, and would run into her from time to time. When I would see her I would feel like vomiting and I'd go to bed, or start crying. To say the least, I couldn't pull myself out of shock. The pain was nearly unbearable. How was I to let go of a 34-year-old relationship with one of the people closest to me in the whole world? At times I felt like I was vaporizing, I couldn't picture being in this life without her. I remember one month that I became so bitter that I felt as though I was going out of orbit. I didn't want to crash, so I made myself come to grips with my bitterness.

How could my sister ever believe such a story? How could she believe that my parents could be associated with Satan or with murderers? And, the really bizarre thing to me is that she really seemed to believe it. The belief itself seems too bizarre to me to even comprehend, but the worst thing about all of it is that she broke contact with our family: me, my children, my parents, my other sisters and brothers. Children were split from grandparents. What I wish that these therapists who are inducing false beliefs of sexual and satanic abuse would realize is that their own misperceptions have caused pain deeper than actual death, and that the pain penetrates beyond the therapy office into relationships between children, cousins, nieces, nephews, grandparents, sisters, brothers, parents, husbands and wives. I think that because of the serious consequences of this bizarre belief, these therapists doing this kind of work need to take a much deeper look into what they are actually doing. I can definitely vouch for the fact that there are many good therapists doing very sound work, and I want to be sure to give credit to the good therapists out there. I think that therapy is very serious business with very long-term effects.

Anyway, I knew that our family was not alone. I had asked area health-care workers if they had ever heard of satanic ritual abuse therapy. I found out that it was going on in at least two hospitals and two clinics in town. I received a hand-out from a course about satanic ritual abuse that said 350 cases had been treated in one year alone in our area. I just cannot believe that this town is full of Satanists. Personally, I believe that the whole satanic conspiracy is made up.

About this same time I heard about the False Memory Syndrome Foundation. I ran to the phone and started crying. I knew that they knew about false sexual abuse allegations, but had they ever heard about satanic ritual abuse therapy? Because of the damage this had already done to our family, and because my ability to trust people was so blown, I was afraid to call, but in so much pain and desperation that I did call. One thing that I have found that false accusations affect is trust in people. To connect with others who actually understood helped me to come out of shock.

After reading the FMS Foundation materials, I decided to call my sister's therapist, so that I knew she had been informed that my parents were not Satanists nor had they ever been. If families don't speak up, how is the therapist to know? I will also say that two other attempts had been made to discuss that my parents had not satanically abused my sister and that we were very worried about her. I also described to the therapist the symptoms I had seen in my sister that seemed so unusual to me. I did not request a meeting. The therapist called me back a week later to say that my sister wanted to meet with me and my husband. My husband met with my sister to find out why she wanted to meet. My sister told my husband that I was the one who requested the meeting. Another conflict. I cancelled my participation in the meeting, because I figured it was just a set-up and at the time I was still in too much pain to give my sister a chance to tell me good-bye forever. I kept hoping that we would be friends again. After I cancelled my participation in the meeting, my sister forbade her children to come to my house ever again.

Last week, I called my sister. She hung up on me once she heard my name. I am healing from this, not only with the support of my family and the FMS Foundation, but also with the support of a group of wonderful people who also happen to be therapists. I love my sister, and if she ever comes to my door and wants to come in, my door is open. As far as I am concerned, she has been brainwashed by a licensed professional in our state. I believe that the therapist is not being intentionally vicious, but that she just believes in what she is doing. I certainly do not believe in what she is doing. I do believe that a lot of lies are being told, and that with our family separated from my sister, my sister will never hear our side or our disbelief. The choice of whether or not she comes back is totally hers.

I understand that clients being treated for supposed Satanic Ritual Abuse are told that their parents can trigger them to kill themselves; that these people (Satanists) appear to be nice as part of the deception; that the parents are educationally minded so that the children can learn the satanic verse; that the reason often only one child can remember is because only one is chosen to be abused; that parents sometimes are only allowed into the cult for a short period of time until they serve their purpose and that's why they don't practice Satanism for a long time; that Satanists have doctors who cover up abuse and hospital records; and that Satanists play mind tricks to make a person forget and that they can only remember with help in therapy. There seems to be an "answer" to everything. I wish that the therapists would have this investigated by the law, in order to protect people who really may be in danger, if there is an ounce of truth in this. But the answer I hear on this is that even policemen are involved in the cover-up.

The question that I would like to have answered from these therapists is this: Why are you using hypnosis/trancework for the recovery of memories? I understand that hypnosis is not accurate for memory recall. If this is so, then why are therapists using invalid techniques to help people regain memories that are not true, and destroying entire families?

In closing, I am walking away from this pain. My sister is

a big girl, and is the one who chooses to live her life as she sees fit. I do not feel responsible for her anymore because, for the first time in my life, I can truly see that people believe what they do based on their own perceptions. I don't have the energy to try to make her believe what I call reality. Besides, she won't talk to me anyway. I do hope that some day we will be friends again. Granted, I have felt emotions during the past two years that have surprised me, but the baseline is that I still love my sister and I miss her very much.

A Sad Reunion

My oldest sister just left this morning to go back to her home in Oregon. She and her husband and six-year-old son stayed at my home here in Southern California for four days. It had been nearly five years since I last saw my sister. So much has happened in the last few years I don't know where to start.

For two nights while she was here, my sister Pat and I sat up very late talking about the events of the last few years. Here is a short version of our family's story.

There are nine children in our family—six boys, three girls. I am 36, the middle daughter and the fourth child. My older sister is 41, the second child. While I myself have felt anger and sadness about things that happened in my childhood and young adult life, I have come to understand that my parents were simply overwhelmed financially, emotionally, and in every other way by their task of raising so many children. We were loved, kept clean, safe, fed and sheltered. My father did his best as sole supporter and religious trainer and mom was busy beyond belief with simply keeping us fed and our house clean. So, needless to say, we all feel that we lacked the kind of personal attention we would have liked and needed. My parents were not perfect, but they were not the cruel, vicious people Pat now claims they are.

It seems to me that my earliest memories of Pat are that she was bossy, negative, rebellious and self-centered. I often thought she resented all of us younger children. She had a way of making everyone feel dumb, that she was always smarter and *always* right. I believe she felt picked on but she was usually the one who started the arguments.

I figured her out quickly, though. I knew that under the boastful, self-righteous exterior she was just as shy and unsure of herself as all of us were.

Our parents were homebodies and raised a family of homebodies. Our whole lives were lived inside the walls of our home except for school, which was very important to our parents. Our father taught school for about 15 years and we all did well in school.

Pat was quite popular in high school, got good grades, was a member of the drill team, pep squads, and was involved in many other activities. She is very intelligent and I always looked up to her because of that, as well as her artistic talents. I always felt, and still do feel, that she could accomplish anything she wanted, but in some ways she seemed lazy, indecisive perhaps, and always blamed her problems on everyone else. Once when she was a teenager my parents talked to her about her bad attitude and she remarked, "I'm just a product of my environment." The blaming started early.

After graduation she started dating a young man a few years older than she was. We all liked him very much. Pat got pregnant and couldn't decide whether to marry him or not. I must admit that my parents were not very supportive of her. She needed a *lot* of help with her situation and I think that they really did not know how to help her. The year was 1970 and unwed motherhood was not accepted. My father's Catholic beliefs made it an even more difficult situation. Our mother was also pregnant with my youngest brother and my grandmother, who was living with us, was dying. There was an incredible amount of tension in our home at that time.

Pat decided not to marry, and the father of the baby was killed in an automobile accident before the baby was born.

Pat gave the little girl up for adoption. My poor sister! So much trauma for a girl of 19 who had really lived a very sheltered life.

Things went from bad to worse for Pat. Next came years of bad relationships with men, involvement with drugs, a marriage that ended with a nasty divorce and two little children who were eventually raised by their father after years of being passed back and forth like footballs. Pat just couldn't seem to get her life together. She couldn't, or didn't want to, work and she was always depressed. Yes, she had some extremely difficult things to deal with, but she continued to blame everyone else for her problems and didn't take any responsibility for her life.

After her divorce and since her ex-husband had custody of their two children, Pat was free at last to do whatever she wanted to do, which ended up being an incredible journey through self-help programs, new-age and holistic lifestyles, feminism, vegetarianism, spiritual quests, psychic phenomena such as palm readings, tarot cards, communal living, experimenting with homosexuality, more drugs, massage therapies, studying eastern religions, and reincarnation and every other new trend, good or bad, that came along. Here in Southern California there are many, many trends one can choose to follow. Pat got totally, fanatically involved in every one of them. All the while she became more negative, more unhappy and extremely intolerant of anyone who was not living the "enlightened" lifestyle she had chosen for herself.

Over 10 years ago Pat started to talk about her "horrible" childhood, and her memories were about "raising" her younger brothers and sisters. Of course, our parents did require her help a lot as she was one of the older children, but we all helped out. I had five younger siblings myself and spent lots of time after school doing dishes, laundry, helping to prepare meals and babysitting. Now when I remember those days I realize how poor we were and how stressed-out our parents must have been. But we never knew it then! They raised us with so much love and a great sense of humor.

But our parents became the villains in Pat's life. She began to talk about beatings our father had given her with a belt and how our mother did nothing to stop him. This is so hard for me to believe because I received one spanking in my entire life from my father and he immediately apologized after finding out the facts of the situation. As for our mother, I remember the many, many times she confronted other parents about spanking or disciplining their children in public. It is hard to believe our mother would allow anyone to harm one of *her* children.

I began to really worry then about my sister's mental health. She sank deeper into a dark, gloomy despair. I wondered if she had a chemical imbalance. Was she manic-depressive? I knew that she needed real therapy instead of the trendy new-age stuff that just seemed to make everything worse. I knew that she suffered a great amount of guilt from having given birth to three children that she didn't parent.

Pat became a migrant worker and lived in tents in orchards and talked about being a gypsy in one of her past lives and met a man, also somewhat a drifter, whom she eventually married.

They had a son, bought some property in Oregon and moved a trailer onto it. I can't tell you how happy I was for her! These were the first positive, responsible things I had seen Pat do in 15 years. But it didn't last long. She was always unhappy, tired and stressed. I knew she started seeing a therapist and I thought that was a good sign, until three years ago when she wrote me a letter telling me that our father had molested her as a child.

She cut all ties with most of our family except for occasional contact with a few brothers and me. I have kept in contact with her these last few years.

I told my parents about the accusations. They then understood Pat's behavior for the last few years. Both my mother and father told me the stories weren't true and they were very sad to think how Pat must hate them. They have written many letters to her with no response.

After many months and phone calls Pat finally felt strong enough for a visit. When we finally sat down to talk, I told her that I had years' worth of questions and she said she would be available to answer some of them. Sometimes I could see my questions were difficult for her, but mostly I could see that she has repeated her story many, many times. Pat is still in an incest survivors group that meets once a week and she has been in almost constant therapy for nearly five years. She sees therapy as a life-long process and doesn't know when, if ever, she won't need therapy. Pat quotes John Bradshaw often and talks about "doing the work" to "heal the child within," which has included hypnosis and role-playing.

When I asked why she first went to a therapist, Pat told me she originally went to talk about her relationship with her teenage daughter and ended up seeing the therapist regularly about her depression. After several visits the therapist told her that she had put together the information Pat had given her and told Pat that she had probably been sexually abused as a child. The therapist said, "How does that sound to you?" Pat said, "Dark and scary." She was "instantly transported" to a closet in an old house in which our family lived in the late 1950s. Since then she has retrieved other memories. It seems our father wasn't the only one to molest her; there was also a friend of our parents and a man who was the school librarian. She is still working on that memory and also a memory or dream about one of our brothers.

When I asked her about details of various incidents she is vague and uncertain of times, places, or her age. Her memories are dreamlike and unclear. She says she relies on intuition. She just "knows" and her "body remembers."

When I asked her when the incest stopped she told me that the time she fell off a tall slide on the playground and landed on her head wasn't an accident; she remembers now that it was a suicide attempt. Pat was seven then and she thinks our father got scared and stopped molesting her.

When I asked Pat about her therapists, I only got their first names and the impression that she admires these women greatly. Pat talks about what great role models they are and how she feels better about herself because of their praise and support. She has become so very dependent on them it scares me. And the first therapist who "helped" Pat retrieve her first memories was an incest survivor herself.

Of course I have been talking with my parents and siblings about the accusations and the recent developments. Most of the people in our family think it's very typical behavior for Pat and since she has alienated herself from most of them, they feel quite helpless.

Our parents live in a nearby community and came over to my house yesterday to see Pat. I thought it was very brave of them, and also of Pat for hanging around until they got here. I'm afraid I had great expectations of the beginning of dialogue or understanding. My mother and Pat made small talk but both Pat and her husband totally ignored our father. When the atmosphere got too tense our parents left. Pat's husband felt "nauseated," he said. Of course he believes everything Pat has told him and when I tried to talk to him he didn't listen very well. He was surprised to hear that I don't believe the stories and brushed right past me when I mentioned a little about False Memory Syndrome. He treated me coolly for the rest of their stay.

After the visit I felt very sad. I was hoping they'd talk or even yell, but nothing happened. I do understand why my parents didn't express their feelings. We all feel that there's nothing we can say or do that would make a difference. I wanted to help my sister and was so sure there must be something I could do! I want my sister back.

So now Pat is on her way back home. She told me her real reason for coming here was to see if she could stick to her story around the family. Well, she did. I'm very sad and even more worried. Our parents aren't sad anymore; they are now angry. We all wonder what will happen next. Where will Pat go from here? How much more time, energy and money will she spend trying to get healed? And our parents, what about them? They worked so hard the last 40 years raising nine children, eight of them healthy, intelligent, worthwhile and happy people. Our father retired last year after years of hard work and sacrifice and my wish for him and my mother is that they could enjoy themselves now instead of worrying about their children.

I hope that someday soon we'll arrive at an answer for our weird situation, and that all heartache will end so we can get our family back together.

Another Family's Tragedy

My story is probably unique, but one that everyone can learn from. What happened to me exemplifies how potentially dangerous it can be when unsupported accusations are made and how misery can spread through a family.

My sister, who is five years older than I am, has a history of emotional problems. She tried to kill herself about 15 years ago. She has been going to therapists or psychiatrists for as long as I can remember. My first experience with a therapist was when I went with her to her therapist about a year ago. This came about after she told me she was having flashbacks of being sexually molested and raped when she was a little girl. She was suicidal. I left my family for a week and traveled across the country to see her. I didn't want to later regret not having gone to try and help her. I feared that when I arrived she would drop a bombshell! She did! She said it was our father who abused her.

At this time, she had a list in front of her of helpful things I could say or do, and what I shouldn't say or do in order not to upset her any further. At this point I was going along with her and acting as if I believed what she was telling me. I wanted to reassure her that I was taking what she said very seriously and believed her. That was one of the biggest mistakes I've made in my life.

My sister gave me *The Courage to Heal* to read. During the week I was there, I spent four hours with her and her therapist. In an odd way, it was exciting. I had never experienced anything like this before. For every skeptical question I had, there was always an answer. I felt I was becoming a part of something. When I walked down the street, I wondered how many of the women I passed had been sexually abused as children, and had or hadn't remembered yet, since the statistics were so high. When I mentioned this to the therapist she said, "Welcome to the club." I started to believe it.

When I came home, my thoughts were on my five-year-old daughter. If my father had done it to my sister, maybe he's been doing it to her. After all, from what I had read and heard, a person like that never changes, even at 70 years old.

Without intentionally doing so, I questioned my daughter about her grandpop after she told me she was anxious to see him. This was two days after I got home. My radar went up and I felt I had to be careful not to close my eyes to something that may have happened. I questioned her. Why did she want to see Grandpop? More questions and answers. Eventually she told me something that was shocking. I panicked and within two days had her at a children's therapist. My sister and her therapist had told me that this type of specialist existed, someone who was an expert in determining whether a child has been sexually abused or not. My husband and I reluctantly took our daughter to this woman. Within 45 minutes she told us that something definitely did happen with my daughter and her Grandpop. She was sure.

The sequence of events that followed was a nightmare I'd like to forget. I went to another children's therapist for a second opinion. I told her what my daughter had said and about my sister. She had no doubt there had been abuse. She said, "You have to believe the child." Why would she make it up? I was shocked. I now had two experts telling me the same thing. My doubts about what my father had done to my daughter came from my being in denial. A lot of mothers do that. I refused to be like them. I would be strong and protect my little girl. When I talked to my sister's therapist on the phone, she said she was really proud of me. Not every mother would have moved so quickly and handled the situation as well as I had.

I was still very confused. In all this time, my daughter never really said anything concrete. Even though she changed her story and denied anything happened, her therapist reassured me this was very common. I then read in a current publication about children revealing their abuse that many, if not most, say things like, "I was only kidding." That confirmed it. They retract their stories. It doesn't mean nothing happened to them. They are also in denial and want to forget the episodes.

I refused to talk to my father. I was terrified of him for the first time in my life. I was completely paranoid. My mother pleaded with me to go and talk to Dr. Harold Lief. This was right after the Darryl Sifford article came out. I consented. Not very much that he said meant anything to me at the time. Not until many months later would I think back on our meeting and recall something he said that made a lot of sense. Dr. Lief said that sometimes children can get caught up in a lie and it can have a snowball effect. It keeps on building and they can't find a way to get out of it.

About five months after I visited my sister, something unexpected happened. All that time, I had had very little or no communication with my parents. Before all of this, it was not uncommon for me to speak to my mother three or four times a day. We were very much a part of each other's lives. She and my father both were extremely generous and loving grandparents to my children.

My daughter had been to four sessions with her therapist. Sometimes I was in the room with her. At the fourth and last session I felt very uncomfortable. She was badgering my daughter and putting words in her mouth. I didn't like it. I have this on videotape and after watching it later was sure I didn't like what I saw. The therapist told me my daughter was "tough." I assumed that meant it was difficult to break her, to get her to tell exactly what happened. Later I realized this was because nothing did happen.

Then I planned a session with my mother to meet my daughter's therapist. Watching this woman try to explain to my mother about my daughter made me lose a lot of confidence in this therapist. She was not prepared and some of the things she said sounded ridiculous to me. My mother's questions were rational, the therapist's answers were irrational. This is when my mind began to open. Shortly after that I came across one of the first newsletters from the FMS (False Memory Syndrome) Foundation. My mother had sent it to me four months earlier. It didn't make any sense to me at that time. When I read it this time, I couldn't believe they were the same words. It suddenly made all the sense in the world. You are guilty until proven innocent.

The real turning point came when I said I wanted to check out an FMS meeting. I felt strongly about getting my parents back in my life. The emotional pain I felt on a daily basis was beginning to be intolerable. My parents were out of town for this meeting. I went alone. I remember walking outside after it was over on a beautiful spring day. After being with these people and listening to them talk about their "stories" and concerns, I suddenly felt I had an answer. This didn't have to have happened to my sister or my daughter. My father was just one of these unlucky men who had their lives blown apart because of a "phenomenon." A tremendous feeling of relief came over me. I took the first really deep breath in five months and was filled with a sense of hope.

Looking back, I can see I was in such a state of emotional turmoil, and confusion, it had to be affecting my daughter. I kept reading signs into everything she said and did. It still is difficult for me to believe that what I considered to be careful non-leading questions were the source of this mess. But that is the reality. It takes an unbelievable amount of skill and experience to discuss something like this with a five-year-old child and get accurate results.

At this point, I believe my mother and I have our relationship back. If we were able to survive this past year and mend our emotional wounds, we can survive anything. There is hope for everyone reading this.

My father is back to seeing his grandchildren and enjoying them. The time we lost with each other will never be replace but I can't dwell on that. Right now I'm thinking about the present and the future and how I'm going to make the best of the time we have left together.

Unfortunately, my sister is more convinced than ever that her memories are accurate. It's very difficult for us to have a relationship. I will never give up hope for her, but at this point I realize it is beyond my capability to lead her to recovery. Another unfortunate outcome of this tragedy has been regarding the relationship between my father and my brother. When my brother heard of my sister's accusations, he completely disbelieved it. But when I told him about my daughter, he was convinced, although some doubts were always in his mind. When my father was confronted first by my sister and then by me, my brother was present and said something so hurtful to my father that he has not talked to my brother since. My brother seems to still be unsure as to our father's guilt or innocence despite what I have told him. Their relationship seems to be destroyed permanently and the whole family loses.

Unanswered Communications

At my husband Mark's suggestion, I am documenting the conversations and events surrounding my sister Debbie. The situation is, at best, confusing and he feels this will be a useful record. I agree. What follows is a brief synopsis of the past few weeks:

May 12, 1990

Debbie called me. I had not talked to her for some time, perhaps two months. She was angry at me for not having contacted her. I apologized for that. She told me of the seriousness of her problems, that she had Multiple Personality Disorder (MPD) caused by chronic childhood trauma, that she had taken the Minnesota Multiphasic Personality Inventory (MMPI) and that if evaluated by a mainstream psychiatrist, the diagnosis would be schizophrenia. I mostly just listened to her. Then I told her to tell me all about it, even though I didn't really want to hear it. She told me that she had been ritualistically abused by Satanists, including Mom, and that Mom is still trying to "get" her. I asked how. She said a greeting card Mom had sent was a "trigger." Another attempt at a trigger was Mom asking Debbie for some of her checks from the joint account. Debbie felt just seeing Dad's name on the check was supposed to act as a trigger. The third controlling attempt she cited was that Mom wore a crystal to their session with Debbie, and any pendant is also considered a trigger.

I asked who was involved. She listed with no hesitation: "Mom, Richard, the Millers, the Hoffmans, probably the Lowes, Dr. Tillman and the priest from St. Mary's."

I asked what she actually remembered. She said much of

it was body memories and the only actual memory was of robes, candles and an altar.

We ended the conversation by agreeing to keep in touch and that she would send me information both on satanic abuse and MPD.

June 1, 1990

Mark had to work late. I went to pick him up and we didn't get back home until about 10:00 p.m. Five minutes later, Debbie called. I asked what was going on. She said she had the most intensely angry night of her life and she had called Mom and my two brothers, Ron and Bill, and told them all to go to hell. I asked what brought this on all of a sudden and she flew off the handle saying, "All of a sudden? Paula, this has been going on for the last year and a half!" She continued to scream at me, saying Mom is evil and so anyone who associates with her is also evil. She called the family a bunch of chicken-shits afraid to face the "truth," and said they had robbed me of my feelings. I was under Mom's power and that she would destroy me. I got angry and said, "No one has power over me, no one can control me and no one has the ability to destroy me!" She got even angrier and hung up.

I then called Mom to check on her. She was okay. I had the impulse to say we have to talk right now, intending to discuss the issues Debbie had raised. I feared Debbie's retribution, but now that she had opened the door I felt I had to speak up.

June 2, 1990

I spoke to Mom at her house in the morning. I confronted her with everything I had been told by Debbie. She said she didn't know where any of it came from. We talked for about three hours.

Nov. 3, 1990
Dear Debbie,

Thanks for writing. I wasn't sure you would want any communication at all from me, which is why I kept my previous note so short. Yet I felt such a strong need to tell you that I have not forgotten you. I care about you and I love you. I'll always respect your needs with regard to whom you want or don't want to communicate with. I, myself, see Ron three or four times a year, talk with Bill occasionally, and see Mom about every two or three weeks or so. Now I have my own family. Yes, Mark and I have a beautiful daughter, born June 14. Her name is Haley and she is healthy and happy and even sleeps through the night!

Giving birth to Haley was the best experience I've had in my life. To be involved so intensely and intimately with the mystery of life, its beginnings, and the connection between mother and child was very profound for me. I've often wished in the past four months that you could meet Haley, that you could share with me the joy of her babyhood, and that I could share with you my feelings.

Since receiving your letter, I have to agree with you that there may be too many obstacles to renewing a relationship between us. In trying to understand you and our family over the past couple of years since we talked last, I've done lots of thinking and feeling. I don't believe now any of the allegations you have made since entering therapy.

At first I was very confused about your accusations. They didn't make any sense to me, yet I wanted to be supportive of you and I had no reason to disbelieve you, so I did my best to accept your memories of childhood abuse. As time went on and you accused more people of abusing you, and then that the abuse had been a part of satanic rituals in a larger satanic conspiracy, I began to

*realize that these accusations made no sense to me be-
cause they were not, and could not, be true. I had no
explanation at that time for where your memories actually came from, but I knew with my heart that our family
was not involved in satanic rituals, and I knew with my
mind that the existence of a cult of satanic conspiracy
had no basis in reality.*

*Now I've come to believe that you are a victim, not of
childhood abuse, but of misguided therapy. I began to
believe this about a year ago, as a result of my own
research. Recently, I became aware that others, including
respected psychiatric professionals, have come to the same
conclusion.*

*I miss you terribly. I feel like my sister has been stolen
from me. I want my sister back. I will accept any communication from you, and have hope that we can someday
resolve this. Please know that I respect you and I love you
and I will never try to intrude on your life.*

Oct. 29, 1992
Dear Dennis,

*I don't quite know how to begin this letter. It is, of
course, regarding Debbie. I know you may want to share
it with her, and if that is so, Debbie, you can consider this
letter written to you as well as about you.*

*Dennis, I've tried to put myself into your shoes count-
less times over the past few years. Many times I've wanted
to contact you, to discover your feelings regarding Debbie,
her therapy, and her accusations of childhood abuse, but
I've guessed that, as her husband, you have probably
supported Debbie fully through an incredibly difficult
time. I would like to let you know my feelings and share
some information you might find enlightening.*

I don't believe any of the accusations that Debbie has made about abuse that occurred in her childhood based on memories she recovered during therapy. But, if these things didn't really happen, then where did these memories come from? I've asked myself this question many times, and until recently, I had no answers.

I've enclosed some newsletters from an organization called the False Memory Syndrome Foundation. A group of families who have had experiences very similar to our experience with Debbie have formed this organization. A woman, usually in her early thirties, with insurance or other financial resources, enters therapy for depression or relationship troubles. During the course of therapy, with subtle or direct guidance by the therapist (or others in a group situation), the woman is encouraged to "remember" childhood sexual abuse, which seems to explain all of her current problems. However, the families of these women, usually including non-accused siblings, say that the abuse never occurred. An explanation for this phenomenon is emerging through research on the mechanisms of memory. If you are interested, I can send you papers which have appeared in the psychological literature describing false memories and the ways they can be induced.

Please read these newsletters, and notice the doctors of psychology and psychiatry on the advisory board. Dennis, I really believe that Debbie's memories are false and that is why I am writing to you. I don't know how you will react to this information, but I am hoping that it will make some sense to you.

Up till now, I haven't heard from Dennis or Debbie. I look for a letter every day.

Another Sister Lost to Therapy

My nightmare began during a visit to our home by my sister, Sandra, and her boyfriend, Bob. I was almost 34 years old and Sandra was 27. We had eaten lunch together that day in July 1991 and Sandra was playing with my two children; Lori was four and Peter was 18 months. For some reason I spoke sternly to Lori, and suddenly Sandra bolted up, began crying, and ran to the bathroom.

Thinking she was criticizing my parenting, I asked what I had done wrong. That question opened up Pandora's box. She asked that we move out of earshot of the children and, still crying, began telling me that our interaction had reminded her of something from her childhood and that she was afraid that if I didn't open my eyes to reality, I would repeat the pattern. What pattern? She then proceeded to tell me about the most heinous acts that our parents had committed. I saw her mouth moving, heard the words and could only sit dumbfounded as I listened to her describe acts of oral sex. She claimed my father forced his penis into her mouth when she was six months old. She said that both my parents had sex with animals and that my father murdered our cat; he was found dead in our yard one day. Sandra also insisted that my mom and dad were involved in satanic rituals.

My sister and I went upstairs and sat on my bed. She continued to pour out her story, telling me that she would spare me the most horrid of details so I would not be disgusted. She implored me to read a book called *The Courage to Heal*, then I would understand what had happened to our family. I am the oldest; Jay is three years younger; Sandra is four years younger than Jay; and Denise is a year-and-a-half younger than Sandra.

In my shock and disbelief, I became nauseous. I assured my sister that I had absolutely no recollection of any kind of physical or sexual abuse. Sandra also told me that we were all beaten. I remember being spanked only two or three times my whole life. My dad did yell but never beat us. I left the state for a college in New England when Sandra was 11. But I did live with my parents for 18 years and *never* had any feelings of discomfort or questioned their devotion to us.

My parents were and are fine upstanding people. My dad is a semi-retired real estate developer and my mom is a well-respected psychotherapist. They have devoted their lives to their children and have always tried to be fair. All four of us went to college and graduate school. Sandra and I have master's degrees in education with a specialization in counseling, Jay is an attorney who develops real estate, and Denise has a master's degree in social work. My parents assisted emotionally and financially with all of us.

I tried to be supportive of Sandra. I did not want to abandon my sister in her obvious pain. She told me, in no uncertain terms, that if I did not remember all of this, I was repressing the memories. She further stated these kinds of memories are *never* made up. If one has the memories, the incidents happened period! In other words, I had no option. Either I believed her allegations were true, or I was blocking out the truth. I asked her about my truth, my reality, my own memories of my own childhood. Her definitive answer was that her memories were the truth. Anything else was fabrication or repression. I stumbled to the bathroom and dry-heaved into the toilet. I felt my whole world crumbling. My husband held me together for the next two weeks until my parents' visit. I was devastated.

Bob, Sandra's boyfriend, supported her fully. I think she met him at a Codependents Anonymous meeting. My husband says that although Bob seems like a very nice person, he looks shell-shocked. I was the one who referred Sandra to her therapist. I have never met her, but knew someone who had seen her and liked her. I have referred others to her as well. I know at least one other person who sees this therapist who has been presented with suggestions of family incest and/or abuse.

My world, as I knew it, was gone. I have multiple sclerosis. Stress is not recommended. The phone would ring and it would be my parents. I felt nauseous. Had they perpetrated these insidious crimes? I could't look at the pictures of them with my kids. It was almost too much to bear. My husband and I talked and talked and talked. I told Sandra that I needed to confront my parents for myself. She reluctantly acquiesced, but I could not mention her name as the accuser.

My parents arrived for their annual summer visit in early August, 1991. On a Sunday night, we sat down and I confronted them. It has been alleged that . . . They knew immediately where this had come from. Sandra had previously dropped a couple of hints to my mom that my dad had committed incest. The discussion lasted three or four hours that night. My parents were obviously sickened and confused. They looked so hurt. I'll never forget it.

I felt so ashamed that I brought this pain upon them. I needed to know for myself. My sister has never come forward to confront them. My parents were hurt that I ever believed her, but I have explained to them that I was in an impossible situation. Sandra insisted that denial is a common reaction and is to be expected.

I believe my parents and back them 100 percent now,

but have spent the last year-and-a-half in a tumultuous state of upheaval. I only hope that one day we will have our family back. I always thought we were the Brady Brunch. I guess that was never realistic. My youngest sister, Denise, has been in intensive therapy for years. Incest has come up in her therapy as a possibility. She is not sure — but she has almost no contact with our family. Sandra, too, has little or no contact with my parents or brother and only occasionally with me. If we see or speak with one another, we cannot discuss this issue. It is too painful for us both.

Manipulated by New Age Therapy

I am the oldest child of a large family, four girls and three boys. During the 1950s the discipline standards were not like the "hands off" disciplining standards of today. My father was strict and insisted that our behavior and manners be flawless. I am proud to say that not one of us was ever in trouble with the law, addicted to drugs or arrested for drunk driving. My parents were always very proud of us because we did live up to their expectations.

Since August 1991, my sister Catherine has abandoned any bond with our family. Her story is identical to the many stories that were documented in the book *Confabulations*.

It all began when Catherine was approached by a woman at the local Women's Health Club. This woman told her that her body language indicated possible abuse. Shortly after this meeting, at a family gathering, my sister announced that she was undergoing therapy. Little did we know what was eventually to transpire.

I need to tell you that Catherine is a woman approaching 40. She has been successful in the business world and has enjoyed living comfortably. She was always very generous and loving, but at the same time her personality could be called aggressive and demanding. Having an identical twin, she constantly stressed her individuality. Her immature actions during the past two years have also shown how controlling she was with the ones she loved.

My sister had been depressed because she was unsuccessful in conceiving a second child. She was also experiencing migraine headaches from the hormones she was taking. Acupuncture, psychics and other forms of creative treatment were all part of her search for happiness. Therapy promised her a cure to her body's supposed aversion to physical success.

When the holidays approached, Catherine requested that we give her some space at her therapist's recommendation. Along with this, she was told that she was also suffering from "repressed memories." These holiday times always meant so much to us all. It felt odd knowing we lived in the same city and weren't allowed to enjoy each other's company.

During the year, she did keep contact with her identical twin sister, my younger sister and myself. When we conversed with her, she explored ideas regarding sexual abuse that possibly had happened to her and she insinuated that we all could be victims of various forms of abuse. Catherine recommended that we read *The Courage to Heal*. Not one of us could determine how this book related to us.

In the months to follow, she and her therapist scrutinized our behaviors. Our personalities were judged and disapproved of one by one so that she could eventually terminate our existence in her life. We were either accused of acting inappropriately towards our children, being alcoholics or "in denial" due to our strict upbringing. The therapist made sure that my sister had no choice but to turn to the dependency that this type of therapy demands.

The initial therapist my sister saw acted in a totally unprofessional way. She related her own personal history of sexual abuse to my sister. This therapist, with pride, revealed to my sister how long it had been since she'd seen her family. From hearing those facts, I knew that Catherine was aimed in a wrong direction. By this time, the therapist's efforts had succeeded in making my sister disdain her childhood and her family.

Catherine was continuously encouraged not to see any of the family and especially her parents. She made use of the telephone, though. Most of the telephone calls brought about accusations and blame against our parents. We had to sit back and watch the parents whom we loved be destroyed by an evil force that flourished in my sister's new world.

If only she had kept her attack to phone calls. The worst and most painful things were written in her letters. Most of her words were copied out of *The Courage to Heal*. She told my mother that she had enabled my father to sexually abuse her and accused my mother of being spineless, unsupporting and unloving. While a child, Catherine claimed my mother had abandoned her emotionally as well. All this was written with malice and a bitterness so ugly it would turn anyone's stomach. What a blow to my mother and to my father!

Also, during this time, she was having nightmares. Her incest survivors group was helping her "recover" memories that she had forgotten over the last 25 years. Hypnosis was suggested as part of her treatment. Before too long, Catherine had uncovered "new memories" that she never before shared with the sisters who had lived in the same house and shared the same bedroom. Never once, in the previous years, did her face or body portray the pain of a child being sexually abused by her father.

She told us that her survivors' group couldn't believe how badly she had been treated by her parents. Cathy became the "star" of her group. Her controlling personality had found a new audience to pay her the attention she demanded.

Things finally came to a head in the summer of 1992. I received a phone call from Catherine one night. I'll never forget the conversation that transpired between us. For months, I had tried my best to maintain a neutral position, but that night I was lured into choosing a side. She threatened to take legal action against our father. It was then apparent I had to let my feelings be known. I challenged her allegations, much to her dismay, because I couldn't support them.

My sister referred to the movie "Sophie's Choice" in one of her letters to my mother. In that movie a mother is made to choose between her children. One is to be taken to a Nazi concentration camp, the other child she gets to keep. My sister alluded to the fact that my mother had made the decision to abandon her when she was a child. Through Catherine's actions, I know now how it feels to make such a painful choice.

Only a truly demented type of therapy would make a sibling choose between believing her sister and believing her parents. It is a fate worse than death, knowing that one you love is on the other side of an impenetrable glass wall of therapeutic evil.

Because I chose to defend my father, Catherine let me know that I would be considered dead to her. She also accused me of not knowing how it felt to be a sexual abuse survivor. Therefore, anyone who couldn't support her needed to be disassociated from her. That was the last I personally heard from her.

Two weeks after that conversation, a restraining order was sent to my parents' home along with a complaint to the Social Services Department. My parents were crushed. All hopes of my sister's recovery were looking very remote. The therapist she was seeing had "turned in" my father.

Not only had my parents lost a daughter—but they were totally humiliated. My father was not only accused of beating his daughter but charged with emotional neglect and sexual abuse. My sister's therapist warned the authorities that minors were living in my father's home and therefore he was a threat to his grandchildren.

It wasn't enough to attack our parents; now Cathy was trying to hurt the rest of the family.

My father appeared in court as requested. He reluctantly told the judge that he would abide by my sister's request to cease contact with her. That was the last anyone has seen her. At court, my sister and her husband appeared to be shattered people. This was Cathy's last desperate move to get attention from my family. She wasn't a victim before therapy but she certainly appeared to be one in court!

This has driven a stake through the heart of the whole family. Never has any one of us lacked love from our parents. Raised and educated Catholic, we were taught good morals and acquired sound values. Together we are strong and our fragmented lives are on the mend.

To add to this story, I want to briefly mention that my brother-in-law totally supported my sister's allegations. Never once did he qualify any of my sister's accusations with any of her siblings. My little four-year-old niece has also confronted her cousins with tales of her mother's alleged abuse.

Too bad therapy couldn't have brought back good memories. I, along with my brothers and sisters and their families, still have the joy of recalling happy memories of a family together. This therapy has taken away an opportunity for my sister and her family to share them with us.

If only Cathy could see the love and support that has emerged within our family. There is no doubt in my mind and in my heart that we are so very lucky to have each other.

As time goes by, I'm still bothered that this is going on. In their quest for power, do these therapists know what they have done to our family? To other families? They have no right! They take it upon themselves to change patients' former perceptions of their family life with absolutely no accountability. Catherine has claimed her alleged perpetrators have done terrible things to her; actually, her therapists have done terrible things to our family.

How did it get this far? How did someone I have never met take my sister, brother-in-law and niece away from our family? It is manipulation! By someone who is skilled and knowledgeable about how to manage other people's thoughts and actions.

This type of therapy advocates rage, hate and retaliation. Forgiveness is out of the picture. I can't help but feel that the authors of *The Courage to Heal* have taken their bitterness too far. Under the pretext of aid, they have stolen family members and made them victims. Of course we, the whole family, are all victims of this widespread vicious recovery movement.

In the end, we don't blame my sister. My family has come to the realization that Catherine is being victimized by a form of therapeutic abuse. We hope that one day she will be released to a new way of healing, one that is nonjudgmental and one that encourages adults to be responsible for their actions.

Funny thing, we still love my sister no matter what! None of the love we possessed for her has diminished with all that has occurred. We don't expect our lives to ever be the same. We only wish that someday she can once again allow herself and her family to be free to love us again.

I Want My Sister Back

I always thought that the family I grew up in was one of those perfect American families. However, little by little I have learned that my family isn't perfect. In fact, it is difficult to find a "perfect" family anywhere. I guess the image of a perfect family started to shatter once my older and only sister, Lynn, was having problems and sought therapy. This was vividly brought to my attention when we received a phone call one night from a hospital in the town where Lynn was attending college.

Lynn was never the easiest person in the world to figure out. My mom will be the first one to testify that Lynn was always difficult. Even as a little kid, Lynn would push my mother away from her. When she was a baby, she never liked to cuddle. Lynn always had a closer relationship with my father. They were the best of friends. They would play together all the time. There is one picture of my sister and my dad that really stands out in my mind. We were at a friend's house for a Fourth of July celebration. My dad and Lynn used to do these "circus" acts where Lynn would hold one of his hands and place her foot on his knee. In this particular photo, they were doing this and they both looked so happy and dependent on one another.

During Lynn's second year at college, she seemed to be having a lot of difficulty. She was seeing a therapist on a regular basis. My folks and I really noticed changes when she came home for a visit and she had given herself a crew cut. Things started to get really serious in the spring of 1990. One evening, my mom, dad and I had just walked in the door and heard a message on the answering machine from a woman at a hospital in the same town where Lynn was going to school. This woman wanted insurance information for Lynn. We only found out by accident that Lynn had been hospitalized. She didn't want any of us to know what was going on. Because Lynn was over 18, she could be hospitalized for psychiatric help without us knowing about it.

I have a vivid memory of my mom shaking and shivering after the phone call with the hospital. We were all so concerned about Lynn, yet our hands were tied and the only person in control was Lynn.

While Lynn was in the hospital we tried to contact her, but she wouldn't speak to us or let a doctor tell us what was happening. And yet my distraught parents were paying hundreds of dollars a day for her care.

After a couple of weeks Lynn was finally able to come home. I missed a few days of school so that I could go with my parents to pick her up at the hospital. While we were all meeting in a small room with her doctor, Lynn gave us some "ground rules." She said that we could only touch her or hug her if we asked permission first. She wasn't as strict with me about these rules; it was my parents that she was concerned about.

Although Lynn returned to our town she still wouldn't come to our house. She insisted on staying with a friend's family. She had so much stuff from college that we had to rent another car to bring everything home. We arrived at her friend's house late at night and unloaded all of her belongings. My mom, dad and I proceeded to go home without Lynn. Lynn has continued to keep in touch with this family and adopted them as her new family. To the best of my knowledge she gets together with them for the holidays. Now these friends don't talk to us anymore.

For my seventeenth birthday, Lynn and I got together

for lunch in the city. This was something that Lynn and I always liked to do. Whenever we got together, Lynn would always want to talk about mom and dad's bad points. I didn't much like to do that, especially since we were supposed to be celebrating my birthday. I let Lynn know that. In fact she could sense that I didn't feel comfortable about this topic. Lynn said to me, "You don't feel like talking about this do you?" I would say, "No, I really don't see why it is that every time we get together to have fun you feel as though you have to harp on mom and dad so much. I would prefer if we talked about something else and had fun." She paused for a moment and thought about what it was that I had just said. Then she continued to discuss mom and dad as if I hadn't said anything to her. It was as if she wasn't listening to me at all. On this special day for me, Lynn mentioned that there was something very important that she wanted to tell me, but that she thought this wouldn't be the right time since it was my birthday. Lynn procrastinated in telling me about this very mysterious something or another.

I used to go to visit Lynn at her apartment. She was living in a woman's residence and had just one room. In the beginning she would let me come in to her room immediately. Then after a while she would make me wait outside her door until she gave me the signal it was okay to come in. When I entered I could see that there was something on her wall that she had covered up with a piece of cloth. I knew that this is what she was doing because I could hear her ripping masking tape through the door. One day I went to her room and she had forgotten to cover up her wall. I saw the messages. They were notes about making sure that she was taking care of herself. Some of the notes were simple things like, make sure you eat when you're hungry — don't starve yourself. Make sure you go to the bathroom when you have to go. Don't spend money on foolish things. There were also little cards on her wall from herself to herself. They said things like, "Lynn, I love you. Love Lynn."

For the past couple of summers I have gone away to teach on six week long internships. In the summer of 1990, before I left for one of my adventures, I got together with Lynn. Again she said there was something that she wanted to tell me, but she was afraid it would ruin my summer so she decided not to tell me the "great mystery." While I was away, Lynn's new therapist advised her to go back into the hospital so she could "evaluate" her and see what kind of help she needed.

About halfway through my trip, I received a letter from Lynn. It was very disturbing to read. In fact I only remember a small portion of it. She said that she was seeing a new therapist and had been readmitted to a local psychiatric hospital. She wrote in the letter that she was thinking of ways to kill herself. I wasn't sure if mom and dad knew that she was suicidal so I didn't say anything to them. I called Lynn to let her know that I was thinking about her and that I was there for her and loved her. The following Christmas Lynn came home to spend the night. That was two years ago and she hasn't stepped through our front door since then.

The following spring everything started to go further downhill. My parents were still paying for Lynn's therapy and medication, yet they still didn't know what the problem was. There was no proper diagnosis while she was in the hospital, except for major depression for which she was taking Prozac. My parents were getting more and more frustrated with her, not to mention hurt as well.

Lynn told my mom to read a book called *The Courage to Heal*. She didn't say why. The reason that Lynn knew about the book was because somebody at college saw her reading a book called *The Courage to Create*. This person said to her, "Have you read *The Courage to Heal?*" She hadn't, but soon she did get the book and spent much time studying it.

Mom and Lynn were talking on the phone the Friday before Mother's Day. Mom wanted to know why Lynn wouldn't meet with us and a family therapist. Lynn finally broke down hysterically and said, "I was raped!" Mom was stunned. She asked Lynn, "When did it happen, did it happen at college?" Lynn answered by saying, "No. Dad raped me when I was four years old." My mother started to shake as she does in stressful situations. My father, who was sitting nearby during the phone conversation, heard the accusation indirectly. To this day, Lynn has not confronted him. All of the communication from my sister's side has been done through me and my mother. My dad continues to try and communicate with her. She doesn't write back.

I didn't learn about the accusations for another six months or so. I often look back and wonder how in the world my parents managed to keep this from me, but somehow they did. I found out in December, a couple of weeks before Christmas in my senior year in high school. I was at a holiday bazaar across the street from where Lynn was working at the time. I hadn't seen her for awhile so I decided to pop over for a little visit. Her shift was almost over so I waited a little bit and then we went to the bazaar together. We looked around and then went outside to talk. Lynn kept saying that there was something that she really wanted me to know. Finally I said, "Lynn, you have been telling me for some time now that you need to tell me something. You've stalled about it twice before and honestly if you don't tell me now then you'll just keep procrastinating about it." She said, "You're right." Meanwhile I'm bracing myself for her to tell me that she's a lesbian. I really thought that was the big news; however, it wasn't. In fact, that would have been a breeze to deal with. After all, I already have a lot of close friends who are gay or lesbian. As the cold December weather ripped through my jeans and into my body, Lynn's cold words also came tearing through me. She put her mitten-warmed hand on my knee and said, "Natalie, I'm an incest survivor." I didn't know what in the world to think. I was caught so off guard by the whole thing. I felt as though I had just been hit by a Mack truck. After a moment of silence on both of our parts she looked me dead smack in the eyes and said, "You do believe me, right?" I never gave her a definite "yes" or "no" answer. In fact, to this day, I haven't. I'm afraid that if I say I don't believe her, I'll lose her all together. Well, this shocking news really didn't hit me for a couple of hours. I got a ride home with a friend and started to cry. I guess for 48 hours I really did believe this had happened. I went up to my room, grabbed my cat and cried myself to sleep. I tried to get in touch with my advisor from school but had no luck. I didn't talk to anyone until Monday morning when I saw my advisor in the hallway at school. We went into the parking lot and I started to cry uncontrollably. We hugged for a long time.

Finally I was able to pull myself together enough to attend morning gathering. I didn't go to all my classes that day. In fact, I spent a good deal of the day talking with the dean of students and my advisor. I soon realized, to my embarrassment, that my advisor had known about the accusations months before I did. Lynn had called her and told her what was going on. I couldn't believe it. I was so angry and upset that Lynn would talk to her and tell her about our "dysfunctional" family like that. I think one of the reasons Lynn did that was so that she could be certain that I would receive the proper help and support that I needed as my mind tried to sort this out.

After school on Monday I went home and tried to carry on with life. I couldn't do it. I was very tense and testy. Finally I blew up at my mom. I think I said something like, "I saw Lynn. She told me what she believes happened." Of course I was crying during all of this. Mom instantly got frazzled and tried to reassure me. Once my dad came home from work we all sat down in the living room, where Lynn used to play as a happy kid, and talked all of this out. When your parents have both been in therapy for a while you learn how to "talk" about everything! They explained this FMS (False Memory Syndrome) to me. I was instantly more at ease. I don't think I have ever in my life gone through as many emotions as I did in those 48 hours. I was angry, sad, depressed, confused, lonely, scared and then, all of a sudden, I was reassured. Of course it didn't all go that quickly. One of the reasons that my mom was so upset was because Lynn wasn't supposed to have told me about the accusations when she did. Apparently, Lynn had promised my mom that she wouldn't tell me unless we were all in a facilitated session. Lynn broke that promise.

I returned to school and tried to explain FMS to my advisor. She wouldn't listen to me. All she would say was, "Well, Natalie, you know I have a lot of friends who have been abused and raped and this really does happen." Any time I tried to open my mouth she would cut me off. I couldn't get a word in edge-wise. I was so frustrated. How could this woman tell me what did and didn't happen in my own home? She had no clue as to what it was like growing up in my family. I was so frustrated with her that I finally stopped talking to her about the issue.

I didn't see Lynn again until February. I went down on a Sunday afternoon to see her new apartment and kitten. We also exchanged Christmas gifts and she gave me my birthday present as well. I took a quick tour of the apartment and played with the kitten for a little bit. It seemed as though everything that I did with her cat was wrong. The poor thing was only ten or so weeks old. She would tell me to stop doing something because the kitten was biting. Since I've had my own cat I have learned that biting is part of a kitten's every day life. Lynn was trying to control the situation with her kitten. The only thing that I can clearly remember about my visit that day was that I couldn't wait to leave. I felt so uncomfortable being there with her. It was as though I was with a totally different sister. I left and didn't see Lynn for ten months.

Although we didn't see one another for a long period of time, there was a little bit of conversation. My high school graduation was in June. I took the time to write Lynn a personal invitation to come. In it, I said that I would really like for her to be there with me on my special day even though I knew it would be difficult for her. The night before graduation a letter was delivered to our house. It was hand-delivered by a strange man. This too was another disturbing letter to read. Its appearance was very sloppy. It was written on notebook paper that had been torn out of a spiral book. In total, it was about eight pages long, that is, eight pages of deep thoughts that were repeatedly scratched out. I look over it every now and then, just to try and figure it out. I'm still not able to make much sense out of it. Other than the fact that my sister needs serious help, there are two parts of the letter that I distinctly remember. One: She would not be able to make it to graduation because it would simply be too painful for her and she wasn't ready to deal with the family yet. Two: She hoped that at the end of this turmoil with the family, there would be a stack of letters for us like there was in *The Color Purple* for Celie and Nettie, the two sisters who were separated for years. I showed the letter to my parents and my cousin who was living with us for a month.

At the graduation ceremony there was a basket of flowers waiting for me from Lynn. In them was a note that said, "Dear Natalie, Even though I am not here in person, I am still watching over you. Congratulations! Love, Lynn." Through all of the commotion of the ceremony, I was very upset that she wasn't there. I don't think I showed it as much that night as I show it now.

I was very angry for a long time that Lynn couldn't just carry on with life and think about someone other than herself for ninety minutes. I wasn't even asking her to sit with the family. She could have stood in the doorway for all I care. Just so she could have been there to see me on my special day. I expressed this to her in a letter that I wrote about a month after graduation. It took me a long time to get the guts to write her, but finally I did it. I also told her how upset I was that she had talked to my advisor months before telling me. She also talked to some close family friends of ours. My mom and I started to suspect that she had talked to them too after we didn't hear from them for a very long time. We called them and indeed she was in touch with them. I didn't hear any response from Lynn after I wrote her that letter.

Every now and then we would run into a friend who had

seen Lynn at work. We didn't even know where it was that she was living. While my cousin, Eileen, was in town she tried to get in touch with Lynn, but she had no luck. They were very close just a couple of years ago. Again Lynn said that she wasn't ready. She was living in a summer sublet and had next to no money at all. I later found out that she was living on food stamps and welfare. I can't deny the fact that I feel incredibly sorry for her, but at the same time we have all tried to reach out to her with no avail.

One day, my mom ran into a friend of ours in the city. He mentioned that he had seen Lynn where she works. She told this friend of ours about the accusations. She had only met him a couple of times before. It seemed very odd to me that she would be telling something so personal to people that she hardly knew.

By Christmas time I missed Lynn so much that I just had to see her. I wanted so badly for us all to be together like the old days. I got her a pretty pair of earrings that I thought she might like. Since we didn't know where she was living but we knew where she worked, I decided to go to her work place and try to talk with her. I went first thing in the morning. She wasn't there yet, but someone told me when she would be arriving. I called my boss and asked if it would be okay if I was a little late. I told him I needed to see my sister and he said, "This is something that is very important for you to do. Go ahead and take as much time as you need." I went back to see Lynn a couple of hours later. First, I went upstairs and saw her from a distance. Previously when I had gone to see her, I had stood behind a stack of books and hid because I was afraid to see her. This time I knew that I wanted to see her because as I looked at her back from a distance, it was as if she were a magnet and I was being drawn closer and closer. I went up to her and said, "Lynn?" She turned around, looked at me and in a soft big-sister voice said to me, "Natalie." She put her arms out in a hug. As we stood there hugging, she rocked me very gently back and forth as I sobbed onto her shoulder. I couldn't believe it. Finally I had seen her again after ten months. We sat down and started to talk. At first it was small talk. Then she said, "You know I feel like we can't have small talk without talking about the issue at hand." So we started to talk about her being an "incest survivor." The conversation proceeded like this for the next twenty minutes or so:

Lynn: *I feel, Natalie, as if you only love a part of me. And that's the part that is not accusing Dad of incest.*
Natalie: *Lynn, you're my sister. I love you and I miss you. I had to come today to see how you were.*
Lynn: *Well, I feel as if you think I'm crazy.*
Natalie: *(No comment)*
Lynn: *I feel as though you don't believe me.*
Natalie: *Lynn, in all honesty, if there is a perpetrator in the family, and one child is abused, then most likely the other child is going to be abused, too, or at least pick up on the fact that something isn't right. I can tell you that NOTHING ever happened to me when I was little. And I also would suspect that there would have been some acting out on your part.*
Lynn: *(in a very harsh and cool tone of voice) Don't you get it? There was acting out. You know I was always alone and withdrawn and I was compulsively washing my hands!*

Some other things were said, but the next thing that stands out in my mind was her saying that she couldn't come home until we acknowledge the fact that she was abused. Before I left she said, "I really get the feeling that you, Mom and Dad aren't dealing with this." At this point I snapped. I couldn't believe she had the nerve to say that. I responded by saying, "You don't think we're dealing with this? How can we *not* deal with it? You haven't been home for two years. We go to sleep at night and it's there. We wake up in the morning and it's there. The whole family is depressed about this and you think we aren't dealing with this?" I started to cry during my response. I asked Lynn if she had received any of our mail. She said yes. Then I asked her if she had opened it. She said yes but that she almost didn't. She used to open her mail in the presence of her therapist. Some of the pieces were hand-delivered to the store. She didn't like this because it meant we had been in the store. She specifically told me that she didn't want Mom and Dad to come in, but she thought it would be okay for me to go in every now and then. She didn't like it when I responded by saying, "Lynn, this is a public store for crying out loud!" Her immediate response was, "Yeah, well, I work here."

I decided to leave before we started to really push each other's buttons. I didn't want to wear out my semi-welcome before I was able to use it again. A positive note during my visit: She was willing to take down the address of the store where I work. After all, I did point out to her that when she first told me about the accusations she said she was afraid to tell me because she wasn't sure if I would support her or not. Everybody always says it's so important to keep the communication lines open. I told her that I was trying to do so by writing letters, but I hadn't heard anything from her. She said she received my letter after graduation but she thought that it sounded very angry. I thought for a minute. Why was it okay for her to be so angry, but when she doesn't come to my high school graduation I can't be angry with her? That doesn't seem right to me. How can Lynn possibly "heal" if she doesn't communicate with us? This whole therapy language drives me crazy. It's exactly the language that she was using during my visit.

When I got home that day I naturally told my parents about my visit with Lynn. When I mentioned to them about her "acting out" in terms of being alone and withdrawn and compulsively washing her hands my mom said, "She was alone and withdrawn because she wasn't diagnosed as having a total hearing loss until she was eight years old." She had learned to compensate for it very well. As far as the hand washing compulsion, she was nine years old when that happened. After thinking about it I said to myself, "Lynn has been an excellent artist since day one, surely there would have been some sort of acting out in her pictures." We have had her drawings, photos and school reports professionally analyzed and there are absolutely no signs of sexual abuse from those reports.

It has been three weeks since I saw Lynn. I haven't heard anything from her. She didn't even send me a birthday card at the store where I work. I was really hoping that we would be able to start some sort of communication and get things going again. I talked to a counselor after my visit with Lynn. He said, "If Lynn didn't hear the words that you spoke to her, she will at least have seen your emotions and realized that you were upset. Those emotions will have an effect on her like a tornado because you can't hide how you truly feel deep inside."

I hope to God that Lynn turns around some day and realizes that we had a good childhood and that it is safe to return home. I feel as though I no longer have a sister to whom I can turn. Other siblings who have experienced this type of family crisis are a little more lucky in that they are in their 20s or 30s and have other siblings and their own families. I feel stuck because in my family there is just me and Lynn. I'm 19 and still living at home. I wish there was someone else I could talk to. I do have a wonderful support system of friends my age and older. But I want my sister back! The pain just won't go away.

Recovering from Accusations

An 80-year-old man sits alone in his self-care apartment at a large retirement center. His very ill wife of more than 50 years lies dying in the adjacent Nursing Center. It is Christmas week 1991 and his family is coming to celebrate. The old man walks with difficulty. He is verbally impaired and no longer able to express his thoughts with ease. In fact, sometimes he is aphasic. He has marked hearing loss. He is no longer a whole person.

Two ministers visit this old person, bringing typewritten pages, one on official church letterhead. No supporting family member or friend is present to hear what these two ministers have to say, to help the old man understand what is happening. No one is there to interpret the lengthy silences of the old man to the two ministers who can speak so easily. Because no one is present to defend the gracious, verbally impaired old man, his loving family does not know what transpired in its entirety.

While the two young ministers are reading from their typewritten pages, confronting the old man with details of gross sexual acts he supposedly performed on his own young daughter decades ago, there is a knock on the door of the apartment. The old man walks to the door, graciously greets Christmas carolers and smiles as they sing. The carolers are from his church. They leave with their Christmas happiness, and the old man returns to his accusers. Eventually the two ministers leave, and the old mentally impaired man is left alone with his immense grief and shock. He is unable to sleep all night.

His family arrives for the Christmas celebration. Only a few members of the family are missing, although all have been invited. One grandson had to work; the husband of a granddaughter had to sleep so he could work the night shift. The accusing daughter chose not to attend. The old man excused himself from the celebratory dinner at the restaurant, the first time ever he chose not to attend. He said he wanted to be with his dying wife.

It is late afternoon of the Christmas get-together day. The old man's apartment is filled with children and grandchildren, making noise, joking and laughing. The old man brings out sets of papers, and hands them to each of his children present. He says haltingly, "Promise me you won't feel too bad." The children note the official church letter-head at the top of one of the sheets, followed by a hand-written letter. The room becomes silent. The children read about alleged sexual abuse by their kind father and the response requested by the church board. The old man's shakily written letter follows, denying the charges firmly and clearly. One child holds a three-page detailed account of heinous alleged acts. The child reads it to the others present when the old man is absent. The children and grandchildren weep, in pain for their beloved, impaired, sad, tired old father and grandfather.

A few days later, as the old man starts his day with a shower, he has a stroke, and falls in the tub. On admission to the local hospital, he is nearly dead.

I am a middle-aged woman, a daughter of this impaired old man, whom my sister has falsely accused of sexual abuse. How have these unjust actions affected me? In these past eleven months, what has helped me to cope and work at justice? What are my objectives now as I write and reflect?

In the first two months following the December confrontation I felt immense devastation. I felt a sense of unreality, that this whole thing could not be happening. I work full time and continued to go to work, but felt detached, felt that my perspective of the world was off. I forced myself to follow my job routines. I experienced anxiety attacks and felt out of control. I felt on the edge of a complete nervous breakdown.

To have my father publicly accused of a shameful crime initially produced feelings of shame in me. I felt such empathy for my dad, I experienced feelings he also felt. I felt "like a fake" at work, when other staff complimented me. I felt I had a terrible secret, one I certainly did not want to share with my co-workers. My self-esteem hit an all-time low. I felt so little self-worth.

I had thoughts of suicide, but never felt concern that I would act on them. Driving to work I would sometimes think how easy it would be to run off the road and hit a tree. This tremendous stress and strain and pain would be over. I had two breast biopsies done during this initial two-month period. At times, while waiting for the pathology results, I hoped the results would be malignant, and I would die.

I cried every day. My mind was obsessed with this problem I felt helpless to solve. I experienced insomnia, lying awake for hours at night thinking through possible courses of action. I felt immense hatred toward the two ministers and one social worker who counselled my sister, and helped her to believe these acts of abuse actually took place. I felt hatred toward my sister who hurt my father in this cruel manner. I felt consumed by the dilemma and unbelievably sad.

I was unable to eat as I normally did and lost twenty pounds in one month. Food just stuck in my throat. I started to dread mealtimes because I was unable to eat more than a few bites. I felt nauseated a great deal of the time. That which was previously pleasurable no longer produced feelings of happiness in me.

What helped to turn these feelings and unhealthy patterns of thinking around?

My uncle in another state sent me an article he came across in the *Philadelphia Inquirer,* "When Tales of Sex Abuse Aren't True" by Darrell Sifford. The article described situations similar to mine, and feelings of devastation similar to my own. I discovered that I wasn't alone after all. At the end of the article was an 800 number to call, which would connect the caller with the Institute for Psychological Therapies in Northfield, Minnesota. My adult daughter called that number and talked at length about our situation. I felt a glimmer of hope for the first time. I started to receive literature from the Institute, which was extremely helpful. Accompanied by and prodded by two of my adult daughters, we three attended a seminar presented by the False Memory Syndrome Foundation, a nationwide support group for persons falsely accused of sexual abuse. The room was full of families just like mine – good kind fathers and mothers – accused of sexual abuse which never occurred, based on supposedly repressed memories. As I shared informally with others throughout the day, I felt utter astonishment that I was believed as I spoke, that I was not challenged "to prove" my father's innocence. I listened to their stories; they listened to mine. I absorbed a great deal of information, which started to empower me. I saw people who overcame the devastation I was feeling, and saw people who were constructively working at the problem. Some participants even showed a sense of humor and could laugh at the very things which I felt so depressed about. I was able to see that I too could get through this.

Through the Institute for Psychological Therapies I became a part of a study regarding false accusations. To participate felt positive; energy expended constructively to better understand this psychological phenomenon was empowering.

The cohesiveness and caring of my immediate family and my extended family was invaluable. Dad continued to be the role model for parental love he always was. He was able to state he felt sad and broken. He said once that he thinks my sister really believes these abuses occurred. He acknowledged that my sister "tried everything in her power to bring me down." It was stated with such grief. He asked us each to pray for her. When asked what he wants for Christmas 1992, he replied, "The love of my children." Our phone bill was high for several months after the December confrontation. For a long time I phoned my dad daily. Brothers, sisters-in-law, daughters, aunts and uncles phoned and wrote frequently. We shared any articles we could find on the topic of false accusations with each other. We shared our feelings. We prayed for each other. We continued to be the caring functional family we always were. Even though one from our family had pulled away, and had made terrible hurtful accusations, I was able to see that we had indeed not changed. My dad is the same person he always was. I am the same caring, sensitive person I always was. We did nothing wrong. The accusing words began to have less power over me. The love and concern within my family was healing.

With my husband's encouragement, I began to share my experience and feelings. I am a member of a small support group of six women from my church community that has met monthly for years. One Saturday morning I risked sharing my sad personal account of false accusations in my family. My friends listened, cried, showed support, love and caring to me. I found that as others joined to share my sorrow, my burden became lighter.

I was put in contact with two other families in our larger church who are currently experiencing false sexual abuse allegations. One woman became a source of strength and healing for me, as we wrote and shared. She "had been there" and relayed those ideas and actions which helped her cope. One man who recently experienced the devastation an FMS victims sibling can feel wrote to share his pain and suffering. I shared those strategies which helped me cope, and also sent him the book *Confabulations*. His appreciation for shared information, for the book, for a listening ear, also help me to heal. Another small network begins.

Lastly, I found healing as I recognized the need to change my goals. My sister had been making the false accusations against my father for some months before the two minister-counselors confronted him. Prior to that December 1991 confrontation, I had a goal to protect my aged, verbally impaired, kind father from a confrontation over the false sexual allegations by my sister. My dad and I live in different states. My husband, my brother and I informed one of the involved minister-counselors of the absurdity of the accusations, of my sister's manipulative personality, of my father's impaired mental state and verbal skills, of our wish for no confrontations. If he insisted on a confrontation against our wishes, a request was made that one of dad's supportive children be present. It was to no avail. I was not able to meet the goal of protecting my father. My dad is no longer a whole person, and I failed to keep him safe. I have a new goal: to show my dad love and appreciation for being the great dad he is and was. I can meet that goal. I recognize I cannot protect my dad from harmful behaviors of others, including my sister and her counselors. I have a goal to remember the good times when Dad and I spent time together. I talk and reminisce from the past, and we share laughter. We had many happy family times; it heals to remember those times with my dad. His great sense of humor was one of the best qualities.

Eleven months have passed since that fateful December day. It is November 1992. What objectives will I strive to attain as my life continues?

I will strive to keep this family tragedy of violence and injustice in perspective. I work outside my home on a full-time basis, and enjoy my care-giving career. I have a kind and delightful husband, with whom I share life's experiences. I have three adult daughters who relate to me and their grandfather in a warm and caring manner. Life has many pleasures, and I will enjoy them.

I will state clearly my dad's innocence of my sister's alleged sexual abuse allegations, as he is unable verbally to defend himself. I can state it clearly and simply, without anxiety, as it is truth. I cannot make people believe what I say; that is not within my control. I am responsible for my words and actions. I am not responsible for my sister's words and actions.

I will relate to all people in a kind manner, to the best of my ability. I will not be friends with all people. I may never have the chance to be a friend to my sister, as she has estranged herself from me. If I someday have the chance to be my sister's friend, I will decide at that time what is mentally healthy for me. I will always be kind to her, as I have in the past.

In December 1991, a tragedy struck my family. I did the best I could with the resources I had. I will not re-hash that experience, but will move forward with hope and joy, and service to others. I commit myself to educate others regarding repressed memory and False Memory Syndrome.

Jana Never Calls

Abstract

His daughter called to his son, and they spoke, and the son believed all that was said by his sister. The father and the son had argued many years earlier, and the bitter taste had lingered on. So what the sister said fit the brother's image of their father. The sister's new memories were a lost puzzle piece found, and they connected with clarity the foggy times of childhood to the unfortunate remembrances of adolescence.

But the puzzle piece, so fine and neatly shaped, did not fit. It was such an elegant shape that at first all those who saw it assured the brother it fit, and insisted that there was no need to try it.

But the brother was by nature a meddler, not content to accept on faith what might easily be tested against fact, and so he took the pretty piece down from its mantle and placed it firmly into the jigsaw.

It did not fit!

So he rotated it.

It did not fit.

So he pressed it harder, earning a sweat on his brow for his exertion, but still...

It did not fit...

When no one was looking, he even cheated, breaking off a tab, bending and reshaping, nibbling edges like jagged nails, but what was not designed to fit did not and would not fit. Thus the brother surrendered and tossed the smudged and bent piece aside. He sat and rested and thought of the puzzle and the piece still missing. And as he sat, he slept. And as he slept, he dreamt.

The dream, of course, was about a puzzle. A puzzle with a missing piece. The puzzle was a beautiful picture of a fluffy, white cloud drifting on a blue sky. The trouble was that there was no table in the dream to set the puzzle on. In fact there was nothing in the dream but the jigsaw and the brother floating next to it. The two floated together in the sky—a pretty sky, azure with puffy clouds. Now you see the brother's trouble. There was a piece missing. This he knew. But the sky behind the puzzle was identical to the picture the puzzle held, and he couldn't find the hole where the missing piece would go, even if he could find the missing piece. In fact, the harder he looked at the puzzle in search of the hole, the harder it became to see any part of the puzzle at all. It blended in with the sky behind it. It faded away. So that when he rubbed his eyes from the strain of staring and opened them again, he was startled to find that he could not see the puzzle at all. Only the sky. It was as though there was no puzzle there. And maybe, he thought, there never had been. Maybe it had always been just sky.

When the brother woke he knew he had dreamed the truth—or at least about the truth. The lesson he learned is that the truth doesn't need to be clear to be the truth, that clouds are real despite their lack of exact form. He woke to learn that a cloudy truth is better than a crystal clear confabulation.

Preface

I suppose that by now I too am on the list of those accused. My sister has not called me since I went to visit her at about this time last year. Our parting was one of strained politeness.

Intuition, inference, and just plain guessing convinces me that I too am now found "guilty" of sexually abusing my sister when we were younger, despite the fact that I am only three years older than she. When I was old enough to abuse her, I was old enough to remember it. Of course, that statement suggests logical and factual proof, and as we all now know, logic and fact should not stand in the way of gut feelings. Jana tried to make me her ally in this family-crushing battle, and when I proved difficult, when I tried to substantiate what she claimed happened, she turned cold to me and cut me off. Just like she cut off the rest of the family. She abandoned them because she believes they abused her as a child and teen. She has abandoned me now. What should I assume?

This is a hard story to tell, and because of the emotions I don't tell it very well. I hope you'll bear with me. I hope it comforts those who need it. You are not alone.

The Beginning

Jana never calls. I live a long way away and she is my only sibling, but she never calls. She and I have never been terribly close, and this has always pained me. I am a man who loves and thrives on family, and to have a sister whom I hardly know forms a hole in my soul. When the phone rang two Januaries ago, and Jana was on the other end of the line, I was thrilled!

Suddenly, out of the blue, she was calling me, talking to me, sharing her life with me. When, years earlier, I had told my great aunt of our lack of closeness, she had assured me that as adults we would come together. And now, it seemed, we were. If only the circumstances had been better. For the circumstances that finally broke down the barriers between us were catastrophic, unspeakable. Our parents, my dear sister told me, had repeatedly abused her when she had been young.

I was stunned. Shocked! Horrified! My jaw dropped as far as it could, and with every iota of detail she related, I discovered it could drop even further. "This abuse was ... sexual?"

"Yes, sexual."

"And they both were involved?"

"Yes, they, and others."

"Are you sure?"

"YES, OF COURSE I AM!"

I had no choice but to believe her. I was raised to be trusting and loving, and this was my sister talking. What reason had I to doubt her? Who would lie about such things?

I was furious with my parents. I had left home a few years back under the clouds of ongoing arguments with them and, since then, I had been slowly trying to patch things up. This revelation shattered the reconciliations, shattered even the desire to make the effort. With each of the many collect phone calls I accepted from Jana, my parents became more and more strangers, less the people I remembered knowing as a child. When I commented on this fact, Jana taught me about repressed memories. I was frightened beyond description. My entire life was nothing more than my memories of it. If suddenly those were taken away, if suddenly they are found to be fiction, then what am I? I too am fiction. I am the man with amnesia who knows not even his name. I am a 24-year-old adult with no memories of what really happened to him as a child.

It was in the midst of that horror of no longer knowing who the hell I was that I began to search desperately for answers. I needed to find my lost childhood and I needed it fast. I was going crazy. I was horribly depressed. I was afraid of my shadow. Jana called every other day or so to tell me new stories of abuse that had gurgled up from the black well-spring of repressed memories in her unconscious mind. Abuse by groups. Abuse with guns. Abuse with various crude medical instruments. Abuse by physical and psychological torture. The world was a bad place.

It was in this atmosphere of dread and disgust that I discovered I too had been sexually abused as a kid, although for me it didn't seem to have been as bad as it had been for Jana. I discovered my own personal experiences with the help of a psychiatric social worker. I chose her because I was poor and she was cheap. I chose to go to therapy because I was on the verge of a breakdown. I explained Jana's situation and my ensuing depression, and the therapist suggested that it would be odd if I had been left alone while my sister had been so harmed.

This was manna from heaven to me. It was something solid in my past, a past of clouds and illusions. I too had been abused! No wonder I couldn't remember anything about my childhood! It was too horrible to remember! It is an odd joy one experiences learning he was molested as a child. But it is a joy when compared to knowing nothing at all, when compared to my past being a void. What a relief! She recommended I read *The Courage to Heal,* which I never got around to.

Over the next couple sessions she walked me through, what she called "Relaxation Therapy." It isn't exactly hypnosis. I was awake through the whole thing. She simply had me relax and peruse my past. Whatever I should see, assuming it wasn't too happy, I was to consider truth. Using this method I acquired a modest portfolio of molestations.

The clarity of the new memories was striking, photographic. So much better than my old memories, those fake cover-up daydreams I'd used to help me suppress the truth; they had been all cloudy. I was beginning to feel like a survivor, like I was on to the truth and it was just a matter of time until I would feel whole again. The trouble was, the closer I came to being "whole," the worse I felt. I was flunking my college classes. I was calling in to work sick. I was smoking a lot. I didn't shave. I didn't eat well. And I didn't care. I needed help. I needed support from someone who was going through what I was going through.

I only knew one person that fit that description.

Going Home

At the time, Jana lived not far from my parents and grandparents, not far from where I grew up and hung out. It was comforting to be in the places I was so familiar with. It was comforting to know that perhaps something was going to be resolved. Jana and I had talked on the phone before I came to visit, and we had made plans. We were going to visit the nearby cities we had lived in as children in an effort to gain impressions to help memories surface. We were going to visit people who knew us as children to see if they could dispel the "happy childhood myth" we'd been led to believe. We planned to check our school and medical records for anything suspicious. We were going to take Jana to the doctor to look for scars. We planned many excursions. Any proof would be welcome.

When I arrived, Jana explained that our plans were off. All of them. There was no need to prove anything. We had our memories. That was enough. To me this felt like being in a car when the brakes are slammed. Your whole body is thrown forward in the direction it really wants to go, but the belt catches and holds you back. In a car, this is good. The same feeling applied to Jana's little surprise was terribly disappointing. I had come so far, and I was so close to possible confirmation, when Jana hit the brakes.

I shortly found out why. She had already been to the doctor. There were no scars. There was no proof. No one could have walked away from what our father supposedly did to her without some scarring. And for an hour I wished that I had not shared that observation with Jana. She fumed and steamed and would hardly speak to me. She informed me that the doctor was somehow in collusion with our parents, and that it would be the same wherever we looked. I suggested another doctor, a stranger. If I had known on the day I arrived what I would know on the day I left, I would not have suggested a new doctor. It made her angrier. I was doubting her. I was soon to learn many nasty personality traits that I possessed. Jana was all too willing to tell me about them. To insist on proof about the scars was to doubt her memories, and, consequently, to doubt her. Did I not have memories, clear memories, of my own? Would I like it if she suggested that my word that they were true wasn't good enough? I shut up.

The "highlight" of my visit was to be a trip to see Jana's therapist, who, I had been told, was a truly remarkable lady. Her name was Cassandra — not her real name, but the name her "energy" was in. She never told me her real name. Cassandra is a psychic who specializes in past-life regressions. For the uninitiated, that means she hypnotizes you and assists you in discovering who you were in your past lives. It helps if you believe in past lives.

Cassandra was, to me, an utter and flagrant fraud. She was also immensely helpful. She provided me with my first taste of doubt. I may have been dumb enough or silly enough or gullible enough to believe for a while that my parents abused my sister and me, but I am no idiot.

Cassandra's tricks were obvious and transparent. She

"divined" things about me by concentrating extremely hard, and then making absurdly general statements. "You are really into music or photography, I perceive," was one thing she psychically revealed. At 24 years old, I knew of no one my age who could honestly claim not to be into music. What Cassandra relied on was the willingness of her clients to be fooled. There was never a moment that I couldn't have said, "Oh, yes, I know what you're sensing, the (fill in the blank) vague picture you're describing reminds me of the (fill in the blank) specific occurrence/circumstance in my life." And she wasn't even particularly good at it. At one point she divined that I had children, which I do not. Then my wife must have had an abortion some time in the last seven years. No, again. Grasping at straws, she suggested the presence of a lot of children where we live. We live in an apartment community comprised almost entirely of old people, I had the satisfaction of telling her. Jana then saved Cassandra's butt.

"You must be sensing his inner child," she intoned.

What do you know? That was it exactly!

I was angry because Jana was wasting her money on Cassandra. Ten minutes later I was furious for a reason more important than money. I learned for the first time about Jana's "past lives." Jana's beliefs about her current life are grotesque and horrifying. She has been raped by the people closest to her, brutalized by everyone who should love her, stepped on, spat on, and cast aside. She is the only person who believes that, but it is very real to her, and it causes her pain as if it were real. Cassandra has taken that pain and repeated it a thousand times. Every past life Jana has lived has been as bad or worse than the one she is now living. She has been beaten, slaughtered, raped and murdered multiple times in multiple lives, often by the same "spirits" (supposedly, my parents) that have hurt her in this life. As far as I could tell, this therapy served no other purpose but to convince Jana that her sorrow is inevitable. This life, last life, next life. Pain is all she will know. I was infuriated (as it turns out, naively) that there existed a therapist so unethical and incompetent. I was genuinely concerned that Cassandra would drive Jana to suicide.

For the remainder of my visit Jana's attitude towards me oscillated between boredom and snideness. Jana saw my true colors right away: I was cynical, rude, a control freak, and, worst of all, I thought too much. All true, I admit, though I prefer to use the words "realistic, assertive, go-getter, and introspective." By the end of the week Jana learned that I had a scientific, proof-driven mind, that I wasn't about to accept some unknown higher power that Cassandra had invented, that I didn't believe in past lives, and that I firmly believed that the only way to success was to take charge of this life. From Jana I learned that those traits did not make up the ideal personality for the re-pressed memory movement. In fact, I was a textbook case of a victim in "denial." I had realized that I had been abused, and that was good, but it did me scarcely any good to know the root of the problem without cutting down the tree that grew from it. My behaviors, that is, my personal-ity, I discovered, were coping mechanisms I had learned in order to deal with my repressed pain. Control had been taken from me as a child, so I sought to control all, and so on. Unless I changed these behaviors and discovered my repressed personality, I would be alienated from others going through the same pain I was. They wouldn't want to hang around with me. They would find me, well, antago-nistic. In my hour of greatest need, as I was trying to cope with having been abused, I was told that I must either change who I am or be abandoned.

Jana hurt me more than anyone ever had, more than the abuse that I then still believed had occurred. Brothers reserve emotional soft spots for their sisters, and Jana that week took the opportunity to aim her blows where I was weakest. I was learning about the recovery movement, and though I thought I could use some recovering, I didn't like what I saw. And I felt more alone and isolated than I ever had. I had travelled over a thousand miles to try to rekindle a relationship that I had for many years. I travelled over a thousand miles to be a loving brother, to support her and help her, and, as a result, to feel supported myself. That I failed miserably at this effort can be seen in the last conversation I ever had with my sister. We arrived at my terminal an hour early. "You don't have to hang around and watch the plane take off," I joked.

"Oh, great," she replied, seriously, "'Cause I'm paying for parking, you know." With a quick, sterile hug she was gone. I have not heard from her since.

Breakthrough

Life is a combination of hard work and a few lucky breaks. In my case, the hard work was thinking. The week spent with Jana had left me with a tiny slivery splinter of doubt. The more I thought about it the bigger my doubt grew. And as Jana would tell you, I think too much. I worked very hard trying to resolve the doubt. I tried very hard to believe the "truth." I made my best effort to take the "truth" for granted. I was abused and that was that. Period. End of discussion.

But, dammit, a little voice inside of me kept asking, "Really?" It was a little voice asking a little question, but it shook my certainty powerfully.

My faith was shaken, and was still shaking, a month and a half later when I visited Dr. Michael Fane, a psychiatrist. Dr. Fane was my lucky break. He ran the clinic where my therapist worked, and part of the deal was that I had to have one diagnostic session with him before treatment proceeded. I explained to him my situation, my recent discovery of abuse, and the things I believed had been done to me. I was so proud of myself; I was using all the right terms from the recovery movement, figuring this would impress him. After I finished telling him my story he leaned back in his black leather chair, stroked his beard, and said in his thick Austrian accent eight words that changed my life.

"You seem to be taking this very well."

I sometimes wonder if Dr. Fane didn't break some *Psychiatric Guiness Book of World Records* record. Eight words to a cure. By the next morning I would wake up to find my faith in my new memories shattered. Indeed, I kept thinking, I am taking this well. Sure, I've been depressed. True, I've moped around a lot. I've felt really confused. But stopping to think about how one might feel upon discovering he'd been sodomized, I was doing really well. Too well.

All too well. I had never heard of False Memory Syndrome at this point in my life, but I knew that I had had it.

It was near Father's Day by this time, so I took the opportunity to buy a card and explain to my parents, with whom I had shared my previous beliefs, that I no longer felt the way I had. I would have liked to explain to them then how I had come to believe that I had been abused. But at the time, I did not know how. At the time, I simply felt guilty and ashamed for having ever believed it.

Mostly, though, I felt used; by whom I do not know. By Jana? I don't think so; she believes what she says. I don't think she meant to deceive me. By my therapist? I'm not sure of that either. I know she meant well. She thought she was doing the right thing. Again, I don't think she meant to deceive. So who used me? Why do I feel I've been used? A year later I am still not sure who I should fault for this, because, honestly, I don't think there is anyone I could blame. Mass hysteria is like that. It is self-perpetuating, almost as though it was a conscious individual. When you recover from being a victim of hysteria, you feel ashamed and used. Used by the hysteria. Only mass hysteria is not a conscious individual, and, in the end, there is no one to blame.

A year later I have at least been able to figure out how I came to be a victim of this hysteria. My adult relationship with my parents had been much less than what I wanted it to be. It was unsatisfying in its lack of depth. My relationship with Jana was unsatisfying because it was almost non-existent. I wanted so much more out of both. I had a capacity to love that wasn't being used, and it burned like money in a pocket. I was liable to believe anything if it meant I could have the chance to spend that love. And Jana is my sister, and she truly believes her abuse happened. Until I could adequately demonstrate otherwise, I had a responsibility to believe her. I had no reason to mistrust her.

I had no such responsibility to believe that the abuse happened to me, however. This is where I feel the most ashamed, and this is where I must criticize the mental health establishment. People naturally trust doctors, and though therapists aren't necessarily doctors, they occupy a similar role. I have no training in the arts of mental healing, and so when my therapist told me about repressed memories and body memories, I had no reason to doubt her. When she told me that I could discover the "truth" about my childhood by relaxing and concentrating on the past, I could only assume she knew what she was talking about. She did have a Master's Degree. . . .

And I was in a horrible mental state at the time. If I had been rational and happy, I might have laughed at her nonsense and walked away. But if I had been rational and happy I would not have been in therapy. I was on the verge of a nervous breakdown. I needed something solid to hold on to.

And the final answer to the question of how I came to believe I was sexually abused is that my family, until the last year, never communicated well. We all seem to have assumed that if we didn't talk about problems they would evaporate, like fog. But that is not true. Unresolved problems simply build resentment, layer on layer, like sediments at the bottom of the ocean. Little arguments unresolved can become mountains of unconscious anger when they are collected and accumulated over the years. Do a million small, unresolved arguments equal in anger the anger generated by one instance of sodomy? Perhaps. I can't say for sure, I've never been sodomized. But I can tell you that the accumulated anger I carried with me was enough to push me over the edge into believing I had been. Communicate, always communicate.

After I sent my Father's Day card, communicate is exactly what I did. My father and I worked hard at discussing our differences, and I at least was surprised at how small they were considering the anger they had engendered. I now have a better relationship with my parents than I ever had before, and on that note, I am very happy.

This story is only a Jana short of happily ever after. If she's out there reading this, and I hope she'll realize how much we love her and how much we would welcome her back.

To a Brother-in-Law

Dear Larry,

I write to you because I feel that I cannot communicate with Anne in the frame of mind she is in. I appeal to you because she's the mother of your children and ask that you would please hear me through. You can show Anne this letter if you must, but you and I both know that is not wise. To drive a greater wedge between her and her family serves no productive purpose whatsoever.

Larry, I would ask you to step out of this whole thing emotionally for a minute and focus on what you do know, not what Anne thinks or speculates. I realize she's told you I'm too scared to face it and I've left her to go it alone. You judge for yourself whether I seemed irrational or unwilling to face the truth. I totally believed her too when I was there. Now don't you think it strange that I can say without a shadow of a doubt that I made a mistake? The power behind this whole deception is these counselors who rob people of their reality and then insert whatever the person's mind can conceive. Can you not see that Anne has completely lost touch with reality and "her reality" grows more bizarre as her imaginations and dreams grow more bizarre? This counselor is convincing Anne that her feelings are facts. Surely, you can see the danger in this!

Larry, do you not realize by now this will destroy your family and you could lose everything by idly sitting by and doing nothing? This counselor will take it all if you let her. I know if Anne was receiving poor medical care you would not sit by and pay a doctor who was treating the illness. In the same way, this counselor is completely brainwashing Anne's mind and I know she's not getting any better under her treatment. Aren't you suspicious when the hundreds of dollars per month spent on counseling is resulting in back pedalling rather than progress?

Larry, Anne has completely convinced you that something she cannot even remember is the truth! Can you not see the danger in this? She convinced me too, but never once did my husband let off of me about the fact that I was treading on very dangerous territory and the very important missing ingredients were facts! Words cannot express how thankful I am for his intervention today. I realize being on the other side that the things Anne sees as suspicious are not at all the way she perceives them. There is no doubt in my mind that my Dad did not molest her and that she is under some very dangerous influence.

I urge you for the sake of your family and for Anne's sake to do the responsible thing and listen and research the other side of this issue. Don't be so close-minded that you walk the road of destruction blindly. Anne cannot do this for herself right now and you're the only one close enough to her who can hold out a hand to a drowning person.

There are hundreds of families going through this same thing, whose daughters are under the control of counselors much like Cindy. These girls have even become suicidal. Please take some steps to save all of you from so much unnecessary pain.

I love you all and I'm confident that you'll realize the motivation behind this is love. Don't let a closed mind stop you from putting yourself in our shoes. We cannot give up because we love you all too much.

Michelle

To My Sister's Therapists

The following three letters were written by the brother of a woman who recalled grotesque "memories" of satanic ritual abuse during several years of therapy with Mr. Carleton. Initially, she claimed to remember being molested by her father between the ages of four and seven. As time passed, memories began to emerge in therapy of being ritually abused during elaborate satanic ceremonies attended by several men and women. Among other things, she claims she was raped by her grandfather, using the body parts of murdered women, and she believes she was forced to murder and eat babies.

She was later evaluated by a psychologist, Dr. Taylor, because of a custody battle for her children. Dr. Taylor concurred with Carleton's diagnosis and agreed with the treatment she was receiving. Her family later convinced her to see a psychiatrist for another opinion. She was referred to Dr. Hoffmann, who also validated her bizarre memories of mass murder, cannibalism and the most perverted sexual abuse imaginable.

As these letters demonstrate, none of the three therapists attempted to corroborate the woman's memories or were even willing to consider listening to the pleas and rational explanations presented by her brother and the rest of the family. All three therapists apparently believe that their roles were to validate memories no matter how they were retrieved or how unlikely they were to be true.

Dear Mr. Carleton,

I'm writing to clarify some of the things we touched on in our phone conversation August 4. I recall you saying

that as a therapist, you believe your patients in the con-
text of the therapeutic session, regardless of whether their
story corresponds with external reality. You also stated
that your specialized training enables you to distinguish
between a false reporting of sexual abuse and a true one.
In fact in one meeting you frankly told me you believe
my sister's allegations. At that time these were limited to
sexual molestation by my father from an early age
through puberty. Since then those allegations have ex-
panded to include multiple homicide, vampirism, canni-
balism, and membership in a vast conspiracy dedicated
to the overthrow of Christ's benevolent influence on Earth.
I assume you are familiar with the details of her memo-
ries, which she says have been recovered through your
help and that of group sessions with others similarly
victimized.

As I told my sister in a phone conversation on August
6, I have pored over her statements, numerous similar
statements by ritual abuse survivors, read and re-read
Michelle Remembers, *the writings of Catherine Gould,*
Roland Summit and other specialists in the field. I have
also studied cases that have come to court based on
similar allegations: the McMartin Day Care Center, the
case in Lido, Utah, the case of Paul Ingram in Washing-
ton State, the Orkney Islands in Great Britain and nu-
merous others.

I have consulted three different therapists; one a spe-
cialist in hypnotism, one a specialist in sexual abuse and
one a former lawyer. I have read two tomes on trance
and hypnotism by Spiegel and Bliss. I have studied pa-
pers on brainwashing by J.F. Dulles and others. I've also
read some of the works of David Finkelhor, Alice Miller,
Bass and Davis' The Courage to Heal, *articles by Jeffery*

Masson and other authors of like persuasion. I have reviewed proposals to state and federal legislatures concerning ritual abuse and reports from state and federal justice departments on the subject. I mention all this to assure you that I do not take any of this lightly. Nor have I instantly drawn a conclusion as to the truth or falsehood of my sister's allegations. I comprehend what they imply about the condition of this world, our society, my extended family, myself and most importantly, my unborn child. As I told you, my sister's accusations, and the vast conspiracy theory that lends them context, have not triggered any spontaneous inward belief in me.

As I said, I do feel and believe my sister's pain. You asked me how else I account for that pain. I'm not sure if the question was rhetorical, but an abundance of alternative explanations have come to mind. Before I go into them, I'd like to state that I'm not certain you were entirely candid with me when you implied that you come to therapeutic sessions with an objective and unbiased frame of mind. For my own self, I must accept that I am trapped in a bias toward disbelief. I factor that bias into my considerations as best I can. Can I assume you recognize a similarly powerful, though contrary, bias in your own being? Could your own faith in your religion color the impressions you receive from clients? If your faith is such that you see it not as coloring, but as casting on your observation the pure white light of truth, what more can I say? If, on the other hand, you hold that portion of doubt that any objective mind must contain, I contend it is worth our time to continue discussing my sister's case.

Concerning faith, I agree with St. Paul that it has the power to move mountains. Against such power how can my arguments prevail? But Paul goes on to state that without love, you are nothing. The point is that I love my sister. It is that love that motivates this appeal to you despite your apparent writing me off as being "in denial." Sally Jean is my sister, my flesh and blood. She is your patient, or client; at best a soul to be saved or a mind cured, at worst a lucrative business opportunity. I have long maintained to the rest of my family that your intentions in treating her are, in fact, noble. But I also maintain that the course of advice and treatment you have taken victimizes her and my family and, of even larger consequence, will help perpetuate sexual victimization of innocent children for a long time to come.

As to the goodness of your intentions, it is my opinion that equally good intentions motivated inquisitors and witch trial judges throughout history to send untold thousands of wrongly accused men and women to torture and execution. It strikes me that this era of history is being repeated. I feel that the imagery of satanic ritual abuse arising within therapy and amplified throughout the world in seminars, courtrooms and the media is the stuff of phantasm and hysteria today as it was in the past. I believe that today innocent people are accused, suffer the forced removal of their children, and are prosecuted by the same spectral evidence that sent so many to the rack and stake in the not so distant past. And I think that the psychological engine behind that slaughter was driven by the same noble intentions that guide your treatment of my sister.

I don't expect any sympathy from you for the anguish that Sally's accusations against my parents and grandparents has inflicted on me and the rest of my family. I do expect you to take seriously the effect on genuine victims of abuse when their voices are drowned in this torrent of false and fantastic accusation. The responsibility for that predictable tragedy will be on the shoulders of those in your profession who have nourished a chorus of "crying wolf" in their patients and clients. As I said to you, even if those crying "wolf" describe in vivid detail the yellow eyes, dripping fangs, foul breath and even the fleas, the cry is, in my considered opinion, no less a false alarm. If nothing else, the probable consequences are of such gravity that I must continue to urge you to consider carefully alternative explanations for my sister's and other people's pain and therapeutically induced recollections.

To repeat myself, I admit a bias to disbelieve the scenario described by my sister. It is utterly contrary to my own memories and to the fruit of my observation, experience and reflection. Although I trust my own judgment, I recognize that I can fervently believe what proves untrue and likewise find false what I subsequently come to believe. Knowing this, I am slow and careful to draw conclusions. I remain open to argument and evidence intended to compel my belief or dispel it. I beg you to do the same. Please look at and consider the following sources I offer from professionals and concerned individuals that support my position. One article is by Kenneth Lanning of the F.B.I., who has investigated numerous similar cases. The others are from a Christian magazine, Cornerstone, *which I include in hopes that you may attend more carefully to fellow Christians. I have left out the bulk of my research material because it is plainly less even-handed or sympathetic. If you are interested I recommend the book* In Pursuit of Satan *by Robert Hicks, The Institute for Psychological Therapies in Northfield, Minnesota, and the False Memory Syn-*

drome Foundation in Pennsylvania.

To return to your question: how do I account for my sister's pain? I stand by what I told you. Much of her condition is "iatrogenic." The process she has over the years described by analogy as removing a splinter from a festering wound — a process she credits you primarily with assisting — appears to me instead as worrying a minor sore into a full-blown infection or a major tumor. She recently told me that she now recalls over 35 homicides she witnessed my parents committing throughout America. She also said that she must continue to retrieve such memories from her unconscious to complete her "cure." I have come to believe that it is within her ability to enter a state of trance allowing her to invent vivid "memory." I believe that the content of that memory is assisted by a system of belief brought to her therapeutic sessions and by her exposure to material engendered by that same paradigm. I feel that this paradigm constitutes an assault, not so much on the truth, but on the means by which "truth" can be arrived at. I am not alone in the opinion that the truth cannot be discovered without debating contradictory conclusions from the same observations.

It was in the spirit of such debate that I sought to meet with you and Sally. I felt compelled to inform her that I was unable to resolve all I had learned about the phenomenon of satanic ritual abuse in favor of her assertions. I wanted to do so in an environment she would feel protected in, namely your office. I have found that professionals of your persuasion regarding this subject tend to shield themselves as well as their clients from contrary opinion. Unfortunately the cancellation of our meeting of August 11 tends to confirm my expectation. It is a shame that I now feel driven into an opposing camp because we do share a fundamental concern: that the sexual abuse of children must be stopped.

Do not think that because your camp bears this as a standard, that myself, my family, or others who similarly disagree with you can be branded as approving of sexual abuse of any nature. Nor should you rely on the concept of "denial" to neatly categorize and dismiss those of us who doubt your version of reality.

I appreciate that you have staked your professional reputation on your interpretation of my sister's condition. I also realize that you are not alone in that interpretation. In fact you and like-minded colleagues, as well as members of law enforcement and a growing body of elected officials, have arrived at the conclusion that satanism is rampant. Many regard memories such as my sister's as proof. It is apparent to me that the numbers of professionals and individuals of your persuasion constitute a powerful force. I'm not sure you appreciate that power. When I spoke to you of an impending backlash, you responded in tones of one already facing overwhelming odds. I feel, however, that the greater risk is to those who would oppose your assumptions. It frightens me to do so. I hope you will understand that it is your assumptions and not your character that I oppose and that my opposition to them is motivated by concern for my sister and my family.

This has been a difficult letter to write and doubtless unpleasant for you to read. I don't consider it a strictly private correspondence and you are welcome to show it to whoever you please. I will include a copy to my sister and the rest of my family.

Dear Dr. Taylor,

I'm writing to you in keeping with a practice of clarifying and documenting discussions I have with professionals regarding my sister's case. Thank you for considering the materials I left behind; transcripts of my sister's correspondence with family members, my letter to her therapist and the Kenneth Lanning monograph.

I was flattered that you found me bright and well-informed. Indeed I regard you with respect for your sincerity and intelligence. However I did understand your statement to imply that I had merely armored myself in my convictions. In turn I must admit that I question your own conviction that you can flawlessly distinguish testimony that corresponds with external reality from that which does not. So stripped of the mutual eloquence of our conversation, it is possible we spent an hour calling one another fools. If so, I am the greater fool for I left a hundred dollars behind.

I did take with me your suggestion that I hypothetically suspend my doubt and look at those things within me that satanic ritual abuse may account for. One value of the exercise was that it made me appreciate how much that hypothetical model of reality can release one from personal responsibility for shortcomings, sins and failure. Another result was unexpected: I realized that I rather like the person I am. I rarely meditate on this, but I do see myself as a loyal and trustworthy friend and mate. I cleave closely to the rule of doing to others as I would have them do to me. I feel exuberance and pleasure at beauties of life: music, art, the natural world. I participate in them enthusiastically. I feel spontaneous love and appreciation for fellow occupants of this planet. I endeavor to help those I can and seek help from those who will offer it. I have developed a refined curiosity and a kind of gourmet hunger for knowledge. Nor do I think I mistake the accumulation of information for knowledge or the accumulation of knowledge for wisdom. As I said to Jack Carleton, I am slow to leap to conclusions and to fly from particulars to generalities. This was not actually an epiphany, and it did present at least one troubling thought; if I like the person I am, and that person is the result of a satanic upbringing, should I positively credit that upbringing?

When I have thought at all about Satan, I've regarded that being as a metaphor, one that conveniently embodies all the misfortunes of life from spoiled milk to war and world famine. But that being never seems to take personal credit for his deeds. On the other hand, the historical record details extraordinary torture and execution practiced by proud and righteous Christians on human beings suspected of associating with Satan. Does the fact that I find such behavior by Christians repulsive lead me to have sympathy for the devil? I bring this up because I genuinely fear the power embodied in the convictions you apparently share with my sister, her own and other therapists, and the politically entrenched Christian right.

I fear the effect that power can have on those who would disagree with your shared convictions. For the record, I have no interest in Satan or satanism other than how it seems the focus of all my sister's energy.

In order to stay in contact with my sister she has required I take a daunting leap of faith, and I imagine she referred me to you to assist that leap. Your own experience with your son's ritual abuse and the stretch of rational faculties that event required of you, and your stature as a doctor of psychology no doubt qualifies you to offer such assistance. I would like to outline the mental steps I must take: 1) Disregard my memories, which are typified by feelings of love, care and protection, and are vivid, spontaneous, detailed and chronologically consistent. If I understand correctly, I must consider them to be manipulated and tailored by satanic experts. 2) Likewise disregard my sense impressions of the character of my parents and their parents. The feelings I have of their essential humaneness, protection and concern I must dismiss as a product of denial and fantasy. I must replace those feelings with the hatred and vengefulness my sister embraces. 3) Accept as fact that my parents and grandparents belonged to a vast and ancient cult. That this cult required its members to regularly engage in prescribed ritual accompanied by elaborate accoutrements, featuring decapitation, cannibalism, and every manner of rape and sexual abuse of my sister and other victims. 4) Accept that this cult practiced these rituals undetected among an isolated rural population consisting largely of relatives and devout Christians. Accept that these rituals and their attendant murders either escaped detection by law enforcement in specific and varied locations throughout America, or that upper echelons of the law participated in and covered up these crimes. Accept that no disaffected members of this cult were able to escape its domain and reveal its existence to authorities. Accept that those authorities were in fact so well controlled by fraternal members that even non-participating and informed underlings produced not a peep. That no gossip circulated regarding these activities and no rumors surfaced until recently. 5) Accept that the majority of institutions, financial, religious, fraternal, military and political in this country and abroad are controlled by this cult. That its members include experts in evidence disposal far too sophisticated for the detection capabilities of the Federal Bureau of Investigation, or that the F.B.I. conspires with the criminals. 6) That this arch-conspiracy entails more than mere human agency, and is guided by the manifest hand of a supernatural being, namely Satan and his demonic cohorts.

It's a big leap. If I'm correct that my sister expects you to assist me in that leap, it will require more than your assurance of professional acumen in deciphering reality, or even your obvious intelligence, kindness and sincerity. I hope you can come to accept that my assertions and arguments in your office were neither intellectual fencing nor thoughtless protection of a self-imposed or externally programmed world view. I was expressing my thoughts and feelings. An alternative to this leap of faith that I understand my sister to require is the opinion that her world view is in fact delusional; and that her delusion is buoyed up by the profession of psychology. Such an opinion would imply that the profession has lost its intellectual and philosophical moorings, and its rational and scientific rudder, is adrift and infested with verminous catch-phrases, buzzwords and checklists in the place of serious research or cogent analysis. That would be a mournful opinion to arrive at, but maybe you can see why I tend toward it.

You offered me a pair of guidelines in accepting testimony as fact. One was the effect of adult patients in recall, the vividness and detail of their memory, and the assumption that these things could not be imagined or acquired from any source but actual experience. The other is the testimony of children — how their natural innocence should dispel all doubt in the listener. You referred to the statements by my nephew, and to those of your own son. In fact I accept that your son's memory and experience was a real and terrible thing. I do not deny that not only sexual abuse, but abuse involving ritual, does exist. In my nephew's case I would like for you to consider a few things. He has been constantly exposed to his mother's process of recall over many years. Unlike yourself, my sister is a crusader on this subject. Her belief leads her to suspect that her children were abused as she remembers her abuse. She has taken him to psychologists to probe this suspicion. Unlike you, a great number of therapists are not reticent about asking leading questions and rewarding expected answers. I recall your condemning this type of questioning in the McMartin case. My sister also believes in the principle that only a specialist, such as yourself, with a full under-standing and belief in the existence of satanic ritual abuse, can properly treat a supposed victim. From this predisposition I would imagine that the therapists she selected for her son would be of this type. I also would understand that my nephew is in a double-bind regard-ing his mother. What would you do if given the choice of finding your primary care-giver delusional and unstable, or joining with her against an insidious enemy?

Unfortunately you and I don't share your opinion of your ability to objectively determine reality from a victim's statements. Also, unfortunately, it is obvious that my involvement disqualifies me from objectivity. So I am left to persuade with only the power of my opinion and what authoritative sources support it.

I think that the ability to be coerced to believe varies among individuals and their situations, something along the lines of Spiegel's Induction Profile I described. My nephew's family situation and perhaps an ability to be hypnotized I venture he, my sister and myself share, would readily explain the memories unveiled in your office.

But we come back to what divides us. Why should I think my memory is real and my sister's is not? All I can offer is that I have been only minimally exposed to therapy and trance induction. That unlike my sister, my memories are not fantastic or bizarre. I do not subscribe, on a weekly or daily basis, to the influence of groups and individuals devoutly committed to and focused on a specific version of reality. And most distinctively, I do not isolate myself from contrary opinion.

Your personal experience and professional commitment to the satanic paradigm notwithstanding, I expect you to seriously consider my interpretation. If you've gotten this far in this letter, I can hope that your own mind is actually open enough to provide a truly mediative role in future contact with my sister, for myself and possibly the rest of my family.

Dr. Hoffmann,

You have played a brief but significant role in shattering my family and breaking my heart. Neither the ethical concept of confidentiality nor the legal one of privilege that you cited in cutting off my entreaty last month forbid you from reading this. I sincerely hope that you do.

I called you on August 20th because my sister suggested I do so and I assumed that she had granted permission to discuss her case. You have served as a signal beacon in a therapeutic journey which has led her by steps to declare my parents and grandparents rapists, murderers and cannibals. In the course of this journey doubtful family members begged her to seek the opinion of a professional psychiatrist unallied with her own therapist, Jack Carleton. She was referred to you by Sutton Hospital. Your advice, according to her, was to stay the therapeutic course and avoid those "in denial."

Whether or not I am "in denial" I am a member of her family; a brother who loves her and has stayed in close contact with her over the past 12 years. When I revealed that I doubted the reality of my sister's therapeutically recovered memories, I felt your tone turn defensive and your manner become abrupt.

I think it is possible that my sister's recollections stem from a source altogether different than actual experience. I am not alone in that opinion. I am including in this letter articles citing such authorities in case their views have escaped your attention.

I think it reasonable that a professional conclusion as to the reality of allegations of such grave implication — psychological, social, spiritual, not to mention legal — would reflect familiarity with thoughts and feelings of the victim's family. It disappoints me that my offer of such a perspective was so curtly dismissed. It offends me to have my own memories, thoughts and feelings summed up as "denial." It frightens me that this summation from a man of your profession carries with it the authority of diagnosis.

But what most hurts and confuses me is your seeming lack of concern for the consequences of your assessments, to myself and my family, if you are wrong. In fact if you are correct and all my sister describes is true, your response seems even more disheartening. Is it not worth your time to illuminate and help protect a person who your patient contends was similarly victimized?

My exchange with you and my understanding of your role in my sister's current condition leaves me angry and frustrated. Knowing that you may represent a significant trend of thought and behavior among those of your profession makes me weep for the poor souls seeking help from psychotherapy.

Beyond the ethical guidelines you advised me of in our conversation stands that fundamental axiom "first do no harm." A dreadful harm has been done, Dr. Hoffmann, and I directly suffer it. I beg you from my heart to at least consider and investigate that harm as a human being, if not as a man whose business it is to heal and protect.

Dear Pastor

I am writing this letter to you because I feel my story and the information included will be of help to you in counseling my sister. For three years I have been forced to live with slanderous lies and false accusations about my parents and against those who support them. The pain has been tremendous with no avenue of relief and certainly no opportunity for them to vindicate themselves. We have prayed every day for our family and even for those whose actions have fractured our family. We have been praying and waiting for the time when we will be heard and now I believe the time has come.

After reading several articles given to me by caring friends and relatives, I realized that this is not an isolated incident. There are thousands of people across the country and some even in our church who have been accused of horrendous acts that positively never occurred.

As you read my account, please refer to the articles that I have included with this letter. These articles written by highly respected psychiatrists, psychologists and educators will point out that my story is not an accumulation of babbling gobbledegook. This account may seem to be lengthy and time-consuming, but it is real; it is horrifying; it is the truth.

My story is of my sister, at one time my best friend. Not quite a year older than me, we grew up sharing our toys, our friends, some hobbies, our birthday parties and even our profession. We even went to college together with her changing her major on my encouragement to enter into my major. Even though our appearances are very different and our personalities were our own, we had many things in common and enjoyed one another's company. When we had difficult times, we both tried to be there for one another. We loved our family and were proud of where we came from and the values we were given.

My memories of my sister have always been those of one who was very caring, loving and generous. She always gave of her time and herself, someone whom you could count on. She was talented in many ways and respected by all she came in contact with as a friend or a professional. I was very proud when I found that I could work with her professionally and did so for seven years. Spiritually she was my definition of someone who truly walked with God. We cried as a family when her babies died and were amazed at her strength when she counseled women in similar situations. Our family has not been without its problems, but we all have worked together to support one another and have done what we felt was best.

About five years ago, I noticed that my sister's personality was starting to change. The change began when she started to take counseling courses at church. She was also being influenced by a girlfriend who works with Better Living Resources. First she would tell me almost daily what she had learned from these courses; then, what she was learning became more specific. She would inform me how her friend would constantly tell her what was wrong with our family, which I couldn't see or agree with. My sister started to label people, often complete strangers, as to whom she thought was gay, who was an alcoholic, who was probably beaten as a child or beaten by a boyfriend. Never before had I seen her so judgmental. When I finally protested, she would change the subject or ignore what I would say. She began to withdraw from me.

My older brother and parents also noticed a big change in her. As a member of our church and a curious intellectual, my brother decided to take some counseling courses too. He would try to discuss her opinion on topics and she would respond by expressing the opinion of her girl friend and her friend's husband. My sister no longer had her own opinion, but always someone else's.

I knew that not being able to have children, giving up her profession to be a missionary, losing a best friend to cancer and having difficulty in adopting a child would be devastating for anybody. But I honestly thought she was strong enough to handle all this because of the spiritual strength she had displayed in her earlier years at church. It never occurred to me that things would get this bad.

My sister's husband began counseling with Better Living Resources shortly after their return from Kenya. We noticed that he was much more moody than ever before. Unknown to me, my sister started personal counseling with her friend. This, by the way, is not generally recommended in counseling circles, for friends to counsel friends. Her counseling then progressed with her friend's encouragement to see others at Better Living Resources as well.

At least a year went by with this arrangement. I knew something was wrong because I would see my sister every day at work and hear bits of phone conversations and would feel tension when we would be in the same room. Some of our mutual friends at work were beginning to treat me with a less friendly nature. They would be invited to parties at her house and talk about it in front of me days after. I would never know about the parties because I was never invited. I tried to understand

and communicate what was wrong, but was rebuffed.

At least three years ago, my younger brother started to counsel with the same two individuals at Better Living Resources. He had gone through a divorce several years before and was bitter. He asked all the siblings to get together for a session to help him. The session was set up by one of his therapists and focused on blaming our parents for anything and everything. I protested this format and was immediately pounced upon by my two sisters and younger brother and his therapist. According to this therapist, their points were valid, mine were not. We were to meet again, but I was never invited back because I did not agree with them.

Nine months later, one week after Christmas and while at work, my sister informed me that my father had molested her as a child. The shock was enormous. Never had I ever considered such a thing. It was foreign to every fiber of my being. I told her I couldn't believe her but promised her not to mention it to my parents. I hoped her therapy would show her the truth.

Her harassment of me increased to such an extent at work that I sought counseling from my own pastor, an old family friend. He directed me to a woman who worked with troubled women and was herself a Christian pastor. I went to work for another year and a half dreading each day, wondering what and whose comments I would have to deflect. My parents still did not know why they had been completely shut off by my sister and two younger siblings but they helped give me the strength to carry on. Their prayers, my husband's love and God's strength kept me going.

Subsequently, my parents were told to meet with my sister, her husband and my two younger siblings on

September 8, 1990 at Better Living Resources. The meeting was termed "Confrontation with Kathy's Parents" and was directed by her husband. My parents were directed not to respond until each of them had given their statements. A tape was to be made and my parents were to be given a copy following the session. That tape was never received; apparently the original tape was accidentally erased and all record of the session lost. It was at this session that Kathy accused my father of repeatedly molesting her, myself and my younger sister and that my mother knowingly permitted this to happen. When my father asked my younger sister and younger brother if either of them were ever aware of these things having happened, they both said, "No." Several days later my parents were shocked to find out that two Better Living Resources therapists were in an adjacent room with the door ajar during the entire session referred to above. When asked about this at a meeting arranged by a church counselor at a later date, they said that they were there to support Kathy and her younger sister and brother. My parents were not told of their presence in the adjacent room prior to or during the meeting. They were informed not to try to make contact with any of the four until my parents had sought counseling for their problems and then only when my sister and two younger siblings were ready to initiate the reconciliation.

My parents immediately contacted a pastor counselor and informed him of what had taken place. During this meeting he directed them to a psychologist associated with State Medical & Social Services Inc. They had at least two meetings with this man and two more with the church counselor.

During the meeting with these two therapists, my par-

ents asked one of them why he didn't counsel my sister to stop harassing me. His only comment was that he had no control over what his patients did. At the other meeting arranged by the church counselor between my sister, her husband and my parents, my sister made the remark that she wasn't responsible for my feelings.

It seems that my sister and her husband accrued $12,000 in counseling fees that they still owed to Better Living Resources. (By the way, it seems extremely questionable for any therapist to allow any patient not to pay their bills. It ingratiates the patients to the therapist to the extent that the patients are incapable of thinking for themselves. They begin to "worship" their therapist.) My sister was desperate. Her solution in essence was to black-mail my parents. They were told they had to admit their guilt and seek counseling. They had to give her $6,000 if they ever wanted to see her or their granddaughter again. All this was apparently not discouraged by her therapists. Blackmail is not only unethical and morally wrong, but is also a crime.

Other similarities to the situations in the accompany-ing news articles were that her stories, dates, places and times were incorrect and out of order. My older brother and I will not validate anything she claims because they are not what we remember at all. My younger siblings were not even alive when the earliest acts she remebers took place.

She has tried to destroy my own marriage by accusing my husband of being a child molester. My sister has unjustly accused my older brother of being an alcoholic and blames him for her loneliness. She has been rude to old friends who support my parents. She is not the sister I knew. Her personality is now completely different; it is *clouded with vindictiveness; she is cruel, manipulative, hardened and irrational. Is this the girl you knew as my sister?*

She also went so far as to claim that I and my younger sister had been molested. Not once prior to the beginning of my sister's accounting of these events, or in the three years since, have I had any hint of this happening. I have not had any nightmares or flashbacks. You would think that something would have finally triggered my memory. There is simply nothing to be triggered. At my last encounter with her, my loving sister told me that I had embarrassed her my entire life.

Some of the meetings and therapy sessions my parents and my older brother were allowed to attend show the therapist leading my sister to her conclusions. He suggested to my parents that a genetic disorder that caused the loss of her children late in pregnancy was due to trauma in her childhood. When my father, who holds a M.A. degree in biology, countered this, the therapist changed the subject. At one session this therapist suggested that the reason my parents moved from Minnesota in 1956 was because of rumors of my father molesting high school students where he taught. When my brother refuted such leading statements, the therapist again changed the subject. Leading a patient to any conclusions would seem to me to be a highly questionable practice. My sister would have been only two and a half years old at the time and would not have understood such rumors, if indeed there were any.

A final similarity to all these other cases was how my sister came to believe that she had been molested. She told me she was put into a "dream-like state" by the therapist and that the "Holy Spirit revealed all this to her." I questioned several times if she had been hypnotized. Each time she anxiously tried to convince me that it wasn't hypnotism. Just a dream-like state.

My sister has separated herself from nearly all of her family, all relatives and her old friends. Very few people know where she lives and she makes her "safe" friends protect her from people like me. Her appearance and language have changed markedly for the worse and she has become old, haggard and cheap looking.

As senior pastor of our church, I implore you to listen to my parents; to look into this matter and others like it that may have been perpetrated upon other church members. These accusations have much in common with the Salem witch hunts of the 17th century in the eastern United States. For my parents' sake, for my sister's sake, for my siblings', my nieces' and my children's sake and for other possible victims within the community of believers, this activity must be stopped. Heads can no longer turn away and ignore what has been going on.

I am requesting that you keep this communication confidential, especially from anyone associated with Better Living Resources or my sister, until we have had the opportunity to discuss this situation with you in person. I do not want further retribution perpetrated against me or my family until we have had the time to talk.

Accusations of child abuse are feared and abhorred. Our society presumes that those accused are likely guilty and it is on their shoulders to prove their innocence. Many of the accused are tried, judged, convicted and sentenced without any opportunity to defend themselves.

Nazi criminals have enjoyed more rights than my parents have been given. What the whole situation boils down to is that it is my sister's word against my parents' word.

There has been no proof offered, no evidence to verify that any of this happened. Obviously the advice of her friends and therapists is biased. Anyone who wants to remain my sister's friend must believe every word she says without asking any questions. She has manipulated her friendships through clever words and superb acting. Her supporters' knowledge of the facts is greatly limited by my sister's choice and cannot help but be biased. Her therapists also are perpetrating the same biased format of judgment. If they really cared about her mental health, they would want to search out the truth, especially when the accusations are so adamantly refuted. One would hope that a reputable therapist would not place a higher regard on a weekly fee than on the emotional health of the patient. What would a therapist lose by seeking out the other side of the story? It would seem that none of the individuals counseling my sister ever considered the veracity of her claims.

As I see it, there are only two witnesses capable of making a non-biased judgment based on equal experience with the accuser and the accused and that is my brother and myself. We also have two ways to judge, by our hearts and by the facts. Emotionally we stand to lose no matter who we believe, no matter who we support. We could decide to support the one we love the most, the one we could least live without. It goes without saying that my brother and I have known our parents all our lives. We are not willing to compare who is more valuable or who is more worthy of our loyalty. We love them both equally and unconditionally. We therefore have no reason to deny either claim or be in denial. It is interesting to note that only my sister has demanded an either/or condition. If we are to decide, based on facts, we are the only two who were with my sister during the times her "incidents" were supposed to have started. We are the only eyewitnesses. A witness is sworn to tell the truth, the whole truth and nothing but the truth. As Christians we are expected to live by even higher standards. We are not to allow outside influences such as blackmail, fear, threats or mind-altering techniques to impair or change the facts as we know them. We are compelled to tell only the truth. I can assure you that there is not one incident that would confirm even one of my sister's accusations against our parents. Not one flicker of a memory has occurred to substantiate any of my sister's stories.

Since my sister said I too was molested, my affirmation would give me the most to gain. I could sue for monetary gain, I could prosecute for criminal justice, I could settle for emotional solace to know that I am not responsible for any dissatisfaction in my life. We cannot and will not tell anything but the truth. Our parents did not commit these horrible deeds.

Yes, my sister was victimized, but not by our parents. She is a victim of her own self-imposed imagination fueled by books she has read, friends who perpetuated her condition and suggestive psycho-babble from therapists who have dabbled in areas far beyond their abilities.

Since these stories are false, our only concern then is how we must save my sister's emotional and spiritual health. The easiest way my sister and our family situation could be healed would be an admission of incompetence by her therapists, admitting their leading and suggestive techniques. This is the only way she could have come up with the atrociously false stories. But expecting such a humbling act from these therapists is highly improbable. The next choice would be proper counseling from someone she trusts and a professional who is expe-

rienced with False Memory Syndrome.

It is my feeling that if you, as the leader of her church, will take a stand against this kind of emotional butchering, then it would not only help my sister but many more who have been so seriously hurt. It all boils down to what is more important, the reputation of a few individuals or the rescuing of one — her heart, her mind and her soul.

CREATING RAGE

Sisters and brothers who confront the problem of false memories cannot understand the feelings of hatred, anger, and rage that their families are experiencing.

In the last twenty years a theory has emerged which has been repeated in hundreds of books and adopted by thousands of therapists. It is a theory that says families are dysfunctional; it is not only acceptable but appropriate to confront your parents, abandon your "family of origin" and create a "family of choice."

The incest survivor movement has accepted this theory.

What follows is a brief analysis of the origins of the incest survivor movement, describing the ideas of some of its major authorities.

Why Would They Believe Such Things If They Weren't True?

What amazes families and researchers as they hear and document the stories of adult children accusing their parents of sexual abuse is the similarity of the stories. It is as if accusers follow a script as their sordid stories unfold.

When the adult child enters therapy it is usually for a common enough complaint. Perhaps it's depression, an addiction, an eating disorder, anxiety, difficulty with a marriage, problems with a child. The parent can understand, relate to the problem and support the idea of therapy. The parent is often asked to pay for the therapy and often willingly does so. Soon, in a matter of weeks, or months, the adult child begins to distance herself or himself from parents, becoming increasingly remote, not answering phone calls or letters, frequently complaining of disorders such as headaches or flu to provide excuses for limiting contact.

After a while, the adult child writes a letter or telephones to say he or she is dealing with difficult problems and needs to "work" on them. At this time, the adult child often says that he or she was abused as a child, perhaps by a stranger, a neighbor, a baby sitter, an uncle or an aunt, and needs to deal with the abuse issue. Be patient, she or he says, I have a good therapist, group support and am reading some good books about abuse. The parents are shocked, horrified, dismayed and guilt-ridden. Could their child have been abused and they didn't even know it? They are perplexed — they also feel helpless.

The adult child specifies a time-limit during which there should be no contact, usually six months. The time is to work on the issue in therapy, sometimes four sessions a week, to help get back the memories of abuse so they can be confronted and put to rest. If the parent asks to meet the therapist, that request is generally denied.

At the end of this time period either an extension is requested or an encounter takes place. Parents reluctantly agree to the extension, having no other choice, and being told that time is necessary for "healing." If the encounter does take place it is generally in the therapist's office, constrained by strict guidelines. Flanked by the therapist and sometimes a friend or spouse, the adult child reads a prepared statement. It lists a variety of accusations. Not only was the accuser sexually abused as a child by the stranger, baby-sitter, uncle, aunt or whoever was mentioned in the first encounter, but also by dad or mom. The statement may say, "You molested me when I was six months old," "I remember you molesting me when I was in my crib," "You raped me from age three until I was seventeen," "You came into my room three nights a week." "You were abused so you abused me; it's intergenerational. And Mom, you let him do it to me. You were an enabler." Sometimes the mother is accused and the father is the enabler.

Often the accusations come in the form of a letter, with similar letters written to brothers, sisters, grandparents, aunts, uncles, cousins and family friends. Thousands of such letters have now been received by parents. Here is a typical letter received by a parent:

June, 1992
Dear Dad,

I've done painstaking work to remember and unblock memories of my childhood and that is why I'm writing to you now. I blocked those memories as a defense for my survival. For my own safety, until I was strong enough, memories of the first 17 years of my life were kept well-hidden (by dissociation) so I could function at all. The past three months have led me back to recall 17 years, from my infancy, of sexual abuse at your hands. Times, places, dialogue, entire scenes fill my notebooks. To remember, I've relived the hell of the emotions, physical sensations of the arousal, and the realization that my family was shrouded in private secrecy.

Treatment began two years ago in a weight-loss program, but I knew I needed more. I had many symptoms over the years which included compulsive overeating, distrust, fantasizing, memory loss (particularly of my childhood and vacations), inability to communicate, sexual dysfunction and a sense of being an outsider. Above all, there had been the shame and secrecy keeping me from seeking therapy. I've learned why.

You were the perpetrator; you planned the times, the methods and how you needed to use me. No mistake, no misunderstanding. You spoke to me at length about how you chose me, how you needed me, how you'd tell the rest of the family if I didn't comply. I remember the terrifying violence, the daily abuse, the force of objects used and even trips to doctors for damage inflicted by broken objects.

As an adolescent the situation worsened. From the onset of my puberty your demands increased and I was expected to participate as your sexual partner although unwillingly. Several times you fed me Valium beforehand. I had forgotten vacations because the abuse had been so severe then. I was terrified, ashamed, humiliated and isolated from the rest of the world. For my own safety, I created a "bond" believing in how much you and Mommy loved me and needed me. That was a public lie. You both served your own needs.

In my healing I've come to terms with the decades of abuse and deception that have distorted and threatened my life. I'm first learning to trust and develop relationships now. Hopefully it is not too late to get close to my own siblings now. I can't get back the time, the years you've stolen from me. I've read a great deal, kept a journal, and with much help, I'm ready to create my own life under better conditions. I have honest relationships and I'm seeking what I need for myself. I'll be attending an incest survivors conference soon as well.

So I told you what I know. That was my intention. At this point there's little else to say. Having been lied to for so long I don't ask for a response. Why did it happen, aside from negligence and irresponsibility? You got what you needed. Now it's my turn but I choose to survive neither as a perpetrator nor a victim.

Terri

Most often, the parents do not even know who the therapist is. The therapist will refuse to meet the parents saying, "I won't talk with perpetrators."

If a meeting with a therapist does take place it is one-sided. The accusations have already been validated in the mind of the accuser and the therapist. This is not an attempt to have the accused make a defense. The therapist and the accuser already know with certainty that the accused is guilty and he or she will deny all charges. No perpetrator ever admits guilt. The purpose of this meeting is to let the perpetrator know that he or she has been found out. Such a confrontation is considered "empowerment" for the adult child and is considered part of the healing process. The parents are now labeled perpetrators, or one parent a "perpetrator," the other an "enabler" for allowing the abuse to occur.

The accusers often plead with brothers and sisters to believe them. They say, "Why would I say such a thing if it wasn't true?" The therapist may tell a sibling that support is necessary for the survivor. They say the survivor has come to this conclusion and needs support from a brother or sister. Sometimes they say, "Your brother or sister might commit suicide without your support." Imagine the agony of the sibling placed in this situation.

Often the accusations against parents include satanic ritual abuse. Over time it appears to the accusers that they have uncovered the reality of their childhood. They now know the truth and the accused are "in denial" or have repressed memories themselves. Through months, perhaps years of therapy, the accusers have undergone a number of experiences and utilized a number of techniques that altered their memories. The new memories they have created have become their reality. They have, by this time, read dozens of books, filled out journals and workbooks, visualized or imaged the abuse, perhaps undergone hypnosis, had their dreams analyzed, heard dozens of other stories of survivors in their group, re-enacted their own stories of abuse, and role-played rituals of separation from their families. All these activities have taken place in the context of healing in a therapeutic setting. By now, all contact with non-believers is severed. The accusers generally refuse to read letters written by parents, or if they do read them, they often must first be approved by the therapist, so they are virtually cut off from all outside opinions. Is it any wonder they now believe in their own new identity as a survivor of sexual abuse?

The objectives of the therapy are to determine that sexual or emotional abuse has occurred, identify the abuser or abusers, and empower the adult child by taking the shame and giving it back to the perpetrator in an accusation. Guides for survivors suggest public disclosure of the perpetrator and sometimes suing the accused. Hundreds of lawsuits against parents are presently in litigation. Many more suits are settled out of court.

Often during the course of therapy the accusers doubt the memories they are uncovering. However, the therapist, the survivors' groups they join and the books they read encourage them to stay on the course and not waiver. They are told that in order to heal they must trust the therapist and the group.

One wonders how anyone, especially a daughter or son who once loved her or his parents, can come to believe such horrendous accusations when there is no evidence at all to back them up.

Robyn Dawes Explains Why People Believe the Unbelievable

Robyn M. Dawes, professor of psychology at Carnegie Mellon University, responded to the question of why people believe the unbelievable in a paper he presented at the Fourth Annual Convention of the American Psychology Society in June 1992. In his paper, entitled "Why Believe That for Which There Is No Good Evidence?" Dawes states: "Many people believe in the existence of widespread 'repressed' child sexual abuse and organized satanic cults. Such beliefs occur despite lack of evidence supporting them, influenced instead by reliance on authorities and social consensus" (Dawes:214).

In the last twenty years, a body of literature has developed written by people, considered authorities, which substantiates the theories of repressed memories of childhood abuse. These "authorities" have written books, presented numerous seminars, quote one another frequently and present the same statistics, often not verified, over and over again.

A wide "social consensus" has developed around these theories by many, including psychotherapists, members of the recovery movement, feminists, adherents to various aspects of New Age therapy, talk show hosts and some celebrities.

We have in this phenomenon the two components that Dawes says are necessary for people to believe that for which there is no good evidence: A group of "authorities" on repressed memories of widespread childhood sexual abuse and a "social consensus" that has developed with broad support for the theories of these authorities.

We all accept authorities or we couldn't function in society. If we didn't trust our parents, teachers, doctors, pharmacists, car repair person, or the pilot of the plane we fly in, we would suffer an inability to function. Dawes claims, "The completely open mind that questions all authority would reside in a body that is a blithering mess" (Dawes:215).

Good students must trust authorities in order to succeed in an educational setting. If they challenged everything presented to them in textbooks and lectures they would never succeed. They must trust that authorities are responsible. Many of the accusers are graduates of some of the finest universities – Harvard, Yale, Princeton, Cornell – and they are often successful professionals – nurses, doctors, lawyers, psychotherapists, musicians. Their ability, discipline and trust made them susceptible to this therapy, which provides an apparent learning atmosphere consisting of books, seminars, therapists and groups. They are provided with book lists and a structured format of work books prescribed by authorities to reach the stated objective of "healing."

Given the circumstances — of intelligent adults seeking answers to problems, authorities who write books and hold training seminars, therapists to guide the process and groups to provide support — is it any wonder that many adult children believe what they are taught to believe? They are taught that millions of adult children have been molested, any number of ailments are symptoms of the molestation, and that memories have been repressed and can be retrieved in therapy. Therapists and groups then validate the memories.

Once started on a course of regression therapy it becomes a closed system. In twenty years, the ideas formulated by a few therapists have permeated the entire culture and regressed memory therapy is well entrenched. An answer is provided for everything in this type of therapy, as parents and other family members well know, who try to break through the stone wall that separates them from their accusing children. Anyone who questions retrieved memories gained in therapy is considered to be "in denial" — a euphemism for lying, guilt, evil or stupidity.

"Authorities" Emerge and a "Social Consensus" Develops

The women's movement of the 1960s and 1970s alerted the public to the issues of abuse against women and incest. Soon some factions of the radical feminist movement began to define incest as a political issue. It was not just the act of a single person, but a way to keep women under control in society. A body of literature developed around the incest issue, its origins and effects on women and society.

Among the "authorities" whose ideas influenced the incest survivor movement are Florence Rush, Susan Forward, Judith Herman, Jeffrey Masson, Ellen Bass, Laura Davis, Christine Courtois, E. Sue Blume, Alice Miller, and Renee Fredrickson.

Helping to create a "social consensus" around the "theories" of these authorities and thereby giving momentum to the incest survivor movement are John Bradshaw, Marilyn Van Derbur Atler, Roseanne Barr Arnold, Frances Lear, and Gloria Steinem. These are influential people in America, able to gain attention and respect with ease, to the causes they believe in. They have ready access to the media and thereby inflluence millions of people.

Authorities Emerge
Florence Rush Interprets Sexual Abuse

Beginning with social worker Florence Rush's historic presentation at the New York Radical Feminist Rape Conference in April 1971, a new, feminist interpretation of the sexual abuse of children was articulated and accepted, mostly unchallenged. Rush declared: "Sexual abuse of children is permitted because it is an unspoken but prominent factor in socializing and preparing the female to accept a subordinate role: to feel guilty, ashamed, and to tolerate, through fear, the power exercised over her by men. . . . The female's early sexual experiences prepare her to submit in later life to the adult forms of sexual abuse heaped on her by her boyfriend, her lover, her husband. In short, the sexual abuse of female children is a process of education that prepares them to become the wives and mothers of America" (Armstrong:133).

Recalling the excitement of that conference in the introduction to Rush's 1980 book, *The Best-Kept Secret: Sexual Abuse of Children*, Susan Brownmiller said that "it was time to go beyond personal testimony and attempt to make theory, to build from experience, and to piece together from scholarships an analysis of sexual assault" (Rush:viii). Brownmiller had established her radical feminist credentials with the publication of *Against Our Will: Men, Women and Rape* (1975), in which she states, "The unholy silence that shrouds the interfamily sexual abuse of children and prevents a realistic appraisal of its true incidence and meaning is rooted in the same patriarchal philosophy of sexual property that shaped and determined historic male attitudes toward rape" (Brownmiller:281).

The new interpretation of incest included certain doctrines which other feminist writers repeated. The first one is usually established from the onset, as it is in the preface of Rush's book: "It is time we face the fact that the sexual abuse of children is not an occasional deviant act, but a devastating commonplace fact of everyday life" (Rush:xii). While Rush dealt with the broader topic of sexual abuse of children by family members and strangers alike, conclusions were generalized to include both types of violations. By 1980, the feminist definition of incest was ambiguous enough to include any inappropriate sexual behavior, with or without contact, with a stranger, authority figure or relative, regardless of age difference. Florence Rush's influence in the feminist interpretation of incest is significant because, according to Brownmiller, she was "the first thinker to see child sexual abuse not as an isolated incident but as a pervasive pattern with antecedents of social acceptance that reach far back into history" (Rush:ix).

Much of Rush's book deals with a social history of child sexual abuse viewed with a feminist interpretation. She cites many examples – the Bible, the Talmud, ancient Greece, early Christians, Victorian England, traditional fairy tales, modern films – which demonstrate to her the universal acceptance by men of the subjugation, humiliation, manipulation and erotic exploitation of little girls. Rush believes, "Men generally do not take sex with children seriously. They are amused by it, wink at it and allow adult-child sex to continue through a complex of mores which applauds male sexual aggression and denies a child's pain and humiliation, confusion and outrage" (Rush:13). Rush also tries to prove that men who molest children are protected by law and custom. "And since it is men who sexually use and abuse children, the law, written and executed by men, tends to be extremely lenient with the sex offender" (Rush:151). Unfortunately, conclusions based on emotion and intuition, prevalent in the radical feminist political interpretation of incest, took the place of unbiased research based on objective studies of the incidence of incest.

Personal accounts of incest published in the late 1970s, most notably *Father's Days* by Katherine Brady and the stories in Louise Armstrong's *Kiss Daddy Goodnight*, graphically portrayed the emotional trauma incest victims endured. These books were widely read as the topic of incest came out of hiding. A despicable crime, which most people thought relatively rare and contained to the lower class, incest, it was written, happened in every neighborhood, on every street, by men least likely to be suspect.

The major result of the new interpretation of incest was to establish, by repetition rather than by evidence, that incest is a common practice in American families. Sandra Butler restated this position in *Conspiracy of Silence: The Trauma of Incest* (1978): "The widespread occurrence of incestuous abuse has been clouded by the fact that nearly all cases in middle- and upper-class homes remain unreported and may be revealed only to private psychiatrists or therapists. . . . Were it possible to provide a more realistic profile of a typical family in which incestuous abuse occurs, it would more likely be a middle-class family composed of husband, wife and children living together in a nuclear situation. The adults would be Republicans as often as Democrats, involved in their church and active in community affairs, the same people you and I pass on the street each morning" (Butler:8).

Susan Forward Prescribes Psychotherapy

Betrayal of Innocence: Incest and Its Devastation (1978) by Susan Forward was one of the first of many books about incest written for a wide audience. An article by Forward summarizing her findings appeared in *Ladies' Home Journal* the same year. Readers learn that incest "happens more often than anyone realizes." Forward is a psychotherapist and "herself a victim." In the first paragraph Forward states that incest involves "at least one out of 20 Americans" (Forward 1978a:116). This number has steadily increased over the years to one out of three girls.

Forward tells how, at age 15, "my father's playful affection turned into highly sexualized fondling" (Forward 1978a:116). This experience, she explains, was ultimately responsible for her unhappy marriage and failed acting career. "Finally, I entered psychotherapy, and only then did I realize the connection between my problems and what my father had done to me" (Forward 1978a:116).

Forward goes on to describe her work training thera-pists in group therapy techniques and working with hun-dreds of women who always knew they were incest vic-tims. She states – with no reference to how she comes up with the figure – that between ten and 20 million Ameri-cans are victims of incest. Forward makes no mention of repressed memories at this date. Incest as she described it in 1978 leaves the victim "drawn into a silent world of shame and hopelessness" (Forward 1978a:120). This im-plies that the incest victim is more likely to dwell on the memory, not forget or repress it.

Susan Forward describes what she believes to be symp-toms that incest victims carry through life: " . . . pain, fear, revulsion . . . a fundamental lack of self–confidence and self–respect . . . trouble developing relationships . . . a variety of sexual problems . . . Or she may develop a variety of psychosomatic symptoms, including migraine headaches, stomach ailments, skin disorders and severe – and seem-ingly mysterious – aches and pains. Most victims experi-ence periods of deep depression, often leading to suicide attempts" (Forward 1978a:120).

Forward also provides a profile of the incestuous father: "He is rarely a freak, a dangerous criminal or a psychopath. Instead he is usually an otherwise law–abiding, hard–work-ing guy–next-door who has lost the ability to control his impulses . . . often regular churchgoers" (Forward 1978a:120). She describes the mother as the silent partner.

Without documenting her statistics or sources, Forward states that "various experts have ventured guesses that incest occurs in as many as 40 percent of all families with daughters" (Forward 1978a:122). Forward makes the jump from one in 20 Americans to 40 percent of families with daughters without explanation – this is indicative of the methods used by those determined to create the awareness that incest is rampant. The concept "expert" becomes meaningless as it applies to anonymous "specialists" speculating without evidence.

Forward recommends therapy and claims she has been successful treating incest victims. "My goal with my incest patient(s) has been to help them gain the courage to reveal the incest and to encourage them to work out the experience and the accompanying guilt. . . . Therapy works well for the vast majority: their headaches decrease or disappear . . . they develop self-confidence" (Forward 1978a:233). The emphasis at the end of the article is again on the prescribed method of healing from the wounds of incest: ". . . anyone who has been involved in incest can do something about the trauma *now* – through psychotherapy" (Forward 1978a:233).

Forward, elaborating on the work of her predecessors, reaffirms several of the doctrines that are now gospel in the incest survivor movement:

1. Incest is much more prevalent than anyone ever imagined.

2. Incest is defined by the victim and can be any inappropriate behavior toward a child, whether sexual or not.

3. Women suffer a variety of physical and emotional ailments – headaches, low self-confidence, trouble developing relationships, skin disorders and mysterious aches and pains – as a result of incest.

4. Perpetrators of incest are the typical guy-next-door, often active in the community and church – the last person anyone would suspect.

5. The mother contributed to the incest by allowing it to happen.

6. Psychotherapy is the way to heal from the long–term emotional trauma of incest.

7. Group therapy is particularly successful for incest victims.

Judith Herman Provides a Political Theory of Incest

Judith Herman's book *Father–Daughter Incest* (1981) restated the feminist interpretation of incest. In the preface she states, "This growing awareness [of incest] is largely a result of the women's liberation movement" (Herman:vii). Herman contends, "It is not possible to write dispassionately about incest. The subject is entirely enmeshed not only in myth and folklore, but also in ideology. We have found that a frankly feminist perspective offers the best explanation of the existing data" (Herman:3). Herman's book provides a political interpretation of a now sensational topic: "Father–daughter incest is not only the type of incest most frequently reported but also represents a paradigm of female sexual victimization. . . It is no accident that incest occurs most often precisely in the relationship where the female is most powerless" (Herman:4).

The first chapter is titled "A Common Occurrence." Herman's first sentence states, "Female children are regularly subjected to sexual assaults by adult males who are part of their intimate social world. The aggressors are not outcasts and strangers; they are neighbors, family friends, uncles, cousins, stepfathers, and fathers" (Herman:7).

Like Forward, Herman attempts to make the connection between women's emotional problems and the probability of incest. "Any serious investigation of the emotional and sexual lives of women leads eventually to the discovery of the incest secret" (Herman:7). This notion comes from a theory Sigmund Freud originated and then rejected nearly a century ago.

Because several of his female patients related stories of childhood sexual experiences, Freud suspected that childhood sexual trauma was the cause of many female psychological ailments. Freud later repudiated his "seduction theory" because he realized that his patients' stories were all similar because of the methods used to retrieve the memories, including hypnosis. Freud was a skilled hypnotist and used dream analysis and trance induction to search his patients' unconscious minds for early traumatic experiences. He later recognized that his patients' memories could have been triggered by his suggestions. Many present-day therapists use similar techniques and suggest that sexual abuse is at the root of many emotional problems.

Florence Rush was the first to incorporate the "Freud was right the first time" dogma into the new interpretation of incest. Herman and other therapists have resurrected the belief which Freud later claimed to be unfounded. The modern theory of repressed memories of early childhood sexual abuse is based on Freud's original, later discarded, assumption.

Judith Herman claims Freud changed his mind to protect the power of patriarchy. "Since much of psychoanalytic theory originated in the refusal to validate a common and central female experience, it is not surprising that Freud and his followers were never able to develop a satisfactory psychology of women" (Herman:10). And since Freud's time, according to Herman, psychiatrists have conspired to make sure that women's claims of incest were simply fantasies. Herman says, "The legacy of Freud's inquiry into the subject of incest was a tenacious prejudice, still shared by professionals and laymen alike, that children lie about sexual abuse. This belief is by now so deeply ingrained in the culture that children who dare to report sexual assaults are more than likely to have their complaints dismissed as fantasy" (Herman:11). Herman believes psychiatrists who are skeptical of adult claims of remembering childhood incest during therapy is similar to ignoring claims by children.

Herman's study also set out to determine the aftereffects of childhood incest. Flaws in her study are evident: "We chose to restrict the study to women who had therapists because we believed our work could not be carried out without causing pain. . . . Informants were located primarily through an informal network of therapists in private practice in the Boston area" (Herman:68-69). It is obvious that women who are in therapy are not representative of the general population. The accuracy of patients' memories was not questioned. "Each individual's testimony had the vividness and integrity of well-preserved memory, and the accounts of many informants were so similar that they tended to validate each other" (Herman:71).

Herman also included in her study 20 women who had seductive but not incestuous fathers. These women, whom Herman calls victims of "covert incest," suffered similar aftereffects (implying that certain inappropriate behaviors might be just as devastating as incest). "For every girl who has been involved in an incestuous relationship, there are considerably more who have grown up in a covertly incestuous family. In reconstructing a picture of this kind of family, we expected to find many similarities with the families of incest victims, and thus to establish the concept that overt incest represents only the furthest point on a continuum — an exaggeration of patriarchal family norms, but not a departure from them" (Herman:110). Herman's conclusion: "The pathological effects of overt and covert incest were similar in nature and differed mainly in degree. . . . The complaints of the women we have interviewed about their experiences are so similar as to suggest the existence of a syndrome common to all incest victims" (Herman:176).

The end of Herman's book deals with "Remedies for Victims." The remedy is psychotherapy with a therapist informed about the widespread prevalence of incest. Herman suggests a new approach for healing from incest. Therapists have traditionally been trained, she says, by reporting to a supervisor. However, since Herman denounces what she considers a century of denial by the mental health establishment, inexperienced therapists do not receive proper guidance from their superiors when dealing with claims of incest. " . . . The tradition of institutional denial has resulted in a situation in which supervisors are no more knowledgeable than beginners. Until recently, there was little professional literature to offer the therapist intellectual support" (Herman:180). So the experience and wisdom of a supervisor who might have a moderating influence on unlikely claims of abuse is considered by Herman to be irrelevant. Instead, what becomes relevant is the growing feminist literature that repeats the same theory over and over again.

Herman's remedy is to question the patient about childhood incest and if there is that possibility (it could be *covert* incest), proceed as if all her problems stem from the incest. "Questions about sexual abuse should be incorporated into any clinician's ordinary history–taking. The prevalence of child sexual abuse even in the general population is great enough to warrant routine questioning. . . . The burden of responsibility for obtaining a history of incest should lie with the therapist" (Herman:vii).

According to Herman, a possible diagnosis of incest as the source of psychological illness should be considered if certain symptoms are present, even if not mentioned by the patient. "In certain situations incest should be particularly suspect, as with women who are alcoholic or drug dependent . . . women whose mothers have been ill or absent . . . failure to raise the question in these cases amounts to negligence on the part of the therapist" (Herman:178).

Judith Herman's "study" of incest – a political rather than psychological study – made a significant impact in the field of psychotherapy as thousands of women entered this profession. Much of the theory behind the present-day search for repressed memories of childhood incest was established by Herman and like-minded researchers.

Jeffrey Masson Interprets Freud from a Feminist Perspective

The thesis of Jeffrey Masson's book *The Assault on Truth: Freud's Suppression of the Seduction Theory* (1984) is that because of a "personal failure of courage," Sigmund Freud denounced his original theory that childhood sexual abuse is the cause of neurosis in adults. In doing so, "Freud had abandoned an important truth: the sexual, physical, and emotional violence that is a real and tragic part of the lives of many children" (Masson:190). Masson claims this changed the course of psychoanalysis as it has been practiced for nearly a century, causing women's reports of sexual trauma to not be believed by psychiatrists.

Masson's interpretation of Freud's rejection of the seduction theory has rekindled a widespread fervor for a return to that belief. Masson, a psychoanalyst and former projects director of the Freud Archives, had access to

Freud's personal letters. Masson's belief that Freud backed down from his original position because of cowardice was hailed by feminist psychologists as proof that Freud's original theory was valid. With this interpretation, Masson allied himself with the feminist theorists. He supports the theories of incest created by Florence Rush, Judith Herman and other feminists: "From these authors I learned that the problem was far greater than I had realized. . . . There is no doubt in my mind that it was the feminist literature of the 1970s that finally broke the silence about the incidence and prevalence of incest," said Masson (Masson: xvi, xvii).

Masson believes, as Freud originally did, that traumatic memories of sexual abuse are hidden in the unconscious mind and the abuse is the cause of various adult neuroses. The memories must be found in order to heal. Without explaining how a memory becomes repressed or recalled decades later, Masson makes a general statement that would be repeated as scientific fact in dozens of subsequent books on incest: "No doubt much of the humiliation, hurt, and rage of the abused child would, in order for that child to survive, have to be repressed" (Masson:191).

Jeffrey Masson did more than just agree with the feminist contention that the history of psychoanalysis is based on a lie. In the conclusion of his book, Masson appeals to the mental health profession to believe memories of childhood sexual trauma recalled during therapy as historical fact. Otherwise, Masson states, "The silence demanded of the child by the person who violated her (or him) is perpetuated and enforced by the very person to whom she has come for help. . . . If it is not possible for the therapeutic community to address this serious issue in an honest and open-minded manner, then it is time for their patients to stop subjecting themselves to needless repetition of their deepest and earliest sorrow" (Masson:192, 193).

Judith Herman Validates Repression

Judith Herman attempted to prove the validity of repressed memories in a study of 53 women. *Psychoanalytic Psychology* published her results in the article "Recovery and Verification of Memories of Childhood Sexual Trauma"(1987). Herman emphasized the importance of group therapy in "remembering" sexual abuse from childhood: "Participation in group proved to be a powerful stimulus for recovery of memory in patients with severe amnesia. Almost all of the women who entered the group complaining of major memory deficits and who defined a goal of recovering childhood memories were able to retrieve previously repressed memories during group treatment" (Herman and Schatzow:8). These patients had previously been "preoccupied with obsessive doubt over whether their victimization had been fantasized or real. Some had previously sought treatment with hypnosis or sodium amytal" (Herman and Schatzow:8).

Under the subheading "Validation of Traumatic Memories," Herman begins: "Participation in group therapy offered an opportunity for many patients to gather corroborating evidence of abuse" (Herman and Schatzow:9). (However, she does not explain how this happened.) The patients worked toward the achievement of a personal goal. For some the goal was "disclosure of the abuse to a family member, recovery of memories, confrontation with the perpetrator" (Herman and Schatzow:9-10).

In a scenario now familiar to thousands of families, Herman describes how three participants in her study "confronted families who united in absolute denial of the abuse. This situation proved extremely distressing to the patients, who felt obliged to choose between their own perception of reality and any sense of connection to their families. The most dramatic resolution of this conflict occurred in one case in which the patient severed all ties with her family, changed her name, and occasionally mobilized alternative social supports for family occasions such as birthdays and holidays" (Herman and Schatzow:11).

Herman concludes by stating that her findings verified Freud's original seduction theory. "The presumption that most patients' reports of childhood sexual abuse can be ascribed to fantasy no longer appears tenable. . . . No positive evidence was adduced that would indicate that any of the patients' reports of sexual abuse were fantasies. In the light of these findings, it would seem warranted to return to the insights offered by Freud's original statement of the etiology of hysteria, and to resume a line of investigation that mental health professionals prematurely abandoned 90 years ago" (Herman and Schatzow:11).

Nearly 30 years after Freud first rejected his seduction theory, he wrote: "Under the influence of the technical procedure which I used at that time, the majority of my patients reproduced from their childhood scenes in which they were sexually seduced by some grown-up person. With female patients the part of seducer was almost always assigned to their father. I believed these stories, and consequently supposed that I had discovered the roots of the subsequent neurosis in these experiences of sexual seduction in childhood. . . . If the reader feels inclined to shake his head at my credulity, I cannot altogether blame him. . . . When, however, I was at last obliged to recognize that these scenes of seduction had never taken place, and that they were only phantasies which my patients had made up or which I myself had perhaps forced on them, I was for some time completely at a loss . . . " (Masson:198).

Herman redefines the role of the therapist and opens the way for feminists specializing in treating incest victims. "It is our impression, however, that the retrieval and validation of repressed memories has an important role in the recovery process. With the return of the memory, the patient has the opportunity as an adult to integrate an experience that was beyond her capacity to endure as a child. . . . In addition, the relief of particular post-traumatic symptoms following recovery of memory is often dramatic" (Herman and Schatzow:12). In short the role of the therapist is "to protect, to bear witness, and in so doing, to make it possible for unspeakable things to be told and unbearable feelings to be borne" (Herman and Schatzow:13).

With this article, which Herman alleges is a scientific study, she claims that repressed memories are real, thus validating Masson's theory. By enlarging the definitions of incest vicims to include those who had forgotten, or repressed it, the number of victims grew considerably.

During the late 1980s and early 1990s, many books and articles appeared on repressed memories of childhood sexual abuse. The same studies are referred to, the same experts quoted, the same advice offered. Carol Tavris, a feminist critic of the excesses in the incest survivor movement wrote in a *New York Times* article (January 3, 1993), "In what can only be called an incestuous arrangement, the authors of these books all rely on one another's work as supporting evidence for their own; they all endorse and recommend one another's books to their readers. If one of them comes up with a concocted statistic — such as 'more than half of all women are survivors of childhood sexual trauma' — the numbers are traded like baseball cards, reprinted in every book and eventually enshrined as fact. Thus the cycle of misinformation, faulty statistics and unvalidated assertions maintains itself" (Tavris:17).

Ellen Bass and Laura Davis Write the Incest Survivors' "Bible"

The most popular guide book for surviving incest is *The Courage to Heal* (1988) by Ellen Bass and Laura Davis. Bass is a creative writing teacher who says that many students in her seminars for women wrote stories about incest. Laura Davis recovered "memories" of her grandfather molesting her from age three to 10 many years after her grandfather died. Their book is widely recommended by therapists who help patients recover incest memories. Judith Herman's endorsement is on the back cover: "This book advances the empowerment of survivors another major step — from breaking silence to sharing recovery." This book is often referred to as the "bible" of the incest survivor movement.

Although Bass states in the preface that "none of what is presented here is based on psychological theories" (Bass and Davis:14), many psychotherapists have adopted the methods used in this book, and many of the statements are now widely accepted psychological theories, such as:

> Forgetting *is one of the most common and effective ways children deal with sexual abuse. The human mind has tremendous powers of repression.* Many children are able to forget about the abuse, even as it is happening to them. . . . *This capacity to forget explains why so many adult survivors are unaware of the fact that they were abused.*

(p.42)

There are many women who show signs of having been abused without having any memories.

(p.71)

Memories are stored in our bodies, and it is possible to physically reexperience the terror of the abuse.

(p.74-75)

If you think you were abused and your life shows the symptoms, then you were.

(p.22)

Children often leave their bodies during sex with the abuser.

(p.37)

Many survivors have a difficult time with the concept of the child within, even though forgiving that child is an essential part of healing.

(p.111)

To say 'I was abused,' you don't need the kind of recall that would stand up in a court of law.

(p.22)

According to *The Courage to Heal*, expressing anger is an important part of the process of healing from sexual abuse:

As you become more familiar with experiencing and expressing your anger, it can become part of everyday life.

(p.131)

. . . anger doesn't have to be suppressed or destructive. Instead, it can be both a healthy response to violation and a transformative, powerful energy.

(p.123)

Therapy and support groups can be ideal places for stirring up anger.

(p.126)

You may dream of murder or castration. It can be pleasurable to fantasize such scenes in vivid detail. Wanting revenge is a natural impulse, a sane response. Let yourself imagine it to your heart's content. Giving yourself permission to visualize revenge can be satisfying indeed.

(p.128)

There are nonviolent means of retribution you can seek. Suing your abuser and turning him into the authorities are just two of the avenues open.

(p.128)

Another woman, abused by her grandfather, went to his deathbed and, in front of all the other relatives, angrily confronted him right in the hospital.

(p.128-129)

When you meet your anger openly — naming it, knowing it, directing it appropriately — you are liberated.

(p.128)

The Courage to Heal encourages incest survivors to confront their suspected perpetrators, even disown their families. The authors provide techniques for confronting and discarding families:

You may want to make the abuser, nonprotecting parents, or others feel the impact of what happened to you. You may want to see them suffer. You may

*want revenge. . . . You may want financial repara-
tions of payment for your therapy.*

(p.133-134)

*You must be willing to relinquish the idea that your
family has your best interests at heart.*

(p.135)

*Preparation for an actual confrontation can be as
important as the event itself. You can role-play
possible scenarios in therapy or with supportive
friends.*

(p.138)

*. . . take a friend with you as a witness. Be careful
about whom you pick to do this. Choose someone
who won't get drawn in by your family.*

(p.139)

*There are many ways to confront or disclose. You
can do it in person, over the phone, through a letter,
in a telegram, or through an emissary.*

(p.139)

*The initial confrontation is not the time to dis-
cuss the issues, to listen to your abuser's side of
the story, or to wait around to deal with everyone's reactions. Go in, say what you need to say,
and get out. Make it quick.*

(p.139)

*You do not gain by remaining part of a family
system that undermines your well-being. In fact
many survivors made great strides in healing by
cutting the cord.*

(p.294)

*Although most people follow customs established by
their families, religion, or culture, it's possible for you
to create new ones with people of your own choosing.*

(p.300)

*Giving up your family and the anguish that causes
deserves recognition.*

(p.305)

Tens of thousands of therapists who specialize in healing from incest have endorsed this book and recommend it to their clients. It is even used as a textbook in some college classrooms. Well over 650,000 copies of *The Courage to Heal* have been sold.

The authors of *The Courage to Heal*, travel the country conducting workshops for "survivors" and training seminars for therapists. Continuing education credits are often given to the therapists who attend Bass and Davis seminars. Thousands of women with recovered memories credit *The Courage to Heal* with helping them to remember their abuse.

Many adult children believe they become empowered by publicly declaring themselves "survivors of incest." They have become a major political force, helping to lobby state legislatures to extend the statute of limitations on sexual abuse that is recalled years later in therapy.

Laura Davis Instructs Husbands and Friends of Survivors

Laura Davis, coauthor of *The Courage to Heal*, wrote two additional books: *The Courage to Heal Workbook* (1990) and *Allies in Healing* (1991). The workbook is a powerful teaching device with the goals of determining that you were abused, identifying who abused you, encouraging anger against the abuser, all in the name of healing. Writing exercises encourage fantasy and vivid use of the imagination. The user of this workbook, if she has any doubts whether her hazy memories are real or not, will likely have no doubts that she was abused after reading this instructional manual for confronting parents and adopting the "liberating" lifestyle of an incest survivor.

Allies in Healing emphasizes the need for partners of survivors to give their full support during the long healing process described in *The Courage to Heal* and the workbook. Davis describes to spouses, who might question how someone can recall something 20 years later that had been forgotten, how repressed memories work: "Children actually forget the abuse happened; they store it away in a part of themselves that isn't available to their conscious minds. . . Then ten or twenty years later, these repressed childhood memories surface, often creating havoc in their lives (and yours). It may be difficult for you to accept the idea that memories can suddenly surface 'out of thin air,' but the process of recovering traumatic memories years after the original trauma is a well–documented psychological phenomenon" (Davis 1991:115).

Davis relates other pseudoscientific notions about memories to mental health professionals, whom she trains. Davis states, as if it is an established fact, "Memories are stored in the body, and physical touch can bring them to the surface. You touch the survivor in a particular way and he goes numb, disappears, or thinks you're his brother on top of him in the narrow bed he slept in as a child. Survivors remember during massages, bodywork (therapies that integrate touch and movement), physical exercise, or in the course of other body changes, like losing or gaining a lot of weight" (Davis 1991:116).

Again emphasizing, as in her other books, that actual memories are not necessary in coming to realize you were abused, Davis notes, "The important thing is for survivors to eventually reach a point where they can say, 'Yes, it happened. The effects are imprinted in my life. I'm going to accept the fact that I was abused and make a commitment to heal, even if I never remember the specifics.' Memory is not a prerequisite to healing. Willingness, determination, and courage are" (Davis 1991:118). Davis responds to the possibility that a partner might doubt the reality of a repressed memory: "It's natural to have doubts; but ultimately, if you want to be her intimate supporter, you need to find a way to believe the abuse happened, even if the survivor never recovers another memory. The survivor is full of her own doubts; she doesn't need yours to deal with, too" (Davis 1991:118).

Davis advises partners, "If you're struggling to believe the things the survivor has told you or to accept the fact that the abuse is still affecting her, keep working at it. With support and information, you will eventually be able to believe her fully" (Davis 1991:53).

Mike Lew's Manual for Men

The same publisher of these three books offers a book for men recovering from sexual abuse, *Victims No Longer* (1988) by Mike Lew, a psychotherapist and "leading expert on recovery from child sexual abuse . . . he gives public lectures, professional training, and workshops for survivors nationwide." His cover biography also notes that he has appeared on Oprah Winfrey and Sally Jessy Raphael.

Victims No Longer is basically the male version of *The Courage to Heal*, complete with a cover endorsement from Judith Herman. Lew acknowledges his debt to the feminist movement: "There is no doubt that the active work of the feminist movement has forced our society to recognize the existence of incest. . . . Judith Herman, M.D. (author of the book *Father–Daughter Incest*) has referred to the need for 'a movement' to insure that information about trauma doesn't need to be 'rediscovered' every hundred years. Without a movement to remind and reinforce, the best research data are ignored" (Lew:38-39).

Lew restates the same fallacies about memory and the same belief that sexual abuse is the root of psychological problems that is evident in *The Courage to Heal*. Lew states, "A great many incest survivors have little or no memory of their childhood. In fact, this method of dealing with childhood trauma is so common that when clients tell me they have no recollection of whole pieces of their childhood, I assume the likelihood of some sort of abuse" (Lew:69).

The theme of *Victims No Longer* is the same as *The Courage to Heal*. In a passage on revenge, anger and hatred are encouraged: "You need the freedom to express your desire to punish the people who abused you. An incest survivors' recovery group or workshop is a particularly appropriate place for you to do so. One of the most exciting aspects of the group experience occurs when a participant begins to share his thoughts about taking revenge against the perpetrator. These can range from lurid fantasies of torture and physical violence to elaborately thought out plans for confrontation, public exposure, and/or legal action" (Lew:257).

Christine Courtois Adds Another Influential Voice

Christine Courtois, a Washington, D.C., clinical psychologist, published a paper titled "The Memory Retrieval Process in Incest Survivor Therapy," an expanded version of her presentation to the 1990 American Psychological Association Annual Convention. Courtois's academic style and presentation gives the impression that she is taking a rational and scientific approach. However, some of the more pseudoscientific concepts surrounding memory retrieval are presented: "Memory can return *physiologically*, through body memories and perceptions. . . . His or her body might react in pain reminiscent of the abuse and might even evidence physical stigmata as the memory of a particular abuse experience is retrieved and worked through. . . . Memories might also return via dreams and nightmares . . ." (Courtois:22,23).

The author emphasizes the importance of a defined therapy program by a "qualified specialist" as a requirement for healing. "An atmosphere of support and validation is also conducive to memory and, in and of itself, is often a memory retrieval cue." (Courtois:22). The therapist has another role — to explain to the client the theory of repressed memories and suggest that sexual abuse might be the reason for her problems, as evidenced by the emotional symptoms. "The therapist further assists the client by explaining the traumatic stress syndrome and, in particular, normative post-sexual abuse reactions. The therapy and remembering process must also be described in detail. . . . Education precedes formal recall strategies to insure the survivor a cognitive framework within which to process emotions which accompany recall. . . . At times, it may be necessary for the therapist to put the pieces together and *speculate* about the emerging picture and its significance. . ." (Courtois:25,26).

Courtois suggests other memory retrieval aids: "Courtois [citing herself] has listed a number of experiential/expressive-cathartic techniques including hypnosis, guided imagery, writing, drawing, guided movement, body work, and those drawn from the schools of Gestalt therapy and psychodrama as well as exploratory/psychodynamic techniques to assist in memory retrieval" (Courtois:27).

According to Courtois, family pictures or childhood toys might trigger a memory. "Group therapy also functions as a memory stimulus and should be considered as a very important adjunct in this stage of the treatment . . . Groups are very powerful in eliciting memories since survivors associate or 'chain' to each others' recollections and feelings" (Courtois:28,29).

Authorities with various backgrounds and credentials, from clinical psychiatrists to self-proclaimed experts, are promoting the same theory: Women who seek psychotherapy and have certain identifiable symptoms are most likely victims of childhood incest. There are dozens of copycat books that have been published by both small and large publishers. Survivor books are big business.

The Merger of Two Popular Movements

During the late 1980s the recovery movement became a billion dollar industry for publishers, authors, lecturers, substance abuse clinics, and therapists. The model of Alcoholics Anonymous was applied to those "recovering" from all sorts of addictions. It became popular to join a 12-step group such as Codependents Anonymous, Adult Children of Alcoholics Anonymous, Debtors Anonymous, Sex Addicts Anonymous, even Messies Anonymous. One had to search within for the real cause of the "disease," which was beyond personal control. The cause was often found to be the wounded "inner child" whose needs were never met because of the dysfunctional family.

The majority of people "in recovery" are women. Membership in a 12-step program often leads to therapy. In fact therapy is strongly encouraged, if not required, to do the "original pain work" necessary to heal. A whole language of recovery was created as the movement flourished with the influence of PBS superstar John Bradshaw. Bradshaw has presented hundreds of seminars, and has written books and produced tapes that are best sellers. His teachings reach millions of people, including therapists who can receive continuing education credits for attending his seminars. The credits are required for maintaining a state license to practice psychotherapy. Bradshaw was not the first recovery guru but emerged as the most influential. Bradshaw claims that all families are dysfunctional. Millions of television viewers were introduced to the idea that they grew up in sick families and that traditional relationships with their families may no longer be desirable if one wants to be happy and healthy. Those not in recovery are "in denial," since every family has issues that must be dealt with.

Bradshaw encourages everyone to join a 12-step program and to go to a psychotherapist. Only a therapist can help one get to the deep pain. It is necessary to regress to early childhood, discover the wonder of one's inner child – symbolized by the stuffed animals that patients are encouraged to constantly hug – and continue a lifelong process of healing, for no one is ever recovered, just recovering.

Because of the recovery movement, hundreds of thousands of baby boomers enter psychotherapy to heal the inner child. They are called "adult children." This created a huge demand for psychotherapists and thousands entered the field. Unlike the traditional scientific training required for psychiatrists and clinical psychologists, which Judith Herman criticized as outdated and not serving the needs of women, the new breed of therapist is trained to deal with codependency and childhood trauma, with many specializing in sexual abuse.

Here was the beginning of the merger of the inner child with the brand of therapy already established to search for hidden memories of incest. By the time *The Courage to Heal* was published (1988), healing the inner child and searching for traumatic memories of incest went hand in hand. Thus the recovery movement provided thousands of "clients" for therapists trained to search out "memories" of incest using hypnosis, guided imagery, psychodrama, visualization, body massage, trance writing and other New Age techniques. Those who attend Bradshaw's seminars and other recovery seminars are primed to break off relations with their "families of origin" and to form "families of choice." For therapy clients already acquainted with the victim philosophy of the recovery movement, accusing Dad and Mom of incest is a natural progression of their anger. Thus, the recovery movement and the concept of codependency, which became popular in the 1980s, were natural allies for the incest survivor movement.

Susan Forward Writes Another Book

One book more than others, and there are dozens of others, best illustrates the marriage of the recovery and incest survivor movements – *Toxic Parents* (1989) by Susan Forward. Forward, as previously mentioned was instrumental in, as she puts it, " . . . efforts to raise public awareness about the epidemic proportions of incest" (Forward 1989:140). *Toxic Parents* has a cover endorsement by John Bradshaw: "I consider Susan Forward to be among the foremost therapists of our age. In *Toxic Parents* she offers us a penetrating model of how to heal the frozen grief of our dysfunctional past."

This book is a guide to identifying personal problems and failures and placing the blame on the parents. Step by step exercises and checklists lead to the goal — Confrontation: The Road to Independence. "The process is simple, though not easy. When you are ready, you calmly but firmly tell your parents about the negative events you remember from your childhood. You tell them how those events affected your life and how they affect your relationship with your parents now. You clearly define the aspects of that relationship that are painful and harmful to you now. Then you lay out new ground rules" (Forward 1989:233). She stresses the necessity of this confrontation: "If you don't deal with your fear, your guilt, and your anger at your parents, you're going to take it out on your partner or your children" (Forward 1989:235).

Getting rid of your "toxic" parents, according to Forward, is a positive step toward personal well-being. As a psychotherapist, Forward firmly believes in disowning imperfect parents rather than working toward reconciliation. She offers step-by-step advice on how to discard your parents after confronting them for their shortcomings. She advises her clients to write each parent a letter if they lack the courage for a face-to-face confrontation. If a personal confrontation is preferable, it is important to rehearse what you will say and to anticipate typical parental responses. Forward says, "They'll insist that your allegations never happened, or that you're exaggerating, or that your father could never have done such a thing.... *Your response:* 'Just because you don't remember doesn't mean it didn't happen'" (Forward:247). Forward also advises, "If you are in therapy, you might want to have the confrontation in your therapist's office. Your therapist can orchestrate the confrontation, make sure you get heard, help you if you get stuck, and most important, be supportive and protective" (Forward:243).

The reactions of other family members also have to be considered. Forward adds: "Just as your relationship with your parents will never be the same after confrontation, your relationship with your siblings will change as well. Some siblings have had experiences similar to yours and will validate your memories. . . . Some siblings feel extremely threatened by your confrontation and may become enraged at you for upsetting the precarious balance of the family. . . . They may call you names and do all they can to convince you that you're either wrong, crazy, or both." Forward suggests an appropriate response to a nonsupportive sibling: "My relationship with you is very important to me, but I won't bury my own needs to maintain it" (Forward:258, 259). Relationships with other relatives and close friends may also become strained, but Forward assures her readers: "This is never easy; it may be one of the more painful prices you must pay for emotional health" (Forward:261).

Forward also takes the opportunity in *Toxic Parents* to give her updated views on healing from incest. She presents the current recovery movement's all–inclusive definition of "psychological" incest: "Victims of psychological incest may not have been actually touched or assaulted sexually, but they have experienced an invasion of their sense of privacy or safety" (Forward 1989:139). This is a continuation of Judith Herman's 1980 concept of "covert incest." Bradshaw uses the term "emotional incest." As incest keeps getting redefined, an increasing number of people are becoming part of the incest survivor movement.

Forward states what has come to be generally accepted as fact by survivor therapists, despite the lack of any proof at all: "The only way many victims can survive their early incest traumas is to mount a psychological cover-up, pushing these memories so far beneath conscious awareness that they may not surface for many years, if ever. . . . It is also common for these memories to surface if the victim is in therapy working on other issues, though many victims still won't mention the incest without prodding from the therapist" (Forward 1989:152).

She believes that a "disproportionate number of incest victims, particularly women, allow themselves to become overweight as adults" (Forward 1989:163). The implication, which many therapists share, is that if an overweight woman comes to therapy, assume incest is the source of the problem. According to Forward, there are other obvious signs of incest. "Recurrent headaches are also common among incest victims. . . . Many incest victims lose themselves in a haze of alcohol and drug abuse" (Forward 1989:163).

According to Forward there is only one way to overcome the devastating effects of incest, real or imagined: "Professional help is a *must* for adults who were sexually abused as children. Nothing in my experience responds more dramatically and completely to therapy, despite the depth of the damage. . . . It is important to shop for a therapist specifically educated or experienced in working with incest victims. . . . If he or she has not attended any workshops, seminars, conferences, or classes on incest treatment, I suggest you find someone else" (Forward 1989:273,275).

"The best way to work through the incest experience is to join a group made up of victims like yourself led by a therapist who is experienced and comfortable with the issues" (Forward 1989:276). Forward describes familiar techniques for "healing." She requires her group members to write letters to the perpetrator, to the other parent who allowed it to happen, to the damaged inner child, to the victim's partner and each of the victim's children. It is easy to see how clients come to depend on the therapist and the group. By encouraging clients to hate and break off relations with their parents, the clients have no other life than therapy, no one to relate to except the therapist and the other group members.

Her biography on the book cover indicates how ideas presented by Forward have become so widespread (*Toxic Parents* was a #1 New York Times Bestseller): "Susan Forward, Ph.D. is an internationally recognized therapist and writer . . . In addition to her private practice, for five years she hosted a two-hour daily ABC Talkradio program. She has also served widely as a group therapist, instructor, and consultant in many southern California medical and psychiatric facilities. She has testified as an expert witness in numerous trials, and she formed the first private sexual abuse clinic in California." Susan Forward has had a great influence on tens of thousands of people, giving them advice on how to break away from their families.

E. Sue Blume Develops a Checklist for Incest Survivors

Another influential book validating the theory of repressed memories is *Secret Survivors* (1990) by state certified social worker E. Sue Blume, regarded as an expert in treating incest survivors. Blume developed "The Incest Survivors' Aftereffects Checklist" — a list of symptoms that

helps readers who have no recollections of incest to consider whether they might have repressed the traumatic
memories. It is also intended as a guidebook for therapists.
This list of nearly one hundred symptoms listed in 34
different categories is used by therapists and clients to
"validate" their "memories" of incest. Some of Blume's
symptoms of incest are: nightmares; gastrointestinal problems; arthritis; wearing baggy clothes; eating disorders;
drug or alcohol abuse; depression; constant anger; high
risk-taking; inability to take risks; fear of losing control; low
self-esteem; high appreciation of small favors by others;
feeling crazy; feeling different; pretending; having dreams
or memories; compulsively 'seductive' or compulsively
asexual; avoidance of mirrors; desire to change one's name;
quiet-voiced; stealing.

Secret Survivors has a front cover endorsement by Gloria
Steinem: "Explores the constellation of symptoms that result
from a crime too cruel for mind and memory to face. This
book, like the truth it helps uncover, can set millions free."

According to the author: "The Incest Survivors' Aftereffects Checklist has spread from its downstate New York
origins to international distribution among incest survivors, professionals, conference attendees, participants in
self-help and recovery groups for sexual and substance abuse, and adult children of alcoholics. The feedback I have received from these diverse and unrelated
survivors and therapists has validated the universality of
the profile" (Blume:xv).

Blume explains how her checklist can be used by therapists: "Among women who had not been aware of childhood sexual abuse but who recognized characteristics in
themselves on the checklist, a surprising number began to
uncover previously repressed incest. Thus we found that

the Aftereffects Checklist can serve as a diagnostic device for suggesting childhood sexual victimization when none is remembered. It also serves as a road map for a therapist treating someone whose amnesia or denial is total. Whether or not actual memories are uncovered, the checklist then presents a structure for identifying and addressing the consequences of incest" (Blume:xxiv). In case anyone is skeptical, Blume assures the reader: "Current research studies are validating the observations in the checklist" (Blume:xxiv).

Blume discusses the different degrees of incest: "It can be the way a father stares at his daughter's developing body, and the comments he makes. . . . It can be forced exposure to the sounds or sights of one or both parents' sexual acts. . . . Or it can be a father's jealous possessiveness and suspicion of the boys his daughter associates with, his inquisitorial insistence on knowing the details of her sexual encounters. . . . Horribly, increasingly, it can occur as part of a cult ritual activity engaged in by a network of adults and involving many children — violence and abuse of animals as well" (Blume:8-9). This last reference is of course to the growing claims of satanic ritual abuse that many therapy patients are describing.

On ritual abuse Blume adds: "The chilling stories told by unrelated victims around the country are virtually identical. The truths of this abuse are so shocking to society that the victimizers are protected by our disbelief. . . . Ceremonies may include sacrifice of animals, human torture, or cannibalism; victims have been forced to participate in the rape and murder of another child. . . . Their flashbacks and memories may represent an unwanted truth, but a truth nonetheless. Believe them. . . . And seek out the experts" (Blume:60-61). She does not consider the possibility that the patient's "memories" may have actually been stimulated by a book, movie or stories.

The concept of repression is accepted as fact by Blume. She expands on the concept with no indication, other than intuition, of how she arrived at her conclusions: "She [the incest survivor in general] denies that she was abused by repressing the memories of her trauma. This is the primary manifestation of the 'secret': incest becomes the secret she keeps even from herself. *Repression in some form is virtually universal among survivors*" (Blume:67).

Some therapists are using this "logic" to conclude that if a client reports no incident of incest in her past, then she must have been abused and repressed the memory. Blume later states: "Indeed, so few incest survivors in my experience have identified themselves as abused in the beginning of therapy that I have concluded that *perhaps half of all incest survivors do not remember that the abuse occurred*" (Blume:81).

Tens of thousands of clinical social workers have entered the mental health field. To renew state licenses, therapists are required to earn continuing education credits each year. Forward, Blume, Bass, Davis, Bradshaw and hundreds of others provide seminars and workshops for therapists. Therapists crowd these workshops because of the required credits they need to accumulate. State licensing agencies have essentially "validated" the techniques presented as scientific by proponents of the repressed memory theory.

The idea that millions of women enter therapy without the knowledge that they were sexually abused in childhood is widely accepted by tens of thousands of psychotherapists and counselors. Much of therapy today is based on the theories of Forward, Blume, Bass and Davis and

Bradshaw. It is no wonder that thousands of women (and men) are coming up with similar memories, memories learned in therapy using the same techniques and guide-books which teach those techniques.

Renee Fredrickson Embraces the Repression Theory

Another book receiving much attention was published in 1992 – *Repressed Memories: A Journey to Recovery from Sexual Abuse* by Renee Fredrickson. Fredrickson describes how in her therapy practice she has come across thousands of women who had repressed memories of in-cest. In her guide to "recovery" she says: "I hope all of you read this book with a journal nearby and a support net-work of a therapist, group, Twelve–Step organization . . ." (Fredrickson:18-19).

Fredrickson expands on the concept of repression and gives her explanation of why this phenomenon has hap-pened only in recent years: "Your repressed memories were held in storage not only for your readiness but also for society's readiness to deal with them. There has been an evolution of consciousness in our culture, resulting in a renewed awareness and ability to humanely respond to abuse. More and more of you are remembering your child-hood suffering as you sense the increased capacity for validation and healing from the world around you" (Fredrickson:24).

Fredrickson relays the same message that if your life shows the symptoms that you were abused – eating disor-ders, career struggles, nightmares, depression, etc. – then you were sexually abused and need to locate a therapist experienced in retrieving the memories that were re-pressed. Only until you recall the abuse and face your fear can real healing begin. "Facing what you do not remember about your past is a challenging odyssey. Yes, it will hurt for a while, but you are probably already suffering from the damage from the abuse. Uncovering repressed memories will give you the chance to end that suffering" (Fredrickson:51).

Fredrickson is a therapist who suspects repressed memories of sexual abuse are the source of almost every problem for every woman who enters therapy. "This form of amnesia lurks in the backgrounds of millions of ordinary, high-functioning Americans" (Fredrickson:53). Millions? For Fredrickson, every person is suspect, because " . . . if you have some of the warning signals given in Chapter Two, you probably do have repressed memories. You are unlikely to be the exception to the rule, no matter what your denial is telling you" (Fredrickson:53-54).

New Age techniques and beliefs appear throughout this book, especially in the section on Memory Retrieval Methods. "Currently, seven major methods of memory retrieval are being used for retrieving memories. . . . Please seek out an experienced therapist to help you with this work" (Fredrikson:97). She then lists and explains each technique: imagistic work; dream work; journal writing; body work; hypnosis; feelings work; art therapy. Fredrickson alerts the reader that repressed memories when recalled do not seem like normal memories. "You will gradually come to know that they are real, but not in the same way you remember something that was never repressed" (Fredrickson:99-100).

Fredrickson discusses the problem many "survivors" have believing their retrieved memories using the New Age techniques she recommends. "You may become overconcerned about making false accusations in particular. You do not want to claim that someone abused you when that is not true, but this need for justice can take on an exaggerated importance. Having been blamed so often in your family, you can become too sensitive to fairness issues. . . . You can also become too caught up in seeking external proof rather than internal relief. . . . Looking to your family to provide validation is especially risky" (Fredrickson:160-162).

Renee Fredrickson on ritual abuse: "If your memories are unusually grisly or bizarre, you may be a survivor of ritual abuse. . . . The ceremonies may even include human sacrifice and cannibalism. . . . Cults use all measures of threats and mind-warping techniques to ensure silence and loyalty to the group. . . . Since cults thrive on the disbelief of the public, another purpose is to set up the children to appear crazy if they should try to tell someone about the abuse. . . . An informal working group studying the phenomenon estimated that ritual abuse accounted for 7 to 10 percent of all sexual abuse survivors" (Fredrickson:164-165).

Fredrickson presents indicators of the authenticity of repressed memories. Generally, "If a memory fits your sense of your past, and, in the long run, you feel better for having dealt with it as real, then accept it as true. . . . The existence of profound disbelief is an indication that memories are real" (Fredrickson:167). It is also important to disclose the recalled abuse to friends and family. "Avoid being tentative about your repressed memories. Do not just tell them; express them as truth. . . .You cannot wait until you are doubt-free to disclose to your family. This may never happen"(Fredrickson:204).

Not surprisingly, adult children with newly recovered memories are met with denial when they confront their parents with horrendous accusations. Fredrickson tells accusers what to do: "The part you are probably dreading is how to handle your family's denial of your repressed memories. . . . You do not have to counter every argument or attack they make. You only have to assert your reality, even if you are the only one who perceives it. . . . You may want to suggest that the abuser has repressed all memory of the abuse." And finally, "The pain of confronting your family is equal to the strength you gain from doing it" (Fredrickson:205-206).

This book is actually the logical outcome of the method of research started by the early incest theorists. By stating assumptions based on intuition and ideology, it wasn't a far road to Renee Fredrickson stating that millions of people have repressed their memories of incest. She cites several inferences: if you dreamed you were abused then you were; if you have physical sensations in your genital area, this is absolute proof of body memories of abuse; bizarre images in dreams or hypnosis might mean you were forced to kill and eat babies. Fredrickson is a nationally recognized expert in the field of healing from incest.

A Social Consensus Develops
John Bradshaw Helps Search for More Survivors

In a monthly column for *Lear's* magazine, John Bradshaw presented the current recovery/incest survivor movement state of "knowledge" about incest. He begins with, by now, a very familiar approach: "Something in the neighborhood of 60 percent of all incest victims don't remember the sexual abuse for many years after the fact" (Bradshaw:43). He continues by saying that many people who can't remember their entire childhoods are worried that they may part of this statistic. "They are bound to wonder whether they were abused and whether the fact that they can't remember anything is a clue to that" (Bradshaw:43).

He then encourages his readers to try and find out if they were sexually abused and forgot it. Without any explanation Bradshaw states, "Offenders may literally instruct their victims not to remember certain events" (Bradshaw:43). Bradshaw explains how repression works according to the prevalent model presented by *The Courage to Heal* and other popular survivor guides.

"How do we begin an investigation into the past?" Bradshaw asks. "Often the journey is through therapy. . . . Depression . . . may sometimes be a clue to early sexual trauma" (Bradshaw:44). Everyone should be suspicious and study the checklists of symptoms for more validation. If you have many symptoms such as the ones usually presented — overweight, alcohol or drug addiction, sexually promiscuous, etc. — but no actual memory, Bradshaw offers this advice: "Accept the *theory* that you were sexually abused, live consciously with that idea for six months in context with an awareness of the traits you acknowledge, and see whether any memories come to you. . . . If you have suspicions, talk about them in an appropriate context. See a therapist. . . . Join a group of people who are also looking into the subject" (Bradshaw:44).

Marilyn Van Derbur Atler, Miss America, Incest Survivor

On May 8, 1991, at a meeting for therapists and survivors in Denver, Colorado, Marilyn Van Derbur Atler, Miss America 1958, announced that she is an incest survivor. A newspaper writer was in the audience and the story was national news the next day. Atler said she was sexually molested by her father from age five to age 18. Atler explains why she did not remember the 15 years of incest until she was 24 years old: "The trauma was so severe that I did what so many children do in order to survive. I split or, to use the psychiatric word, I dissociated." Atler says that she was actually two separate persons: the "day child" who became the over-achiever and the "night child" who was sexually abused in her bedroom during late-night visits from her father. "As difficult as this is for most people to understand, until I was 24, I, the day child, had absolutely no conscious knowledge of the night child. During the days, no embarrassing or angry glances ever passed between me and my father because I had no conscious knowledge of the traumas and the terrors of the night child."

Since going public as an incest survivor, Atler gives speeches throughout the country. She encourages others to go public as she did. She begins her talk addressing the incest survivors in the audience: "We were violated as children and as teenagers by fathers, stepfathers, grandfathers, uncles, husbands, older sisters, yes, even mothers. By teachers, ministers, priests, coaches, neighbors, strangers."

She tells victims of incest they must work hard in order to heal. Atler regrets that "there was no *Courage to Heal* when I was in recovery." In addition to group support meetings and years of psychotherapy, Atler's "work" included "over 100 deep massages, over 100 rolfing sessions as I tried to free my body from pain. At least 60 acupuncture sessions, acupressure, perhaps 50 sessions of hypnosis, neuro-linguistic programming, dance therapy, bioenergetics, self-defense therapy . . . I read hundreds of articles and 72 books as I have searched for relief and healing."

The overwhelming response Atler received propelled her to a leadership role in the incest survivor movement. She says it gave her a whole new identity. "Thirty–four years ago I won a title that became an extension of my name. Until May 8, 1991, if my name were in the paper, my name was Marilyn Van Derbur, former Miss America. As of May 8, 1991, and forevermore, my name is Marilyn Van Derbur Atler, incest survivor. That is the way it should be. Just as Jonas Salk will always be known for his greatest accomplishment – the discovery of the polio vaccine, I will be known for my greatest accomplishment – I survived incest."

Roseanne Barr Arnold, America's Most Popular Television Star, Incest Survivor

Following Marilyn Van Derbur Atler's public announcement, Roseanne and Tom Arnold met with the Atlers. Roseanne explains, "And then, both her and I and our husbands, Larry and Tom, thought, 'Well, what if Marilyn and I – give it a one, two punch, that it could never go back in the closet again?' "

On September 21, 1991, Roseanne Barr Arnold addressed a crowd of 1,100 people, mostly incest survivors and therapists, assembled in a Denver church: "My name is Roseanne and I'm an incest survivor" (Darnton:70).

During the next few months, Roseanne's story became publicized as she and husband Tom Arnold appeared on several popular television shows. Some details of Roseanne's "memories" and how she recalled them were revealed. It started when Tom recalled, during drug addiction treatment, that a male babysitter molested him as a child. When he called Roseanne on the telephone to tell her this, she claims it triggered her early childhood memories of both parents sexually abusing her, beginning when she was six months old. Roseanne said, "I remember my mother molesting me while she was changing my diaper" (*Sally Jessy Raphael*, October 10,1991). On *Larry King Live*, Tom Arnold told how he insisted Roseanne "go through the steps and do the work" and he helped her find a therapist (*Larry King Live*, September 25, 1991). Roseanne was in therapy for two years, and says she "didn't remember it before that." In a June 1993 interview in *Playboy* she says, "When I first started to have therapy and recall my memories, I really couldn't handle anything. It came so fast and furious. I couldn't even walk" (*Playboy*:72).

Roseanne told Oprah Winfrey, "When someone asks you, 'Were you sexually abused as a child?' There's only two answers. One of them is, 'Yes,' and one of them is, 'I don't know'" (*Oprah*, November 8, 1991). Roseanne's response to her parents' public repudiation of her charges rings familiar: " . . . it's so typical of all incest families to blame the victim . . . so I expected that because I've been in an incest survivor group for two years. . . . My counselor, Arlene Drake, who has been doing this for 20–some years and she never has once, not once, seen where the family goes, 'God, we're sorry we did this to you,' not once."

Roseanne tells how appalled she was when an interviewer questioned whether her announcement was worth all the pain her parents had to endure because of the publicity: "I looked right at her and I said, 'To ask such an offensive question like that to a survivor makes me wonder that maybe it's happened to you too and you haven't had your memories yet or you're still repressing or you're in some sort of denial about your own parents because only somebody who was protecting somebody would ask a question like that to a survivor'" (*Oprah*, November 8, 1991).

Roseanne told a national TV audience that "both Marilyn Van Derbur Atler and myself have totally committed the rest of our lives, basically, to try to do something about this problem. And we find ourselves in a weird position, because we have to educate the media, too" (*Sally Jessy Raphael,* October 10, 1991). Apparently Roseanne is successful in controlling some of the media. *People* magazine put her story on the cover of the October 7, 1991, issue. Roseanne claims she got to have final say in the content of the article. Her story was further validated by *Newsweek* magazine, which stated that Roseanne and Marilyn "are among thousands of people only now confronting a searing childhood pain – abuse inflicted not by strangers (or kids playing doctor) but by parents and older relatives" (Darton:70). Later in this article, complete with photos of Roseanne, Marilyn and *The Courage to Heal* co-author Laura Davis, it is reported, "The sudden recovery of traumatic memory is common to incest survivors. . . . Most often, the child forgets because remembering is simply too painful" (Darton:71).

Television talk show host Sally Jessy Raphael was also quick to validate the truth of Roseanne's memories of being abused at six months old: "I have been greatly moved by what I believe is a great deal of courage to speak out. . . . So if you are saying to me, 'What do you think? What do you feel? Do you believe her?' The answer is, darn right, I do" (*Sally Jessy Raphael,* October 10, 1991).

The Media Jumps on the Bandwagon

By late 1991 articles about repressed memories of incest were appearing throughout popular magazines. *Cosmopolitan* magazine ran an article on incest in the May 1992 issue which condensed the information repeated for the past decade or so, now treated as fact: One in three American girls were sexually abused; children protect themselves by repressing the memories; incest does not necessarily include touching. The symptoms repeated by therapists are readily recognized by clinical social worker Nita Daniels–Levine. She declares, "I would automatically suspect sexual abuse in someone with an eating disorder" (Yudkin:248-249). This last statement seems to be the consensus among many therapists, because this is what is taught at seminars authorized by the profession, despite the lack of any creditable evidence.

Self magazine published an article in October 1992 by its beauty editor, A.G. Britton. Britton tells how her psychiatrist, an adjunct lecturer at the Mount Sinai School of medicine and a faculty member at Cornell College of Medicine, described repressed memories: "He explained how repressed memory emerges: first in the body, then in the emotions and finally as an actual memory. . . . Because of his training he was able to translate the language my body and emotions were using to cry out for help. The inability to eat, the insomnia, the alternating fear and numbness, helped us to calculate that I was in the reliving phase of traumatic–memory return" (Britton:191).

Britton's traumatic childhood, she "reasoned," was why she endured a succession of career misfortunes. "I would lose the ability to speak. My tongue would get all gummed up as if I were an infant" (Britton:192). Because her "symptoms matched the developmental stage of an infant between the ages of six months and two years" (Britton:192), her doctor concluded that she must have been abused during this period of childhood. She says she had her first memory of the abuse within a couples of weeks after meeting with her psychiatrist. She remembers seeing herself at age one being sexually abused by her father in a cabana at the beach. Everything appeared to make sense to her now. "There it was: the answer to 30 years of pain and anguish and confusion. I would remember more of the facts of my life over the next 12 months, but the basic truth was that my father had sexually violated and otherwise tortured me from the age of six months to the age of 18 months" (Britton:192,200). Britton gives advice on getting the proper therapist: "Groups of clinicians around the country have responded to the growing crisis by developing new psychotherapeutic methods for treating incest survivors, and experts are likely to be up-to-date on what they are" (Britton:202). Britton tells of the grueling memory-return process and the list of rules she kept during this process. One of her rules was, "Do not talk to anyone who doubts your veracity. They are part of the problem" (Britton:202).

Lear's ran a 28-page cover story, "Incest: A Chilling Report," by Heidi Vanderbilt in the February 1992 issue. The cover page exclaimed, "Every word of it is true." Among the experts quoted in the article are: Sue Blume, Mike Lew, Judith Herman, Jeffrey Masson, Christine Courtois, Alice Miller and Laura Davis.

To sensationalize the topic of incest, the author inserts short case studies such as: "Rikki and Nick's parents were members of a satanic cult. The children were sexually abused and tortured. When the parents left the cult, they got their children into therapy. Rikki is three. Nick is four. Both have full-blown multiple personality disorders" (Vanderbilt:50).

In a section subtitled "Recovery," Vanderbilt explains, as Judith Herman did, how psychiatrists have been traditionally trained to ignore or disbelieve patients' reports of incest. She writes, "Over the last ten years, however, therapists who were influenced by the feminist movement began to listen to their clients, believed them, and pioneered new and effective treatment. Other therapists followed. Now survivors can use talk therapy, group therapy, art therapy, and body and movement therapy – the last two of which help release memories locked in the body. . . . Now there are dozens of books on incest and its consequences, self-help workshops, and 12-step programs to use in conjunction with other therapies" (Vanderbilt:73-74). Vanderbilt then summarizes the new long-term "treatment" described in *The Courage to Heal* and dozens of similar books.

In another section of the *Lear's* article, dealing with legal aspects of incest, a form letter is provided as readers are exhorted to take political action. The appeal to readers exclaims: "Reform legislation is imperative if we are to protect children against incest and sexual abuse. We urge our readers to send this letter, or some version of it, to their political representatives at the state level, including governors and legislators" (Vanderbilt:69). One of the three "reforms" readers are urged to support is: "Abolish or extend statutes of limitations for civil and criminal cases pertaining to incest and child sexual abuse" (Vanderbilt:69). Explaining that there has been success in this area, this legislation is needed because victims "may repress memories of sexual assaults for many years (studies have shown the average age of discovery to be between 29 and 49); statutes of limitations should be based on the special circumstances of the crime or case" (Vanderbilt:69).

The Popular Press Reports About Satanic Cults
A growing number of therapists are reporting that some of their clients recall "memories" of violent abuse during

devil-worshipping rituals. The stories are very similar and usually include cult members dressed in black robes, sacrificing and eating babies, and the most perverted sexual activity imaginable. Seminars to instruct therapists and law enforcement officials to uncover "ritual abuse" perpetrated by a secret, international satanic cult – which supposedly includes government officials and other powerful professionals – are well-attended throughout the United States and Canada.

Maclean's, Canada's largest national weekly news magazine, reported about satanic abuse as fact in a June 22, 1993 article by Tom Fennell, "The Satan Factor: Bizarre Cults Promote Sexual Abuse." Fennell alerts readers that "across North America, a growing number of respected mental-health therapists have come to the chilling conclusion that the tormented ravings of patients who claim to have been sexually abused as children by members of satanic cults are true reflections of their experience" (Fennell:29). Readers of the article learned that "such memories are usually deeply suppressed because Satanists employ a process of almost incomprehensible painfulness to brainwash their victims. . . . Sometimes children are sodomized in group ceremonies. . . . almost invariably the victims refer to 'breeders' – adolescent girls who are impregnated by a Satanist. The resulting children are abused by the cult sexually, or sacrificed and eaten, often with a mixture of blood, vomit and urine. . . . The cults' highly organized secretive activities also make detection difficult" (Fennell:29). While accusations of satanic ritual abuse are plentiful, there is no evidence that supports any of the accusations, yet hysteria is spreading throughout Canada.

The January/February 1993 cover of *Ms.* magazine shows a drawing of a baby in the clutches of Satan's tail. The cover declares: *Believe It! Cult Ritual Abuse Exists.* The story, "Surviving the Unbelievable," is a personal account, written under the pseudonym Elizabeth Rose. Rose tells the nearly–identical story that all self–proclaimed survivors of satanic ritual abuse relate: "I had been involved in a generational satanic cult and had been ritually abused in that cult setting. My thought patterns were altered through brainwashing and severe psychological abuse. . . . I personally witnessed the murders of two children, one of whom was my baby sister. . . . The sacrifice was followed by a communion ritual, during which human flesh and blood were consumed" (Rose:40-41,42). The author describes one scene which appears to come right out of the movie *Rosemary's Baby*: "The victim was strapped to the altar table in front of a ritual gathering and systematically gang–raped while the fertility rites were chanted. The purpose was to impregnate the victim. The resulting fetus was sometimes used in ritual sacrifice" (Rose:44).

This article differs from many similar articles encouraging the public to believe these incredible stories, despite any evidence, in that it includes a feminist, political overtone. The implication is that if you refuse to believe murderous satanic cults exist, you are contributing to the suffering of these tortured women. Rose tries to prove satanic ritual abuse is the extreme form of women's subjugation to men. She claims that ritual abuse exists "because violence is perpetrated against women and children and then passed on to the next generation. . . . People would rather believe that survivors – particularly women survivors – are crazy. This keeps many survivors from coming forward. . . . We were told that because Eve had accepted the fruit from the serpent, women were inherently more wicked and evil than men, and so were more capable of carrying out Satan's work. . . . Women were maligned, humiliated, and abused. . . . The abuse was aimed primarily and directly at the women and children. . . . The idea of female wickedness and depravity was pounded into my head at the impressionable age of four" (Rose:41, 42, 45).

The end of the article gives advice on how to stop these elusive cults and their bloodthirsty rituals: "For a start, we can believe that it exists. . . . The truth is that *ritual abuse exists* . . . if we want to stop ritual abuse, the first step must be to believe that these brutal crimes occur. Society's denial makes recovery much more difficult for survivors" (Rose:45). Advice is offered for healing from ritual abuse: "It is essential to have a good therapist when working through these issues. Ask specifically if the therapist is experienced in ritual abuse issues. . . . Many health insurance programs cover the cost of counseling" (Rose:42). Three of the six books recommended are: *The Courage to Heal, The Courage to Heal Workbook*, and *Allies in Healing*.

Gloria Steinem Looks Inward

Feminist celebrity Gloria Steinem's latest book, *Revolution From Within: A Book of Self-Esteem*, embraces many of the concepts of the recovery, New Age, and incest survivor movements. Getting to know your inner child and searching for repressed memories of childhood abuse are two ways Steinem recommends to gain self-esteem. Steinem takes readers on a New Age journey to unlock the hidden secrets of the unconscious mind, using self-hypnosis to meet not only your inner child, but also your future self. Having been through the journey herself in therapy, Steinem is excited about relating her experiences of the path inward.

In a section called "Voyaging to Time Past," Steinem begins with a quote from John Bradshaw: "I believe that this neglected, wounded inner child of the past is the major source of human misery" (Steinem:157). This idea comes from Swiss psychiatrist and author Alice Miller whose books have been translated into several languages. Bradshaw and others in the recovery movement have popularized Miller's ideas in America. Miller claims that every child has repressed traumatic memories of childhood which in turn hinder self-awareness and personality development as an adult. Society, especially the healing professions, discourage people from discovering their real childhood memories. Miller believes that it is essential for everyone to retrieve their memories of the horrible acts committed by their parents. Memories that remained locked in the unconscious mind, she believes, like Bradshaw, to be the source of all human misery. Miller explains in her book *Breaking Down the Wall of Silence*: "What remains is the vicious circle of repression: the true story, which has been suppressed in the body, produces symptoms so that it could at last be recognized and taken seriously. But our consciousness refuses to comply, just as it did in childhood – because it was *then* that it learned the life-saving function of repression, and because no one has subsequently explained that as grownups we are not condemned to die of our knowledge, that, on the contrary, such knowledge would help us in our quest for health" (Miller:142).

The ideas of Alice Miller are central to the theme of Steinem's search for her true self. Steinem explains the interaction between the adult and the inner child: "What makes self-rescue possible, says Alice Miller, is one condition: *at least one person* in our childhood who affirmed our true feelings, and thus let us know that our true self could be seen by others and did exist. I've come to believe that this hopeful 'one person' theory is true. But something more: that even if there was no such person then, it's possible to *become* that 'one person' for ourselves now; to journey back to a lost child, recover and experience what that child experienced, and become our own parent" (Steinem:82) She later seeks a psychotherapist to guide her to her journey into the unconscious — "that timeless part of our minds where events and emotions of our personal past are stored along with the wisdom of our species" (Steinem:157–158).

Steinem instructs her readers about the childhood trauma repressed in the unconscious mind: "Frequently such memories are so painful that they don't surface fully until years after the events occurred. The more extreme and erratic these events, the younger we were when we experienced them, and the more dependent we were on the people who inflicted them, the more repressed they are likely to be" (Steinem:163). Steinem lists some of the tell-tale signs that someone may be repressing traumatic memories: " . . . fear of expressing anger at all; substantial childhood periods of which you have no memory of emotions or events . . . depression . . . severe eating disorders . . . Trust these clues — there is substantial as well as personal evidence that the conditions they point to are widespread. Perhaps a third of the children in the United States (and many other countries as well) have been subjected to sexual and other kinds of severe neglect . . ." (Steinem: 162–163).

Finding the right therapist to guide someone on the journey to the repressed mind is very important. Steinem states, "The good news is that there are now many more therapists who are experienced and empathetic in recognizing the causes and helping with the results of such trauma. . . . And remember that credentials may have meaning, but none can substitute for what you feel. If a therapist puts you at ease, gives you the freedom to express yourself and the confidence that you are understood and believed, and also challenges you and cares, she or he is the right therapist for you" (Steinem:163).

At the end of her book, Steinem offers what she calls "bibliotherapy" to guide readers to books she strongly recommends. Included under the topic "Healing Childhood and Other Wounds" are *The Courage to Heal* and *Toxic Parents*. Considered to be one of the ten most influential women in America, Gloria Steinem has the power to help form opinions among millions of women.

No Word of Caution

Nowhere in the writings of all these influential people, either the authorities or the consensus builders, do we find any word of caution. They never say that it is possible to make a mistake, that a repressed memory might be inaccurate, that a dream could be interpreted in many ways, that symptoms such as depression or headaches could have a variety of causes, that to accuse someone without being certain could be a terrible injustice. By blaming every ailment on repressed childhood sexual abuse, they make it unlikely that many families will ever reunite, because the alleged abuse is unforgivable. This "expert" advice can mask the true reasons for the problems that brought the person to therapy in the first place.

STORIES OF RETRACTORS

Years have been lost that can never be regained. Words have been spoken that cannot be retrieved. Anger and rage have been expended that cannot be recalled. For thousands of adult children it may be too late. They have started on a path of alienation from their families, encouraged by therapists, books and groups that take them into a world without parents, brothers or sisters. They are charting new territory, in a land where "families of choice" have abandoned "families of origin."

But some have realized that the new territory is a land of lies. They were encouraged to look for memories of abuse and, when the memories weren't bad enough, they were encouraged to look deeper and visualize abuse perpetrated against them. They were abused by the therapy and they wrote their stories to explain the tortuous journey into and out of the world of false memories.

Three of the women chose to be identified. The others prefer to be anonymous.

Memories Not Mine

At one time I had a past filled with childhood memories much as anyone does. Though not all of them were like the Waltons', I had a sense of family and origin. That all changed with the help of a few therapists who took me into hell where on an emotional level I lost my parents, the past I thought I had, and my sanity.

As far back as I can remember I was an emotionally distant person with many fears and phobias. I needed help and when I finally sought it I was misled and misunderstood. The trauma that finally brought me to the therapist's office was the birth of my youngest daughter. She was born with a rare brain disease and we were told she would die. The first months with her were bitterly sad. She spent time on and off life support machines and had more problems than I could recount here. I could no longer sustain myself as a distant person who constantly hid my fears and tried to escape life by burying my emotions.

Although I could easily explain my desperate situation, my therapists insisted that all of my problems were based on my childhood. I received little or no help in dealing with the life-threatening illness of my baby, my marital problems, or the unresolved breakup of my first marriage. To this day I can't understand how they could have been so blind!

My first experience as an "incest survivor" was when I began seeing my pastor for emotional help. He was a licensed therapist with the Marriage and Family Counseling Association and also with the American Pastoral Counselors Association. He referred me to another therapist who specialized in Adult Children of Alcoholics and offered to see me up to three times a week for extra support. He quickly gained my trust.

It wasn't long before he started asking if my father ever touched me or tried to look at me when I was taking a shower. My immediate response was "No!"

I was able to relate several stories about inappropriate behavior from other adults of my childhood, true memories about being raped by a friend's brother, and sexual harassment as a teen by older men. Even so he seemed more interested in pulling out stories about my parents.

As our relationship grew he was able to convince me that I must find the "truth" and work through it. He said this was the only way I could learn to overcome my anxiety. I thought I must be wrong for experiencing so much fear at the thought of my daughter's possible death because all my therapists seemed concerned about was my childhood. I began talking to my sister about my therapy and found that she too was in this kind of treatment. She said that she had no real memories but that her therapist said she was certain that my sister was an incest survivor. She seemed confused to me. At the same time I saw her anger grow towards my parents. I listened as she told me what a terrible childhood she thought we had. I started reading all the books she recommended. All of them were designed to bring back repressed memories. I learned a whole new language from my sister and the books. I learned that you call people like me and my parents sick and that if you don't admit your sickness you are "in denial" and you will never get well.

During the emotionally draining conferences I was having with my pastor I was able to dig up enough false memories to satisfy his hunger for the "truth." My life seemed in such disarray and I was grasping for anything that could put it together. I read hundreds of women's stories about their incest experiences. I hoped I could fit in somewhere, anywhere, if it would give me some healing from what I was being told I suffered from.

I was slowly pulled into an ugly and abusive relationship with my pastor, who preyed upon my insecurities to initiate a sexual relationship that later served to further devastate my life. In retrospect I see that I was duped into believing he was the only one who loved me and cared for my well-being. After all, he was my pastor and counselor. He said he wanted to help me heal from the abuse I suffered at the hands of my childhood caregivers. He convinced me that my family was evil.

My sessions involved no real hypnotism, but I have no doubt that I was brainwashed. He leaned over from the chair seated directly in front of me, just two feet away, and talked in a soft, luring, almost monotone voice. He constantly made suggestions about what might have happened to me as a child and dug for stories. When I came up with nothing he prodded me further by saying he cared for me and wanted to share my stories. I remember being in such a state of desperation that I would take any piece of true memory and watch as it became a detailed fantasy which I wasn't sure was the truth or a lie. I was told that people don't make up things like this and that these things were in my mind for a reason, and therefore they must be true.

At the same time I was working in group therapy and individual therapy with the Adult Children of Alcoholics counselor who I was referred to by my pastor. There I was trained to talk the recovery talk: denial, risk-taking, caretaker, etc. It became a way to hide from real life and only focus on the things I was being taught in therapy.

Because of the relationship with my pastor, the lies, and

the memories, I became dependent on the relationship. "Without it," I thought, "my life will surely end in insanity." Later I came to realize that this was the beginning of my becoming insane.

A few months into the sexual relationship he became increasingly violent and I realized how many problems this man must have. I convinced my husband that we should move several states away, using our daughter's health as an excuse. We knew the cold weather of New England aggravated her disease so we moved to Arkansas. That was the end of the relationship with my pastor.

The trauma of leaving New England and all my friends, coupled with the confusion of the counseling I had undergone, was more than I could bear. I quickly relapsed into my previous state of constant fear and phobias. I fell into a dark depression. I was addicted to the therapy and immediately sought help in the form of another counselor who would carry on with the treatment I'd been having. My new therapist was a Christian counselor. He was not trained in childhood sexual abuse; he specialized in short-term adjustment problems. We started talking about sexual abuse within two weeks. In one month I was so distraught that I thought my only answer was death. I wanted so desperately to die and put an end to the conflict that was going on inside my head. Although part of me was aware that all the accusations I was making were false, another part truly believed that these so-called experts knew what they were doing. My therapist offered to refer me to someone who had expertise in this field, but I had developed an attachment to him and was terrified that he might abandon me. He agreed to continue seeing me three times a week. "If you would only stop protecting the people who hurt you and come out of denial and voice your memories you would get better," he told me time and time again. So I dug for memories, I dug for answers, and I began to dig a deep grave for the person I used to be.

When I could no longer stand the conflict within my head I broke down and would have preferred death to the sad and painful life I was living. My therapist listened while I verbalized my death wish and he made arrangements for me to go to a hospital psychiatric ward to treat the depression and anxiety I was suffering. He also knew it was out of his control and that I would surely die if I wasn't protected.

When I walked into the ward and the door was locked behind me I entered a chapter of my life I will never forget. My daily routine began with a 7:30 AM appointment with the psychiatrist who was the only admitting doctor to the ward. He had utter and complete control and gave the whole experience a nightmarish effect. He insisted that I was severely sexually abused as a child and that I MUST remember and talk about it in group therapy or I would never be a productive member of society. He said that my psychiatric test scores showed that I was a borderline personality and he could see that I was a selfish and childish person. He also diagnosed me with Post-Traumatic Stress Disorder. He wanted me to talk about the abuse I'd suffered at the hands of my pastor. I consistently flew into rages whenever I was forced to listen to things about me that I knew were not true and was punished like a child when I wouldn't conform. The staff routinely took away things that were important to me. At one time I was denied use of my flute, which was a major source of comfort to me and which I'd been given permission to bring with me prior to my admittance to the ward. At another time the staff took my sketch pads, charcoal and pencils. I was often put on probation and not allowed to eat meals with the other patients. I was forced to acknowledge anything they "saw" in me and when I realized I was losing all control of my life I asked for a discharge. I was told that if I left I would be discharged AMA (against medical advice) and that none of the $21,000 I'd racked up would be covered by my insurance. I was forced to stay and devise a plan to get out. I decided my only hope was to go along with whatever was expected and try my damnedest to believe that my parents had abused me as a child.

My days were filled with taking drugs that sometimes altered my ability to understand what was happening to me, group therapy, listening to others' stories of abuse and various visualizations and individual therapy. I was once told by my therapist that I hated men and that was why my therapy wasn't productive. When I tried to deny it he became enraged. I flew out of the tiny cramped room screaming and crying, "Why are you doing this?" I remember thinking this was a nightmare. How could my therapist send me to a place like this. I called him at home and at his office and begged him to get me out. He apologized and said he couldn't do anything. He said he had no idea it would be like this for me. Later I learned he quit referring his clients to this place.

When I was finally granted a discharge I was severely depressed and suicidal but managed to hide it from the all-seeing staff. They reported to the psychiatrist how much I ate and even my toilet habits, but I succeeded in keeping my state of mind from them. I walked out of that hospital despising myself, my parents and anyone who resembled a doctor or a nurse. I was belittled and badgered and all pride was stripped from me in a short five weeks.

From that point on everything I did was flavored with childhood sexual abuse. I ate, drank, breathed and slept the torturous loss of believing that this insanity might be true. I read *The Courage to Heal, The Courage to Heal Workbook, The People of the Lie* and countless other books that I hoped would give me some concrete memories.

I continued in incest survivor therapy and began writing poems and drawing detailed pictures of my false memories. I wrote long stories about what I thought might have happened to me and when I finished I couldn't believe it was true. Often I told my therapists that these things were lies but I was encouraged to believe them and to "act as if." This, I was convinced, would bring recovery. I was encouraged to keep this up and to talk about as many memories as I could come up with. I hated myself more every day. I wondered how I could be so confused and messed up. One day I sat on my bed after looking in the mirror for what seemed like hours without recognizing myself. I began hearing voices and was certain I'd never return to reality. With a .22 rifle pointed at my head I tried to convince myself that I could blow my head off my shoulders. According to what I'd learned I would never get better because I couldn't bring myself to confront my abusers. Nothing felt real except the stabbing pain. I was living in an unreal world set up by the so-called recovery movement. The gurus of the 1990s had taken my reality away and I was unable to live the life I was meant to have.

For days and sometimes weeks at a time I only got out of bed to go to my therapy appointments, where I would spend an hour rehashing my dreams and memories. Afterward I would drive along the twisting back roads to my home fighting with myself about whether or not to crash my car into a tree or bridge. In between sessions I slept and read books about other so-called survivors. I didn't make any friends during the time I lived in Arkansas and had only two people to whom I ever spoke outside of my therapy appointments. The relationship with my husband and daughters deteriorated. I suffered great loss.

Soon I began having memories of ritual abuse and when all hope seemed lost I made arrangements to travel to Indiana to another hospital that offered a treatment program that I thought might help me. My therapist didn't want me to go. As it turned out, the treatment in Indiana was my salvation. While I was there I did some continued work in incest survivorhood and also some inner child exercises and visualizations, but the thing that made it all worthwhile was the self-esteem work I was given to practice. I wrote my own affirmations and recited them three times every day in the mirror. I was taught a new sense of spirituality, which was something I had lost thanks to my preacher friend. At this hospital I gained a new outlook and began to trust my own intuitions. Although I was encouraged to do some of the same damaging things that I had been previously taught, the majority of my time there was productive and I am alive and happy today only because I made the decision to go into treatment again at a place where the staff puts the needs of the patients first. It is disturbing that even the good therapists and treatment centers are involved in this damaging movement.

For the first time in four years I was able to listen to my heart and distinguish between lies and truth, not because I was encouraged to find out the real truth of my past but because I was given tools to learn better who I am. I was able to enjoy my daughters again and as I got well I was able to see my daughter recover from her own illness. Throughout the whole terrible ordeal I never obeyed the

demand to confront my supposed abusers and I am grateful to the inner wisdom I must have had in spite of the
garbage I was being fed.

I had one final chapter in my story as an "incest survivor." When I moved from Arkansas to my current home in
Michigan I was still taking medication for depression. It
was important to find a psychiatrist to monitor my dosage.
I had two sessions with my new doctor before realizing
what I was getting into. During the first session he wanted
to know about my history and what kinds of therapy I'd
had. I explained as much as time allowed and left with
another appointment for the following week. When I returned he had already planned my next several months
saying he wanted to continue working on the incest issues.
I told him that I wasn't interested in doing that kind of
work any more. I said that I'd come to realize I was on the
wrong track in my therapy and that my main objective was
to learn to live my life productively and to eventually come
off the anti-depressant. He told me to beware of denial and
that if my previous therapists had picked up on abuse in
my past that it must be there and we should schedule
appointments for three times a week. He reminded me
that my insurance would allow me to have as much therapy
as I needed. "This way," he said "I could get a lot of work
done quickly." I maintained that I was more concerned
with recovering a relationship with my parents than in
trying to make more memories and that I felt I'd been
misunderstood by the psychiatric profession in the past.
When he insisted, I agreed to go to an incest survivors
meeting that week and to reconsider the therapy he prescribed. Within the first half hour of the meeting I knew I
was in the wrong place. I'd never felt surer that I could

trust my own memories and that so many of these women were sadly misled. Some spoke of having multiple personalities due to not being able to recover their memories. I was appalled. I left knowing that I had also been where these women were and that I no longer was there.

During the next several months I worked to stabilize my life by trusting that I was making the right decisions for myself and to regain some of the ground I'd lost within my family relationships, but I feared that I was emotionally weak for allowing myself to get caught up in this ugly false recovery movement. Then one day I received a magazine that talked about other people who had similar experiences in therapy. I will always be grateful to that writer, Andy Meacham, who wrote an article titled *Presumed Guilty* in *Changes* magazine. He went out on a limb to talk about the truth of this devastating problem.

Unfortunately there are many true incest survivors and it is a horrendous abuse, but how many others are being taught to believe that because they are having problems in life that they too are incest survivors? My parents drank a lot of alcohol when I was a child. It is said that incest is common in alcoholic families. Maybe False Memory Syndrome is also a common occurrence for people who grew up in homes where parents were alcoholics.

As far as I know my sister is still involved in the incest survivor movement. She has adopted a new family within her "recovery community" and has abandoned her family of origin.

It's extremely frightening to know there is a movement that is so powerful it can turn ordinary people into powerless monster hunters. It's horrifying that helping professionals are misleading others who are in need of guidance. In coming to realize what is actually taking place in the self-help and therapy circles, my hope is to help guide others into an understanding of the process that seems to be taking place and to see those people re-educated. It is sad that it may be too late for some to make their retractions.

I hope that I can offer hope to those on both sides of the damaging effects of False Memory Syndrome – both the victims and the parents who are being accused of things they didn't do. Just as I released myself from this cult-like movement so can others. Since my "recovery from recovery" I have been able to come completely off the drug I was given for the consuming depression and am leading a productive life as a writer.

I find that after recovering I love and respect my parents even more than I ever have and am striving for a healthy relationship with them in their later years. With the wicked lies behind me and an understanding of False Memory Syndrome, I am determined to give my parents the daughter they deserve now. I accept the parents I have always had with a heart full of love and admiration. I am certain that they did the best they knew how when they raised me. It feels good to take full responsibility for my own life for a change. I have a good life after having gone to hell and back. And believe me, I've been to the gates of hell and I am back!

Who Made Her God?

"Like an alcoholic can smell another alcoholic, an incest survivor can smell another incest survivor." My therapist continued, "Emily, I'm convinced you were sexually abused as a child. You need to just believe it and start working through this book." That being said, she handed me her copy of *The Courage to Heal* and thus, I began the most bizarre and frightening experience of my life. I'll never forget that particular day in her office. After she made the dramatic diagnosis I remember looking at her and feeling a tremendous rush of anger. Inside, my mind was flooded with questions: "Who made her God? How does she know what happened to me as a child? Why am I sitting here?" I wanted to run out of the room. I thought about her credentials. Sue was a "licensed counselor." She was in her 30s, a recovering alcoholic and an "incest survivor." I didn't know how much formal training was required to become a licensed counselor, but my gut feeling was that Sue's comments were very inappropriate for a therapist. I left Sue's office that day reluctantly taking with me her copy of *The Courage to Heal*. I drove home in total confusion. I passed a cemetery and thought how life wasn't worth living. Why would Sue have said these things to me if they weren't true? It must be true, but I had no memories — no memories at all.

My story does not absolve my parents of all responsibility for my emotional well-being as an adult, for I was raised in a mentally unhealthy environment. However, several aspects of subsequent therapy led me on a road to sexual abuse fabrications that further alienated me from my parents and complicated my mental well-being for many years to come.

I started therapy in November of 1988. I was having marital problems and also had been estranged from my parents for six years. My first therapist, Robert, was a social worker with Catholic Social Services. My first two months of therapy were concentrated on my marriage and when that part of my life strengthened, Robert and I began focusing on the problems with my parents. Every week I would give Robert a play-by-play of my life. I was born in 1957, the fifth and last child. I had four older sisters. My mother and father had five girls in six years, so we were very close in age. We grew up in a beautiful home. My mother, a full-time homemaker, kept the home spotless, both inside and out. All of our neighbors constantly commented on the lovely landscaping surrounding our home. She'd spend hours at a time doing yard work. When darkness came and she had to come inside, she'd do housework or bake one of her many delicious recipes. My mother strived for perfection in everything she did. My father kept very busy with his job. He'd leave first thing in the morning and come home around dinner-time. After dinner, he'd take a long walk in the forest that bordered our property. He took this walk daily. During the winter he'd carry big salt blocks into the woods to leave for the deer to enjoy.

My earliest memories of growing up are rather normal. I remember grade school, my neighbors, favorite toys. When I was in second grade I started to gain weight and spent most of my childhood, through the eighth grade, overweight. I was teased a lot at school and suffered from extremely low self-esteem. As I became older and less naive, I began to realize that my parents were different from most of my friends' parents. We seldom had company. On the rare occasions when we did have visitors, they never made it past the family room in the basement.

We had an outdoor entrance to the family room, and that was the entrance visitors always used. Visitors never went upstairs. My parents were very protective of our home. I always felt as if there were a barbed wire fence protecting our property.

When I was in the seventh grade, I came home from school one day to be greeted at the door by my mother. Usually the first thing I did when I got home was to go to my room that I shared with two of my sisters. My mother informed me that because we didn't keep our room neat, she moved all our belongings to the basement. She told me we'd have to stay down there until we learned how to be neat. Our room was messy. With three teenagers in one room it was hard to keep the room organized and in perfect order like my mother required. It got to where I didn't even try, so when she moved us to the basement, I didn't fight her. I felt guilty and ashamed and figured we deserved to be down there. Actually, it didn't seem so bad at first. The family room was down there (paneling, wall-to-wall carpeting) along with the television. I thought this could be fun. Much to my disappointment it wasn't the family room where she moved our stuff. We were put in another room near the furnace. This room had concrete walls and a cement floor. All of our clothes were piled up on a homemade ping-pong table. Our dresses hung from the water pipes overhead. We slept on the floor on out-door furniture cushions. I hated being down there. My mother would conduct periodic inspections of our quarters to see if we were being neat. One of my sisters managed to keep her belongings up to Mom's standards and she was allowed to move back upstairs. That left two of us. We spent about six months down there and then eventually were allowed to return to our old room. I don't know if we earned the privilege or my mother needed the space downstairs for something else. But in any case we were back in our old room, and it felt good to feel slightly normal again.

The bulk of my remaining memories of growing up center around one of my older sisters, Beth. My mother and Beth clashed terribly. There was fighting almost every day. There was always tension in the air. I tried to stay an outsider, either spending a lot of time by myself or staying involved in many extracurricular activities at school. By this time I had reached a normal weight, felt more confident and was involved in pom-pom girls, the school newspaper, National Honor Society, etc. The friction at home continued until Beth was kicked out of the house. I pretty much separated myself from what was going on between them, but I always received more attention from my mother if I squealed on Beth.

Two weeks after I graduated from high school I moved to Washington, D.C., to work as a secretary with the federal government. I stayed there for three years before I left to begin school full-time. Four months before I left D.C. I met Gary, the man who would eventually become my husband. After I got settled into college life, Gary relocated to be closer to me. In February of 1980 Gary and I became engaged. I was afraid to call my parents to give them the news of my engagement. They were both always nonsupportive when it came to boyfriends. The more in-dependent I was the more approval I received from them. My fears were justified, for when I called them, they were both extremely disappointed. My mother lectured me for two hours on why I was throwing my life away by getting married. They didn't know Gary very well, so it wasn't him they were against. They just didn't want me to get married yet. This was the beginning of serious problems with my parents. After that phone call to them announcing my engagement, I only heard from them once — a letter from my mother putting in writing everything she had said to me on the telephone. I would not hear from my parents again for two years. Gary and I were married on August 30, 1980. My mother and father did not attend the wedding. The only immediate family member to attend was my sister Beth.

The first two years of married life were difficult. Without my parents' blessing, I always felt as if I had done something very wrong by getting married. As feelings of depression came and went, my weight fluctuated up and down. I didn't feel very attractive and was isolating myself most of the time. My relationship with Gary began to suffer and in August of 1982, I felt the need to get away so I could try to put things in perspective. I didn't know where to go, so I mustered up the courage to call my parents. Not having seen or spoken to them in two years, I apprehensively dialed their number. My mother answered and I broke down crying and told her I needed time away from Gary. Knowing that I was having marital problems, my parents welcomed me home with open arms. After a week at my parents' home, I returned back to my town driving a new car that my father had bought me. He also bought me new clothes, gave me a blank check and cash for a hotel room, and made me very strongly aware of his wishes for me to end my marriage. The day I planned to see an attorney, I went to see my pastor instead. I then returned back home to Gary. When my parents realized this, they came to my town and took away the car, the blank check, and stated that I was no longer their daughter. This was August 30, 1982, the last time I saw them.

I was depressed often during the next few years, but I think my depression reached a higher level after the birth of my son in May, 1986, a grandson my parents never met. I continued to cope with the estrangement by overeating. When I felt my life was falling apart, I finally sought professional help. This was in November of 1988 when I began therapy with Robert. Robert was a strong advocate of cognitive therapy (an approach to therapy that tries to change some of the patient's habitual modes of thinking) and tried it several times with me. I resisted it most of the time because it required so much work on my part. It was so much easier to continually rehash old memories and blame my parents for all my problems. It felt good when I had an appointment with Robert and could talk about my childhood. I made it a point to always discuss the most traumatic of my memories for this would ensure much crying on my part. This would be accompanied by a sympathetic face from Robert. I felt this was an easy way to get the affirmation I didn't receive from my parents. Down deep inside, though, I felt I was playing a strange game. The more dramatic I was, the more I enjoyed my therapy.

After awhile Robert became increasingly frustrated with me. I wanted to act like a hurt child, but Robert encouraged me to be the adult I was and take responsibility for my life. At one point he questioned whether he could be of any further help to me. Eventually, due to Robert's busy schedule, he informed me that he'd only be able to see me every other week. I remember leaving his office that day feeling very angry and abandoned.

Through some connections at a 12-step group I had been attending, I found out about a "core issues" therapy group that was forming for Adult Children of Alcoholics and Dysfunctional Families. This sounded perfect for me, so I immediately signed up. We met once a week for two hours. One thing that appealed to me about this group was that it was facilitated by a "licensed counselor." That title sounded so professional to me. I hoped that the therapist would be clever enough to see through my dramatics and stop me in my tracks. This was not to be the case, unfortunately. The therapist, a woman in her mid-30s named Betty, fueled me with suggestions that I was physically and sexually abused as a child. At one point she asked me if I was sure there was nothing satanic going on in the basement of my house while I was growing up. I soon became the star of the group. Each week when the group ended I was hugged by every group member, each commenting on my bravery and courage. As the weeks passed, I became more and more dramatic. Down deep inside I hated being in the group. People would do anger work by taking baseball bats and beating a couch or going outside and violently tearing apart cardboard boxes, all the while screaming obscenities directed at their parents. Betty would be beside you cheering you on and motioning to the other group members to join in with her. The more dramatic you were the more affirmation you received from Betty. Betty saw a few of the group members individually during the week and would update the group as to who was remembering childhood sexual abuse. It felt strange that my goal of becoming a happier person disappeared with a new, more trendy goal of remembering childhood sexual abuse. I had such a sick feeling in my stomach. The group was the epitome of negativity. The bulk of the time was spent blaming members of our "families of origin," doing anger work, etc. I never complained of my discontent with the group for fear of being labeled someone "in denial." Instead, I conformed to the group and became the perfect

role model of a "victim." After about six weeks of this
group, I became suicidal. I felt as if I were living a lie. I felt
like I was being brainwashed into a cult. I had to get help.
After discussing my condition with Betty, she advised me
to immediately quit the group and begin counseling with
one of her colleagues. This is where the real horror in my
life began. My therapy with Sue would be the force that
catapulted me into the darkest time of my life.

I began this story describing just one particular session I
had with Sue. There were many. In December of 1990,
after only two sessions with Sue, I admitted myself into a
psychiatric center. I was very depressed and had no desire
to live. In retrospect, I believe the major force that drove
me to such despair was the therapy I was receiving, rather
than anything that occurred in my childhood.

I spent over 10 weeks in the hospital. I was diagnosed
with major depression. The hospital psychiatrist, Dr. Taylor, administered many different drugs to me and at one
point diagnosed me with bipolar disorder. With that diagnosis came a regimen of lithium and a few other drugs. At
the time of my discharge, I was still on lithium and at least
two other medications. These drugs were of no benefit to
my condition – in fact, they produced terrible side effects.
Three times a week during my hospitalization I had therapy
with a psychologist, Dr. Richardson. Dr. Richardson never
once made any suggestions that I may have been sexually
abused as a child. However, I did go into the hospital
believing that there was a possibility this may have happened. When I began to discuss this with Dr. Richardson,
she suggested hypnosis. The thought of hypnosis made me
very uneasy. It wasn't so much that I might learn of some
horrible abuse in my past as it was that there might not be
anything of that nature in my past, and I wouldn't have

anything major to blame my problems on. I became so upset at the idea of hypnosis that Dr. Taylor began administering anti-psychotic medication, and I was moved to the Intensive Treatment Unit (ITU). I was eventually discharged from the hospital. The "unresolved sexual abuse" was "put on the back burner" for me to deal with when I was ready. Dr. Taylor felt I could continue with that subject during out-patient therapy.

So there I was, out of a psychiatric hospital and back into the care of Sue. Sue reminded me so much of Betty, my former group therapist. It was during my first appointment after my hospitalization that Sue made her convincing diagnosis that I had been sexually abused as a child. At home her copy of *The Courage to Heal* sat on my dining room table. I would not open it. The next week I returned it to her and told her I did not want her to use the word "incest" during our appointments, because I believed that this was not a part of my past. She agreed not to use the word, but asked if it was okay if she called it something else. I felt like I was in a no-win situation. She was so determined to get me on this "incest bandwagon." After about a month, I was so confused and frustrated that I announced to Sue in one of our sessions that I did not want to continue this type of therapy until I underwent some form of hypnosis to see if incest was indeed a part of my past. I felt at that time that hypnosis was the foolproof way to find the truth in one's past.

The only person I knew who was certified in the practice of hypnosis was Dr. Richardson, my psychologist from the hospital. I wrote her a letter describing what was happening in my therapy with Sue. I told her that I did not feel comfortable "acting as if" I had been sexually abused and putting myself through unnecessary trauma by working through *The Courage to Heal*. I asked for Dr. Richardson's opinion, but she was unable to give it to me due to "ethics" in the field. As long as I was undergoing therapy with another therapist, she could not intervene. I was livid when I received Dr. Richardson's letter stating this. I thought of how a person could get second opinions for heart surgery, but not for what I considered mental surgery.

By this time I was completely fed up and abruptly stopped all my therapy. I occasionally saw my psychiatrist from the hospital, who by this time had taken me off all medications and reversed his diagnosis of my bipolar disorder. I was still haunted by the childhood sexual abuse suggestions that had been made to me by "professionals." So haunted that I eventually bought not only *The Courage to Heal* but the accompanying workbook as well. I decided that I would work through the book on my own. The book became somewhat of a "God" to me. I worshipped every word in it. It played into all my vulnerabilities. The more I read, the more convinced I became that incest had been a part of my past and that I had somehow blocked all memories. Reading *The Courage to Heal* mentally immobilized me. I lost touch with reality and was dangerously coerced into a trap. Any valid doubts I had about my past were belittled by statements in the book like, "If you are unable to remember any specific instances . . . but still have a feeling that something abusive happened to you, it probably did," and "If you think you were abused and your life shows the symptoms, then you were."

It didn't take me long to fall back into the depths of hopelessness. Again finding myself contemplating suicide, I readmitted myself into the psychiatric center that I had been a patient of less than five months before. This time I was not only diagnosed with major depression, but also with Post-Traumatic Stress Disorder. My goal during this hospitalization was to once and for all deal head-on with the childhood sexual abuse that by now I was almost convinced had happened to me. Dr. Taylor and Dr. Richardson were once again my psychiatrist and psychologist, respectively. They both enthusiastically encouraged me to continue reading *The Courage to Heal* and complete the exercises in the workbook. The therapeutic atmosphere at the hospital made me feel uncomfortable. Patients were pressured to discuss their childhoods in depth in hopes of finding unacknowledged abuse. The more childhood abuse you endured, the more attention you received from the hospital staff. Again, I felt like I was involved in a strange game. I quickly conformed to the atmosphere, and dramatically performed anger work toward my parents, even to the point of having to be transferred to the ITU for a day to calm down. I was widely respected by the other patients and soon was elected president of our "community" (a word the hospital used to describe the patients in a particular unit).

My sessions with Dr. Richardson during this hospitalization began with discussing hypnosis. I still had many fears about using hypnosis, and Dr. Richardson assured me that she would not do anything that she felt I wasn't ready for. I remember feeling relieved that hypnosis wouldn't be done, mainly because I still had this gut fear that incest was not a part of my past, and I didn't want to be found out. Three times a week I had sessions with Dr. Richardson where we reviewed my childhood in intricate detail. That coupled with my continued reading of *The Courage to Heal* led me to concentrate and expand on a few of my memories. I still had no concrete memory of any sexual abuse, but according to every staff member at the hospital who cared for me, I had all the symptoms of a "survivor."

I entered the hospital with a mission of remembering the sexual abuse in my childhood, and I remember thinking that I had better get started. I started with a "memory" I had of my mother. I don't know where this scenario came from, but all my life I always thought about how as an infant my mother gave me a bath in the kitchen sink, wrapped me up in a big white towel, and laid me on the kitchen table to put baby powder and a diaper on me. This is something my mother may have told me when I became older. In any case, when I began talking to Dr. Richardson about this, she was concerned that I could remember something that happened to me at such a young age. I detected a feeling from her that I had read about in *The Courage to Heal* regarding the ability to remember very early incidents in childhood if they were extremely traumatic. She wanted me to try and visualize the kitchen and what my mother looked like as she laid me on the table. Dr. Richardson spoke to me very softly and very slowly. I felt as if I were in a trance-like state. I then began going into extremely vivid detail of my mother abusing me. Having doubts about the horror I was relaying to Dr. Richardson, I shouted out "What's real here, Dr. Richardson? What am I making up?" Dr. Richardson very calmly answered, "That's not important right now. I want you to stick with the image and keep telling me what you see." This session lasted two hours. I was visibly shaken as I left Dr. Richardson's office that day. As upset as I was, there was a part of me that felt satisfied that I finally "remembered" some sexual abuse. I finally had something tangible to blame my depression on, and it was bad — bad enough to qualify for extra attention from the hospital staff.

During the course of the next six weeks, I would "remember" sexual abuse from my father and one of my sisters. I would also have additional memories of abuse from my mother. During the "memory sessions" with Dr. Richardson I would continually question the validity of my memories. She always answered me by saying, "That's not important right now." I always wondered when it would be important. During two of these sessions, I became so angry that it necessitated Dr. Richardson moving me into the "safe room" where we finished our session. The safe room was a small room in the hospital that was carpeted everywhere but the ceiling. If a patient became out-of-hand or needed somewhere safe to be, this was the place to go. I became enraged in the safe room. I screamed at the top of my lungs. I beat the walls with my fists. At one point a mental health technician ran into the room to make sure Dr. Richardson was in no danger. I was told later how the other patients in my unit had been instructed to stay in their rooms until I was finished. I really created a scene. I was angry, but the core of my anger wasn't about these new "memories." I was angry about the trap I had let myself fall into.

Throughout all of this, there was a small chilling voice inside me that spoke louder than any screaming I did. I would battle this voice for months and months to come. Inside I felt that these "memories" were all fabrications, but I felt helpless and trapped. There was such a powerful treatment fighting my doubts: two doctors, several therapists and nurses, and the book, *The Courage to Heal*. Never at any time did any part of this treatment question the validity of my memories. It was quite the opposite. I would receive insurmountable validation from the professionals and the group. It was too easy. I would wake up in the morning and tell myself that today I would remember sexual abuse by my father, and sure enough I would come out of my session with Dr. Richardson with memories of my father abusing me.

I left the hospital and threw myself into an overdose of out-patient therapy. I had a new therapist, a survivors' group, and my 12-step groups, all providing me with just enough validation to weaken the doubting voice inside of me. Then, in November of 1991, I was reading my local newspaper when a heading caught my eye. It read "Accusations of sex abuse, years later." As I read the column by Darrell Sifford, chills went up my spine. Here was the voice inside me in print. Someone else had the same feelings I did. I shook as I read the article. I finally had validation for my doubts. Two months later another of Darrell Sifford's columns appeared in our paper with the heading "When tales of sex abuse aren't true." These columns were practically an account of what had happened to me. I was scared in a way, but so relieved that I was finally freed from this horrible nightmare.

In September of 1992, I contacted the False Memory Syndrome Foundation in Philadelphia. By reading the literature I received from them and also from speaking to various people across the United States who had been affected by this syndrome, I became convinced that this abuse in therapy was more widespread than anyone could ever imagine.

In retrospect, I don't know if there is anything I could have done to prevent what happened to me in therapy. There is no doubt that one of the most crippling steps I took in therapy was reading *The Courage to Heal*. The book masterfully primed me for fabrication. With the exception of my first therapist, Robert, all of the mental health "professionals" who cared for me (both as an inpatient and outpatient) were "caught up" in this new wave of repressed memories of childhood sexual abuse and in blaming parents for all the problems one may have in adulthood. My biggest regret is not listening to that little voice inside me. That little voice was smarter than any of the "Ph.D.s" I had helping me and also wiser than any statement found in *The Courage to Heal* — all 495 pages of it.

I am very content with my life now. I no longer attend any therapy or 12-step groups. I have a loving family. My husband, Gary, is gainfully employed and very supportive. My son is now six years old and the joy of my life. I spend my free time writing, volunteering as a den mother for my son's Cub Scout Pack, doing crafts, and playing the piano. I'm actively working on my weight by following a sound nutrition program and exercising three times a week. I hope to have more children in the future. I have also made peace with my parents, and we are in communication with one another. My family and I are planning a trip to visit them sometime this year. My son will finally get to meet his other grandparents.

I am very grateful to Darrell Sifford for writing those columns. Through his work, I was finally able to do something that I had never been able to do before. I validated myself and the little voice inside me. If only I had listened to that voice sooner, I would have avoided immeasurable grief and saved thousands and thousands of dollars.

My Recovery from "Recovery"

My personal descent into hell began with a visit to a health fair in California. I had been feeling depressed for quite some time and I wanted to get a complete physical and emotional checkup.

The symptoms of depression had been going on since a previous marriage ended in September of 1988. It had been a painful marriage because of an accidental pregnancy which my husband was unhappy about. I had a beautiful baby daughter and couldn't think of leaving her with a stranger to go back to work, and my husband's intense unhappiness with the situation and personal conflicts about his sexual preference caused me to begin to develop a low-grade chronic depression. When my daughter was two, I faced up to the fact that I didn't have a real marriage and I made the difficult move of obtaining a divorce and trying to make it as a single mother.

During the time that my divorce was being finalized, I met a wonderful man and began dating him. He was warm, caring and supportive. After all the unhappiness and bad feelings of my previous marriage, I felt that I owed it to myself and to my daughter to give us the home and family we had always wanted, so I married Dan after eight months of dating. Unfortunately, we were met with many pressing problems right away. I had taken a government job and I had a boss who made lewd remarks to me every day, and Dan was being passed over on his promotion at his job. My daughter was struggling with repeated ear infections and we were having trouble with Dan's ex-wife meddling into our lives. I became very ill with sudden kidney infections and was hospitalized. I was forced to quit my job and file sexual harassment complaints against my boss. Our stress level was so high, it seemed like things were never going to get smoothed out for us. We decided to move out of the area and to try to make a fresh start. Dan was offered a good job in southern California, in the town where I grew up, so we made the big move.

I instantly went into some kind of culture shock after the move. The smog was terrible in southern California. It had been 10 years since I had lived there and it had changed a lot. I had moved out of there in 1979 up to Lake Tahoe and thought I would never have to come back, and here I was. After living in the mountains with snow and beauty all around, I was now stuck in a dirty, crowded rat race. I was unhappy at the prospect of raising my daughter in such an environment. My depression got worse and soon I couldn't even get out of bed or take care of my daughter who was now almost four. I sent my daughter to stay with her father in Lake Tahoe while I got myself back together. I was also troubled by unspecific digestion problems, urinary problems and pelvic pain during my depression. Things had just piled up on me, and all I could stand to eat was ice cream. All I could do was sleep and cry, and read my self-help books. I felt bad all over.

I had good medical insurance from Dan's new job, so I set out to get well. I went to urologists, gynecologists and general practitioners hoping they could help me. I wasn't able to sort out my problems; I just knew that I felt bad physically and emotionally. The medical doctors couldn't find anything wrong. I even underwent a laparoscopic exploratory operation, which proved negative. I wasn't sure where to go for help or what to do next.

A False Belief Is Implanted

I saw an ad in the newspaper for a women's health fair

that was free and would screen a person's health thoroughly. In addition to getting blood tests and a breast exam, I was given a questionnaire to fill out to see if I was depressed. I began crying as I filled out the questionnaire. The nurse who interviewed me was employed by a hospital. She told me that the hospital could help me. She explained what a nice hospital it was and how my insurance would pay for everything. I felt that this was exactly the answer I had been searching for — time and medical help to get myself straightened out and back to functioning normally again. Little did I know the horror that my life was to become for the next three years as a result of this decision.

I wanted to get better very badly and I was highly motivated. I had been reading John Bradshaw's books and Alice Miller's books and other books about the "inner child." I had also been attending Al-Anon, AA and ACOA groups on and off since 1984. In the past two years, I had been very wrapped up in reading "self-help" books about recovery. At last I felt I had the time and space to really concentrate on myself and get over the pain of the past few years. My daughter was being cared for, I had medical insurance, and the time was right to go into this thing with everything I had. When treatment began, I was in a very open and vulnerable mental state and I soaked everything up like a sponge. I was reading John Bradshaw's *Healing the Shame That Binds You* as I entered the hospital for treatment.

Right away I was met with questions about my parents. Other than a few brief questions about my marriage, my assigned psychologist did not seem to be interested in hearing about any of my current difficulties. He kept asking me about my childhood. I kept wondering, when I was going to be able to talk about the divorce and the job and everything that had been happening the past couple of years. I was never even asked about the stressful events in my life. The divorce was never even mentioned. My therapist asked me several times if I had ever been touched in a sexual manner. I replied, "No, not that I remember." He placed great emphasis on this possibility, as though I were withholding something very important that would explain my emotional problems. I started to think, "Well, if he thinks this is so important, maybe it is." So I began to try to remember my childhood.

My childhood was a combination of good and bad, I guess you could say. In many ways it was good – we had a house with the biggest and most intriguing back yard on the block. We had this giant tree that towered above the whole neighborhood and it had a fort in it and a tire swing. I remember spending many happy hours swinging and climbing in the tree. I also loved animals and had a dog, a parrot and many guinea pigs. My parents didn't have much money but I always felt loved. My mom stayed home to raise us while we were young, and we even moved to a house with a swimming pool when I was about 11. I always had pets and plenty of books to keep me happy.

The bad part of my childhood was due to my parents' personal lives. We had some neighborhood friends who we played with and my parents were best friends with their parents. At some point, my mom decided she wanted to have an "open affair" with the man, and then my dad started having an affair with the woman. In order to understand this, it helps to realize that they were a young modern couple of the 1960s. The sexual liberation movement had begun with the advent of Elvis, among other things.

I guess that this stuff about my parents and their open

marriage had always bothered me, but not really that much. I don't believe now that it affected my adult life one way or another. I had talked it over with my first husband and had felt that I could forgive my parents for their mistakes and get on with life. I definitely feel that no matter what the extent of any problems may have been back then, it was not causing my current depression. I had plenty of other good reasons to explain my symptoms.

I told my psychologist about my parents' past affairs and he seemed to perk up at this information. It was as though all of a sudden he was interested in me as a patient, when before, he seemed quite bored when we had our sessions. He told me he thought I had grown up in a "very sexual atmosphere" and that it was very likely I had been "touched." At first this confused me, then I figured out he meant that my father had done something to me. I couldn't remember any kind of abuse — I don't even remember ever getting spanked — but I kept thinking, he must be right because he's the expert.

For the most part, I was enjoying the social part of my stay in the hospital. I liked talking to the other women, even though it seemed like the main topic of conversation was sexual abuse. We went to groups all day and into the evenings. A common theme in the groups was whether we could "get angry" or not. If you could get in touch with your anger and feel your rage, you were looked up to and revered by the other patients. It was common knowledge in the hospital that there was a special room available for rage work, in which we could use a piece of equipment called batackas. This equipment resembled a pair of padded bats that patients were allowed to hit with — I never gained access to that special room so I don't know what the actual target was that the women were hitting. "Rage work" stems from a currently popular theory that anger is like a hydraulic mechanism in which pressure is supposedly built up and requires release, but in reality the end result of this kind of "therapy" is that it encourages patients to be consumed with anger, hatefulness and spite.

I talked in groups about my problems and my parents, and I especially enjoyed the groups that were about the "inner child." In one group I drew a picture of my inner child being a beautiful, spoiled little girl and my grown-up self being a stressed-out, bug-eyed monster. The other women in the group all drew their inner child as a starving stick figure and they seemed even envious that my inner child on paper looked to be thriving. It was the adult part of me that I was having problems with, not my "inner child."

My psychologist only came in to see me late at night, around ten or eleven o'clock, and his visits only lasted about 15 minutes at the most. Whenever I saw my psychiatrist, he just prescribed medications for me. For some reason, I lost my appetite as soon as I went into the hospital, and I couldn't sleep, either. My husband had been forbidden to see me by both my psychiatrist and my therapist. I think that if I could have had some kind of contact with anyone in my family, I might have been able to keep in touch with reality. As it was, I felt abandoned by my family because I hadn't been told that they were not allowed to see me. I just drank glasses and glasses of water, as it was the only thing I could get down, but I don't think that the nurses ever took notice of that. The only close contacts I had were with other women, many of whom were constantly complaining about being sexually abused as children, and with the nurses who treated us as though we were children. If someone had purposely designed an environment to reform and change a person's thoughts, the environment of this hospital would fit the bill perfectly. We were insulated from the outside world; our diet was controlled; we were given medication, literature to read, and kept constantly busy in groups that focused on our emotions.

The therapeutic focus on childhood sexual abuse soon became a routine. Every time my psychologist saw me, he asked me again if I had been sexually abused as a child. I continued to reply, "No, not to my knowledge." The women in my groups just kept talking about their dreams of sexual symbols and their anger at being abused. After about seven days of intense brainwashing sessions with my therapist, feeling extraordinarily pressured to "remember" a single incident that would explain everything, I had a mental breakdown. To say that this was a frightening experience would be a great understatement.

It is still hard for me to sort out what this breakdown felt like, but I remember it being very scary. I was in one of the many classes about our "inner child" when all of a sudden it felt like it had all clicked in — like I had integrated my inner child with my adult. Apparently things were not as together on the outside as I suddenly felt on the inside, though. I was talking in disjointed sentences to the nurses, leaving out prepositions. I remember that I kept saying that I had to "say goodbye to the trees." I believe I was trying to express my great sadness at having to leave the mountains which I had grown to love. The nurses interpreted these ramblings as a declaration of my intent to commit suicide, which never even entered my mind. I think that if I could have just gone back to my family and to life in the real world at that point, I would have come out of the confused and disoriented state I was in and would have gotten better. But this was not to be, for quite some time.

Something in me seemed to have gone "snap" and I suddenly felt quite together, very centered, and I packed my bags and told them I was leaving the hospital. Suddenly I was surrounded by several hospital employees and they were physically pushing me into a padded room. I couldn't believe what was happening to me. I stayed calm and cooperative, and I went quietly into this little room that contained a sparse bed without covers, and a little square window through which I could view the hospital staff going through the contents of my purse and my luggage.

They brought me pills to take which I can identify now as being Trilaphon, Ativan and Benadryl. A couple of times I told them I had to go to the bathroom so they would unlock the door and about five people, men and women, would accompany me the few short feet to the bathroom. Even in my distressed state, I wondered incredulously why they were treating me as if I were a dangerous armed criminal. At one point, I asked for a sanitary napkin because I felt like I was starting my period and a woman told me that she would have to see for herself if I really needed a sanitary napkin. I remained calm. I stayed in there for what must have been hours and then I went up and tried the door again, which was unlocked, but there was a man sitting in a chair outside the door blocking it. I weakly pleaded with him to help me, and he came in and talked to me. After awhile, he led me out of the room and in to eat dinner in the critical ward dining room, where I was afforded my first experience with schizophrenics and psychotics. They were weird, they were scary, and for the life of me I could not figure out why I was in with them.

That night I was transferred from the relatively luxurious women's unit to the sparse and prison atmosphere of the co-ed unit. I shared my room with a very rough-looking lesbian who had both of her wrists stiffly bandaged from suicide attempts. The lesbian's lover, a very young and pretty blind girl with a beautiful golden retriever guide dog, would visit her and they had terrible arguments. At other times I was afraid that they were going to make love right in the bed next to me. I felt like I was in a loony bin and that I was never going to get out. They had a male guard posted right outside my door and for 72 hours I was not allowed to go anywhere without him.

Late that first night after the transfer, my therapist visited me very briefly. He seemed very upset and even angry. He stood outside my door, and I will never forget how he said, "I still think you were either beaten or abused." That was it. I knew that I was never going to get out of that place until I said the one thing that he and everybody else at the hospital had been digging for. I began to cry like a little girl and said, "I think I was raped by my father." He replied something like, "I knew it," and for a moment he looked like he was going to hit the wall, he looked so angry. That was the end of our most important "session" and the beginning of my journey into a nightmare so engulfing that it nearly destroyed my life. My therapist was satisfied that he had done his work.

The next day, my therapist told me that he had called my mother and she was going to come in so that I could tell her what my father had done to me. He told me to write my father a letter, so I wrote to him and accused him of raping me. My parents lived about half a mile from the hospital and a reply was delivered to me shortly afterward in which my father denied the abuse. I showed my therapist the note from my father, and he told me to forget that my father ever existed. I think that down deep, I was willing at this point to make any personal sacrifice in order to get out of that hospital, so I went right along with my therapist's wishes. After all, what choice did I have? Was I in any position to question, to critically pick apart the treatment I was getting in this insular environment?

I was becoming paranoid and I felt pressured all the time to relate details of rapes by my father. A male hospital worker told me that I should get a book called *The Courage to Heal*, so I had my husband bring me the book. My doctors wanted details and more details, so I wrote pages of scenes for them in which my father raped me in various locations. In one scene, my father supposedly raped me at the age of three or four on the bathroom floor. I had taken the knowledge that I did have my arm dislocated once when I was young, about which I had no memory, and I incorporated it into the scene and wrote that my father had dislocated my arm during the assault. I weaved my scenes of fantasy in with reality, the whole time feeling sure that this was going to secure my liberation from the hospital. I think I knew the whole time that I was certainly making it all up, but underneath I was driven by an urgent and desperate need to survive, and this is what I felt I needed to do in order to appease my doctors.

The confrontation with my mother went badly because I was obviously very confused and disoriented. I kept changing my age at the time of the abuse from four to five to seven. I wasn't very convincing and my doctor seemed quite disappointed in me. After that, his visits to me in the hospital became infrequent, and cursory in their quality. I felt quite abandoned by him, but I continued to tell the hospital workers that I felt obsessed about the rape, and at one time I even pleaded to my psychiatrist to help me with it, to which he replied, "You are obsessed," and then increased my various medications.

At the same time that I was in the hospital, my husband entered outpatient group therapy sessions with this same psychologist. The therapist had diagnosed my husband as an alcoholic even though my husband only drank two or three beers a week. Every person in the group had been diagnosed as an incest survivor, even the males, I found out later. Any time anyone would complain of marriage problems, the therapist always recommended a divorce. He told my husband several times that he should divorce me because he thought I would "never get well." He also told my husband that I was a "drug addict" and would always be one. He failed to mention that this was because the hospital had placed me on all these drugs, under his treatment. He made it sound like I was popping pills of my own free will.

I kept wondering when they were going to let me out of the hospital. I desperately missed my husband, my daughter and my life. I finally realized that they would keep me in as long as I was willing to stay, so I picked a date and informed the staff that I would be leaving then. They didn't forbid me, but at the same time acted like they disagreed with my decision to leave after six weeks.

Following my long-awaited discharge from the hospital, I was faced with rebuilding my life, but it was very difficult to do much of anything. I was heavily sedated on major tranquilizers, Ativan and Halcion. I hated taking all these pills but I was frightened of what would happen if I stopped, so I managed to keep seeing a psychiatrist in order to stay on medication. I didn't like the way the pills made me feel, but if they were protecting me somehow from being crazy I wasn't going to question it. I slept a lot and tried even harder to remember what had really happened to me so I could get rid of the constant and tormenting doubts. I read *The Courage to Heal* over and over, trying to get a concrete memory of the rape that would truly convince me it had happened. It was all I talked about. My husband didn't know what to think. He had also cut off contact with my family, at the insistence of our therapist.

My obsession was placing even more of a strain on our marriage and so we saw the same therapist in weekly marriage counseling sessions. During one of the sessions, I brought in a taped phone call I had made to David Viscott of KFI talk radio. David Viscott is a well-known psychiatrist and author, and I had called him to tell him the story of how I came up with my memory of the rape. I told him about the mental breakdown, and surprisingly Dr. Viscott completely contradicted what I had been told by my psychiatrist and my therapist. He said that I had made a terrible mistake and that I needed to apologize to my parents for the accusation. Feeling as though I finally had some confirmation to back up my doubts about what my therapist was telling me, I played the tape for him and told him of my conflict about whether or not this had really happened. My therapist brushed it off, and replied, "It doesn't matter." Apparently he didn't think it was important that he had pushed me to confront both of my parents with the accusation, but now he had changed his mind and decided that the truth didn't matter to anyone. This man is a marriage and family therapist with a lifetime membership in the California Association of Marriage and Family Therapists, and he was saying that a false accusation has no importance in a family and that I should disregard it. I thought, "What about my parents if it isn't true? What in the world have I done to them?"

My marriage seemed to get worse with each counseling

session with our therapist. My husband was also seeing our therapist alone. I quit after finding out that my husband was being advised to divorce me. I went to groups a few times with my husband and even though our therapist was billing the insurance company under his name, the therapist had his undergraduate secretary lead the groups. The therapist used to tell us in these sessions about how he had been abandoned as a child and had to eat out of garbage cans. He also told us that he had suffered several psychotic episodes in his life. You'd think this would have made us question his competency and motives for the advice he gave, but for some reason we didn't think much about it at the time – we felt sorry for him.

Finally, our insurance had run out and we were told that we could not continue treatment. We were left on our own to tangle out the great mess our lives had become. We were living three short miles from my family, with whom we had vowed to cut off contact, and we were miserable, so we planned to move back to the mountains. Coincidentally, my husband's company was having problems and notified him that he was to be laid off. By this time, we were feeling very strongly that we had made a huge mistake in moving to California, so we happily moved back to the mountainous area we had left.

Within a few short months of returning to our town, my husband left me and filed a quick Nevada divorce. He had had enough of my sickness and so had his family. He had been told by our therapist that I would never get well, and he was losing hope. This abandonment was devastating to me. I was broke and without family or friends. However, my desire to survive always wins out, so I was able to get work and to keep supporting my daughter somehow. In order to function, I had to put my abuse issues on the back burner for a while. Over the next few years, I saw a total of two more psychiatrists and three more psychologists, and one hypnotherapist. My psychiatrist placed me on lithium and it was really hard for me to function on this drug.

The book *The Courage to Heal* played a very large part in my life. I particularly related to a long story in it about a woman named Giselle. This is because she suffered from manufactured memories, too, although of course I didn't realize it at that time. Giselle had gained her memories through the use of MDMA, a hallucinogenic drug that therapists used to use back in the 1970s and is now illegal. I wrote to the authors of *The Courage to Heal* and asked what Giselle was doing now and if I could write to her. They replied that she had dropped out of sight. I have since wondered many times if that is because she realized that she falsely accused her father, too. In fact, I would bet on that's what happened. "Giselle," if you are reading this, I hope you will contact me.

I took out a loan and bought a computer, in the hopes that I could do medical transcription at home, but even this kind of activity was too difficult. I started calling computer bulletin boards as a hobby and became involved in an electronic support group for incest survivors. For those who don't know how this works, when you call out to a large computer using your phone line, you can type messages to other people. They call this "e-mail," which is short for electronic mail. I easily found other survivors and we sent a multitude of messages back and forth to each other every day. I felt as though, if I told my story over and over again, it would certainly one day begin to feel real for me and then I could get over the horrible abuse I had suffered as a child. Gradually, I taught myself so much about computers that I was able to set up my own bulletin board service that other people called in to. I was the systems operator for a board called "Adult Victims of Child Abuse."

It was through this medium, the computer, that I met Lindsey, a woman who had her own small company that she called "Sexual Abuse Victims Salvation." She lived in a town near mine and I soon became friends with her and one of her "clients." She is a self-appointed "mental health advocate" who gives support to victims and referrals to therapists and lawyers. She came out to my home to interview me as a client. She does not charge for her services, but takes donations that arise out of the proceeds of lawsuits brought against perpetrators. She was a real sexual-abuse survivor, who actually had a child by her step-father, although she had lost both her children through a custody battle because she was on welfare and not able to take care of them. Lindsey was remarried and mainly supported herself through Social Security disability. Her diagnosis? Post Traumatic Stress Disorder (PTSD) presumably from the past incest.

I told Lindsey the extent of my "memories" which at that time consisted only of "body memories," a pelvic sensation that I believed was sort of an echo of past sexual abuse. On this basis, she concluded that I was an incest survivor and that I should sue my father. She referred me to an attorney and set it all up. The attorney in California took my case over the phone and began the process of drawing up the papers. Lindsey had convinced me that my father should be paying for my therapy, and by this time I had been influenced by *The Courage to Heal* to believe that getting revenge was vital to healing, so I agreed. Fortunately, my father was never served the papers.

Meeting Lindsey and starting the lawsuit had the effect

of getting me back into my obsession full-time. I was intent on remembering the abuse and I was feeling alone and abandoned by everybody. I had no family, and no friends other than Lindsey since we had returned to our city. I looked around for an incest survivors group and when I could not find one, I started one. It was pretty easy to do. I sent away to SIA (Survivors of Incest Anonymous) in Baltimore for literature and instructions on how to organize a 12-step survivors group. I called various churches and public facilities until I found a church where we could have our meetings for only $20 a month rent. Using my computer, I made up flyers with a picture of a teddy bear on them and I went around town and posted them in public places, like Planned Parenthood and the libraries. I also mailed my flyers to counseling centers, hospitals and schools. I placed an ad in the paper in the free section about support group meetings. From there I just had to go to my meeting and sit and wait. I didn't have to wait long before women started showing up.

Incest Survivors

Soon my meeting grew and settled into a basic core group of about 12 women. Their personalities and methods of approaching this subject were as varied as can be. As I look back on it now, I believe that many in my group had false beliefs and a few had really detailed false memories. There were also women in my group who really had been sexually abused.

Donna was the most outspoken one in the group and the one whom I felt the most kinship with. She had a lithe body and a harsh face, and was proud that she held a black belt in karate. She had spent most of her life teaching self-defense to women, although she seemed to be chronically unsuccessful as far as her personal life and her finances went. She lived with a meek younger man who was totally dependent upon her to control his every move. He would not hold down a job as long as they were together, but preferred instead to work from their tiny, dark apartment with his computer. She said they lived "on credit."

Donna came to my group with no memories of abuse other than being very unhappy as a child. She had somehow come to the conclusion that she "must be an incest survivor" as she felt that would explain all of her lifelong difficulties with men and also the lack of success that she longed for. I introduced Donna to my hypnotherapist and she began going to him for hypnosis sessions. While I was in the group, Donna did not come up with any detailed memories of abuse except for a vivid dream of her father looming before her and something about a snake. However, toward the end of my time in the group, she told me that under hypnosis she had uncovered the memory of her mother holding her legs apart while her father did something to her, and there was lots of blood. She mostly just had "symbols" that convinced her there was sexual abuse somewhere in her past.

Carla, a prostitute, was another interesting survivor. I was impressed by the details of her recovered memories. When I asked her how she got her memories, she told me that she had been attending 12-step groups for many years when suddenly in one group she broke down and cried about a feeling that she had been punished by her mother for some sexual acting-out. Apparently, this brought about a flood of memories of being sexually abused by her uncle, who lived with them for a time. She also claimed she saw her uncle kill someone. Her life as a prostitute seemed like evidence that she had been abused, but the more I got to know her, the more I began to doubt the things she told me. They were too bizarre and detailed. Here was a woman whose profession was to engage in sexual fantasy, and it seemed as though she was really quite good at it in more ways than she knew.

Debbie was overweight and worked as a teacher. She told how when she was an infant, her father carried her cradled in his arms when he would suddenly "stick his finger in her" and she cried at how painful this was. She had confronted her parents with memories of sexual abuse, to which her father said that it was "physically impossible" to do the things she was accusing him of (such as rape). Debbie was sure that her problem of depression and overweight was directly related to abuse. The reason why I now believe she had false memories is because I was always trying to get her to relate the details of her abuse (thinking it would help me remember mine) but she couldn't come up with anything convincing — just this memory of being two months old, which we all know is impossible.

Then there was Diana — always searching, never finding. She admittedly had no memories of sexual abuse but was convinced that "something happened." We heard how she questioned her neighbors and friends but didn't come up with any suspects. She didn't think her father or mother were guilty, but one time she seemed quite excited because she had remembered that her grandfather used to take her for rides in his car. While she had no memory of what happened on these rides, she felt that something did. Perhaps it was the answer she had been searching for, to explain all of her years in Codependents Anonymous groups and her painful recovery.

Among the women whom I genuinely believe had been

abused were Tanya and Carol. Both these women were assertive and articulate, but they never elaborated on the specifics of their abuse. They said they "had always had their memories" and didn't feel there was any benefit in describing the abuse and having to relive it. They both lived alone and were struggling with how to have an intimate relationship with a man. They also got quite upset when the others in the group insisted on describing their abuse in detailed terms. They felt they were there to gain new survival skills and not to hash over old memories. Carol started her own SIA group in another location on another night.

Besides the women who made up our "core" group, there were also women who came and went. One woman who I will always remember came to the group and sat there silently the whole time, with a shocked and panicked look on her face. She came up to me afterward and told me that she had been in a John Bradshaw workshop and doing a left-handed writing exercise when she wrote, "I wish my father would respect my body." She seemed broken, she was in tears. Of course we reassured her that it must mean something very important and that she should pursue it.

Of all the women in my group, the one who stands out most in my memory is Cathy. She was a shy introvert who seemed to be unsuccessful in her life except for her artistic talent. She was a loner. She dutifully worked at her job as a public servant until one day she had saved up enough money to quit work and to try to make a living as an artist. Her paintings were unusual and beautiful, yet she lacked the marketing skills to support herself as a self-employed artist. Cathy had been in hypnosis for about six years. The hypnotherapy was accomplished over the phone. Apparently she had a male friend in another state who had been her long-distance therapist and he would actually spend hours hypnotizing her over the phone. She had been doing this for years when suddenly she came up with graphic tales of sexual abuse and rape by her father, and sodomizing by her mother. She would describe the scenes in great detail, with the color of the tile in the bathroom as her mother leaned her over the tub and sodomized her with a hairbrush to punish her. Another favorite scene was how her father raped her in his lap and forced her to "oink" like a pig. When I tried to talk to her on several occasions, she had such a hard time concentrating that it was almost impossible to hold a rational conversation with her. Cathy is the one I worry about to this day. I feel she was deep in the grips of her visualizations and if she is still working and living half-way productively, I would be surprised.

It really began to bother me that the women without any memories of abuse seemed more ill and dysfunctional than the ones who had always known about their abuse. I watched with fascination as many of these women then entered therapy to gain memories and each became increasingly disturbed.

Memories and More Memories

Despite my regular group meetings, and my contact with Lindsey, I still did not feel as though I was improving. Lindsey kept preaching to me about "mental health" and about how important therapy was, but I was broke and didn't have insurance to cover therapy. At last I found a psychologist who would take me for a very low fee, but I felt that I needed something more, something stronger that would force these elusive memories out of hiding, so I consulted a hypnotherapist. Hypnotherapy to uncover repressed child abuse started me well on my way to my second and final nervous breakdown.

From the very first hypnosis session, my therapist diagnosed me with having Multiple Personality Disorder. He didn't see it as a "disorder," though, but a way of coping. He admitted he was a multiple personality too, and so were most — if not all — of his patients, although I never saw any other personality than the same muddle-headed man that he always was.

I turned out to be an excellent hypnosis subject and after the first session I was able to go under immediately upon entering his office, without any hypnotic induction process. With his help, I relived the supposed rape scene and many others, including being molested on the changing table at the age of one year. The only problem was that with all this "cathartic" therapy I was getting worse, not better. I began to feel at times like I was slipping into a trance state spontaneously. I became frightened that I would fall asleep or go unconscious and another personality would come out and take over. The hypnotherapist had me draw all the personalities, so I set to work imagining all these various different people inside of me and drawing them. I perceived that he wanted some real art, so I drew portraits and colored them with colored pencils. I had one part of me that I determined was a little boy and he was the trouble-maker. One personality was an older wise woman, and so on. I was quite proud of my creations but when I showed them to the therapist, he seemed disappointed. I think that what he had in mind was stick figures and I was giving him much more. I was getting discouraged. I really thought I was a good patient and I was doing everything I knew to try and get better, but it seemed like nothing ever felt resolved. I decided to change my name and I used "April" in every situation I could. To me, my old name reminded me of an abused, hurt little girl. I never got around to making the name change legal, thank goodness, but I still have people approach me from time to time who knew me as "April" and it makes me cringe.

About the time that I entered hypnotherapy, I had enrolled in a few college courses. One of the courses was psychology and I found the literature on neurology of particular interest. I began studying the brain and found it fascinating. I was also very involved in my literature class and it really forced me to do some deep and critical thinking. I ran across one book that stands out in my mind in particular, *In the Palaces of Memory* by George Johnson. What I was getting out of it was basically that memory is mostly chemical and that much of what we experience gets lost forever. This was a direct contradiction to what I had been reading about memory in the incest survivor books. Slowly, the thought was beginning to surface that maybe this sexual abuse belief just might not be true. I tried to discuss what I was learning with the women in my group, but I couldn't seem to interest any of them. Deep down inside of me, there were some major changes taking place, but they weren't to become apparent until some weeks later.

What was my family doing through this period? Well, I hadn't spoken to my father in years. My few phone calls with my mother were very tense and upsetting. I felt completely betrayed by her because she insisted on a neutral stance. She wouldn't say that she believed me, yet she wouldn't say that my accusations were impossible either. With the hypnotherapy, my phone calls became abusive toward them. I called my younger brother about twice a day to report to him my new memories and I pleaded with him to go to a therapist so that he would remember too. I told him that I had seen my father sodomize

him when he was two. I gave him minute details of the
scene — I must have been very convincing because I heard
much later that he confronted my father and said, "If it's
true I'll kill you." To this day, I think I feel the worst about
what I put my brothers through.

By this time I had an incredible amount of pressure to
remember abuse; pressure to come up with details for my
lawsuit; pressure to report new memories to my group —
after all, I was their "leader"; pressure to report new memories which meant progress to Lindsey; and pressure to
report new memories to my new therapist, a clinical psychologist. My new therapist wrote in his records that I had
experienced a "flood of memories" during my first
hospitalization and he just assumed that it was all true. Our
sessions consisted of having me stare into his eyes for the
entire hour while I related scenes of abuse. I have since
found out from experts in mind-control techinques that
this is a form of trance induction; however, my therapist
believed that it was a method which extracts real feelings
and real memories. He was just not seeing the pressure I
was under and how I was caving in to it with a form of
compliance by manufacturing memories.

At the same time, I was also under tremendous pressure
to get healthy and to stop my medications. My therapist
and my hypnotherapist were both adamantly against psychiatric drugs. I was very tired of popping pills so I was
willing to give it a try and quit cold-turkey. I had been on
Tegretol, Ativan, Stelazine and Desipramine under care of
my psychiatrist at the state out-patient clinic.

I was now fully embroiled in the cult-like atmosphere of
the repressed memory/incest survivor movement. I started
cutting on my arms and my thighs with a razor blade
because I had gotten the idea about self-mutilation in my

survivor books – I read that it afforded the victim a feeling of relief and of release. I did not find this to be true at all. Those cuts hurt and stung, and it was hard to hide them with my clothing all the time. Thankfully, this practice of mine didn't last too long.

Being raped once as a child became insufficient to explain the great pain I was in now. For some reason, the fixation on abuse by my father now gave way to visualizations of being raped by a family friend who had died in the Vietnam war. The visualizations stepped up into an all-consuming frenzy of being trapped in the past and fear of slipping into an altered state or personality at any moment. On my way home from my psychologist's office, I began having flashbacks of watching the family friend murder young girls and bury them in a junkyard. I had vivid pictures of him threatening me with death if I told. I felt that the only thing that could explain this horror was that he was a Satan-worshipper and a serial killer. I couldn't believe the horror of the things I was remembering – could I really have repressed all these blood and gore scenes? On one trip home from the hypnotherapist's office, I took an overdose of Ativan. I woke up to see two policemen who insisted on taking me to the hospital. Lindsey was there with them and I'm not sure to this day how they found out I had overdosed. They took me to the hospital and I was checked out and it was found that the dose I had taken was not toxic enough, so they sent me home.

At home, it was back to the same thing. I was starting to crack up. Lindsey had me call the police department in the small town I had grown up in to check into my story about the missing children. Of course, nothing came up and no children had been reported missing for those years that I gave. I began to get really confused. I began to wonder if I could have witnessed all these murders and forgotten them, then what else could I have done? I began to think that maybe, just maybe, I had not been able to break the cycle of abuse and that I had actually murdered children in my sleep or in an altered state of consciousness. I stopped sleeping and lay awake all night wondering if I had done anything as horrible as murder and repressed it. Whenever I saw a poster of a missing child or a picture in the paper, I went into an instant panic that felt like intense guilt. Could I really have done something so unthinkable as killing someone? Perhaps I was not where I thought I was everyday and one of my "alters" was killing people when I believed that I was taking a nap or whatever. I really think that I was having guilt on a deep level over the false accusations I had brought against my father. I also felt extraordinarily pressured by my group not to "deny" that I had been abused. The pressure and the guilt were pressing down on me so hard by that time, I could not keep myself together. The intense conflict was causing me to split off from reality.

At last I could not stand it any longer. After another sleepless night, I looked all over the house for something to kill myself with. When the only thing I could find was a small steak knife, I was left with only two choices: to either push that knife as deep as I could into my stomach, or to go to the hospital. I thought of my sweet little six-year-old daughter sleeping in the next room – and packed my bags to go to the hospital.

With no medical insurance, I had to go to the state mental hospital. I was placed directly in the critical ward, with schizophrenics and psychotics everywhere. It is a dark, cold, hard, depressing place, but for some reason, I felt relieved and euphoric to have my attention directed outward from myself and I soon began to improve, for a brief amount of time. I found it a challenge to talk to the schizophrenics locked up in there who seemed so far gone and some of them actually responded to me. One girl was in a completely frozen catatonic state, bent over at the waist and her hair was all matted. I kept talking to her and talking to her. I told her that it was time for us to make peace with ourselves and with our families. Much to my astonishment, and that of the hospital staff, she slowly began to come out of the catatonic state. She ate for the first time in weeks. I told the hospital staff that I had falsely accused my father of sexually abusing me as a child and they seemed incredulous at this. I think I was racked with guilt over the accusations I had made to my family. I managed to get the staff to let me use a phone so I could call my father. My grandmother had just died and it was the day of the funeral. I told my father I had been very wrong and I asked him to please forgive me and he said, "Yes, of course." I still felt horrible over what I had done to him. I was teetering on the edge of some kind of snapping or splitting again, but the hospital felt that I was okay and so they discharged me.

The next events are hard to remember, difficult to comprehend and even worse to try to explain. I went home from the hospital, got dressed up and went to have all of my long blonde hair cut off short. My daughter was being taken care of by her father in the next town. I packed a bag, cleaned out my purse, and drove myself to the police department where I turned myself in for murder. To me, it seemed it was the only possible thing to do at the time. The only problem was that I wasn't sure who I murdered. I thought maybe that I had murdered each and every one of the children whose pictures were posted on the wall at the police station. But I wasn't sure. Maybe I was a psychic who dreamed it, I argued. At any rate, I felt I was being an obedient citizen by telling them that maybe I had done it. I was interviewed by two detectives in a small room for quite a while. I'm sure I was very polite and cooperative. I know that I asked them several times if they were going to handcuff me. They kept saying no, that they didn't believe I had committed any crime. I argued with them. I told them that Jeffrey Dahmer had been cool and logical and cooperative, too. I longed for them to put me in jail so I could be out of my torment. I was trapped in a world where there was no one true reality. One of the detectives brought me back to a room and opened a photo album. In the photo album were various pictures of a small black child who had been beaten, drugged and tortured by his sick mother. I was revolted and started crying. At last, I asked them, "Do you think I am suffering from delusions?" They replied, "Yes," but I still didn't believe them. They drove me back to the state hospital.

At the hospital again, I endured another nightmare. I was given a large dose of liquid Haldol, an anti-psychotic drug. At first I had severe stiffness in my neck from the drug, and it turned into grand mal seizures. I cried out to the hospital staff that I needed medical attention as I was helplessly thrashing around and all they did was reply, "You are already in a hospital," as they took my bed down off the frame and placed it on the floor so I wouldn't fall off. There, I thrashed and thrashed uncontrollably. I managed to call over a fellow patient and asked him to put his hands on my head and pray for me. I was sure that I was in hell. He prayed for me until I fell asleep to the sound of the mental health workers laughing in the background.

The next day I was brought up before a group of psy- chiatrists, social workers and staff psychologists. They questioned why I was back in the hospital. I couldn't speak. I went into some kind of an internal withdrawal and became catatonic. Hospital staff were called and they dragged me away and threw me into a small, cold, padded room. There wasn't even a bed. I had to sit on the floor and I was shaking from the cold. My psychologist handed me an MMPI, a test with about 800 questions, and told me I was not getting out of that room until I finished the test. I worked on the test, but I was so confused and paranoid that I had an extremely difficult time deciding what to answer, and anybody who has ever taken this test can tell you that it has some very tricky questions, some of which are repeated in various ways. I would work for awhile, and then I would lie on my back and stare up at the cold bright light and try to will my soul to leave my body. I thought that maybe if I concentrated hard enough, I could leave my body forever and go past that light and into heaven.

I finished the test and went to sit in the day room. By this time I was getting very tired from the strong drugs they had given me and the days of no sleep, and I needed badly to lie down. Every time I slumped in my hard chair, a big burly mental health worker would come by and shove me. If I put my feet up on another chair, he would roughly yank the chair out from under me. If I thought I was in hell before, I knew it by now. To make things even worse, the psychologist came out and told me that my MMPI test had proven to be "invalid" and that I must take the whole tortuous thing over again. I was not allowed to eat with the other patients. I knew I was being punished for something, but to this day I wonder what. They treated me just like a horrible criminal, and from their attitude I assumed that maybe I really had done some terrible things. I kept wondering when I was going to be hauled off to prison and to court and then put to death in the electric chair.

Over the next three weeks I existed in a world of insanity all around me. People were talking to themselves and no one seemed to care about anybody else's comfort or pain. I was so stiff from the Haldol that it was difficult to walk, to brush my teeth, to stay awake in the hard chairs. We weren't given anything to amuse ourselves with all day. TV was not allowed, except for a short time in the evening. It was just me, a big ugly room and all these crazy people you couldn't even talk to. They were either shouting, singing, or picking their noses all the time. The mental health workers weren't there to talk to the patients, like they had been at the luxurious hospital in California. They were there to needle, discipline and basically babysit. A particular social worker there became extremely verbally abusive to me. I asked him if I was ever going to get out, and he replied, "They never let people like YOU out." Soon, I was served with formal court papers saying they were going to try to commit me for six months. It seemed that I was trapped in a virtual never-ending nightmare.

Liberation

Somehow I survived the next three weeks in the hospital. I spent my days lying on my side on the hard, dirty floor, facing the wall and trying to doze off into oblivion. At last my court date came. I had no problem convincing the judge that I was really sane and not a danger to myself and to others. I had figured out in the hospital that I had been horribly duped and that everything had been a figment of my imagination – all the abuse, all the murders, and especially the rape by my father.

Coming out of that hospital was like being born again. I had been given a new lease on life and this time I was not going to blow it. After I got home, I took the longest bath of my life and then I immediately tore up all my self-help books and I changed my phone number so that the women in my group could not call me. I started looking for a job. I was so tired of being sick.

It was a few months before I was able to tie everything to my first therapist who implanted the false memory. If I had never seen him, I believe that I would have sooner or later pulled myself out of the depression on my own, but instead I was pushed into a spiral of certain self-destruction and unreality.

When I realized I had been duped, I didn't even know about False Memory Syndrome. One day I ran across a message about the FMS Foundation over a computer conference and was overjoyed to find that there had actually been others who had been through the same type of experience. I called the Foundation and I can't remember anything that I said, but I do remember all the anger I was beginning to feel at what my first therapist had done to me in starting this nightmare. I got hold of another woman in Texas who had been through this and I can tell you that the feeling of finding out that you are not alone in something so bizarre as FMS is a very unique feeling. I was shaking as I spoke to her.

But soon my euphoria at my new found health and freedom met with a shock. I went to my door and there stood Donna and Carla from my group. I should have known better, but I let them in. They proceeded to tell me that they wanted me back in the group. I told them that I was not an incest survivor, but that instead I had False Memory Syndrome. They became very angry and very insistent. I tried to tell them that although I had been very sick before, I was now well and very sorry if I had misled them. They told me that I was in deep denial and that they hoped I would come out of the darkness. They both looked pale, thin, and had dark circles under their eyes. I felt deeply sorry for them. I asked them to leave and they refused. Donna said she had been called over to my house many times in an emergency when I was having flashbacks and that she had stood behind me and the only thing I could think of to say to them was, "I was sick." I went to the door and held it open. They still sat there staring at me with hate. I told them if they didn't leave, I would call the police. They left. A few days later, I found a note on my door from them. It was an old poem I had written back in the days when I believed I had Multiple Personality Disorder. The poem revolted me and it still scares me to this day to think that I actually live in the same town as these women. I feel very sad for them because I think that most of them are still stuck in the same destructive cycle of FMS. I send them literature and articles whenever I can but they ignore it. I feel certain that if any of them come to realize that they were suffering from FMS too, that they will contact me.

I have been off psychiatric medications and out of therapy for a year now and I can confidently say that I feel I am at last fully recovered from this nightmare. I work hard, I sleep well, and my life is what it should be. I don't let small anxieties and depressions get the best of me any longer. I have no further desire to pay a therapist large amounts of money to listen to my self-obsessed ruminations. Most important of all, I have grown up and have learned how to take complete responsibility for my own life and not to trust so easily. I learned that life is not simple for anyone and no one has promised it would be fair. My life now clearly shows the symptoms of health and my well-being proves that I was not abused like I had been led to believe.

I have filed a lawsuit against my first therapist, and I have contacted my other therapists and often send them articles to try to educate them about FMS. I do not ever expect to experience mental illness again. I know what the difference is between my imagination and reality, and I know that people do not repress the knowledge of horrible events like rapes and murders. If anything like that had ever really happened to me, I feel sure that I would have much difficulty in forgetting it, not remembering it! Not everyone goes along with me on this. When I confronted Lindsey about her part in my deception about my memory, she became very angry. She called the psychologist I had been seeing and reported several lies about me, saying that I was a "drug abuser." I suppose she thought that if she were to convince everyone that I was some sort of drug addict, it would make me look crazy and she could then feel absolved of the errors in judgment she had made. Lindsey thinks that my health will not last. I plan to call her every year on the anniversary of my liberation from the state hospital (April Fools Day, coincidentally) to let her know how well I am and how I still have no memory of sexual abuse. I doubt if this will convince her. She will probably only say I am "in denial."

My family and I have been reunited, thanks to the assistance of the FMS Foundation. At first, my parents found it difficult to really forgive me until they read the literature that the foundation sent them. Now they know that it was my first therapist in the hospital who implanted the false memories and who started me on the downward spiral of FMS and mental illness. My brothers have had a tougher time understanding and we are not completely reunited, but I feel sure that some day we will be. We all have a lot of healing to do, but we have come far.

My life now is normal. Not dramatic. Not exciting. Just normal, and I love it. I have a great job and I work hard for the FMS Foundation in my spare time. I edit and publish a newsletter called "The Retractor" for other survivors of False Memory Syndrome. I am trying to gather us all together for a nationwide support network. Right now, there are only a handful of us, people who will admit to FMS, but I feel certain that in the next 10 years, our numbers will be many and then perhaps we can help bring an end to this insane abuse going on in the mental health profession. I have a special concern about the children who are undergoing this type of therapy that pushes for memories of sexual abuse. I know that for the rest of my life, I have a purpose — to help stop abusive therapists and to help educate the public about their undue influence.

I think that the authors of such misleading books like *The Courage to Heal* owe the public an apology for the hoax they are perpetrating with their misinformation about "repressed memories." Ellen Bass and Laura Davis need to write a new book about false memories that is a complete retraction of much of the garbage that they put forth in their early books. I also believe that recovery movement gurus like John Bradshaw owe an apology to the many new victims they have created with guided visualization and inner child therapy. Universities need to teach people about mind control and cults so that they can protect themselves from being duped. People do not seem to be aware of the great influence that they have over others and how easily people can be misled.

Melody Gavigan

Surviving "Therapy"

The following is a candid summary of my four-year battle with False Memory Syndrome (FMS). It is my hope that my experience will shed some light on this phenomenon. I also hope that by telling my story, it will serve as a warning beacon to others so that they may avoid the senseless suffering that my family and I endured.

My husband John and I began marriage counseling when I was in my early 20s. We had been running the gamut of what I now understand are typical marital spats, which were increasing in frequency and intensity. Along with a good dose of pride and stubbornness on both our parts, our relationship was affected by the unrelenting stress of a variety of crises we struggled through together. Beginning shortly after we married, we had moved steadily from one crisis to another without any let-up. Preoccupied with coping, we hadn't had much energy left over to get to know each other and to build our relationship. To John and me, both of us emotionally and physically drained, our marital problems felt overwhelming.

There was also another motivation behind our decision to get marriage counseling. My childhood had been extremely difficult, involving numerous traumas any one of which individually would have been challenging to cope with. Together, they wreaked havoc on my emotional well-being. In general, my family life was very unstable. During my childhood, my dad turned to alcohol as an escape from marital problems. He became violent with my mom when he drank. My worse childhood memories are of witnessing his violent abuse of my mom. My dad never struck me when he was drunk, and only on rare occasion did so while sober. Afterwards, he would apologize. My mom, however, was physically abusive to me. Emotionally, she struggled to "be there" for me while I was growing up. Because of a number of circumstances including my dad's drinking, she was usually stressed out. For these reasons, I felt closer to my dad than to her. Both of my parents also had extramarital affairs during my teenage years, which I was aware of.

My anxiety over my dad's drinking, both parents' violence and their marital infidelities caused me great suffering. During my teenage years, the toll of my suffering began to evidence itself. Along with depression, I was plagued with an eating disorder and a sexual compulsion.

The depth of my emotional pain and my compulsive behavior frightened me. I didn't understand what was happening to me. After marrying, I felt less compulsive, but remained chronically sad. I still didn't understand myself, and I didn't trust myself. Of course this affected my relationship with John. And so in the hope of doing my part to resolve our marital problems, and of alleviating my pain, I entered into marriage counseling with John.

We chose to see Tom, a licensed therapist with a masters degree in social work. He lived in our neighborhood, and was spoken of respectfully as a professional. We knew him only as an acquaintance. In counseling we primarily learned communication skills. As we put them into practice, we argued less. We had renewed hope for our relationship. I felt better. Crediting Tom with teaching us how to save our marriage, both John and I admired and trusted him. I had discussed very briefly with Tom some of what happened during my childhood, but nothing was said about the stress John and I had been through during our marriage.

Around the time John and I were contemplating ending counseling, Tom turned to me and asked me a question that was to forever alter my life. With the tone of a parent sympathetically asking a child with cookie crumbs on her mouth if she ate the last cookie out of the cookie jar, he asked me if my father had sexually abused me. At first I couldn't tell if he was somehow confronting me or if he was confusing me with another client. He looked at me searchingly, as though he knew something I didn't know. It became apparent he had earlier drawn the conclusion that I was an incest victim. I was shocked. He told me I had the classic symptoms of an incest victim. He said he could even tell by the way I looked at him (seductively, he said). Another client of his recently told me he bragged to her about being able to diagnose an adult victim of childhood sexual abuse after just being in the same room with her for a couple of minutes. Currently he was working as a therapist at a school for delinquent girls and saw clients like John and me after hours. He said most of the girls he saw were sexual-abuse victims and it was his area of expertise.

I thought of my dad. Was this possible? I had never suspected my dad of sexually abusing me, and I had absolutely no memory of any such thing. Tom insisted this was totally irrelevant to whether or not it had happened. He told me I had probably repressed — hidden away in my subconscious mind — all of the ugly memories because as a child I was too emotionally weak to deal with it. He said it had stayed buried all of this time, until as an adult I could deal with it.

I stumbled out of his office like a zombie the night he out-of-the-blue sprung his diagnosis on me. I felt like I had been diagnosed with a terminal disease. I respected his diagnosis like I would have a doctor's, and it was presented with the same authority. I respected therapy as a science. I had seen therapists on TV and read their advice in magazines. They were given the final say so on everything from potty training to criminal behavior. They were above reproof, except by old fogies who called them shrinks. Therapy was presented as a science. Tom had an advanced degree, a license; and my insurance, with its many exclusions, was willing to pay part of his hefty hourly charges. I felt light-headed. I could barely think straight. Tom told me I was dissociating, which was my mind's way of protecting me from the incest memories I was yet too emotionally weak to deal with. To him this was further proof I had repressed memories. I wondered in amazement at this proof. His prescription was for me to go home and see if I remembered anything.

I spent the next week on a vigil pressing myself to remember something. My world had been turned upside down. I was in a state of emotional limbo. It was like sitting by the phone waiting to hear if a loved one was a casualty or a survivor of a plane crash. Was nothing as it seemed to be? My dad's not who I think he is? Nor my mom? Not even my childhood? Who am I? This precarious state felt torturous. I looked through my childhood photo album and read old poetry I had written, thinking this might bring back a memory. I pressed myself so hard to remember that I worked myself into a frenzy. Still, I could not remember anything about incest.

At the time, I had very limited contact with my dad and the rest of my family. They lived in other states, and once in awhile we'd speak over the phone. I saw them less than once a year. My dad had divorced my mom, as he had been involved in an extramarital affair. I tried to be open minded and nonjudgmental, but I felt devastated and angry at him.

I felt rejected and betrayed. My family had essentially died when he divorced my mom. Because of the divorce and other frictions between us, I had come to feel that he didn't care about me anymore. I guess I wasn't sure he still loved me. I felt very emotionally and physically removed from him. When I thought of him, I felt hurt and rejected. When I really strained to get in touch with my feelings after Tom's suggestion that my father had probably molested me, I felt a sense of violent victimization. Maybe it was possible.

I also experienced a sense of relief that there was a possible explanation for all of my problems, especially my eating disorder and sexual compulsiveness. If it were true, then to unrepress it would bring me inner peace. John too told me it was a relief to think there was now a clear explanation for my emotional pain and some of our marriage problems. I had been hurting for so long, and though I tried, I couldn't shake my pain or make my compulsiveness go away. I too had heard somewhere that most eating disorders are caused by sexual abuse. Could this be the reason I couldn't help myself?

In agony I went with John to our next appointment. After hearing I couldn't remember anything, Tom asked me what it would take for me to remember. I said a safe place – some psychology lingo I picked up along the way. With the goal of ending my agony by remembering being sexually abused by my dad, he had me close my eyes and visualize this safe place. This visualization eventually developed into a scene of my dad violently sexually abusing me.

Tom instructed me to say whatever popped into my mind. Throughout this hypnotic state, a variety of the details I "saw" were real memories of objects, and non-abusive experiences which I had previously remembered as having taken place under different circumstances totally unrelated to sexual abuse. In between picture-like flashes of these, were many gaps during which nothing picture-like would pop into my mind. At these times I would follow Tom's instructions and mentally strain waiting for "thoughts" to pop into my mind. Believing that whatever popped into my mind about sexual abuse had to be real, I felt great anxiety when details of sexual abuse actually did pop into my mind. I cried and shrieked as they came. They were laced with feelings of terror as I had experienced during my dad's violence toward my mom. I was aware of my mind trying out different thoughts of sexual abuse (by visualizing them) and their corresponding emotions, looking for those that flowed in the context of the developing sexual abuse scene.

Tom asked me questions during this hypnosis about what "was happening." He told me to visualize himself at one point talking to my child-self I was visualizing. I did this while he actually said things as the voice of my visualization of him. He said things about my dad being a very sick man and about me not having to suffer anymore. This visualization of Tom felt as real as when I filled in the gaps with whatever thoughts popped into my mind.

I was very upset during this hypnotic experience. It was very intense and my thoughts jumped around very quickly. After the visualization, Tom told me this scene of sexual abuse had really happened to me when I was a child and that it had been repressed since. He commended me for my strength. I felt some relief, in a sense, that I was able to remember something. I also felt some confusion.

Shortly thereafter, although I could clearly remember what I had visualized and said, I felt like I had just made up a story. The objects and the non-abusive parts of the visualization I had "seen," which I had previously remembered as being unrelated to sexual abuse, felt real to me. The emotions of terror and victimization I had felt as I visualized myself as a child being molested by my dad also felt real, but the sexually abusive details I had visualized did not feel real at all. They didn't even feel like a dream.

Tom reassured me that it was normal for women to doubt the validity of the memories they unrepress. He maintained I was dissociating again because I was still too emotionally weak to deal with the truth. He was confident that in time, the scene I'd visualized would feel more and more real until one day I would finally accept it.

Later, after I'd had time to ponder, I had a pressing question on my mind. I asked Tom if my symptoms of repressed memories of incest couldn't actually be related to the traumas I had suffered as a child that I had never forgotten? Again I had spoken only briefly to him about them. My symptoms were chronic sadness, loneliness, poor self-esteem, insecurity and an eating and sexual compulsion. Oh, and also the way I looked at him. I remembered my childhood feelings of terror, helplessness, and shame related to my dad's drinking. I also had some feeling of responsibility and guilt about my dad's drinking. Both of my parents had said things out of anger in the past, claiming that because I was a demanding child it drove my dad to drink. I remembered feelings of victimization during my childhood from my dad's drunken attacks on my mom, and my mom's violent outbursts. I remembered feeling unwanted and rejected at times growing up. At the time of our marriage counseling, I had barely begun reflecting on the stress John and I had been through and its effect on me. It felt to me my symptoms stemmed from my childhood experiences. However, I wasn't too sure about the compulsiveness.

It did seem logical that sexual problems came from sexual abuse. Although I remembered nothing about incest, I had never forgotten two other experiences of sexual abuse. During childhood a teenager had exposed himself to me on a playground. He shouted obscene things at me, saying how much I enjoyed what he was doing. Also when I was alone walking one morning at age eleven, a group of boys I didn't know approached me and threatened to take off my clothes. Obviously these experiences scared me.

Tom insisted that none of what I remembered experiencing, even though he only knew bits and pieces, could possibly be enough to cause my problems. I ran through my list of childhood traumas again with him. He said I was making up excuses trying to hide from the truth. I was "in denial." He told me he was 95 percent sure my dad had sexually abused me.

Soon after this I went to a therapy session alone because John couldn't make it. Tom said I was much more open when John wasn't around and told me to come alone from then on. I had felt uncomfortable at times sharing such intimate details about myself with another man, especially with John sitting next to me. During our individual therapy, Tom did hypnotherapy, and I did self-hypnosis at home. I was still confused about my repressed memory of abuse that had come out. It still didn't feel like a real memory, but Tom still insisted it was real.

During hypnotherapy, I didn't visualize any more sexual abuse scenes, but I did remember a few miscellaneous childhood memories. Tom, however, adamantly insisted these were somehow related to sexual abuse. He concluded my mind was stopping short of the abusive parts to protect me. For example, during hypnotherapy I "saw" my dad in swim trunks and it felt like a real memory. Tom then, encouraged me to describe to him what my dad was doing, with the goal of having me remember a sexual abuse scene. At first I drew a blank, but then the thought popped into my mind that he was lying on his bed and then I visualized it. From then on I drew a blank and nothing popped into my mind. My doubts only served to make him more sure. Tom didn't plant the picture of my dad in swim trunks in my mind; he interpreted it.

It would have been wise at this point to say so long to Tom and run, but I didn't. My mind, by not having any memories and by refusing to accept that the hypnotherapy scenes were accurate, was telling me I didn't have any repressed memories of incest, but confused and self-doubting, I chose to believe Tom instead of myself. I honestly accepted that he knew more about my childhood relationship with my dad than my own mind did. Certainly with his education, he knew more about the mind and memory than I did. He represented, by virtue of his profession, a model of emotional health. He was older than I was and extremely self-confident. I was a chronically sad and lonely young woman, distrustful of myself because of my past compulsive behavior and at times overwhelming emotional pain. I trusted him more than I trusted myself.

I became obsessed with trying to reconcile my memories, thoughts and feelings with his beliefs about my childhood, which were based on repressed memory theories. Through this means, the evidence was growing that my dad had molested me. When I would search my soul in agony for an answer as to whether he really had or not, my mind would draw a blank. I could not remember anything in a way that felt real to me that indicated he had. What I did feel was that familiar emotional ache I had been suffering from, that subtle sense of violent victimization, and very, very sad feelings about my dad. Was Tom right? Were the ache, the sense of violent victimization, and the sadness the emotional residue of sexual molestation? Was it really just as much proof as if I remembered? I only remembered bits and pieces of my childhood. How could I know what really happened?

According to his repressed memory theories, Tom had an explanation for all of my problems — including even my doubts that I had repressed memories. According to his theories, there was an explanation for every mistake I'd ever made. Although the explanations might indicate that I had acted in a dysfunctional way, they also cleared me of any real responsibility, because it was my parents who had caused my dysfunction. I, however, was now responsible to go through therapy to overcome my dysfunctional ways.

Actually, the repressed memory theories had an explanation to discount anything that opposed them and an explanation to justify anything that validated them. They were a hodgepodge of ideas including those associated with healing your inner child and healing from sexual abuse that was not repressed. In reading books based exclusively on each of these two theories, I noticed that repressed memory theories included, among other things, everything from both theories with some omnipotent ideas about memory tacked on.

Despite my wholehearted attempt to accept the idea that my dad had molested me, I was continually racked with doubts. I bounced back and forth, sometimes in the same day, between believing Tom's charges against my dad and believing my dad was innocent. When I bounced in the direction of believing my dad was a child molester, I had very dark thoughts about my childhood. The idea that he had hurt me in such an ugly way caused me indescribable emotional pain. My dad, the dad I loved, albeit the dad I was angry with, died to be reincarnated as a pervert who used me in the ugliest of ways. The many happy times I did remember from childhood now seemed pitiful, and any love or attention my dad had shown me I now interpreted as "sick." And then to think my mom let such a thing happen. I began to detest them both and questioned how my extended family could not have noticed – accomplices by omission. And so certain members of my extended family suffered similar deaths in my mind.

When I bounced in the direction of believing my dad was innocent, I felt a terrible guilt. Tom had previously commended me on being an ideal patient because I was so quick to follow his counsel. I felt like a failure because I couldn't make myself come out of denial. I wanted to please him. I felt inadequate. Something was wrong with me for not being able to remember, and for not being able to believe the hypnotherapy scenes were real experiences from my childhood.

I also felt guilty because he had made being "in denial" out to be emotional weakness. I felt angry and distrustful of myself for being in denial, similar to my feelings about my compulsive behavior. I couldn't control myself and make myself remember. I pleaded with my own mind to show me the abuse. I begged God to let me remember. Believing Tom's contention that my denial was standing in my way, I would resolve to fight any doubts that came into my head about whether or not my dad had sexually abused me. But I could never fight my doubts off for long, and soon they'd be parading through my mind again.

Some of the repressed memory theories themselves were especially strong motivators for me to take them seriously. My dad's fiance, with whom he was living, had a young

daughter named Sarah. Another woman he had dated also
had a young daughter. Had he chosen these women so he
could abuse their daughters? I was being taught that child
molesters rarely stop molesting, even with therapy. I hated
myself for being too weak to remember my molestation,
fearing Sarah was suffering sexual abuse and I was not
helping her. And then there was my own daughter, Marie.
I was taught adults who've been sexually abused as children often abuse their own children unless they go through
therapy and heal. I lived in fear that one day I might wake
up and be an abuser if I didn't stop denying. Whereas I had
been physically affectionate with Marie prior to therapy, I
now hesitated to hug her and bathe her for fear I might
have some perverted impulse from my subconscious. Whenever I pondered dropping the whole idea that I had repressed memories, I thought of Sarah and Marie. What if I
was wrong? Tom was so sure. I had to stick it out until I
was strong enough to come out of denial.

In whatever direction I bounced, I was full of worry and
emotional pain. I felt an insecurity unmatched by anything
I had felt before therapy. I could barely concentrate and
found myself doing things at an ever-increasing pace. I was
totally preoccupied with coming out of denial. I did all of
the things I usually did as a homemaker and mother and,
with Tom's advice, I scheduled fun activities, but these
were but brief distractions. My thoughts were focused on
trying to heal.

I just couldn't figure out how to go about my life not
knowing whether or not my dad had sexually abused me.
It struck me as irresponsible to go about life as usual while
Sarah's safety was uncertain and dependent on my healing.
What was I supposed to do about my relationship with my
dad and the rest of my family? I'd cringe when the phone

would ring, hoping it wouldn't be one of them. What would I say? How would I act? Should I visit them anymore? I woke up thinking about my dad and went to bed thinking about him. The only thing I wanted to talk about was my repressed memories. John soon got burnt out. I told near strangers about my therapy. I was searching for someone who could make some sense of it all. No one knew what to make of it. Many thought it sounded off the wall, but wrote it off as a complex thing you must need a psychology degree to understand. Some of my friends cried.

I decided to phone my mom and see if she could give me some information. I told her my dad had molested me as a child. I tried to conceal my own doubts for fear she wouldn't accept what Tom said about doubts being proof it had really happened. I wanted her to take me seriously and I was afraid she wouldn't if she knew of my doubts. Her response was mildly hysterical. First she denied my dad was capable of such a thing, and told me that despite his faults, he never would hurt me like that. She was angry at Tom and accused him of incompetence and trying to fill his wallet at my expense. I maintained that my molestation had happened, but avoided going into any detail because I didn't know the details myself! I had kind of formulated a scenario based on my hypnotherapy experiences, but if pressed I would be at a loss to offer any solid information. That's why I was calling her — to try to get some information. She sounded confused. For a minute her anger turned toward my dad and she said if he really did that to me, she would buy a gun and shoot him. Then her anger was directed toward Tom again, and she defended my dad. She was torn by her doubts about the accusation and her trust in me.

I felt obliged to defend Tom, and I felt a familiar angry frustration with my mom, like when I was a teenager when my parents would put their foot down about some not very wise, teenage scheme I'd come up with. Now even though I was a young mother, she had still been offering me all kinds of advice. She said she did it only to be helpful and because she loved me. It registered with me as a put-down; she thought I couldn't take care of myself. Now talking to her on the phone, I thought to myself: "I'm an adult now! I don't have to listen to her!"

Tom and I interpreted her angry and jumbled response as further proof the incest had occurred. I had become competent at filtering my past, my thoughts, and my feelings through repressed memory theories. No wonder I hadn't told her about the abuse when I was a kid — look at how she responded now. She would have blamed me. Or maybe I had told her and she did blame me. I'd have to think about it and see which explanation felt right and try to do self-hypnosis to remember. She was most likely a sexual-abuse victim herself and was in denial. Before she could acknowledge my abuse, she'd first have to unrepress her own. It was common for sexually abused women to marry sexually abusive men. During later phone calls I asked her questions about her own childhood, looking for evidence that she too had been sexually abused.

My therapy took a twist when I started to get the strong impression that Tom was in love with me. He told me he watched for me in our neighborhood and when he saw me there, he wanted to run to me and take me in his arms. He said he enjoyed looking at me and he liked my feminine, gentle ways. He told me I had a beautiful mouth. He said he loved me in a special way because I appreciated him, unlike his other clients who just paid their bills.

At that time I had few friends. John and I were still trying to patch up our marriage. John's family lived in other states and my family was "sick." I felt very isolated and lonely. And then there was Tom. He adored everything about me. He gazed at me adoringly while I spoke. After a session we would embrace and he would tell me he loved me. If I reciprocated and told him I loved him, he'd sigh.

At first I idealized him. Whereas I had problems going into marriage counseling and was somewhat distrustful of myself, now, trying to deal with my repressed memories of incest, I had even more problems that I was absolutely helpless to deal with on my own. I needed Tom. He could make sense of my repressed memories. He was there to teach me how to overcome my denial and subdue my confusion. He was there to assure me that I was being heroic. Once I got the knack for applying repressed memory theories to my life, he was also a sounding board to validate my suppositions as facts.

To him everything about my therapy was going as expected and with his professional help, any day now I'd come out of denial. According to him, the only way to alleviate my emotional pain was to accept the truth that my dad had molested me. Tom was the gatekeeper of my mental health and I was continually praising him as such. He was always available to hear about my repressed memory pursuits, unlike John. I could even phone him at home.

He would see me in his office in the basement of the girls' dorm where he worked. It was in the evenings and I rarely saw anyone around. Our sessions were two hours long, once a week. One night the session lasted for three hours and I didn't get home until after midnight.

My idealization gradually turned into infatuation. I felt scared about my growing attraction to him, which came to include sexual attraction. When we first started meeting without John, Tom had told John and me that he was going to intentionally take the role of my dad and that I would probably become very attached, and maybe even attracted, to him. However, this attraction sure didn't feel like a dad/daughter relationship to me. Rather it felt like good old male/female attraction. It was clear to me that the attraction was mutual. I felt scared. I was starting to feel compulsive feelings. I loved John and our family and I did not want to be unfaithful. I told John about my sexual attraction to Tom, and of my fears. I decided to confront Tom. He denied having any sexual attraction to me, assuring me it wasn't that I wasn't attractive to him, but that he didn't want to compromise his relationship with his wife. As far as my feelings go, he said I was transferring my childhood sexual feelings for my dad onto him. He said that was a normal part of sexual abuse therapy and that he would help me keep them in check. This was another application of the repressed memory what-feels-real-isn't-real theory.

Tom had told John and me during marriage counseling that he was a cross between a boyfriend, brother and father to the girls at his school who had been sexually abused. He maintained this was therapeutic. He said some of them were very attractive; they would come for therapy, and spend the whole session trying to seduce him. He would patiently endure it and then gently reject their advances with the intent of teaching them how a real father/daughter relationship should be. Thus my suspicion of him and my sexual attraction to him were further proof I really had been molested by my dad.

John met with Tom and was given the same explanation. John too was confused about my repressed memories. As I was becoming increasingly emotionally unstable trying to deal with the revelation about my dad being a child molester, he felt it was critical to do his best to support me. He was primarily upset with Tom, however, because he was giving me marriage counseling without him present. Tom would side with me about the fights John and I had, which were occurring more than ever now and were primarily sparked by my therapy. Tom questioned whether John really wanted to be married to me. John no longer trusted Tom.

John was under tremendous stress. He felt that I was in danger. He was aware that I was becoming more distant from him, increasingly less self-reliant and emotionally unstable, while becoming more dependent on Tom. He asked me to find another therapist, but I refused. I threatened to divorce him if he wouldn't agree with me. I had been taught that dysfunctional people don't like it when someone gets well because they don't know how to have a relationship in a healthy way. I questioned John's motives for wanting me to leave Tom's therapy.

Tom became frustrated, defensive and angry. He told me he didn't trust John anymore and that John was undermining my therapy with his immature jealousy. I had grown as dependent on Tom as if we were the only two people on the planet.

John and I had turned to an older couple in our neighborhood for support. They knew Tom. The woman, Marge, told me something sounded really wrong about my relationship with Tom. Our friendship, based entirely on her listening to my problems, progressed, until one day she asked me if I'd be interested in visiting with her older sister, Maxine. She said Maxine believed she had a gift for healing through massage. It sounded odd, but I was willing to try anything to come out of denial. I made arrangements to meet with Maxine. One evening the two sisters arrived at my home. They set up a massage table in the middle of the living room. Maxine believed in auras. She ran her hands just slightly above John's arms and hands and couldn't say enough about how friendly his aura felt. She was particularly interested in him and her tone bordered on flirtatious as she visited with him.

Among other things, she questioned whether I had been sexually abused because I tensed up during the massage when she worked on the parts of my body near my pelvic area.

After the massage therapy, I took a bath while the two sisters visited with John. I then headed off for a session with Tom. The massage therapy was planned to precede my appointment with Tom, to help me be more open. As I drove away, I waved goodbye to John and Maxine standing together by her car.

Hours later I returned home to find John and Maxine sitting together on our couch. I immediately felt suspicious. She had left and then returned to our home, saying she had felt inspired to come back and tell John that God loved him. John, a normally stable person, had been worn down by the unrelenting stress from my therapy and had burst out sobbing. At the time I arrived, Maxine was discussing my therapy with John and telling him he needed to forget about me and to take care of himself. She went on to question me about my therapy, and to freely ramble on, offering us very personal information about herself including that she was a rape victim, had a therapist, that men she did massage therapy on usually fell in love with her, and that she had almost had an extramarital affair with a male friend. She was really weird. I felt very distrustful of her.

When I went out of town for a few days Maxine and

John continued to see each other. I was very disturbed by their growing friendship. He refused to stop being friends with her unless I found a new therapist. He compared his relationship with her to mine with Tom. Although I disagreed adamantly, I knew deep down he was right.

With our marriage hanging by a thread, I agreed to meet with John and our clergyman. He advised me to immediately find a new therapist and for John to avoid his "new friend" at all cost. The choice was clearly between my marriage and Tom. I had begun to have doubts about Tom's competence and I loved John; thus, I chose my marriage. Even though John told Maxine he didn't want or need her support anymore, she was quite hard to shake off.

And so that was the end of my therapy with Tom, but not the end of my battle with False Memory Syndrome. For with time, I was able to break free from the dependence I had on Tom, but the seeds of suspicion about my dad had been planted and unrelentingly nurtured by Tom. I believed I probably had repressed memories but had chosen the wrong therapist to help me. Shortly after I ended therapy, Tom moved away into an affluent area and set up his private practice in an office with other therapists.

I was scared off enough from therapy that I decided not to find another therapist. I hoped the whole repressed memory thing would somehow fade away. However, after having another baby, I had the blues. I was scared it might somehow be related to repressed memories. I was very confused at this point.

And then I got a referral to Ann, a therapist with a doctorate in marriage and family therapy. She was a middle-aged widow and mother of a large family. She said she had suffered sexual abuse from a relative as a child. She did not say if her memories had been repressed. She said that she,

too, like other therapists, had gone into psychology to try
to figure out her own problems. In time, it became apparent she was a feminist. Another model of emotional health,
she condescendingly told me she was just a little farther
down the road of emotional health than I was. I met her for
a 50-minute session once a week.

When I first met her, she claimed to be a faithful member of the same religion as myself. However, during the
course of my therapy, she made many comments undermining the religion's basic belief system. Once when a
woman commented to her about a certain therapeutic
practice she (Ann) used not being Christian-like, Ann defensively boasted that one could get more of Christianity in
therapy than at church.

I told her about my indecision over whether or not I had
repressed memories. She listened to the summary of my
hypnotherapy. She also had me do therapy with anatomi-
cally correct dolls, during which I was to act out a scene
between father and daughter dolls. She told me to say
whatever popped into my head. The idea was that too
weak to remember my own molestation, I'd be able to
express it from a distance through the dolls. Words popped
into my head about the daughter feeling responsible for
her father's sexual abuse of her. The emotions of guilt and
shame I felt as I did this were very familiar to me. I believed
Ann — that this was my inner child speaking about my
incestuous relationship with my dad. Shortly after this
experience I could remember what I had said, but it didn't
feel like anything more than a dramatic story I had made
up. Because the emotions felt real, did that mean that my
dad had molested me? I had heard that children often
blame themselves for sexual abuse they suffer. Accustomed
now to writing off my doubts as denial, I wondered if I was

keeping myself from remembering because I blamed myself for the incest.

Another therapy technique she used was to suddenly turn to me and ask me if my dad had molested me as a child. She told me to say the first thing that popped into my mind and not to try to think about it; just let it come. I couldn't help but think about it. I sighed and wearily said yes. Of course, once the element of surprise was gone after the first time she did this, I knew what was coming when she tried it again in the future. Once using the same technique, she spontaneously asked me what I didn't want to see when I was a child that caused my eyesight to weaken so that I had to start wearing glasses. Picking up on her implication that my bad eyesight was caused by my molestation, I gasped and felt spooked.

She too was convinced I had repressed memories of incest. She told me the fastest way to get at them was to do hypnotherapy. She talked with such confidence about hypnotherapy that it sounded like there was no way it could fail to bring me out of denial. Throughout my therapy Ann, as had Tom, repeatedly spoke of my coming out of denial as being just around the corner. Any day I could overcome my doubts that my dad had really molested me.

During other sessions, we did do hypnotherapy although everything told me not to do it. My body would turn cold and I could see the sweat literally in puddles on my palms. I felt afraid I was going to mentally walk into a horrible nightmare. Not knowing my own childhood history, anything could have possibly happened. I was afraid I might remember something so appalling, I would lose my mind. Ann told me these were the emotions of my terrified inner child. I had been reading a book she had recommended called *Reach for the Rainbow*. In it the author, Lynne

Finney, herself a therapist, describes her own once repressed memories of sexual torture inflicted on her by her
father. Reading it had so upset me, I had begun to wonder
if perhaps I wasn't coming out of denial because my abuse
had been torturous like hers.

The results of hypnotherapy were similar to my experiences with Tom. I "saw" some real memories of objects
from childhood and some real scenes of violence I had
never forgotten combined in a very disjointed way. There
were many gaps of time in which I'd sit and nothing would
pop into my mind. Upon Ann's suggestion, I'd mentally
strain until a thought popped into my mind. Nothing about
sexual abuse popped into my mind. Ann, like Tom, decided that all of this was related in some way to incest, but
that my mind was stopping short of the abuse to protect
me. Again, although some two years after Tom had diagnosed me with repressed memories, I was still emotionally
too weak to come out of denial.

Time and time again I questioned Ann as to whether my
symptoms couldn't be related to the traumas I remembered from childhood. Time and time again she firmly
rebuked me with the pet phrase, "Trust me! It happened!"

Getting nowhere with hypnotherapy, I worked on other
problems with her. Counter to her repressed memory
theories, the other therapy she did with me seemed logical
and practical and I resolved some problems unrelated to
sexual abuse. As a result, I trusted her. I tried to put the
repressed memory idea in the back of my mind and enjoy
the progress I was making, but I couldn't.

Still, I hadn't told my dad anything about thinking he
had molested me or even that I was in therapy. Ann
suggested attending one of her group meetings for adult
survivors of childhood abuse. She told me it would be

amazing how much "work" I'd be able to do "piggy-backing" off the other women. Having discussed with me my need for a surrogate family to take the place of my dysfunctional extended family, she also mentioned that friendships often develop among group members.

I told her about my experience with Tom. She urged me to report him to a licensing board, even giving me the phone number to call. She said that mine wasn't the first story she'd heard about him. She told me that he had repeated the incestuous relationship I had had with my dad by isolating me and using me to satisfy his own emotional needs. We discussed the likelihood I hadn't come out of denial because I had become unsure about whether or not I could trust Tom.

I called the appropriate office and expressed my concern that Tom had serious "boundary" problems. The man who took my call assured me my case would definitely be investigated and said it sounded like Tom was in love with me. He instructed me that because his office was so back-logged, it might take several weeks before I heard back from an investigator, but to be patient. No one ever contacted me. After quite a run-around, I was arrogantly told over the phone that the investigator had found no justifiable reason to warrant an investigation.

Group therapy met one night a week for two hours and forty-five minutes. The group was made up of eight women, all of whom considered themselves survivors of some type of childhood abuse — usually sexual abuse. Those who came into group for other forms of abuse, with rare exception, always came to question whether or not they had been sexually abused as children and had repressed their memories. Even those who had never forgotten their childhood sexual molestation often came to question if they had repressed memories of molestation by a different perpetrator also.

Some of the group members, upon Ann's suggestion, brought a stuffed animal or a doll to group to comfort their inner child, like a security blanket. Ann mentioned that sometimes she'd find her roommate, another therapist, curled up with her stuffed animal at home when she was feeling particularly down.

With rare exception, all of the group members had previously divorced, divorced during therapy, or were working on a plan with Ann to divorce in the near future. I too came to question whether I should divorce John. I was struggling to function as an individual, let alone in our relationship. I questioned if I'd heal faster without the marriage problems weighing on me, too. I loved him, however, and decided not to.

The majority of the group members were seeing or had seen Ann for individual therapy, which is where they had originally heard about her group. Some had come back after a significant period of time. Some were seeing a different therapist individually. The vast majority of the group members also attended a session of Ann's assertiveness class for which she charged an additional fee – some attended more than once. Ann enthusiastically recommended this class during group therapy. Something about it didn't appeal to me and every time Ann brought it up with me, I felt like she was a salesman trying to sell me something. I was uncomfortable with her hefty charges for therapy in the first place, although I was more fortunate than some because my insurance was covering part of it. In early 1992 she was charging $70 for fifty minutes of individual therapy and $20 a night for group. There was usually a waiting list to get into the group.

Group followed a regular format. The time would start with a "brag session" during which each woman would tell of something good that happened to her the past week. After that, three or four women would work with Ann for twenty minutes each about some problem, usually a relationship problem. If Ann thought the woman had acted in a dysfunctional way, she'd respectfully guide her into seeing her mistake. If she thought the other person involved in the problem had functioned in a dysfunctional way, she'd dramatically belittle that person. Once a woman questioned her on this, asking why she didn't empathize with others outside the group, only with group members. She said her loyalty had to be to her clients and that it was her job to validate them. She said if the person outside the group was her client, she'd validate and gently guide them too, rather than belittle them. Her double standard left me with an uneasy feeling.

In the group therapy I came to understand what she meant by "piggy-backing" off of the other women. When one group member would talk, it was sure to remind someone of something they were working on and bring out corresponding emotions. It was very upsetting for all to listen to the horrible and shocking stories of the women who had never forgotten their childhood molestation. It was heart-wrenching and emotionally draining. At times all of us would be crying and there was a box of tissues for us to pass around. My heart went out to these women who had suffered at the hand of those who were supposed to love and protect them, but I did not relate to their experiences.

The women I related to were the ones trying desperately, like myself, to remember the repressed memories they had been diagnosed with, so they could heal. They too expressed doubts about the validity of the memories they had recovered during hypnotherapy and other treatments. They too felt angry at themselves for being in denial. They too were estranged from their extended family. They too were confused, frustrated, scared, and in tremendous emotional pain. They too were having trouble functioning in their day-to-day lives. One woman told me it was therapeutic for her to hear about my repressed memories because she had trouble accepting hers as real, and felt more confident about hers after hearing mine. I knew what she meant. Sometimes in or after group, women would compare notes about their therapy for repressed memories of sexual abuse such as hypnotic experiences and bizarre fears. The similarities were mind boggling. There had to be something to the repressed memory theories if all of us were having similar experiences.

Some of the group members uncovered grisly repressed memories during group. One therapeutic technique for this was "make-up-a-story." A woman would describe unpleasant emotions she had felt at some time during the past week or during a nightmare. Ann would ask her to sink into the emotions, really letting herself feel them. She would ask her to describe where she felt them: in her stomach, in her throat, in her pelvic area. Then she would tell her to go back to a time when she was a child and had felt the same way. Sometimes the woman would remember an experience that appeared to be related to her current problem. If she didn't, Ann would tell her to make up a story — say whatever popped into her mind without thinking about it. No matter how the woman strained, she often couldn't come up with anything and would apologize in frustration. But sometimes she would start emotionally describing a scene of sexual abuse. Ann, at times obviously disgusted, would then have her do "chair work." Chair work involved putting an empty chair at a distance from the woman. The woman then pretended the perpetrator was sitting in the chair. Ann would tell the woman to pretend she was a little child again and to talk to the perpetrator about her feelings about the victimization. She'd also tell her to talk as her now-adult self about her anger and her victimization. Ann would dramatically supply the sentences and the woman would repeat them. Sometimes the woman would take off on her own, expressing her pain or anger at the perpetrator. Sometimes she'd come up with questions she wanted to ask him. The woman would then sit in the empty chair and pretend to be the perpetrator addressing the allegations against him. She was to speak as the perpetrator, saying whatever thoughts popped into her mind without thinking about it. Then she'd go back to her own chair. Sometimes the woman would use a padded club and pretend to beat or kill the perpetrator as she struck the empty chair with all her might. Afterwards the woman would look exhausted, distraught, and often embarrassed. Ann would ask her if she needed a "reality check," during which the woman could ask any or all of the group members if they thought she was crazy or had looked stupid. Everyone always responded kindly with words of commendation and support, and often disgust for the perpetrator. Once a woman described a scene so bizarre, Ann looked uncertain, but the woman describing the scene insisted it had happened. Ann nodded her head.

Another technique used to uncover repressed memories was based on body memories during which a woman would link some bizarre physical sensation to an event of sexual molestation. After observing this in group and reading about it in self-help healing books, I started noticing a tightness in my jaw that would come and go. I wondered if this was a body memory of my molestation. As Ann had taught me, I tried to sink into my emotions when I was feeling the tightness. One after another, a train of thoughts went through my mind building to an energetic climax with the final thought being that I was gagging as though someone were forcing my mouth open. I decided to see my dentist. After an examination, he asked me if I was under extreme stress. He told me he suspected my tightness to be a common stress-related condition caused by clenching my teeth. Upon his advice, I started checking myself throughout the day to see if I was clenching. Sure enough I was. I had also been experiencing daily headaches and shortness of breath that my physician suspected as stress-related. I was chronically tired.

Many times after group I would approach Ann and apologetically question her about her repressed memory theories and why I wasn't coming out of denial. She grew impatient with me and started avoiding me after group. Afraid of her rejection and feeling inadequate, I asked her in individual therapy what she thought about me as a person. It was very frightening to think this person who knew not just my outward self, but my very soul – my most private thoughts and fears – might not like me. She assured me she respected me for my courage and commitment. She said other women had come to her, learned of their repressed memories and never came back. They were, unfortunately, in denial.

I spent most of my effort in group working on problems unrelated to the repressed memories. But when the other women would talk about their repressed memories or never-forgotten memories, I'd start feeling guilty. This was especially true when they would emotionally speak about how their adult relatives had known they were being abused, but did nothing to help them. I felt like scum thinking about my father's step-daughter, Sarah. Would she grow up to hate me?

I spoke privately to Ann about my guilt and worries. She told me she feared Sarah was in real danger. She encouraged me to report my dad to his state's child welfare services so they could investigate him. She said they would interview Sarah's schoolteacher and others. I told myself that I had to stop denying and protect Sarah. I just couldn't report my dad, however, and I hated myself for it. I just couldn't decide if my dad had really molested me or not. I had remembered some repressed memories, but they didn't feel real. The serious possible repercussions in my dad's life would most likely be permanent. Ann told me it was my decision to make, although there was no doubt in my mind that she thought reporting him was the healthy thing to do. She said I had to take care of myself first. I felt cold-hearted and selfish.

I phoned my paternal grandma who was like a mother to me and tearfully told her that her son had molested me. She tried to comfort me and told me that everything was going to be okay. I repeatedly asked her if she believed me, and she said she did. In my journal I recorded how her love for me was a true love because she believed me. Whether or not she believed me was a measure of whether she really loved me. According to the repressed memory theories, it also was a measure of her own emotional health, whether or not she was sick and in denial. She asked me for details about what had happened and I vaguely told her a few bits and pieces from my first hypnotherapy experience. I again was careful to conceal my doubts. My grandma couldn't understand how I could have been molested without her knowing about it. We were very close as I grew up and I often confided in her. She was accepting and warm. Over and over she asked me why I hadn't come to her and told her. She also wondered out loud how my dad was capable of such a thing. He had no history of anything even vaguely similar. She asked what could make a person do such a thing. I hesitatingly told her that usually the man had been abused himself as a boy. She had been a stay-at-home mother and wondered out loud who could have hurt him. She gasped and said that my grandpa, who she'd been married to for over fifty years, would never have done such a thing. She asked me if I wanted her to confront my dad, or if I would do it right away. She said she was worried about him and she needed to get him some help as soon as possible. I could hear the agony in her voice. I told her I would confront him as soon as I felt able to, and swore her to secrecy. I reviewed our conversation with Ann over the phone right after I hung up from the call to my grandma. Ann enthusiastically offered me her congratulations for facing my fears.

I questioned Ann as to how my grandma could have mothered me as a child with so much respect and kindness, but to have mothered my dad so poorly that he turned out as a molester. After all, the premise was that this was a learned inherited illness. She said it was possible that my grandma has a problem with men and not with women. I began to analyze my grandparents, looking for evidence of dysfunction.

I also felt guilty in group when there was talk of a woman outside the group who had recanted her repressed memories of sexual abuse and had reunited with her family. She was spoken about as being weak and uncourageous.

It was now approaching four years since Tom first diagnosed me with repressed memories of incest. Time was flying by. I was running out of things to work on in group. As a young mother I could see many other places, besides therapy, where I could be spending my money. My relationship with my extended family was growing increasingly distant. I hadn't been home to visit them in a couple of years. Sometimes I'd make snotty comments to my dad on the phone in a passive aggressive way. I always felt so confused after talking to him because I could not feel the "perverted dad" in him. Ann said maybe he had repressed his memory of the incest also, or maybe he had been drunk during it. I was taught that alcoholics frequently sexually abuse children.

In group therapy I had listened intently as Ann explained her philosophy about therapy. She said the whole therapist-client relationship was about trust. She said the therapist asks her client to take risks. She compared this to being told to jump off a cliff, saying the client may feel the risks are life threatening, literally like being told to jump off the edge of a cliff. All her instincts may tell the client not to jump. However, only if she trusts the therapist that all will be well and jumps will she heal. She also had added that those clients who were willing to trust her the most were the ones who healed the fastest and ended therapy the quickest. I was upset. I had jumped off the cliff so many times I had lost count. Rather than feeling healed, I felt like my sense of well-being lay smashed in the ravine below the cliff. Was I ever going to be happy? Was I ever going to come out of denial? Other women supposedly had done it. What was wrong with me?

I discussed with Ann the consequences of never coming out of denial. She had no doubt my repressed memories would follow me and at some time come out. I wanted it over with once and for all! I decided I had to get back into individual therapy — I had been only attending group — and once and for all stop denying. I was desperate.

Determined to come out of denial, I began hypnotherapy again. This time it went differently. Once or twice as a teenager my mom had been in the room when I was dressing. I remembered feeling uncomfortable. Ann and I decided to "check out" my mom with hypnotherapy. Could it be my mom who molested me, not my dad? Or could it have been both? With the cue of going back to a time when my mother touched me in a way that made me uncomfortable, I "saw" a few scenes of violence with my mom that I had never forgotten and that I had been thinking about before hypnotherapy. Pressing me, Ann asked me if there were any other times. As with my other hypnotherapy experiences, I drew a blank. I tried hard to let something come, but to no avail. I pleaded silently with my mind to please show me the abuse. A thought came into my mind that my mom was lying on her bed. I visualized it. There was a gap of time. Nothing was coming. A thought popped into my mind that my mother was sexually abusing me. I visualized it and shuddered. The face of the person I'd visualized was foggy, but the thought had been that it was my mom. The scene I visualized had looked familiar in a way. Actually, I couldn't decide if it was my mom or my husband who I had seen. If it was my mom, perhaps that's why she acted so odd when I had told her about my dad molesting me. She might have been afraid I was going to remember what she had done to me. I was even more confused now.

After this hypnotherapy, I felt very uncomfortable. I felt the need to assure Ann, who was holding her open collared blouse closed, that I wasn't a lesbian. She nervously told me that she knew I wasn't. I told only one or two people about the visualization. It didn't seem socially acceptable to talk about as my dad's molestation. I had feared that some of the acquaintances I'd told about my therapy would fear I might hurt their children since it was an inherited type of mental illness. My fear was compounded to think what the reaction would be if someone thought my mom had also molested me.

I told John what I'd seen in hypnotherapy and we both cringed. We'd really have to protect our children from my family. John had started questioning his own family also. Some of his sisters had some peculiarities. Could they have been . . . ?

If in one lifetime I had experienced all that I remembered, plus sexual abuse by both of my parents, I told myself I had to be near crazy. My fear of losing my sanity was growing. Preoccupied with the repressed memories about my dad, I tried to put this latest development on the back burner, and there it simmered, always in the back of my mind. I pondered if I was in denial because I'd been through so much and my inner child feared I'd lose my sanity if I came out of denial. I had questioned why I could remember the traumas related to my dad's drinking, but not the incest. Maybe to not repress the incest would have actually caused me to go insane as a child? Repression was talked about with reverence as a God-given gift to spare children emotional pain until they could understand their abuse and heal as adults. But why could some of the women in group remember their childhood abuse and others repress it? The unsatisfactory answer was that everyone is different and comes from different circumstances.

Throughout my therapy I was plagued by a variety of fears. Feelings of intense insecurity, grief and loss would overwhelm me. There was no telling what would trigger them, be it a movie or a song, or even hearing someone speak affectionately about their family. Ann again urged me to create a surrogate family referred to as a "family of choice" — friends of various ages who take on the roles of mother, father, sister, brother, cousins, grandparents — to fill my longing for a family.

Many of the fears I had never experienced before, and were bizarre. During an overnight visit with my mom, while I was in therapy with Tom, I had a bizarre fear that she might try to kill me while I was sleeping. On different occasions, I experienced spells of anxiety during which I felt in physical danger. Once after telling some acquaintances about my repressed memories, I feared the police were coming to arrest me. In the daytime, home alone with Marie napping, I'd get spooked and feel like my dad was hiding in my house or following me when I walked. At night if John came into our room while I was asleep, I'd wake up and scream. According to the repressed memory theories, these bizarre fears were said to be the actual feelings I had felt as a child living with the horror of incest. I felt sorry for myself. Ann had me pretend my inner child was sitting in a chair and directed me to tell her I would protect her and never let those things happen to her again.

I also had fears relating to John and my children, aside from my fear that one day I might wake up and be a pervert. I feared John's death and our children's safety. I went to the extent of having my will changed stating that under no circumstances should my children be alone with my parents. I'd have anxiety attacks in bed when I'd lie down to sleep involving my children being kidnapped by one of my parents or by a stranger, or of John and me dying and there being no one else in the world to love them. I told myself I couldn't live if my children had to suffer the things I had endured.

There were times of such extreme misery that I questioned whether life was worth living. At these times I clung on to my spiritual convictions like a life raft. Throughout my years of therapy, I prayed, and I prayed to God to let me come out of denial. In all of my confusion, pain and fear, there were times when I fell on my face on the floor sobbing, and pleaded with Him to help me and to protect me from losing my mind. I prayed before therapy sessions that He would guide me to the truth and consecrate my sincere desires to be a good person and to help Sarah. There also were times when I screamed out at Him as to why as a child I had to go through so much, and why my life was just one obstacle after another. Why wouldn't He let me remember my molestation?

I began having dreams of being raped, of my mom being raped, and of being sexual with women I had had close friendships with throughout my life. Ann told me the dreams were symbolic of the repressed memories of incest in my subconscious mind. This was a good sign in my healing. She encouraged me to concentrate on my repressed memories and other problems right before falling asleep. She said my subconscious mind would work on them while I slept. She directed me to keep a notebook and pen at my bedside to record my dreams, saying they would reveal details to me about my molestation and my denial. While still groggy in the morning after first waking, I was to do self-hypnosis. She said that was a good time to try to access my subconscious mind.

Whereas I had done self-hypnosis once in a while in therapy with Tom, in my current desperation, I was now doing it once a day. I was taught that everything that had ever happened to me was on file in my mind. Now, daily, I would talk to my mind like it was a computer, saying pull up such and such a file. During the former times, telling my mind to show me my abuse, I had visualized a variety of bizarre scenes without any details of sexual abuse. As Tom and Ann taught me, I interpreted them as being symbolic of my repressed memories. For example, I pictured myself as a girl badly beaten up. From that I deduced that as a girl being unloved and sexually abused, my body felt sick. I used these various impressions in formulating the scenario of my incestuous relationship with my dad.

In self-hypnosis and in hypnotherapy, sometimes in the expressed pursuit of remembering being sexually abused, I "saw" scenes of violence from my childhood related to my dad's drinking and physical abuse of my mom. They were scenes that I had long since forgotten. There was absolutely no doubt in my mind that what I "saw" had actually taken place. These were without a doubt real memories. When I mentally strained to develop them into a more detailed account with whatever following thoughts popped into my mind, the authenticity of the details felt uncertain. I had never forgotten that during my childhood, my dad had at times beat my mom while he was drunk. I had forgotten some of the specifics, although I had never previously seriously tried to remember them. These scenes I "saw" of violence in hypnosis felt real to me, unlike the thoughts that popped into my mind during hypnosis of sexual abuse that I would visualize. I also had been having "flashbacks" since childhood that I clearly related to my dad's violence toward my mom. I felt a quick onset of fear when I'd smell beer, particularly the combination of beer and cigarette smoke, of which my dad's clothing reeked when he'd come home from a tavern. Inadvertently stumbling upon a fist fight or boxing on TV would fill me with panic.

In the course of my therapy, I came to question not only if my dad and mom had molested me, but also if my uncles, paternal grandpa, and maternal grandpa had molested me. My suspicions were primarily based on picture-like flashes of faces and objects I saw during self-hypnosis and hypnotherapy. This list does not include the other family members and friends whom I questioned because of their "symptoms" or the "symptoms" of their adult children. The suspicion of one of my grandpas stemmed from the following experience: As I was trying to fall asleep in bed, a picture flashed into my mind of knickknacks at my grandparent's home. Following a therapy technique Ann used, I then imagined myself slowly walking through the rooms of my grandparents' home, analyzing the way I felt in each room. In a storage room in the basement, I had a nervous feeling. Ann was confident "something" had happened to me in that room.

I'd do self-hypnosis whenever I'd feel an intense emotion. On three such occasions, in self-hypnosis, I visualized my dad sexually abusing me. The first time I was feeling very depressed. I sat down on my couch and began self-hypnosis. I "saw" a picture of a motel room I had stayed in as a girl with my parents on a vacation that I had never forgotten. The thought popped into my mind that my dad was on top of me on a bed. I visualized a foggy picture of this. I "saw" a photo-like flash of fabric which I recognized as that of a blouse I wore as girl. The motel and the fabric felt like a real memory to me, but not the abusive part. I felt doubtful about the validity of this memory, but thought this time there was physical proof to overrule my denial. I ran to get my childhood photo album. I knew there were photos of this vacation in the album. I had studied them along with the other photos many times, looking for a facial expression or an inappropriate pose that would tell me about my repressed memories. I flipped quickly to the photos and sure enough – there I was, wearing the exact blouse that had flashed in my mind. But, although I was wearing the blouse in a photo taken in the same state, it was taken years after the first time we had visited the state and stayed at the motel I had visualized. Now that was odd.

My repressed memory therapy had crossed over into much of my life. During times of intimacy with John, sexually abusive images would pop into my mind, and sometimes in the dark, I'd think John was my dad or someone else. It became predictable that after intimacy, feeling victimized and lonely, I'd sit and sob. "Healing" books warned that this often happened. This was testimony of my dad's molestation. John struggled to understand and to endure.

Healing books were an important part of my therapy. In group Ann recommended, along with *Reach for the Rainbow*, the book *The Courage to Heal*. She said it was good if you were okay about some of the lesbian stuff in it. Off to the bookstore I ran. *The Courage to Heal* was sold out, but there was a copy of *The Courage to Heal Workbook*. Relieved, I bought it. As I began reading it, I got spooked. According to the repressed memory theories, I was accessing my inner child. On page seven of the workbook, I had been warned and had even underlined "If you start to feel things you haven't felt before, or if you start to feel overwhelmed, know that you are not crazy. You are feeling. You are remembering. You are receiving images from the past." With my reaction and the overall despair I felt as I read, I decided I had to have repressed memories.

Everything Tom and Ann had told me about repressed memories was validated in the workbook. The author of the workbook, Laura Davis, in describing the details of healing, described much of what I'd been experiencing almost to a tee, especially my denial. On page 224 I read:

> It is often difficult for survivors to maintain the belief that they were abused. One day you may be certain that you were abused, and the next you may find yourself doubting whether it really happened or questioning whether your experience counts as abuse. This process of doubt and reaffirmation, doubt and reaffirmation, is a natural part of the healing process. If you have doubts, it doesn't mean you weren't abused. It just means you're not yet ready to live with the consistent knowledge that you were abused. Sometimes this process can take years.

I went to group and told Ann my reaction. She smiled and nodded her head and said it was a powerful book.

One evening as John and I were talking, we reminisced about our experience living in another city. I felt sad just thinking of the city. I remembered being afraid when John had been working out-of-town while we lived in that city because a rapist had attacked women in our subdivision. I couldn't remember much detail about our time there. It bothered me. I had been taught that gaps of time for which one doesn't have any memory is a common symptom of repressed memories of abuse. I went to group therapy with the goal of understanding why I felt so sad about the place and couldn't remember much about it. Using one of her regular therapy techniques, Ann asked me what would have been the worst possible thing that could have happened to me there. I wasn't supposed to think about my answer, just let it come.

I accepted that whatever popped into my mind would

be a fact. The first thought that popped into my mind was that I had been raped. As I said it out loud, I cried out and near hysterical, began shaking and sobbing. I couldn't bear it. On top of everything, now I had repressed memories of being raped less than four years earlier! Was I a walking amnesic zombie or what? The precarious state of not knowing my own childhood was terrifying. Not knowing what my history was only a few years prior was indescribably terrifying. Over and over I screamed and begged, "No, no, it didn't happen!" Ann took my hand and firmly told me that it had happened. She asked me if I remembered any details of the rape. I told her I searched my mind for more details; a picture flashed into my mind of a hand trying to push open a door. After my turn, a couple of other women "worked" as I sat numbly in my chair, tears running down my face. After group Ann told me I was going to have a rough week ahead of me and that I could call her at home if I needed to. I threw my arms around her neck and sobbed. She was stiff.

Another group member offered to drive me home after the meeting. She, herself a rape victim, said she never would have believed I could have forgotten being raped if I hadn't reacted so emotionally. She said no one could fake that much pain. At this time, however, although I was filled with anxiety, I did not feel like I had ever really been raped. It didn't feel real. I felt the same sadness about the city as I had previously, and there was my subtle sense of violent victimization, but now I felt spooked as well. Was I in denial about this too? As mentioned earlier, I had been afraid of the rapist who had attacked women in my subdivision while John was out of town. I remembered being nervous about going outside, and calling the police to report an odd man I'd seen in the neighborhood. I even moved a desk against our apartment door at night. I had been really afraid. Currently at night when I went out alone, I still was very cautious. Other women I knew didn't act so cautiously when they were out at night by themselves. Maybe my fears were a symptom that I had really been raped. Maybe it had happened.

I went home and told John that I'd been raped. It was the oddest of feelings. I felt like I needed to act like a woman who'd just been raped, but the feeling just wasn't there. John was noticeably racked with grief. He blamed himself. He should have quit his job and not gone out of town. Tormented, he asked me over and over why I hadn't told him.

I called Ann and arranged to meet her at her office with the intention of doing hypnosis to unrepress the rape. I was very grateful she was willing to meet me on such short notice. Under regular circumstances, I had to schedule appointments to see her weeks in advance, she was so booked. She finally decided not to take on any new clients.

Before my appointment, I tried self-hypnosis at home. I visualized that hand again trying to push open our apartment door. The memory of the hand felt kind of real and there was an element of surprise feeling to it all, but I couldn't decide if it was John's hand one of the times we were playing around, if it was a rapist's hand, or if I had just made it up.

During hypnotherapy I drew a blank. Ann was disappointed and asked what happened with the hand pushing the door. I visualized the hand and went on to emotionally describe a rape scene. As with my other experiences with hypnosis, the scene was made up of real memories unrelated to sexual abuse, thoughts that popped into my head with emotions of powerlessness, fear, and shame that felt real, and many gaps. In the gaps, Ann asked me specific questions like whether or not the rapist penetrated me. With no thoughts coming into my mind, I'd say whatever seemed likely to fit in with the thoughts that had popped into my mind.

Throughout this experience, my mind kept telling me that I was making up a story. My mind had interjected with such comments during other hypnotherapy experiences also. At times I was aware of my mind trying out a variety of thoughts and emotions in attempting to make a scene flow from those non-sexual-abuse, picture-like flashes that did feel real to me. I questioned Ann about this. She told me it was very normal, and that as my subconscious was describing the repressed memories, my conscious mind, still in denial, was coming in and out.

Because I had unrepressed the rape and was having trouble functioning, we questioned if I was in "flooding" — a time of high anxiety when memories flood out. I had read on page 69 in *The Courage to Heal Workbook*:

> Most survivors have suicidal feelings at some point in the healing process, usually in the emergency stage. If they didn't feel suicidal before they started to heal (many survivors have been suicidal their whole lives), the intensity of the healing process may cause them to contemplate suicide for the first time.

My fears of losing my sanity were intense. I went home and told John I wasn't going to be able to function in a normal way for awhile because I was entering flooding. I warned him I might even become suicidal. Like a self-fulfilling prophecy, I felt so emotionally overwhelmed and confused, I began to panic. John didn't know what to do. Did I need to be hospitalized? Overwhelmed, he angrily expressed that he didn't know how much more of this he could take. I began having fears of leaving my house.

In anguish John asked our clergyman to come to our home. He sat next to me on the couch and listened to me retell the horrible news. Expecting him to offer his sympathy, I was shocked by his response. He looked me right in the eye and said, "Maybe it happened and maybe it didn't, but you can't go on like you are." At first I was angry. Tom and Ann had taught me that anyone who questions the validity of my repressed memories is denying my pain and doesn't really care about me. As I listened to him further, however, his words touched my heart. He didn't say he thought I hadn't been raped. Rather he pointed out my obsession, telling me I couldn't go on like I had been and that I was obviously heading for a nervous breakdown. Despite nearly four years of preoccupation with coming out of denial, I hadn't realized I was obsessed. Ann and my fellow group members certainly didn't think I was obsessed. To them I was in a healing process. I had even come to believe I was a hero saving my external family from an abusive cycle. My clergyman told me I was needed in the present and that John needed a wife and my children needed a mother. He reminded me of the value of positive thinking. This stood in direct opposition to Ann's direction to sink into my pain as a method of overcoming it. I felt a long forgotten sense of inner peace. I was smiling and laughing before he left.

A day or two later, however, I started feeling angry at him again. How dare he say I should not deal with the pain of being raped for my family's sake. I went for therapy the next week. I told Ann I was angry about the counsel my clergyman had given me. She became furious and told me he had no right to deny my pain. She said he should stick to his own profession and leave the therapy to her. We were both unaware at the time that psychology had been his undergraduate major. I had even been warned in healing books to avoid at all cost any psychiatrist or the like who expressed any doubt about the validity of my repressed memories of sexual abuse. It was dangerous to my emotional health and healing to allow anyone to "deny my pain."

I had brought with me a list of frightening experiences I had had unrelated to sexual abuse — graphic movie and TV rape scenes I had seen, some during childhood, and stories I had very recently heard on talk shows that were all unmistakably similar to the thoughts that had popped into my mind during hypnosis. One by one I apologetically read them off to her. I asked her if the rape I'd described in hypnotherapy couldn't be related to these things I had seen and heard. Again she insisted I was in denial — hiding from the truth.

I told Ann about how hard I was trying to come out of denial and how I was totally stressed out. She told me not to pressure myself and that when the time was right, I would come out of denial. I felt a twitch of anger. Wasn't four years long enough?

John couldn't take much more of my obsession. He asked for a date when I'd be done with therapy. I told myself he was trying to control me and that he was putting himself before me. Ann and I were angry with him. How could he demand such a thing?

I myself, however, was pretty tired of the whole thing too. I knew Ann's therapeutic techniques like the back of my hand and was correctly anticipating the particulars of how she'd do therapy with the other group members. By this time I had discussed all of the childhood traumas I remembered, and most of the stress John and I had been through together. I felt at peace about them. I had long ago run out of problems to work on independent of my repressed memories, and had just been waiting to come out of denial. After my brush with a nervous breakdown, I decided to stop trying to come out of denial and to get on with my life. My anxiety subsided and my fears calmed. Denial or no denial, enough was enough. I'd have to cope with the confusion about my family and all of the surrounding heartache. I'd have to create that "family of choice" and learn to live at an emotional distance from my real family. I'd been doing both for four years and had started getting used to feeling orphaned. Living far from my family made it easier. I told Ann I was going to be leaving group in the near future.

Tying up loose ends, I met individually with her. I for the who-knows-what-time asked her why I still was in denial. She looked at me with a straight face and said, "I don't know. Maybe it (being molested by my dad) only happened one time. What do you think happened?"

After four years, three and a half of which I was in therapy . . . After me asking time and time again whether my "symptoms" couldn't be related to the childhood traumas I remembered . . . After being rebuked time and time again with, "Trust me. It happened!" . . . After all of the emotional agony, time, and money I had put into obediently trying to come out of denial . . . SHE WANTED TO KNOW WHAT I THOUGHT HAD HAPPENED!

I was shocked. What? Just one time? Which one was the one? I numbly rambled off the scenario I had pieced together based on the repressed memory theories. I knew no more about what had happened during my childhood than the night Tom diagnosed me as an incest victim. I knew a lot less

about my childhood than I knew one second before Tom
diagnosed me as an incest victim. I didn't know what had
happened during my childhood. I guessed I'd never know.

I ended individual and group therapy with an expression of thankfulness for the growth I'd made through each,
and a silent hope that I wouldn't be haunted for the rest of
my life by my repressed memories.

One morning about two weeks later, as I was leaving the
house, I noticed a newspaper to which we did not subscribe
on my porch. Curious, I took off the rubber band and skimmed
the front page. The leading story was about something called
False Memory Syndrome: therapist-induced false memories
of childhood sexual abuse. My heart started racing. I read
faster and faster. I felt an incredible sense of freedom and
jubilation, like I had been stranded by myself on a desert
island for years and someone had finally found me. I could
clearly relate to what I read. It was the first time I had heard
anyone, besides my mom and my own mind, question the
legitimacy of the therapy I had received for repressed memories of sexual abuse. Now for every doubt I had had that I had
repressed memories of an incestuous relationship with my
dad, there wasn't some omnipotent response to discount my
own sense of reality, and pacify me. Rather, there were
common sense answers that validated my every doubt that
my dad had ever molested me, let alone any one of the
multitude I had suspected at one time or another. Miraculously, I finally woke up.

For every ounce of ecstasy I felt, I also felt intense anger.
I asked myself what kind of science is this? I had taken a
four year casual stroll through hell carefully catching all
the sights with two highly paid "model of mental health"
escorts prodding me on from the door of the pit. Isn't
there a word to describe forcing an individual to reject old

beliefs and accept new ones by subjecting him to great mental pressure? The Oxford American Dictionary suggests the word BRAINWASHING.

Is it possible that educated, licensed, mental health professionals intent on becoming part of the financially lucrative and ego-building crusade to slay the world of child abusers could inadvertently brainwash an intelligent client into believing she was sexually abused as a child by people she loves? Could books, TV talk shows, and TV therapists who zealously sell "healing" contribute? Could other women who had no idea they'd ever been sexually abused until they went into therapy, who have been convinced to embrace their natural doubts of it all as proof of the reality of their victimization, contribute?

I and many of those who love me have suffered indescribably during my battle with False Memory Syndrome. And for what? There is an ugly irony in the destruction wreaked by those who proclaim to be teachers of healing. What kind of science is this?

As my family and friends gather around me to help me pick up the pieces of my life, where are Tom and Ann? I know where they are. They're sitting in their offices slaying the world of some other appointed child molester and destroying a family.

I'd like to close my summary of my battle with False Memory Syndrome with an excerpt out of my journal written about three and a half years after I was diagnosed with repressed memories of incest, and six months before I ended therapy.

"I feel like yuk. All this stuff. I don't know if I'm making it up, going nuts or incapable of ever processing it out. I really fear I'll never get it out and will live the rest of my life in pain of wondering . It is so hard to be at the

mercy of my brain. Why can't I just say show me and it will show me, or remember and I'll remember. The uncertainty of it all feels like it's going to kill me. It is like waiting to go into labor. Nine months big and pregnant, uncomfortable, preoccupied. Just waiting for pain, then relief and joy."

Let there be no uncertainty that I thank God for watching over me, and credit Him with guiding me into the truth that my dad never molested me. I thank Him for His Son Jesus Christ whose teachings transcend man's shallow acclaimed wisdom, and bring me enduring peace as I apply them in my life. And I thank John for riding the storm with me.

There is an unmistakable moral to my experience. God-willing I hope it echoes off this page into the hearts of all those who stand dizzily on the edge of a cliff a therapist has created for them. It's the message on a sign on the edge that reads: WARNING! DON'T JUMP!

The Truth Set Me Free

I am a survivor – a survivor of sexual abuse, physical abuse, emotional abuse and spiritual abuse. I remember all of these abuses. I have total recall of them. I was not abused by my parents. I am also a survivor of another type of abuse. This abuse is from a therapist. It is something that will anger me for a long time. I'm not sure when the anger is going to stop. I have gone through a lot of crises in my life. I have total recall of all the bad times, all the times I was molested, the times I was raped, by whom and what the circumstances were. But the person who really victimized me the most, I believe, was my therapist. I am going to relate the story of that abuse.

I started going to my therapist in June 1991. I had many problems in my life – eating disorders, an overactive gag reflex, anxiety and paranoia. If you open the cover of *Secret Survivors* by E. Sue Blume, you will find her "Incest Survivors' Aftereffect Checklist." I checked off every single symptom except one. I didn't believe I had a split personality, but every other one some seemed to fit – some applied to me now and some applied to me at times in the past.

I was in therapy for approximately three months before a big tragedy hit me in my life – the passing of my father. I loved him very much. His death drastically affected me. I couldn't sleep and I was overcome by some disturbing physical symptoms, which I found out later, after consulting a doctor, were indications of anxiety. He put me on medication for anxiety. The symptoms of paranoia and panic, such as shaking and the feeling that something was lodged in my throat, all subsided as I continued to see my therapist.

But somehow things escalated. In an attempt to explain all my symptoms my therapist started putting things together about my life. All at once, she hit me with a bombshell — a big one. This bombshell was supposed to be the reason for everything — for who I am today, what type of person I am, and the reasons for the disorders in my life. Everything that was wrong with me was all because of this one reason. She said, "I know everything about you and, anywhere between the ages of four and six, you were sexually abused as a child by your father." I was in shock. I trusted her very much. I am one of those people who has a very trusting personality and she knew that.

I believed what she said. Yet there is a difference between being gullible and being stupid. I had doubts, and I questioned her many times. I referred to the checklist in *Secret Survivors* and I asked her, "Couldn't these things be true about me because I was molested several times between the ages of nine and 14?" I really was molested and had always remembered it. The first time, I was nine. I was at a shopping-center carnival and met a man who seemed very nice. He took me behind a store and we walked and sat down and talked. He touched me and took my hand and put it down his pants. I was really scared. I never repressed or forgot that incident. To this day it makes me sick. Another time, I went on a vacation with some neighbors, but I didn't know they were nudists until they took me to a nudist camp. I wouldn't take off my clothes and some adults tried to get me to do some sexual things. One molested me while I was sleeping and this really scared me. I had also been raped by a strange man when I was 13 and the physical pain from this had been horrible and lasted for months. I had developed a fear of sex for at least five or six years. I feared that sex might feel the same as the rape did.

There were other abuses also.

I said to my therapist, "Are you *sure* that all these signs and symptoms aren't because of that?" She replied, "Oh no. We have top psychiatrists throughout the United States who put these symptoms together. If you check off a certain quantity of these things, then it means that you were sexually abused as a young child." She meant that this was gospel truth — it was carved in stone. Okay, that hit me. That must be the answer. This was why I have been the person I was all my life. This was why I had a problem with obesity, with an overactive gag reflex, with claustrophobia, with *everything* on that list except for multiple personalities. So I believed her. She increased my visits from once a week to twice a week. She knew that I would be needing that therapy. After hearing something like that, I suppose anyone would seek more therapy.

I got worse. In my therapist's eyes the ball was now rolling and recovery was to begin. With this new knowledge — that I had been abused by my father when I was small — healing could begin. I went faithfully to therapy twice a week. As the weeks went by, my anger and hatred towards my father got worse. The pain of this was unbearable. How could he do this to me? Every week I would hear more. My therapist talked quite a bit. Sometimes, I think, she talked more than I did in therapy, which is something I now realize that good therapists don't do. A good therapist is there to listen carefully and to let you figure out your own answers to your own problems.

The feelings continued to get worse with therapy. My parents' wedding anniversary passed and I got very depressed. The therapist said to me, "Isn't it strange that you would be feeling this way at this time? It's like your father was 'your husband', and it was 'your marriage'. Isn't that a coincidence?" I would think, "Well, it does make perfect sense." I very much believed in everything she said. Her word was gospel. I questioned my mother about childhood trouble I had. I was desperate and wanted answers. She said that I wet my bed when I was very little. It started when I was around four or five and didn't stop until second grade — another sign of abuse. Again, it all added up. I also remembered that I used to be afraid of many things and I used to be scared of the devil.

One time, I was relaxing with my husband and we were lying side by side. As we embraced in each other's arms I suddenly envisioned my father there. I closed my eyes and thought it felt really strange. I had been forewarned by my therapist that there would possibly be a flooding of memories, and that this was the healing process that she had mentioned. I shook my head and thought, "This is ridiculous. Why would I be thinking about my father? I feel very safe at this moment. If my father had molested me then why would I think about him when I am feeling safe?" I lay there with my eyes closed and, in a twilight state, said to myself, "Okay, it's time to face your devil." My therapist had told me that the fear of the devil that I had when I was small was because I actually feared my father. As I was lying there, I became extremely fearful. I opened my eyes and started to see a shadow. A voice inside of me pushed on, "Face your devil. See who it is." I wanted my husband to wake up and snap me out of it. I shared this with my therapist and she said, "You know who that was, don't you? You weren't ready for the memory to come back. The reason why it happened is because you were calm and lying on your back, just as you were as a child, and your father came and violated you." She told me that the memory of my father molesting me was trying to enter into my consciousness and that I would not allow the memory to emerge. Of course I believed her because it made perfect sense to me.

I have a daughter who was molested at the age of four by a man who was a friend at the time. He is now in jail for the crime. I had gone out one night to help a friend with an emergency and at the time I had no reason to fear he would ever harm her. It turned out this guy was very obsessed with me. I believe now he molested her to get back at me. Following this very traumatic event, I suffered a nervous breakdown and I was hospitalized for about two months. The fact that my daughter was violated so terribly crushed me to the core, and there were a lot of other things happening in my life at that time which contributed to the breakdown. My daughter was very traumatized and went through a year of therapy. But she remembers *everything*. She remembers it in detail even now, five years later, and talks about it to me. Even though he had threatened her and told her not to tell, she told me about it the next day. I know that she will never forget or repress the fact that this happened to her.

When this happened to my daughter, I was riddled with guilt, depression and shock. As I discussed this past event with my therapist, she told me the reason I broke down so badly was because, not only was I experiencing the pain of my daughter's abuse, but I was subconsciously re-experiencing the occurrence of my own abuse at the same age. Again, it made perfect sense.

As time went by, the anger grew stronger and so did the hatred and the bitterness. I shared it with some friends and siblings. I asked questions. I wanted so badly to find out the truth, but my sisters and my friends begged me not to tell my mother. Thank God I did not confront my mother. I believe now that the Lord spared my mother, as I think it would have destroyed her if I had said that dad molested me. At the time, though, I didn't really care much about what my mother felt or thought because it was often a topic in therapy about how uncared for and unprotected I was and how unloved I must have felt by my mother. My therapist always told me that mother was not there for me. The hatred toward my mother started to grow.

Because my therapy was based on unreality, I had lost the time to grieve for my father. At times I was encouraged to feel glad that he died because of what he had supposedly done. My right to grieve was taken away from me by my therapist. She cultivated hatred for my father in me that was supposed to be "healing." The natural cycle of grief did not take place. My symptoms of depression grew stronger, my anxiety increased, and the anger, bitterness and resentment toward my mother grew and grew. My therapist said that I didn't need my mother and it was okay to give her up in my mind. She said that I had other people in my life who could replace my mother or my father or sisters. She or others could replace my real mother in my life. She said that anyone who did not support me in what I believed had happened to me just didn't care. If anyone doubted me, then they weren't my friends and weren't to be trusted. Fortunately, my sisters and my friends are intelligent and, knowing what a trusting and gullible person I am, they realized that I had been easy prey to these lies because of the circumstances in my life, both present and past.

What is therapy? Why do people go to counseling? People go to counseling to get better, to heal their wounds. But what happened to me was that I wasn't healed and I didn't get better with therapy. I was taught that being angry was healthy. I want to say that no one gets better with bitterness and hate and anger. I am here now with a clear mind and I can tell you there was no healing in my therapy. I went along with something that I didn't even remember, an abuse that never happened. How could anyone be healed by something that isn't real and that desperately rips them apart inside? Only after I came to believe that my father abused me did I begin to feel suicidal and this was not because I was trying to protect his memory or anything like that. I could not handle the conflicting feelings day after day, night after night, and I would call my therapist to tell her about it. She would say to me, "You are having a flashback. Memories are going to start returning. Do not be afraid. This is healing." I was living a nightmare.

I was not healing, I was being destroyed – all over an event that my therapist said happened, an event that I didn't even remember. I was blind, I was fooled and I was deceived. You don't have to be a stupid person in order to be deceived. People from all walks of life can be deceived, especially by a person whom they trust. While I was going through this, a few of my sisters and friends picked up *Secret Survivors* and they all started to wonder if they, too, might have been abused even though they didn't remember it. They too checked off many things on the list. They got very upset for awhile, and almost believed it too.

I wasn't only deceived by a therapist, a woman whom I deeply trusted, I was deceived by an evil book called *The Courage to Heal*. This book will tell you that if you have any number of symptoms, it means you were abused and molested even if you don't remember it. I never got those memories. I had little flashes of things that I imagined and I would call my therapist. She would put it all together for me and tell me what my flashes meant.

I depended on my therapist for everything. She became more important to me than my husband and my family. She became more important to me than myself. In my mind she was all that I had. She controlled me and she manipulated me. She became my God. Call it what you want to call it, but never call this "healing." If I had been healing, I wouldn't have become as sick as I did.

My therapist sent me to an incest survivors group. It was quite astonishing to see a group of about 12-15 women in which more than half of them said, "I am a survivor of sexual abuse but I do not have the memories yet." To me, it made perfect sense because so many others believed it too. It was the one and only reason for all my life's problems. I believed it all. Every pain in my life, every hurt, every fear must have had its origins in this unremembered abuse. The pain was so intense. But still my therapist told me this was part of the healing process, and I got sicker and more desperate.

During this time, I had an opportunity to move from the suburb where I lived. However, I would not move because I could not leave my therapist. She had that much power over me. I desperately needed her. Week after week she spoke about how I was robbed, how I was cheated, how I was violated, and about that poor little child inside me. She explained how all these bits and pieces and dreams meant that my father had molested me. She would interpret every dream to mean that I was abused and neglected. This went on twice a week for about 10 months. During the latter part of these months, I became suicidal. I felt that there was no reason to live and I would sit on the side of my bed and think of ways that I could end my life. I lived in constant fear of a memory surfacing at any time, and I'm here to tell you that there is no true healing that is such a living hell! Any time I would have certain feelings, certain sensations, my therapist would connect it all to the abuse. I could not sleep for fear that the memory was going to come forth. And this was supposed to be a "healing process." My healing process consisted of getting angry with the people I loved the most, and living in fear, dread and paranoia.

I had always been a spiritual person and so had my family. I truly believe when the blinders fell away, a miracle happened in my life thanks to the prayer and support of my family. I could no longer tolerate how I was feeling. I woke up one morning in tears. It was Father's Day. A loud voice inside me said, "You were not abused by your father. It's a LIE. It's all a lie!" I believe now that it was the Lord speaking to me in His loud voice. About a day or two after my realization, I was told about False Memory Syndrome (FMS) by my sister. I called the FMS Foundation and I started to cry when I read the information they sent that explained everything that had happened to me. I began to look at it all with new eyes. I became aware, relieved, and crushed inside knowing full well I had been deceived, *again*.

I called my therapist and said it wasn't true, that I no longer believed the horrible things about my dad. She told me I was "in denial." When I told her that I no longer needed her, another whole set of problems arose. She was very intimidating, and she wouldn't accept that I was well. I no longer needed her services and she didn't like that at all. She didn't want to let go. She told me that I had to come in and talk about this with her. My sisters got very upset because they knew that going to see her would not be in my best interest. They knew she would try to talk me out of the truth once again. I finally felt good — as though a ton of bricks had been lifted from my shoulders – because I was no longer living a lie and walking through hell. I didn't need any more of her misguided therapy. This relief, that I at last knew the truth, was what I had been searching for the last 10 months. The phone conversation with my therapist was very disturbing and I was beginning to wonder at this time "who needed whom." I knew I was well because I finally felt very well, but she would rather have me stay sick. I tried to make it easier for her because I didn't want a confrontation. I told her that she had helped me enough and had served her purpose in my life. She asked me, "What have you learned from therapy?" This was almost comical. I paused and thought to myself, "Think of something quickly." So I replied, "I learned some good breathing techniques to aid anxiety." I could tell she knew I felt strong and well, but she didn't like that. If she had been a good therapist, I think she would have been happy with what I told her and with how well I was feeling. But instead she said, "It's a cop-out."

I have not confronted my therapist personally because I am afraid of what she would do. I have heard stories of people who have been forcibly committed to mental institutions for less, and I wouldn't put this past her. I look back on what happened to me now and believe that the therapist used a form of mind control. I believe that she – unintentionally and without malice – used suggestion on me. It was just like a one-on-one cult.

I was involved in a religious cult once, many years ago, and this was much the same. It was like walking a thin line between the truth and lies. Just like the leaders of the religious cult, my therapist was mentally controlling, and getting out was very difficult. In both experiences I was told this is where you need to be, and everything makes perfect sense. The members of that religious cult told me that they were the only ones who really loved me; my therapist made me believe that she was the only person I could trust. When I woke up and made the connection, I became very frightened. The therapist told me, "I am going to keep your time slot open for the next two months because you are going to be needing it." I have been out of her cult for about 11 months and I have no desire to see her. The more I grow and learn, the more I realize the wrong that she did. I was mentally hurt more during the therapy and during the false memories than at any other time of my life. I was indoctrinated by the leader of the cult years ago, and then I was indoctrinated by a therapist. I couldn't see the forest for the trees and I isolated myself from my family and friends.

My therapist had a master's degree and I believe that she must have gone through some kind of "New Age" training. I had been to other therapists in my life before her, and none of them ever mentioned an early unremembered molestation as the cause of my problems. If this is what therapists are learning in school, then I will never seek any kind of counseling or therapy again. This is a sure way to keep a person ill, and dependent on therapy for the rest of his or her life.

Sometimes I am angry with myself for believing my therapist's lies. My husband has been angry at me for believing such foolishness, and I feel a lot of shame over that. I am a trusting person, which has been an asset at times, but this time it was my downfall. My only counselor now is God, and He is the only one I can really trust. I am no longer easy prey for any psychotherapist. I have been affected by this, but God has been good to me and I believe that He intervened in the nick of time. I really believe that

I would have died if God had not opened my eyes when He did. I always pray for wisdom; the Lord knows my weak points, and he hears me.

I am now beginning to grieve for my father, which is what I should have been able to do after his death. My real memories are of a loving, caring, nurturing father. The loss of my father has left a tremendous void in my life. He was a very affectionate father and husband. My parents regularly displayed their love and affection for each other through-out their 37 years of marriage. Sitting next to my father, hugging him, talking with him, I always felt protected. I now think the way this twisted therapist tried to distort my memories of this wonderful man is sickening. He might not have been a perfect father, but I am sure that he never sexually abused me. I miss him very much.

It has taken me some time to go back and tell my friends that I was wrong, but I need to clear his name because he is an innocent man. This has been a "real" healing process for me to say, "Guess what — it's not true." They all said, "Thank God. I didn't ever believe that he did that anyway, but I didn't want to say that to you because I was afraid I would lose all contact with you and your friendship." Some cried with relief. I feel very sad about the way this therapist not only affected my life, but affected my husband's life, and my family and friends as well. I feel much wiser for the experience. I have a sense of peace now and I don't believe that I will fall into the hands of deceit ever again.

To other women in therapy I say: If you're feeling worse, and feeling uncomfortable and feeling fear, reconsider your therapy. If you are being told things that don't feel right in your gut, a light should go on inside your head to warn that something wrong is happening. Listen to your family and friends because they are probably right about what is happening to you. Look at your feelings. Be aware. If I could do it all over again, I would listen to myself and to my feelings and ask, "Why am I getting worse?" When you are going to someone for help, you should begin to feel lighter, not heavier. Every time I came out of my therapist's office I felt as though weight was being added on to my shoulders, not taken away. There was always another thing I had to think about; there was always that fear of when the horrific memory was going to emerge. You aren't supposed to start feeling fearful and suicidal from therapy. It isn't normal. If you are being told that bitterness and rage are "healing" then you need to take another look at what is happening in your therapy. In a healthy therapist/client relationship, there should never be any suggestions from the therapist about anything as an answer to all your problems. This "New Age" cure to remember imaginary sexual abuse from your childhood is not right. Books such as *The Courage to Heal* and *Secret Survivors* are misleading many women and tearing apart families. I know; I experienced it.

One of the things my therapist used to say to me repeatedly was, "You were robbed." Yes, I have to agree with her now. I was definitely robbed. Robbed of grieving for my father whom I loved dearly, and robbed of my life for almost a year. I'll close by saying I'm very well now and very sound. My father in heaven has already seen to that. No one can ever tell me I don't give the credit where credit is due. Thank you Lord for giving me everything — personal power, love and a sound mind!

—Gerilena Spillios
(pseudonym)

Misplaced Trust

This story is dedicated to my precious daughter, Jennifer, who went through this nightmare with me and loves me anyway.

With the exception of my former counselors, the names in my story are real. I decided to use my real name for several reasons. First, I feel I will be better able to help those who read this, and as a result, they might realize their therapy may be causing them similar problems and want to come out. In addition, I lived each and every moment of this nightmare. The gray hairs on my head were earned through every incident in my life, especially this one. This story is mine. I do not wish to share my experience under a pseudonym. My attorney's name and his firm's name were used with his permission.

Monday, November 18, 1991. My appointment is for 4:00 p.m. I arrive early, but then, I always do. Simpson & Dowd, a law firm in Dallas, specializes in mental health issues. I am to meet with Skip Simpson, Attorney at Law, along with several other families who have been polluted by a perverse group of therapists. Here I am, meeting an attorney with a family that I heard for years were Satanists. Imagine my shock when I read their story in an article in a popular Dallas magazine. False accusations, devastation, hurt, pain, humiliation, the separation from their only daughter, a daughter they felt much love for. A daughter I knew well. A young woman in the same sort of circumstances I was in. Needing a reason why she felt so "abnormal." A daughter I watched accuse her parents before the rest of the group, to her therapists, to anyone who would listen, just as I had done. Now here I was, joining forces with her parents to help put an end to this senseless destruction of the family system.

As I look back, I wonder how it got this far. How could a relationship with a therapist become the sole focus of my life for four long years? How could I have sold my soul to a mere human being? A man, who it turns out, has issues in his own life that he has never dealt with. A man so sick he needed me and other women to stay "sick" in order for him to excel. I trusted this man with my innermost soul. I shared my dreams with him, confessed my sins to him. Steve was my mother, my father, my brother, my sister, my best friend, my husband, boyfriend, decision maker, choice maker, teacher and pastor. He had become everything to me. If Steve said it, it was so. My life became so enmeshed and intertwined with his life, my ability to think for myself disappeared. I thought what he wanted me to think. I believed what he wanted me to believe. I became what he wanted me to become. How in the world did I allow therapy to become the most important activity in my life?

It began on Friday, December 20, 1985. Steve was supposed to be a specialist in treating eating disorders and man, did I have an eating disorder. Since I was ten years old I would eat and then force myself to throw up. By the time I got to Steve I was nearly 32 years old. That means for 22 years I had been forcing myself to vomit. When I began therapy, I was binging and purging sometimes 15 to 20 times a day. I would gain weight, lose weight, then gain weight again. I abused laxatives, diuretics and diet pills. I couldn't deal with feelings of any kind. Any emotion would trigger a binge, then a purge. Food was my best friend and my worst enemy. My parents did not know I had bulimia. I didn't even know it had a name until 1981. I read an article in the paper and it said that this disorder was coming out of the closet and was a widespread problem. At first I was relieved because I had felt so alone and different from other people. Then I became frustrated because there seemed to be no one out there who knew how to treat it. Then I heard about Steve. He was supposed to be the expert.

I was told: "Steve will save your life." "Steve is your answer." "Go to him, trust him, do what he says and you will get well." Only God knows how badly I wanted to get well, how badly I wanted to be normal.

I began my journey with Steve by sitting on his couch and spending the next hour with him staring at me. He was overweight and balding but seemed very confident and sure of himself. He seemed to be looking right into my soul. It was very uncomfortable. What few things I was able to tell him did not even seem to faze him. He seemed cold and uncaring and unfeeling. I told him I didn't like him staring at me and he asked, "Why is that?" I said, "Hell, I don't know, I just don't like it." After that he only seemed to stare harder. I left my first session feeling confused but I was so desperate and determined to end this terrible disorder that had plagued my life since childhood that I was ready to do anything to get my life in order. "Trust him, believe him, he is your answer." So I put everything into my therapy. Although much of the time Steve was staring, he also did something else. He was listening. I was so hungry for someone to listen to me, just listen. To hear what I had to say, no matter what it was. Nobody had ever done that. If I felt something, I might be told, "You don't really feel that way." "That's not the 'right' way to feel." "You don't really think that." "If you think about those kinds of things, you're gonna make God mad." "He's ashamed of you, I'm ashamed of you, you should be ashamed of you." So God, before you stomp me in the ground for having a "bad feeling or thought," could you maybe tell me how not to have them? Now I had met a man, a parental figure, an authoritative figure who would listen to anything that I had to say and not once did he say, "You should be ashamed." Needless to say, he won my trust. I began seeing him every week, then twice a week. Soon into my therapy Steve would tell me to close my eyes. He would make me keep them closed throughout most of the session. Before long, I was saying anything and everything that came into my mind. There were thoughts, ideas, images, feelings and I had never shared them with anyone until now and this guy was listening to me. I never believed that I was worth listening to. My heart was so empty and lonely and for so many years the only comfort I had found was in binging and purging, and then binging and purging some more. The endless cycle. Gain weight, lose weight, eat and vomit, eat and vomit some more.

In the beginning of my therapy, I brought with me some very real hurts and disappointments. I had lost one of the most important relationships of my entire life. My life seemed out of control. I had external problems that caused me great distress. Steve didn't seem too concerned with those. The pain had to be deeper, had to be buried, "repressed." For me to have a "death wish" of the magnitude I had and to be so self-destructive, I had to have repressed something so horrible and so traumatic that only a lengthy therapy, hypnosis and hard work were going to make me better, according to Steve. Well, by this time Steve controlled me. He had bought my loyalty and dependence by giving me the one thing I was starving for: attention. It was attention with absolutely no boundaries.

Week after week, session after session, eyes closed, under hypnosis, going deep within myself, strange images began to appear. At first they were images of a tiny little blonde child with the biggest, saddest eyes I have ever seen. Steve said it was my "little girl," my child within. It was as if I were sitting on a chair as high as the ceiling watching her. Steve wanted me to reveal to him each and every image or movement the "little girl" made.

My first "flashback" came while I was home vacuuming the floor. I had been to my therapy session earlier in the day. All of a sudden, I broke out in a sweat and I couldn't breathe. I was in a total panic. I was unsure of what age I was or what time period I was in. I had images of a young boy holding a pillow over the face of an infant. It was a terrifying experience. I called Steve and he "walked" me through the "flashback." After I was calmed down, he literally put me to sleep on the phone.

My next session was very uncomfortable. Steve kept drilling me: "When are you going to accept the fact that your brother tried to kill you?" I argued that it wasn't reality. It was just a dream, a nightmare. This could not have happened, not in my family. Over and over he said, "You'll have to accept the fact that your brother tried to kill you."

This "flashback" got Steve's attention. All the ones after that held his attention. The images in my head got more and more bizarre. I began going to therapy more frequently. I was going to the group room to write, a place where Steve said I would be "safe." Every flashback I had was judged to be actual, factual data from my past. Every dream, no matter how bizarre, was what had happened to me. The images grew. The scenes became more and more frightening. Had all of this junk been hidden in my mind? Were these horrible scenes things that really took place in my family? Was this reality? What was reality? I got caught up in a full circle of flashbacks. They would reach out and snatch me up and engulf me in them at almost any moment. I cannot say where my logical mind was at this point. The flashbacks took control.

Steve said for me to ask my doctor for Xanax, a mild sedative. I did. I began taking it, as Steve put it, "to take the edge off." I was swallowing them left and right. Soon I needed two, then three, then more. I was playing Russian Roulette with my life and I didn't even understand it. I had never played these kinds of games with my life before. Why now? I would take a few too many pills and end up in the emergency room and guess who I called? Steve.

Now, you have to remember, what was I starved for? What was Steve giving me? The worse the flashback, the more self-destructive I was, the more attention I was getting from the main source for all things in my life. Steve kept telling me, "You have to get worse before you get better." Well, I was definitely getting worse. I was over-medicating, vomiting more and more and my life seemed more out of control than ever before.

In addition, no matter how many times I over-medicated myself or ended up in an emergency room, the doctor kept prescribing Xanax to me. Not only Xanax but numerous other pills. Pills to sleep, pills to not be depressed, pills to "mellow out my rage." Pills for literally everything. My therapist would goad me, make me angry and push me to the edge and then the doctor would step in and medicate me so I wouldn't be in such a rage. The group in the hospital would get on a subject and harass me until I was livid and then the nurse would come get me and put me in a little room because I was angry. The nurses at the hospital said they had to take the "control" away, yet when I did what they said I was tagged with being "over-compliant." The messages were extremely confusing to someone who had grown up with confusing messages. My mind was apparently gone, although at the time I was convinced this was the only way I would ever get well, and be a whole person.

I lost control on many occasions, and Steve was the only one who could calm me down, make me "think right" again. I wanted more than anything in the world to be well, to be "normal." In spite of the still small voice inside of me, doubting, questioning, and wondering, I trusted this man to know the truth. That voice would soon fade for some time to come. I believed in him so deeply. I began telling other people, "Trust him, believe in him, he will make you whole." I believed in him so completely, in 1986 I spent five months coordinating a retreat for women suffering from bulimia. In a five-month period, I talked with over 350 women suffering from this disorder. I wanted them all to know about Steve. The retreat was called "Hope for Hungry Hearts" and was held in a beautiful wooded retreat campground in east Texas. There were 77 women and one man who came to this weekend retreat to hear the "truth." Of course, Steve lectured. If Steve said it, I believed it.

During my therapy I wouldn't admit that I was desperately dependent on him, even to myself. I was unusually strong and independent in some areas of my life, so to have to admit that I was dependent to that degree and controlled so heavily by this man was unthinkable.

It wasn't long until the "repressed memories" of child abuse began to come up. The visions in my head were of severe physical and sexual abuse. The images were so incredibly bizarre but seemed so real. My picture of my family became distorted. Was it the drugs that the doctors had me on? Was it television shows or traumatic events I had witnessed over the years, or was it actual memories? I just don't know, but Steve said they were fact, and to deny them meant that I didn't want to get well, I was "in denial," I was running, I was "protecting" my family, I was staying sick to "cover up" for my family. He had all the answers. He was always right.

Looking back, I can see a clear resemblance of my flashbacks to the movie "Sybil" and the last horror film I ever went to as a teenager called "Deranged." It was only after filing a lawsuit and looking into things more clearly that those movies came to mind and I saw a correlation between them and the "memories" I had while having flashbacks.

I was put into group therapy. This is where my therapy team grew to include Steve's partner, Dave. I did not want to go but Steve said I was just transferring the fear of my family onto the group. He said I must go. At first we all just talked and I found a common ground with the other girls. Then, slowly the group emerged into a room full of "victims." We began as Eating Disorders, then Sexual Abuse Victims, then Incest Victims, then Satanic Ritual Abuse Victims, then Multiple Personality Disorders. There were endless tags placed on us. All of the women systematically had similar flashbacks, uncovered repressed memories and severe abuse. It was really eerie at times. Each week we sat in a group and the stories were enough to make a strong stomach sick. One woman might have a flashback one week about her parents or someone else in the family and then the next week another one would have a similar memory come up. My mind became so confused and tormented. It wasn't long before my own flashbacks got even more bizarre. There was "group sexual abuse," a dead man hanging from a rope — my grandfather having killed him — being sexually abused by animals and much more.

Most of the time, members of the group were advised to stay away from their families and/or anyone who challenged their therapy. There was so much anger aimed at all of the parents. If someone had some doubt that a flashback or memory was reality, Steve and Dave would goad them, then the whole group would join in — "You're in denial," "You want to stay sick for your family," "You don't want to get well." This type of input from people we trusted so very much kept us enmeshed in their treatment program.

There were many times when a group member was instructed to write to her parents (the perpetrators) very hostile and mean letters, divorcing them, accusing them of terrible acts they had commited. These letters were coached by the group and group leaders. They were always read out loud to the group to get the support.

Steve instructed me to write to my mother and list every mean thing that she had done to me, what I believed she had done at the time. Then, he stood beside me reading every horrible word in the most hateful, hostile tone imaginable. I was standing there with balls of clay, throwing them into the wall. The louder and meaner he read, the harder I threw those balls. It was a very intense session. This was supposed to release my repressed anger. After sessions like this one, I was exhausted.

I now believe if you constantly fill your mind with hate, it will spit out hate. Being placed in that situation, I had my mind filled with a constant flow of vile images: drinking blood, killing babies, sexual abuse of everything imaginable, incest, torture, murder, you name it.

I would like to note here that out of all the women in my

particular Monday night group, nearly all of them have since realized their "flashbacks" were not in fact reality. Most won't speak up. I'm not sure if it is loyalty to Steve and Dave or maybe fear, or maybe just lack of guts. Whatever it is, it makes me angry because I believe if they would be outspoken, more women would come out of this delusional state much quicker.

One woman who was one of my favorites accused her family of being Satanist. She "divorced" her parents and her in-laws helped her through the toughest parts of her therapy. She had some of the most horrible flashbacks of a baby, supposedly her twin, being hung in a tree. She questioned Steve and Dave about the fact that her birth certificate had "single birth" on it. Steve said that the coven had people who took care of all of those things to cover up. Later on in her therapy when she seemed to be doing well, she said she wanted to drive to the nearby state her parents lived in and talk to them about all of her "memories." Steve was livid in group and kept trying to talk her out of going. "What about the coven?" he said. He was furious and yelled at her. This beautiful, petite woman said, "I don't care, I've got to find out." She went home to her parents, talked everything out and made peace with them. Shortly afterward, her mom died of a heart attack. I talked with her just recently and she told me when she went home that time there was absolutely nothing to substantiate her claims of satanic ritual abuse. She said to me, "You know, I live with guilt each and every day of my life about what I did to mom."

My relationship with my family became extremely troubled. My sister would not allow my nephew to spend the night in my home. I looked at my parents with suspicion. Steve had me believing my mother had been trying to kill me for years. Not in an obvious attempt, but in the things she would do for me. I was bulimic. If Moma bought us groceries and they were easily ingested "binge foods," Steve convinced me it was to kill me. At one point, I took some badly needed groceries back to her and asked her if she was trying to kill me because there were some cookies and chips in the bag. I looked at her with disgust. I suspected her every move, her every motive. I questioned every remark. I missed many family functions and when I did attend, I was cold and suspicious of everyone there.

For years, I was consumed with suspicion, anger, fear, confusion. Could anyone in the whole world be trusted? Even my pastor, who was also my dear friend, became suspect when he began "doubting" my therapy. I was losing everyone and everything who meant anything to me. Police officers who were friends of mine and who I worked with (I am a Dallas Police Department employee) would tell me I was turning into a "pill head." They said I was not acting normally, that I was depressed all the time, that I had changed. I argued back that I was sick and "had to get worse before I got better." The group members were the ones who I talked to, the ones I was friends with. Steve and Dave would tell me, "The group is your 'new family'. Move away from your family, divorce them, they are dangerous, you will never get well living near them." They even wanted me to quit my job of fifteen years because they said I was trying to shut my "little girl" up with the violence that was part of police department work.

Desperate to be normal, feeling abnormal, I was in a constant rage for years, furious with every single thing that ever happened to me, or that didn't happen to me. My family members had become my enemies, people placed on this earth to destroy me. I could not distinguish memory from reality. Nothing seemed real anymore.

Now, in all honesty, my parents made mistakes, plenty of them. But let's be real, is there any human being, parent or child, who hasn't made mistakes? I know I make them every day with my daughter Jennifer. I believe that the key is to acknowledge them, ask for forgiveness and move forward. The question is, in my case, were my parents intentionally trying to destroy me? I don't think so, although this is what my therapy team, my group family made me believe. The simplest things that my family said were twisted to be "evil."

Their response to accusations I made would not have mattered. If they said nothing, it was because they were guilty. If they proclaimed innocence, they were trying to hide something. If they didn't remember something the way I remembered it, they were in denial. There was always an answer. This was ingrained into every conversation and thought I had. I was told to read books about evil, sexual abuse, dysfunctional families, co-dependency, and on and on. Some of the required reading included *People of the Lie*, *Courage to Heal*, *Healing the Shame that Binds You*, *On Becoming a Person*, and *The Child Within*. I "lived" therapy. It was always on my mind. When I wasn't at therapy, I was calling my therapist. When I wasn't talking to my therapist, I was thinking about my therapy. The entire ordeal consumed every ounce of energy I had and every penny I could get my hands on. All of this was "necessary" for me to "get well." Again, remember, Steve repeatedly told me, "You have to get worse before you get better." I continued to get worse. I honestly believed what he told me. He was, after all, the "expert." I, on the other hand, felt abnormal, unimportant to anyone. I was desperate.

Never underestimate what a desperate person will do. No matter how bright or intelligent a person may be, if desperate enough, he or she can fall into the same pit I fell into. I had worked in the jail for the city of Dallas since I was 19 years old. I knew the correct name for every charge in the Texas Penal Code, the Penal Code number and the penalty class. I could tell you what kind of time you could get for nearly every crime listed in our penal code. I could catch an error on an arrest report with a simple glance, book a drunk in 30 seconds, and usually determine the elements of arrest if I chose to read the report. I mastered county and city computers. I could research a criminal history and "find" just about anyone. I know literally hundreds of police officers and most of them would do nearly anything for me. Before entering this therapy situation, I had many commendations and was nominated by my sergeant for Non-Sworn Employee of the Year. After getting into therapy, I was still good at what I did, but my work, the officers, my daughter, everything took a back seat. By the time I left therapy, I had expended all of my sick time, my vacation time and come close to being fired over one of my stays in the hospital. Was I getting worse? I would say so.

I believe the hardest part of this type of therapy is living through the flashbacks. To this day, I still do not understand what was happening to me. Sometimes I wouldn't know where I was or how old I was. It was frightening and left me empty and drained. I would literally "feel" pain of the things I was seeing in my head. My mother became my sexual abuser, then my brother and grandfather. The sexual abuse was vivid and seemed so real. Ordinary objects terrified me because they were sexual abuse tools in my flashbacks. It started out with simple fondling or molestation, it ended with torture, torment and indescribable pain.

I would emerge from one of these "flashbacks" and feel tremendous rage. At times, I believe, I was homicidal. My nostrils would flare and I would throw things, rant and rave and scream. I used to pray, "God, why did you let these things happen to me? What did I ever do to deserve this kind of pain?" Confusion at this point was a way of life to me.

My anger was constant. My therapy also included "rage reduction." It consisted of throwing things like clay or bean bags, ripping phone books, beating with bataaka bats and shrill screaming. I personally got the most relief from breaking glass. I would drive down the street and throw coke bottles into the ground. When they would shatter, it was like a sedative. These things were supposed to decrease my "repressed anger." In essence, the more anger I expressed, the madder I got. I was in a constant state of rage. After a flashback, Steve would have me direct that rage at Moma. He literally hated my mother. He would insult her, distort everything that she said or did. Once, she wrote a check for my therapy because I simply did not have the money and he tore it up in my face. "I don't want her money," he said. He then added it to my bill. My mother knew better than to speak against Steve. I just would not tolerate that. He was the expert. He was going to "save me." I wish someone had saved me from him.

I spent four years with this therapy team. After four years, I wanted to do more. I wanted to be more. I was at the point of feeling like I would never get well. There was no hope for me, I was too far gone. I just wanted to make the best of my life. I called Steve on December 20, 1989, exactly four years after I had walked into his office. I said I wanted to write a book about my experiences in the jail. I had contacted an author of a book about the police and felt sure he would help me. Steve was real quiet. I asked him if he thought I could do this, "Wouldn't it be exciting?" I waited, listening like a child waiting for approval from a parent, and the words that followed stung me to the core of my being. "You are not through with the flashbacks."

Disenchanted, angry and frustrated, I terminated my therapy. I grieved so much that I had to enter therapy with another counselor to get through it. I went to her, telling her the same stories I had come to believe in therapy about my family. I spent the next 22 months still convinced these things had happened to me. I would have doubts, confusion. I might "just know" it didn't happen in the daytime and at night go to bed wondering why it happened. I went to bed every night believing my moma wanted me dead.

In October, 1991, I picked up the article on a family who had been accused of horrible abuse by their daughter in therapy. I was at Kroger supermarket and never left the parking lot until I had read every single word. I was in therapy with their daughter. I knew her. I had listened to her pain and suffering. Now, I was getting another side of the picture. Steve and Dave insisted these people were Satanists, the cruelest, meanest people in the world. They had committed indescribable acts on their children. Could Steve and Dave maybe have lied to me? Lied to us all? I was glued to the article. Then, after I read it, I drove home and read it again. I wanted to know these people. I wanted to meet them and see for myself that they weren't really what I had heard they were. In meeting these people and seeing the severe contrast to what I had heard, I was able to discover reality. Just because Steve said it, just because I had a "flashback," did not necessarily make it so. He had lied to me, the con job of all con jobs.

This therapy has snatched something from me that I can never get back: years off of my life; years where I was emotionally distant from my family and my daughter. It created pain, humiliation, fear and frustration. It caused me to be paranoid. I have problems trusting anyone. Professionals scare me to death and I drive them crazy because of my lack of trust, of even those there to truly help me. It caused me to waste years before I was able to obtain competent help. My daughter and I had no financial security and nearly lost our home. I do not have a car that runs and it will be sometime before I get to a point where I am able to purchase one. I haven't been able to provide for my daughter the way I should. I am a single parent and I should have been there emotionally for her. I wasn't. All my energy, all my being, everything I had went to the therapy.

Now, with the help of Skip Simpson, his law firm, faith in God and the support of friends and family, I will hold these men accountable for what they have done to my family and what they continue to do to others. I was told by a friend, another woman who got caught in this system but has since realized her "flashbacks" were not reality, that "Christians don't sue Christians." I would have to disagree on one point. These people are under not only God's law but the laws of this land. They are responsible for the unethical, unprofessional treatment of me and my child. They injured us and it will take years to undo the damage. When I decided to sue them, I had no idea how big this was. I just knew what they had done to me and my daughter could not be left without obtaining some justice.

At times I sit in awe of all that is going on. All the families involved. If something is not done to stop this senseless destruction of our family system, we will no longer have a family system. I was paranoid while in therapy that everyone I came in contact with was sexually abusing someone.

Seemingly normal people were really abusers, murderers and Satanists by night. How in the world can we live in a society where everyone is suspect, where they are tagged as criminals with absolutely nothing to substantiate the charges? I do not condone sexual abuse. It is the one crime that I have been exposed to, with prisoners coming into the jail, that makes me sick to my stomach. But an interesting point to make here is that I was sexually abused as a child. I was molested by a man, a stranger at a swimming pool. Although my therapist was only the second person I had ever told that story to, it was not dealt with in therapy because it wasn't "deep" enough. It wasn't repressed so it couldn't have caused me problems. Is this not a system of denying sexual abuse, real sexual abuse? I am angry that I spent four years in therapy and never dealt with that issue or countless other issues that, in fact, did cause me emotional harm. The issues we dealt with in therapy were the ones created in therapy. I am 38 years old and even as I write this, I fight back tears at the waste of my life, of my daughter's early years.

If you are caught in the "repressed memory" game in therapy, I urge you to get some corroborating evidence. Something, anything to help you find out what is reality. If you have just recovered one traumatic event, it merits looking into. If you have recovered an entire childhood, several pregnancies, repeated sexual abuse, torture, satanic abuse, I'd say run, don't walk to a competent counselor who deals with reality. There are some good therapists out there. I have found one. She deals with issues and attitudes that I have formed since childhood, but we deal with reality. Get in touch with people who knew you and your family when these things supposedly happened. If you want evidence, do not listen to any group member or therapist who says you are in denial or that you are running or that you don't want to get well. You owe it to yourself and your family to get a reality check. Get in touch with creditable memory experts who can tell you how your memory works. I did. I called after reading that article in *D Magazine*. It was explained to me how my delusions could have happened.

I am sorry that I hurt my family. I am sorry that I woke up one day and Jennifer was 12 years old and I had spent her precious childhood in a delusional state. I am sorry that I trusted the wrong people. I have had to learn a valuable lesson in all of this. No one, not one single person in this world, has all of the answers.

As I look back on my experiences, I remember how many times I heard: " Why would anyone go through this if it wasn't real?" "You cannot make up this kind of pain." I believe with every core of my being that the pain was real, but the flashbacks were not reality. And there is a definite payoff. At no other time in your life do you get the kind of attention, love, support, nurturing from group members, cards, letters, financial assistance, people feeling sorry for you, people calling to check on you, and much much more. We, the group members, clung to each other for our absolute existence. We sustained each other, many times keeping each other from harming ourselves or, in some cases, committing suicide. We became each other's family, just as we had been told we would.

My story is far from over. I am caught up in the legal system. I have an extraordinary law firm supporting me. I have an attorney who believes in me, who is patient with me and who has a heart for people who have been victimized. The legal process is hard. I get frustrated and angry. Is it worth it? At times I wonder. But the bottom line is yes. If these people are not held accountable for what they did to me, how much longer will they be allowed to practice in extreme gross negligence and at the cost of yet another family? I was accused by opposing counsel of being "a woman with a cause." I think I am just a person who does not mind standing up for things that are right. This situation literally scares me to death. I do not want my daughter to grow up in a world full of "victims." I will not believe that people, no matter how normal they seem, are sneaking out at night, killing babies and torturing their own children. I do not believe in the "conspiracy theory" that this is a multi-generational thing that has been successfully kept quiet for many years. I refuse to give this satanic cult conspiracy theory any power, or the simple-minded counselors who have a quick answer for everything from nail-biting to drug addiction. I will work to make my world a better place to live in. I will teach my daughter to believe in herself, to not follow a path, but rather to go where there is no path and leave a trail.

I am now doing well and get a lot of support from friends, co-workers and family. On October 1, 1991, I transferred from the Dallas City Jail and am now employed by the Narcotics Bureau of the Dallas Police Department. I am working on my 20th year with the department. On Christmas 1991, my sister and I presented our parents with a videotape we made with family photos and music dubbed in. It was the first Christmas since beginning therapy that I truly enjoyed the holidays. On June 25, 1993, my lawsuit against my former therapists was settled out of court. We are very pleased with the outcome.

—Laura E. Pasley

Traumatic Therapy

My purpose is to describe where I came from, what happened in therapy, and how I got out of it. I've seen parents of the women with whom I was in therapy live with horrible accusations for two or three years. They often have to sell their homes, hire detectives, have no contact with their daughters, and they are never able to defend their innocence. I've seen them worry and hope that this nightmare will go away and their daughter will come back someday.

I was in therapy with two therapists after treatment for an eating disorder in 1986. I read a book called *The Monster Within*. Some of you may have heard of that book. You can probably get it at Christian bookstores. It was about a woman who had bulimia, went to a hospital, met these two wonderful therapists and got well. I'd had an eating disorder since I was nine. I've been so thin I was paralyzed from anorexia, and I've weighed 320 pounds, so I've spanned the whole spectrum and now I'm somewhere in between the two.

But I can tell you that just because I've had weight problems or an eating disorder does not mean I'm an incest victim. I want to stress this because I hear that a lot today — that if you have an eating disorder, you have probably been sexually abused.

My parents are good hard-working people. They're honest. They never in any way meant to harm me. I didn't come with an owner's manual and they really didn't know what to do with me sometimes. They both were the youngest in their families and both are somewhat passive people.

I'm the older child, and I am fiercely independent. My dad would tell you I'm as stubborn as a fence post. I wouldn't say it was that bad, but I am bull-headed. When I believe something, I really stay on it. Sometimes my parents did not know how to handle me. I got married at a young age so I've never been really meshed with my parents. I've never needed much guidance from them in a lot of ways.

However, the therapists interpreted this to mean that my parents were not there for me, or didn't love me, or that they neglected me. That's not true. It was simply that I did not depend on them a lot. That's just not my personality, or wasn't at that time. Later on, after I got into therapy, I became a dependent person. It is almost shameful to me to admit how dependent I was on my therapists.

When I entered therapy for my eating disorder we began to talk about the family dynamics. I told the therapist that, yes, I had been sexually abused – that's the first thing he asked – by an uncle and that was well-known in my family. My uncle is really sick. My family has known about it for years. It was not anything that I ever forgot. It was not a repressed memory.

But the therapist thought I wasn't showing enough emotion about the abuse by my uncle. I had all the feelings and pain of it but I didn't sit around and cry about it all the time. I think I dealt with it as well as anyone can. My family knew about most of it. It wasn't a secret.

But once I got into therapy, the doctor said if your parents knew about the abuse they must have participated in it. And it wasn't just in the sense that they knew and let it happen. (My parents didn't know what happened at the actual time – they found out later.) Then the therapists said things such as, since you feel uncomfortable hugging your father, your father must have sexually abused you.

I was raised in a home that is sexually conservative. My

brother did not run around in his underwear in front of my two sisters and me. My dad did not talk or make any sexual remarks in front of his daughters. He did not believe it was proper. In my home, I knew there were certain things you didn't do. I wouldn't kiss a boy in front of my dad. I may sound old-fashioned, but that's just the way it was. It wasn't because there was any incest that went on. It's just that we were very conscious about what was and was not appropriate sexual behavior. So if you had asked me if I felt uncomfortable hugging my dad, I would have said, "Yeah, maybe, just like I do other people."

I don't think there's anything my parents could have done differently that the therapists wouldn't have interpreted as evidence that abuse happened. Once they have that agenda, then anything you do can be twisted around to prove abuse. For example, the fact that I didn't like my mother washing my hair when I was eight or nine was seen as an indication that my mother had done more than wash my hair in the bathtub. The fact that my parents moved a lot was also seen as a sign of abuse. The therapists believed this meant that my parents were afraid that people would find out about the abuse. The real truth is my parents never had enough money to pay the rent so they would get kicked out and move from house to house. That's the real truth. But the fact that I wouldn't reveal the specifics was seen as a sign of my denial.

Eventually, after hearing all these interpretations, I began to believe that possibly my parents had been involved in something strange and I even began to have visualizations of incidents. I had been in the hospital only once. I had come in with bulimia and some bleeding ulcers. I did have serious eating disorders, no doubt about that. But I was also on eight different types of medication and psychiatric drugs that I'd never been on before.

I was given a series of psychiatric diagnoses including: Schizoid Affective Disorder, Bipolar Disorder, Major Depressive Disorder, Neurotic Depressive Disorder, Post Traumatic Stress Disorder, Dissociative Disorder, and finally Multiple Personality Disorder. I worked my way up to just about all of them at some point. It looked like I was pretty sick. When you're paying people $100 an hour and they're doing tests that reveal so much about you that you don't even know, and then they tell you you've got Schizoid Affective Disorder, you begin to believe them.

There is also a history of mental illness in my family. Some members of my father's side of the family, including my father and his siblings, have been institutionalized at one time or another. With that type of history, when you go to a psychiatrist, mental health problems are seen as genetic. You are told that you're probably going to be in and out of psychiatric hospitals for the rest of your life. Well, that didn't sound real promising. It wasn't what I'd dreamed of when I moved to Dallas to work for EDS, a large computer company owned by Ross Perot.

Based on the fact that the therapists told me I'd suffered traumatic sexual abuse, and I had from my uncle; that my father and his family had a history of mental illness; and that different tests had shown me to have psychiatric problems, I began to believe what they were saying. My therapists therefore decided that we'd have a joint session with my parents. Now here are two simple people from Oklahoma who are very honest, loving and caring people but who, on an educational and professional level, are below average. My dad worked in the oil fields. He didn't know anything about these big city psychiatrists, was scared about his daughter, and was concerned about what was going on with her. He had no idea of the ambush he was walking into.

The therapist and I role-played what I would say and I wrote up a list of things that they should or could have done differently, as well as my feelings associated with their behavior. My parents were not told what this joint session was going to be about. They were concerned about their daughter and when they were invited they came to help me. They drove three hours in a beat-up pickup truck that I wouldn't drive in for two miles.

Now I look back and feel very ashamed because of all my parents went through. They came to the hospital. The therapist sat between me and my dad and my mom in a little room. He began by telling my parents that I was ill and that I was probably going to kill myself, which was a big shock to my dad and mom because they thought I had an eating disorder. They didn't know that much about it. They sure didn't know about Schizoid Affective Disorder and all this other stuff he was dumping on them.

So my parents just sat there and didn't say anything. They were really quiet, listening to this professional give them his opinion about their daughter. He told them I had had a serious eating disorder for years and he described my medical problems that were related to it. Then he stated that it was essential to my survival that they listen to the things I was about to say; he told them more or less that if they didn't listen, their daughter was going to die.

My parents hadn't said anything and they sat there and listened. As we went down the list I had made with the therapist, my dad didn't deny anything. He didn't deny that sometimes he had gotten too angry, had maybe spanked me improperly or said something wrong. One time he had called me a bitch. I didn't forget that. No repressed memory there, and I said that to my dad.

My dad felt very sorry and that's what he said. His eyes were kind of watery. I wouldn't look at him because I just couldn't do that. But my mother was just blubbering. She was a basket case over all this. When we discussed my uncle, my dad said that they didn't know what had gone on, which I already knew. I knew my parents would not intentionally let someone harm me in that way. But my dad said maybe he should have known better than to let me stay with my uncle. And that's the mistake my parents made.

That is the only real mistake my parents made that I can truly say I hold them accountable for; they entrusted my care to someone who wasn't trustworthy. But they didn't sexually abuse me. The rest of the mistakes were just normal parental mistakes.

We got ready to leave and my dad was shell-shocked. He hardly said anything and his eyes were watery. My mom was still crying.

Upon questioning from the therapist it was revealed that I was conceived before my parents' marriage. I was told by the therapist that I must ask my father whether or not he was my real father. I cannot describe the shock and pain I saw on my father's face. The therapist thought this would explain why my father would abuse me and not my siblings. We gave him a nanosecond to respond and when he did not immediately leap to his feet and announce that of course I was his daughter, the therapist said this was a sign of doubt that he was my real father. Now I know that he was in shock after such an appalling confrontation.

At the end of the meeting I told my dad, "I'm remembering what you did and you know what it is." I didn't actually say that my father sexually abused me because I'm not so sure I actually believed it myself.

I then left my parents in that little room and I didn't see my father again for more than two years. My therapist left the room. There was no closure for my parents. They didn't get to hear anything else. They were just left there to bawl. My parents went outside and my brothers and sisters came into another little room. They heard from my therapist how bad my parents were and that unless I had their support, I was liable to kill myself. I still believe that was emotional blackmail for my brothers and sisters. They were not allowed to tell me, "Lynn, we don't believe these accusations."

The therapist told my brothers and sisters that I remembered that our dad did this and this and our mom did this. So, my brothers and sisters over the next two years would say, "Well, Lynn, Dad didn't do anything like that to us. You really think he did that?" But that's as far as my sisters would go. "He didn't do that with us. You really still believe that?"

I made five suicide attempts in 1987, and in one I ended up comatose. The therapists twisted and distorted everything I thought I knew about my family and childhood. They told me that everything I knew for the past 20 or 30 years was wrong. These people that I loved, that I trusted, the values they had instilled in me as a child, were all garbage.

Such an experience was devastating. It put me in a very serious medical crisis that I hadn't been in before. I'd never tried to kill myself until I started therapy. And by that time I didn't have my parents. On a limited basis I had my brothers and sisters but I didn't trust them because I didn't know whether they believed me or not.

I became part of an incest survivors group. The therapists told me that I needed to make this group of women my new family. I loved those women and still today I love every one of them. I hope they all get better. But we were not a group that was able to depend on each other. You've got a bunch of women trying to kill themselves. Who's trustworthy, who's dependable?

By this time I was so seriously depressed that I started missing work. I didn't communicate with people on the outside because I didn't know what to say to them. All the people in the group talked about was incest, depression and medicine and what their latest flashback was. Normal people on the outside don't have those kinds of flashbacks.

We went to therapy, worked enough to pay for therapy, and called each other to talk about our flashbacks. That's how my life went for a while. I became really sick.

I lost a lot of years doing this but I was fortunate because I was able to come out of it and go on to build the life I have today. One of the women in my group always wanted to have a family. She's been in group now for six years and she's getting past childbearing years. She can never have a normal relationship while she's in this group of sick, dependent women.

I watched one young woman, a wonderful person, die because of the group therapy. In group we regularly talked about explicit sexual abuse in a small room while screaming, yelling details, and beating things with bats. You hear this for an hour and a half every day and sometimes an hour at night, and you get to where you really don't know what went on in your life. We also talked specifically about what we did to harm ourselves. I used a very dangerous substance that induces vomiting and I had to talk about my use of this. One woman went home and tried what she had heard me describe and she died.

There were two different outpatient groups that met regularly. There was a great amount of gossip. Everybody knew what went on, not only in their group but in the other group. A major portion of therapy was the exchanging of flashbacks. If one of the women had a revealing flashback, such as her parents ate another child of hers, someone would get that information to me.

There was never any confidentiality. The other women even knew what I was saying in my individual sessions. My therapist would write it in the chart and afterwards the staff would read the chart entries out loud. Patients could stand near the nurse's desk and hear what all the staff thought about whatever was written.

I do not believe that group therapy is appropriate for someone who has not had individual therapy and who is not strong and individualistic. Group therapy doesn't work for a person who is suggestible or who has just begun therapy. Such a person may not have any sexual abuse issues, but if she is placed in an incest-oriented group, it becomes contagious. If that's all they hear every day of the week, if they're given a book like *The Courage to Heal* or *The Monster Within,* they will come to believe that they are incest victims also. The suggestibility of the women was proven by the flashbacks they reported. If one woman had a flashback of snakes and cannibalism in the woods, a few days later, someone else had a similar flashback.

We regularly had occupational therapy where everyone does all kinds of artsy-craftsy stuff that I don't have any ability to do. The reason I didn't finger-paint when I was a kid was not because my parents deprived me of it and didn't let me express myself. I just never had any interest in finger-painting. If they'd given me a computer, I would have expressed myself as a child, but I wasn't going to express myself by squeezing paint all over my fingers and smearing it on paper.

Well, the therapists decided that I needed to do those kinds of exercises in occupational therapy in order to get well. They then interpreted what I did. If I used red, that meant I was angry. If I was given a choice between red, blue or green, I'd probably choose red. This didn't mean anything about abuse. It just meant that out of three colors I liked red better. But they always found some underlying meaning to it, such as I was drawing the blood that my father made me drink after he cut me with a knife. I drew a house. All I can draw is stick houses. That meant that my home wasn't stable because I didn't put a bottom on it and draw rooms. Well, I can't do that. I'm not an architect. That's all my drawing meant. I just drew the best little house I could. It didn't have any symbolic meaning.

Throwing clay was another thing I was encouraged to do. If I didn't throw the clay like I was really angry, it meant that I wasn't getting in touch with my feelings. They then put me into seclusion where I could get in touch with my feelings. The simple fact was that I was living here, eating three meals a day, and there wasn't a whole lot wrong and I wasn't feeling tremendous anger every day. It didn't mean that I was in denial of abuse by my parents.

On one occasion the therapist hadn't been able to get the "anger" out of me that he believed I should have about my parents and the awful things they'd done. He then decided to taunt me with the stuff my uncle had done, which was real. He talked about details of the abuse, saying, "Well, what did you think when your uncle did this? What did you think when he did that?" It was really gross stuff. This was supposed to help me get my rage out. I don't think I threw the clay any harder. I think I just looked at him and cried.

Another thing I had to do in occupational therapy was draw my own tombstone and put my epitaph on it. Now what therapeutic benefit is that supposed to have? I have no idea why a suicidal person should get that close to acceptance of her own death.

Everything was interpreted as supporting the abuse. When my parents sent a birthday card, it was interpreted as a suicidal message. The question I asked my father during the session was answered indirectly when he sent me letter a couple of days later. He signed the letter, "Love, your father." So he did answer. But to the therapists that was a direct message to get me to kill myself. The idea was that death suggestions were supposed to be coded in messages I received from my parents.

Part of the treatment was something called trance writing. The therapists claimed that trance writing was different from hypnosis but I've yet to understand the difference. Probably trance writing is just more dangerous because the garbage I wrote was sure nowhere near the truth. I can't remember what it was. It was just really gory.

Another technique they used was called "body memories." They believed that certain physical sensations reflected abuse that couldn't be remembered. That is, although there were no conscious memories, the body remembered. They told me that because I had some numbness in my hand, it was a result of holding my father's penis. Actually, the reason I had numbness in my hand was from taking 900 milligrams of Lithium and a large dose of Xanax and Mellaril. This made my fingers numb. My feeling of discomfort did not mean I wanted to cut off my hand because I'd touched my dad's penis. But that is what I was told it meant.

We believed we were being treated by one of the great-est therapists alive. He could heal eating disorders and by that time I'd had mine for 18 years. As a result of my disorder, I also had serious physical problems, so I didn't have a whole lot longer to cure my eating disorder. I believed that my therapist could heal me and that if trance writing would enable me to get to that one thing down there in my gut, I would be well. They convinced me that if I faced the horrible thing that harmed me, I could confront it, and then I would a healthy, normal functioning person. But that wasn't what happened.

Day in and day out I listened to screaming and shouting and to graphic details about abuse. I continued to draw or write or tell about my abuse since that's what the staff wanted to see and that's the only way I could stay out of seclusion. I finally started to say what they wanted to hear. The sad thing is I almost started to believe it.

After a while I said what my therapist wanted to hear if I wanted any attention from him. And at that point I wanted attention from this man. He was about the only person I had left in my life. He told me what I could and could not do. Was it okay to go grocery shopping this day? Was it okay to go see my parents or to call a long lost aunt? Was it okay to go to church? Every event had to be cleared through him. I had to discuss it with him to see if it was in my best interest and then if it was judged to be okay, I could do it. If not, I just called the people back and told them that my therapist said I shouldn't do this.

I began to believe the abuse by my parents was true. However, my feelings about it were totally different from the situation with my uncle. When I said it about my father, my voice wasn't strong and there was a little voice inside that always doubted. There were a lot of tears with it, too, and even today when I recall what I said or believed about what my dad might have done, it still hurts.

I got sicker. I also had insurance difficulties. Aetna had agreed to pay about $250,000 by that time. EDS had paid about $100,000. EDS was a little tougher on those insurance restrictions and the therapists really hated that. So the doctor told me to get a policy that would pay the rest. I told him that the new insurance policy had a two-year exclusion clause for pre-existing conditions, and therefore we would not be able to get anything more for two years. He said that we would use a different diagnosis so it wouldn't look like a pre-existing condition. We tried that but the insurance company had a hard time understanding how suddenly this 27-year-old woman had Schizoid Affective Disorder, Major Depressive Disorder and so forth yet she'd never been hospitalized before. They decided they would not pay the claim.

Well, to say the therapist got mad is to say the least. He came into my room one day and said, "What are you going to do? You don't have any insurance, you don't have a job and you can't see me anymore." He kept yelling at me, "What are you going to do?"

I sat there and, at first, didn't say anything — I didn't know what I was going to do. Finally I said, "Well, I guess I'll just go home and rot." Now, rot in that sense meant go home and not do anything because he just told me I don't have anything to do. I don't have therapy. That's the only thing I've been doing for a year.

The next day some deputies arrived because I had said that I was going to go home and rot. The therapist interpreted that to mean I was suicidal. They got an order for protective custody and I was handcuffed and taken to jail as a criminal.

I'd never been in jail for anything. From there I was taken to a Mental Diagnostic Center (MDC) which is what Dallas County uses to evaluate people who are believed to be mentally ill. This was not a good place for someone who has any type of abuse issues. This shows that the therapist was not concerned with my welfare or he wouldn't have placed me in that environment. Most of the people were untreated schizophrenics.

I was still on a lot of strong and addictive medications, including Xanax, Mellaril, Lithium, two different drugs for ulcers, Ristorel to help me sleep, and Darvocet to help me when I had headaches. But when I was taken to MDC, they did not give me my medication for over ten hours. I began to have severe withdrawal symptoms. They threatened that if I didn't quit crying and get control of myself, I was going to end up being sent to Terrell, the state hospital.

I was very scared of that place. My dad's family had spent time in a state institution and my therapist had used Terrell as a threat if I didn't do what he said. And now he'd gone ahead and placed me in a position where I might actually be sent to Terrell. I was scared. That's probably the only time I've ever called and begged anybody but I begged him to get me out of there, I'd do whatever he wanted, just get me out. But he wouldn't do it. He said that I needed to be in Terrell for ten years.

That was in 1987. If my therapist had his way, I'd still be there and I wouldn't have my son and my husband today. Fortunately, I saw a psychiatrist at MDC who looked at my chart and asked me, "Well, what are you doing here?" I answered, "I don't know." And he said, "Well, you won't be here long." This was Friday and I was released on Monday and I never had to go to court. The psychiatrist did not feel that it was proper that I was there, and didn't know why such an order had been obtained.

I was released with a couple of black trash sacks that had been mine when I was in the hospital, which had all of my belongings. I had no friends because they had told the other group members for their own good not to talk to me or I would harm them. I don't really remember how I got an apartment that day but somehow I did and I began to try to put my life back together.

I didn't do a good job of it for a while. I didn't have my medication. I called the psychiatrist who had given me the prescriptions and he said, "Well, I'm sorry to hear that." I told him I was beginning to shake, I could hardly talk, and I was suffering discomfort. He said I should go to Parkland.

Parkland is the county hospital. If I went there having seizures from psychiatric drugs, they would send me back to MDC to be evaluated again and therefore could send me to Terrell. So I knew I couldn't go to Parkland. Finally I said, "No, I won't do that." And he said, "Well, you will if you get sick enough."

I called Jerry, a therapist I had known before. He didn't get into all this recovered memories of abuse nonsense. He was a behavioral cognitive therapist. I told him the awful shape I was in and he was angry because he hadn't seen me in a year and when he had last seen me I was a normal functioning human being. He knew about the incest with my uncle. He told me that he had a friend who was a doctor and they'd get me the medication I needed immediately and then work on getting me off of it.

Jerry also encouraged me to believe that I could recover from what had happened. At that time it felt like I had destroyed my family. I'd said all these things about them and if they weren't true, then I was really sick. I was some kind of sexually perverted person for even thinking these things about my father. If they were true and I was as mentally ill as the doctor said, then I'm some mentally ill person. Either way, I didn't believe I had a lot of hope.

I didn't have my therapy friends and by that time I had cut off my normal friends. How could I go back to them a year later and say, "Hi, guys, here I am?" I had lost my job at EDS, which I had originally obtained after receiving a four year degree in two years. I felt like I had just blown my life.

But I've found out that I'm a survivor. I got the apartment that day and I talked to Jerry who helped me get some medication and assured me that, insurance or not, he'd stand by me. He'd see me and we'd get through this.

I saw him probably three days a week for that first week or two. I cried about my other therapist and all that went on. Jerry would just sit there and listen. He was angry over what had been done but he didn't get really involved with it. He let me express my feelings and worked with me on getting on with my life.

In desperation, about a week later I begged my previous therapist to continue where we had left off. He said only if I'd agree to go to Terrell and stay for two years and work real hard. And work means you have to say all the right things, play all the right games and talk about the details of the abuse. But I thought I'd told everything so I didn't really know what I was going to do. I couldn't stand to go to Terrell so I didn't see this therapist again.

Finally, after two years, it was time to get off all this medication. For one thing it was eating me up financially. Several people had said I was addicted to it and by this time it was almost chic to be an alcoholic or drug addict. So I went to a drug rehab program.

At first I didn't like the plan they had for me. They didn't want to hear much about the abuse and I didn't really understand it since that was all we had talked about in the other environment. But they weren't interested. Instead, they stressed, "What are you going to do about now? You can't drink today, you can't take pills. You have to do the normal things you used to do. So what, you're depressed today. Everybody has days they feel lousy. You still must go to work, you must eat, you still must take a bath, you still must comb your hair, you still must do these things."

I'd never had therapy like that before. In my incest victimization therapy, I'd been taught that I didn't have to do any of that. If I felt bad, I'd stay home. I'd stay in bed all day. I'd read a book. I'd bawl, I'd take an extra Xanax. I didn't have to be responsible. If I'd had kids I wouldn't have to take care of them because I'm an incest victim. Because all of these awful things happened to me I didn't have to live by the same rules as everyone else does.

But this place didn't go along with that. They thought I was just like anybody else. It was good for me. I had to relearn how to live. This was difficult to do since I'd become used to the sick way of life that I was taught. I'd become used to flashbacks and gory details of sexual abuse, to people saying, "Oh, you're an incest victim. We feel so sorry for you. It must have been horrible."

I got better. It took awhile, though. I'm in a 12-step recovery program today. I believe that it has truly saved my life. It definitely taught me how to live again. Around mid-1989 I got to where I felt I was emotionally healthy. About a year later I began dating the man I'm now married to. He understands what went on and sometimes gets extremely angry when he hears what happened to me.

I reconciled with my parents at a family gathering. I told my sister I'd come and she told me that my parents would also be there. My dad has never asked me for an apology.

He's never told me that we've got to talk about it. He's never said, "How could you accuse me of something like that?" My mom's never been angry at me about it and I'm very grateful for that. I'm very grateful they didn't say, "Well, after accusing us of something so horrible, how dare you set foot in our place?"

I wish that my parents had been more insistent with my therapist that they didn't abuse me. I wish that my dad had made a call, written a letter or something and proclaimed his innocence. It might have kept the doctors from saying, "See, they did it." That's why they turned tails and ran. Because that's exactly what the doctors told me. "They did it. They won't even face you."

My parents really didn't know how to handle such accusations and they didn't have anyone that they could talk to. Today, I have a better relationship with my parents than I've ever had. Also, looking back, I realize this wouldn't have changed either of my therapists' minds.

What allowed me to realize that the "memories" of abuse by my parents were not true was time away from the therapy group. I do not believe that this would have happened if I had remained in the group. I did believe the group and the therapists were going too far when they decided that I had Multiple Personality Disorder, but I wouldn't have been ready to just leave on my own. The group pressure to trust the memories and to believe was just too strong to resist.

The truth did not come to me immediately after leaving the group. It happened gradually as I was putting my life back together. As I was restored to some health and emotional well-being, I was able to get a sense of which memories were based on actual experiences and which were not. It became obvious to me after a while that my dad never molested me. Yes, I felt uncomfortable when he hugged me, and I may have felt embarrassed if I walked into the bathroom when he was there. That doesn't meant he molested me. The fact that I walked in one time while my parents were making love and I was embarrassed and ashamed and turned around and walked away doesn't mean I was abused. It meant that I knew I had seen something I wasn't supposed to see. It wasn't because I thought my mom was taking my lover, as my therapist said. This type of realization became increasingly clear as time passed.

When I look back at that period of my life, it is as if I were this therapist's little child and if he said turn right, I'd turn right. If he said turn left, I'd turn left. If he said have a flashback, I'd have a flashback. That period of my life is confusing. I remember it, I remember being there, I remember what happened. But I have a real sense of numbness and ugliness, kind of like a non-existence. I think that's because I wasn't myself. I didn't make decisions for myself. I didn't act for myself.

Although I lost four years of my life, I'm grateful. I'm a lot more fortunate than some. I got a chance to go on with my life. I remember having to make the choice of facing my parents or moving far away. I seriously considered moving away and denying the existence of my family. After realizing that, the shame I felt was overwhelming.

In Dallas, there are five of us from the same group who have since recanted all of the accusations we made. One woman who had confronted her mother was able to retract those remarks before her mother died. Most have been able to heal their family relationships. One left therapy because the therapist thought he had healed her but she later told her mother she knew her mother did not do all the things she had said. One woman's husband took charge and removed her from the therapy program. After that time she began to get better than she's been in years. Another woman had been in group for seven or eight years and finally just realized that it was sick and crazy. By this time the group was talking about people hanging on meat hooks in trees and other bizarre things during satanic cult activities. She was able to break away for awhile and could then see that this was nuts. But such realizations occur only after getting away.

Today I am very grateful to have my parents and other healthy, loving friends in my life. During the last ten years of my bulimia, the doctors were not sure if I could have children. After marrying a wonderful man, I gave birth to a baby boy in September 1990 and a baby girl in August 1992. I believe these two precious babies to be a miracle and I cherish them daily. I regret taking my family for granted and pray I never will again. I hope to help others who have had similar experiences with therapists. I also hope to help parents who have been falsely accused so that I may symbolically give back to my parents what was taken from them.

—Lynn Gondolf

Diagnosed as MPD

I am Victoria, a 39-year-old female. I am a survivor of a hideous form of mental, emotional and spiritual rape! I was brainwashed for someone else's personal gain. I am telling my story to try to put back together the lost four years of my life, for myself, my children, my husband and my family.

When I was 34 years old I was married and the mother of two children. Both my husband and I had lost our jobs. We were in desperate financial trouble and started having marital problems. As things grew bleaker, so did our marriage. We separated and lived apart for nine months, only to get back together again without dealing with the issues that led to our separation. My husband was back to work but I was not. With all of the stress in our lives I had developed an anxiety disorder that was all-consuming. I had hurt my back and gained quite a bit of weight. I steadily became more depressed. Instead of looking at our communication problems and lack of intimacy, I fell into a sea of self-pity. My depression grew worse until feelings of suicide brought me into a hospital.

At first I had been assigned to an elderly male doctor who thought "electric shock treatments" were the answer for many of his patients. I didn't want to be one of them, so I spoke with other patients and staff about the possibility of getting reassigned and asked specifically for a female. Dr. Daley's name kept coming up, so I fired the first doctor for Dr. Daley.

I had always been aware of the neglect, and physical and sexual abuse I had endured as a child, and felt more comfortable speaking to a female, although I didn't feel it was necessary to dredge up all that old garbage again. I had dealt with it and felt it was behind me.

Dr. Daley spoke rather highly of herself, name-dropping colleagues and referring often to her European practice. She told me of how she had learned so much observing psychiatry in other cultures and that she was a true psychoanalyst and Freudian. We had several conversations about Freud's theories and she told me that many people were misinformed about him.

She asked me to write my life story and explained that she had a very unique way of helping her patients. However, she told me she only treated people with Multiple Personality Disorder (MPD), an area that she was "pioneering" in. So we decided that she would treat me with medication when I got out of the hospital, and that she would call in an associate to do weekly therapy with me.

She continued to see me while I was in the hospital, which was about ten weeks. She asked me to read the book *The Courage to Heal*. As time went on she started to mention MPD as a diagnosis for me, but I tried to convince her that it did not apply to me. However, she told me I had a lot of the classic symptoms such as losing time in my life (like driving somewhere and reaching my destination without remembering the ride). She talked to me about hearing voices, like the ones in your head that tell you not to take another bite because you really are full. I had always assumed that everybody had these types of experiences but she convinced me that it was very abnormal. I was instructed to carry around a notebook and write down everything these voices said and to note if I had lost any time. She explained to me that people didn't have child-like parts to themselves (like when I felt giddy and giggly as I was playing with my children). She said that part of me was not the real me. Even my suicidal thoughts were not mine. I was so taken in by what seemed to be her infinite wisdom and soothing voice that I really started questioning my own sanity.

I left the hospital and went back home with my family. I was seeing her and her associate therapist. The therapist was good to talk to about day-to-day matters, and she strongly disagreed with the possible MPD diagnosis. When I reported this to Dr. Daley, she would give me more proof as to why I had MPD and told me that the therapist was insecure because of her lack of education and credentials. She suggested that what we talked about in our sessions remain between us. She then suggested that I "try the diagnosis on" just to see if it fit. After all, if it didn't then we'd know for sure. Since I felt comfortable with this, she gave me some index cards and suggested that I write down a name (whatever popped into my head) for the child-like part of myself and the suicidal self. I was instructed to relax and to try to remember the first time I felt that way. I was then told that these were accurate memories at actual ages. She invited me to come to a women's group she held in the evening, explaining that a lot of people had the same problems that I had.

I was very afraid to meet these "Sybilish" monsters, but at the same time I was ashamed and afraid for my own sanity. After all, I was hearing voices and losing time. I decided to go once. When I got there I noticed that some of her other patients were people I had met in the hospital. One of the women was someone I had gotten rather close to. I had a lot of respect for her and when she saw me she jokingly said, "I knew I'd see you here soon. After all, it takes one to know one!" (MPD, that is.) I had felt awkward asking anyone in the "real world" about these voices and lost time so I took my chance here. They were all really warm and wonderful women and seemed pretty normal, not at all the monsters I had envisioned. Everyone was very honest and in a light-hearted way we would joke about making lists so we wouldn't forget things. Some of us exchanged phone numbers and would talk during the week. I no longer felt so freakish and alone. It became okay to be MPD. Actually, I was told only extremely intelligent people used this as a safety device in childhood. I *belonged* somewhere! The group became my new family of sisterhood and my life line.

In our group we all shared different stories of how some of us had past therapies and medications, but were only able to escape from our problems for a few years or so. Dr. Daley told us she couldn't emphasize enough how this was confirming our diagnosis even more. Some of the women in the group had been reading books on MPD and sang praises of our doctor and how lucky we were to finally find someone who understood our unique problems. We were told over and over again how other doctors (especially males) would not and did not believe in our mysterious mental quandary. I was told repeatedly about Dr. Daley's feelings concerning male dominance in our society. We talked about how men were almost always the perpetrators in our childhood years and now as adults they were trying to stifle us again. I was given books on goddesses, multiple personality disorders, incest, cults and satanic ritual abuse.

We were to keep everything on index cards and carry journals with us. When I did not cooperate I was told it was up to me how long I wanted to stay *sick*! All friends and family who didn't go along with our "diagnosis" were to be avoided, cut out of our lives, or considered perpetrators.

We (the group) were a team. When we were all together, we were an especially strong team. It's odd that when one of us got sick (back in the psych ward) others from the group would follow. When I was feeling overwhelmed by some of the newly recovered "memories," Dr. Daley would sometimes suggest I go to the hospital for a break from mothering and family. I was not suicidal at these times, but she told me that the hospitals were coming down on her and the only way for me to get a rest was to make up a story about how I was going to end it all. She usually came up with the specifics, and after we rehearsed the story, she would often call the hospital from her office. I was then told to go home and pack a few things so that I could be admitted at my convenience. I didn't like having to lie about suicidal thoughts and tell nurses my plan (all fantasy), but Dr. Daley told me it was best this way. I hated going into a locked unit, but she told me not to worry, that I could check into the hospital in the evening, and guaranteed me that she would come in early the next morning to let me come out to the open unit. I'm surprised none of the staff, at least to the best of my knowledge, didn't question why so many of Dr. Daley's patients were admitted to the locked unit one night and miraculously had no feelings of self-harm the next morning.

Several women in the group had very vague memories also. I was told this was normal. I was also told that anything I dreamed was my altered states reliving the horrors that had happened to me. I was to have a note pad and pen by my bedside and to record every dream or nightmare. No matter how bizarre my dreams were, Dr. Daley would try to get me to relax and remember where they came from. I would think and think and, when nothing came out of it but a severe headache and exhaustion, I would make up something just to satisfy her mind-probing.

In one of our sessions I had told Dr. Daley about a distant cousin who had gone into therapy several years earlier and who thought she was ritually abused. Well, that made it clear to the doctor that I must have been ritually abused too.

A few months later I was back in the hospital and very depressed. I didn't know if I was losing my mind or on the way to recovery. After all, in order to recover I would get worse, a lot worse. This was because I was told I needed to remember and relive my pain to resurrect from it. I remember thinking, "How much worse could it get?" I had felt suicidal, I knew about my sexual abuse, and even though I had some feelings of sadness about it – it was over as far as I was concerned. The "satanic ritual abuse" really scared me, though! I had been raised in a strict Catholic family and mere thoughts of demons frightened the hell (excuse the pun) out of me. I saw the movie *The Exorcist* and I had been told it was based on a true story that took place in the 1950s, only the possessed person was a boy, not a girl. I can credit these words of wisdom to my mother, who was not at all mentally stable herself. For as long as I could remember my mother had also told me that the cleft in my chin was the kiss of the devil, that I was a parasite, and that I was possessed because I was such a horrid child. Now I knew my mother was not a mentally healthy person; however, I still felt there was something odd about me. My father had told me that he felt I had special powers like ESP or something. What were these people trying to tell me? I hadn't felt like I fit in anywhere before this group. I was so confused with fear that I literally became ill. My knees would buckle underneath me. I was having a lot of nightmares and I actually started wearing dark glasses indoors and out no matter what time of day it was. I had a dark cloud around me all the time and was becoming increasingly paranoid.

One morning, after a night filled with nightmares, Dr. Daley took me into a room to have what I thought was going to be a "Hi, how are you today?" visit. This particular day she insisted that I confront my bad dreams head on. The only problem was that we were not talking about my nightmares. She told me to close my eyes and relax. She started describing a cold dark place and asked me what I could see in my mind's eye. I said I saw a large slab of stone. She said, "Like an altar?" I was to continue to look closer and tell her who was there. In my imagination I remember feeling child-like and peeking out of a corner. The doctor then described a baby to me which I saw as a woman giving birth. We then continued as she asked me questions about people in black hooded robes and magically, when she said things, I saw them. She asked about candles. I talked about daggers and, oh yes, I saw those too. She asked me to describe the setting again, and I began to ramble on about the woman giving birth. I know that at some point I asked her to stop. She sounded a bit frustrated, but insisted we continue. Her voice sounded calmer now as she spoke about the hooded people, the setting and the baby. So we looked into this movie as we put it together in my mind. She asked more about the woman giving birth. As we continued, I saw the baby coming out, covered in blood, and then came the afterbirth. It looked pretty gross. I felt frightened. When I had given birth to my second child, not all the afterbirth came out, and I passed it the next day. I felt panicky, like when it had happened to me in real life. Dr. Daley asked me what they were doing to the baby. All I could see was them taking the baby away. It was so strange. When she asked me how many people were there, all I could say was I didn't know, because as I looked at this mind image, one minute there would be three and the next about fifteen. She asked me again about the baby and suddenly my heart began to beat faster as I saw some beings, half human and half moles (mole people, I guess) and they were eating the afterbirth. I screamed out, "They're eating the afterbirth!" Next she asked me what I was doing. I kept saying, "I don't know." Then she surprised me by asking, "Are you eating the afterbirth too?" Suddenly in my mind *I was*! I started screaming hysterically. The doctor shouted for staff and medication. They made me chew a pill as I sobbed, clung to people, and hysterically relived what I at that time had believed to be a memory. Dr. Daley left sometime during this. I don't remember her saying goodbye.

At some point the staff helped my drugged body into my room. The nightmares became worse. I was sure I was going mad. The images seemed so real. I now had to figure out how to put this new knowledge into my life. I grieved horribly about the fact that I had been part of satanic ritual abuse. Dr. Daley kept telling me it wasn't my fault, but I didn't believe her. I ruminated over this scene continuously. I felt as if someone had picked me up and hurled me into a wall. My sanity was on the brink at times and then at other times my mind would say, "This is stupid. These are images I conjured up; and mole people, come on!" I would talk to the doctor about it and she always had an answer. The mole people were "hairy" so they were probably men and as a child that's how I saw them. I was like soft clay in her hands.

On another visit shortly after this, my doctor came back to see me. She brought me into a room where there was another patient of hers (there goes her promise of confidentiality), and proceeded to tell both of us that we shared the same problem. She told us that she was diagnosing us both with Multiple Personality Disorder. We both stared at each other in disbelief and tried to convince her that this was just not so. She became angry, curt and short with us, stating, "If you don't agree with my diagnosis, which there is a cure for, I have no choice but to diagnose you with some other extreme psychotic disorder. You will then be committed to a state mental institution and both of you will lose your children!" She was medicating me more heavily at this time and it took all the strength that I had just to get me out of that room and into mine where I went to bed and cried myself to sleep.

I was supplied with books like *Sybil* and *Three Faces of Eve*. The more I read, the more depressed I became. I knew I had to get myself out of the hospital so she wouldn't have the power to commit me. I checked myself out and started seeing the other therapist again. I was going to the women's groups and seeing Dr. Daley just for medication.

The other therapist let me know that the mental health clinic where they worked was politely asking for Dr. Daley to leave on her own. The therapist explained to me that I should not have been diagnosed so soon. She was helping me come out of the fog a little. I had decided that I would switch to another doctor at the clinic. I did not let Dr. Daley know, though, because I was afraid of her.

The time came for her to leave and I made an appointment with a different doctor, one that the therapist recommended. I went to see him, and in less than 15 minutes he told me that he knew what my problem was because he had seen it so many times with women. He proceeded to tell me that I was a middle-aged housewife with too much idle time and that I was just looking for pity. He then proceeded to take me off the highly addictive medication that I was on. After a few days of withdrawal and what seemed like living hell, I called Dr. Daley for an appointment and asked her to refill my prescription. She said she would but threatened that she would not help me if I left her care again. I was grateful for the medication. I had been having severe visual distortions, vomiting and what seemed like a hard time breathing.

I had talked to one of the women in my group who had told me that her husband had contacted the local university and was told that even if her diagnosis was not accurate, the treatment was basically the same for major depression, and it wouldn't hurt her. Armed with this new knowledge, I decided I was going to be a good patient and group participant. I started writing out my index cards and coming up with all sorts of alters. The group met one night a week. We (the group) decided, with the aid of the doctor, to write a "How to Cope" handbook for others with MPD. I really felt like I belonged there. I was able to call some of the other group members throughout the week and the doctor even gave us half an hour per day when she would take her phone machine off at home, so we could call her during this time if we needed extra help.

One night I went to my group and the doctor told us that she had had a session with one of the other members earlier in the day and that this woman was very upset and talking about suicide. We had our regular group session but hurried through it. We were all concerned about our fellow group member. We called a halt to the meeting early. The doctor was having a hard time trying to describe what to do about this situation. Actually, Dr. Daley seemed more like a group member herself than a doctor. Dr. Daley asked some of us what we thought. I had come up with calling a suicide prevention hot line. One of the women in the group called but was told that if this woman didn't actually call in herself, there was nothing they could do. I had called this woman's home and talked to her as well as other women in the group. She didn't sound good. We were all very worried and asked her if we could come to her home and spend a little time with her. She said it was okay as long as the doctor didn't come with us. (Apparently they had a disagreement earlier in the day.) We let the doctor know our plans, but she insisted on being a part of it. So five people drove in two cars to this woman's home. I asked the driver of the car to speed, as I had given my word to the suicidal woman that I would protect her from the doctor. When we got there her car was still in the driveway but no one answered the door. When the doctor arrived we were told to go inside the house to search for her body but not to disturb anything if we found her. We broke in and searched the whole house. I found her son, then about 13 years old, in bed sleeping. I tried to wake him to ask him where his mom was, but he was very tired and didn't want to talk. As we paced the living room, the doctor became more angry that this woman had left the house knowing we were coming. She hadn't seemed concerned about the boy until this point and angrily she declared that she was going to call the child protection agency and have the child taken away. I knew of another friend of hers that didn't live far away. I called this woman's house several times and left messages on her answering machine. Meanwhile, child protection was coming to take her sleeping son. About five minutes passed and a call came in. It was her. The doctor spoke to her first and they argued. Next I got on the phone and informed her about the doctor's angry call to child protection. She was crying and we talked about how the doctor had something on everyone in the group. We decided on a place to meet. I went into her son's room and shook him awake and told him to dress and get school books for the following day. I was so afraid that the police would walk in at any minute. After all, we were trespassing. The doctor was scolding me for helping my friend, but I couldn't help it. I just knew that this was not right. Another woman and I quickly got the boy inside the car and hurried to our destination. It was hard to believe that we, the group, had been sucked into a trap to harm another group member.

We decided on the way home that at the next week's meeting we were going to confront the doctor about her unethical behavior. However, it wasn't meant to be. Two days later the suicidal woman was in the hospital and so were a couple of other group members because of the trauma of this experience.

At our next meeting only a few of us were there. The doctor asked us, "Where did I lose control?" I remember someone replying, "You never had it." She praised us all for all the help we had given that night. She singled me out to suggest that this might be a field that I should consider going into. I felt so proud, almost giddy. The great doctor had actually thought I might be good at helping others. Yes, I thought to myself, I am being a good patient and that's why I was having this temporary "high."

Hours and days turned into weeks of "Do I have MPD and need to work harder or is all this just weird therapy?" I was having a difficult time because my memory was betraying me again. I just couldn't *really* remember enough things to get better. The doctor told us that we all had to have been sexually abused by at least two perpetrators, that we had all been satanically abused, that we had lesbian personalities, that we had male personalities, that we all had animal personalities and that we had demons.

I would try to tell her that I just couldn't remember. She told me that I wasn't working hard enough and that I could stay sick as long as I chose not to remember these other personalities so that I could become integrated.

I was given more books, like *Daddy's Girl, Silence the Child*, and *When Rabbits Howl*. My concentration was really off and it was hard to read. When I became distraught and my husband would call Dr. Daley, the answer was always the same: "Increase her medication or put her in the hospital." I would increase my medication because my husband and kids were really losing their patience with all of my hospitalizations.

The Truth Serum

One of the women in the group was going to get a truth serum; the doctor was going to put her under "amytal therapy." I was so excited; so was the doctor and other group members. If I recieved this treatment, I wouldn't have to push my mind into severe headaches anymore. We could just get knocked out and the doctor would know all of our other personalities and find out what truly had happened to us. We could then have our perpetrators jailed. There would be justice for all and we would all get healthy.

The first patient to go under the "truth serum" was chosen because she was the most financially secure. Her husband even contributed money for an airline ticket so Dr. Daley could go to a convention somewhere in Illinois to learn more about MPD and administering the drug.

When Dr. Daley returned from her trip she was more adamant than ever about satanic ritual abuse (SRA). She told me that the original sin was sex. I felt really stupid

because I didn't know this and I had attended a parochial
school for eight years. When that feeling passed I began to
feel dirty and sinful. Not only had I had sex, but I had given
birth to two children. I started crying uncontrollably. I felt
as if everything about me was evil. I couldn't trust my own
decisions anymore, and I pleaded with the doctor to give
me a frontal lobotomy.

I was so distraught I was sure I was going insane and
would go to hell! I don't remember how many days or
weeks had passed but I was sleeping 18 to 22 hours a day.
I lived in my nightgowns and had to force myself to bathe,
wash my hair and brush my teeth about every week and a
half. I started reading from the Bible a lot and I would pray
in my head a lot. I got to the point where I truly believed I
was possessed by the devil. I had to be hospitalized. There
was a minister on the mental health unit daily. I would
scurry to try to get closer to him. I thought that if I was
possessed this holy man would sense it. He never said
anything but was soft and kind. I got bolder and started
taking communion. I thought that if I had enough hosts in
me it would drive the demon away. One day I got up the
courage to talk to the minister before his little service. I
told him my concerns about being possessed. He told me
not to take communion that day and said he would get
back to me. I felt like he was looking at me strangely now.
My depression got worse as I pleaded for a lobotomy.
Within a few days a Catholic priest came to see me. I was
sobbing deeply and confessed to him every sin I could
possibly think of, real or imagined. I also told him how the
doctor had told me that the Catholic church was founded
on voodoo. He blessed me, stayed with me and talked to
me for some time. He told me that he believed a lot of this
was nonsense, assured me that I wasn't possessed, and told

me that Jesus had died on the cross for all of our sins, and that Jesus had forgiven me. He told me the best thing I could do for myself was to forgive myself. I felt much calmer the rest of the day. But then in the morning Dr. Daley would come in and taunt me with the fact that my mental health was getting worse because I hadn't accepted her diagnosis.

It had been suggested to me several times throughout this whole ordeal that I switch doctors. The insurance that covered me would not let me change. Even if it did, I was somehow addicted to this doctor. The group that she ran was my new kinship or sisterhood. She was at times like a mother to me. She had a profound effect on me. She was like a wise woman and she could interpret the Bible to me in ways that I couldn't. She was a bit of a "guru" to me.

She promised me that if I stuck it out with her, even against my family's wishes, she would bring me through to sanity and light. She frequently told me that she was praying for me. This made me feel special, but there was still the doom and gloom of that SRA lingering in my mind.

When I told her that my husband and daughter (who was 17 at this time) wanted me to stop therapy with her, she suggested a divorce from my husband and foster placement for my daughter.

She reminded me continuously about men and their oppression of women. She told me that she thought my husband also had MPD, because sometimes he would be supportive and sometimes not. He even joined a men's group to help him sort all of this out.

Dr. Daley came to my home one evening because I was having a "Christmas Around the World" party. I had also invited all of the other group members. My daughter came in from an activity, was introduced to everyone, and then she asked if she could go to another function — I don't remember, but it was something like a high school basketball game. When I told her she could, she hurried upstairs to change her clothes, like any normal teenager. When she did this the doctor suggested that it was terribly odd for her to change her clothes from one event to the next and suggested that my daughter possibly had MPD also. I was so confused!

I continually asked her for the truth serum. It was almost like some carrot on a stick she was dangling in front of me. She decided this time I should see someone she shared office space with, a psychologist who knew how to hypnotize people. She had tried to hypnotize me before but I don't remember if it worked. The doctor told me she was getting some flak at the hospital for using sodium amytal and wanted to see if hypnosis would help. Through hypnosis I found the lesbian and male personalities in me. All I needed now was to find the animals and the demons. I remember having a very hard time relaxing. Soon I was into some altered state of consciousness and all I can remember was making some deep guttural noises and not being able to speak. Needless to say this really had me frightened again. The nightmares became worse and so did I.

The doctor finally agreed to give me the "truth serum." I was filled with hope, yet scared about what she would find. I guess she had a hard time knocking me out. When I awoke I was upset and crying. When I listened to a little part of the tape that evening with my husband I became even sadder. At the beginning of the tape I had stated that I truly believed I had MPD. But there had been a part of me that wanted to prove her wrong.

The next day she came in and was supposed to do another amytal session with me. She told me that the hospital administrators were very upset with her. Apparently they had already warned her not to do this anymore.

I was crying. I needed to find out what had happened, and had been told it would take several sessions. She suggested that I stay in the hospital a few more days, but I told her that I couldn't see the purpose in that, because the only reason I was in the hospital was to get the "truth serum."

I went home and things spiralled downward. I was now so heavily medicated that sometimes I would see things like men's noses slowly turning into penises. This seemed to confirm my illness. As I was getting sicker and sicker, I knew I had to do something. I realized that I would probably be committed soon because I was going MAD. I decided that it was best for my children, husband and other family if I were gone. I decided to take my life. No, this was not a cry for help; I was getting more than enough help. I put together a foolproof plan. I wrote my own will and goodbye letters to my beautiful children and husband. I also wrote more general letters to other family members and friends. I got everything I needed. I set a date. One of the things I wanted to do was to go back and see the women in my group, one last time. I thought I would, in my own quiet way, say goodbye so that they wouldn't know it at the time, but would figure it out when I was gone.

My husband drove me to my group that night, as he usually did. A couple of the women from my group were outside smoking, which was something we had commonly done before our meeting. I joined them. First we chatted about nothing of much importance, and then one of the women to whom I had felt particularly close started telling me about a different medication she was on and how she was feeling stronger inside and it was getting easier to cope. I asked her the name of the medicine and wrote it down. What the heck, I thought, maybe as a last ditch effort, I would try it, but only for two weeks. That night in the group meeting different members were talking about medication. The doctor sat there with her prescription pad and pen in hand. Someone took the *Physician's Desk Reference* from her shelf. We were all passing it around, looking through it and commenting on different medicines we had taken. One at a time we made our requests for medication. The girl before me asked for codeine cough syrup, and Dr. Daley wrote out the prescription. Next it was my turn and I had a slip of paper on which I had written the other medication. I asked the doctor to fill it and she obliged. I said my goodbyes and left. I had the prescription filled and threw out the other drugs. I started taking the new medicine right away but still had a cloud hanging around me. I really didn't want to leave my husband and children, but I just couldn't think of any other way to do it. I lay in bed going over my plan again and again to make sure it would work. I cried a lot because I knew how much I would miss them. But I didn't want to be their dark blemish anymore.

Five days later I woke up sometime in the afternoon. I felt strange. I went into the bathroom and showered, washed my hair, and brushed my teeth. I went back to my bedroom, but I wasn't as tired as usual. I actually got dressed just to be at home. I went to my kitchen and was feeling stronger with every little move I made. I did the dishes and began to hum a little. Next I went to the fridge and proceeded to make my family dinner.

I was smiling inside. I picked up the phone and called my best friend, crying tears of joy at what I had accomplished.

Soon my children and husband came home. They were looking at me strangely. The kids started to giggle and play. My husband stood there with tears welling up in his eyes. I hugged him and went over to play with my children. We all had a big family hug as tears of sorrow and laughter engulfed all of us.

Well, it took me a little while, but I got away from Dr. Daley. All but one person from my group now realize that we were falsely led to believe we had MPD and were ritually abused. After the effects of the medication wore off, I was able to distinguish which memories were real and which were created in therapy with Dr. Daley. My real memories are the same memories I had when I entered therapy. I am fully recovered from this nightmare created by Dr. Daley in order to further her career and obtain long-term paying clients. I'm back in college, majoring in psychology and I'm running the school dance ensemble. I love my children, I love my husband and I love my life!

When I look back I feel sad about the lost time, when my kids didn't have a mom, my husband didn't have a wife. But we are healing. It frightens me to no end just knowing she's still out there practicing. I've filed a malpractice lawsuit against Dr. Daley. I can't bear the thought that someone else could be on the brink of insanity, families destroyed, and maybe lives and souls lost. I have vowed to stop this madness that I consider to be emotional rape!

In the following two stories, Victoria's husband and daughter tell how Victoria's experience with false memories affected their lives.

Victoria's Husband – His Perspective

There is some irony in saying that this story is from my own perspective. For a *perspective* is usually a clear view or balanced focus on a piece of art or an issue at hand. My story is anything but clear. Distortions are the emotional memories that I still struggle with. Distortion and confusion mixed with an ultimate feeling of hopelessness were my intimate companions, more so than my own wife.

Let me start at the beginning. My name is Jim. I am in my late 30s and I have been married to Victoria for 10 years. About five years ago we were having some trouble and separated for about nine months. After getting back together we went through a readjustment phase. We were seeing a counselor, both individually and together. My wife, Victoria, was trying to find a woman therapist with whom she would feel comfortable and who could also help her sort out some very delicate issues from her past. After some time and various circumstances she finally hooked up with a therapist. The therapist seemed perfect because she was a woman, and because she was also a psychiatrist who therefore could deal with some of the greater issues and be responsible for any medications which needed to be prescribed for depression and anxiety.

Well, there was that honeymoon period between patient and doctor when things were on a surface level. Nothing too deep at first, just day-to-day issues. But eventually the sessions got heavier, with my wife revealing her past experiences of being sexually abused, past abusive relationships and more. These issues were hard enough for me to understand and be compassionate about, besides dealing with the issues of our marriage. But, on top of these things, it all got much harder and very confusing when Dr. Daley diagnosed my wife with Multiple Personality Disorder (MPD). Victoria had a hard time accepting this, and so did I, because it just didn't seem to fit. She had enough issues which we could identify without adding something we did not really understand. But Dr. Daley was the authority and claimed to be a pioneer in the field of MPD. At first she presented it to my wife as "a try it on for size" diagnosis. But within a short time it was a definite fit in the doctor's eyes.

I knew my wife was capable of some drastic mood swings and it could be like an emotional roller coaster at our house, but I never observed her slipping in and out of other personalities. I would have noticed that! But Victoria started down that road with Dr. Daley at the wheel. She was told to give her feelings names. Each mood now had an identity of its own. She had actual names for her little girl self, her insecure self, her wild side; her stronger emotions even had male names. All of this was with the doctor's guidance and suggestion. It was a little hard to swallow. After a session Victoria would come home and tell me about another new character. She was really trying to trust the doctor, although it still did not feel right. The doctor said Victoria was "in denial" when she would question the validity of the MPD diagnosis. She would tell my wife to work harder, dig deeper and keep a journal at home to help find more personalities.

After several months of my wife telling the doctor that I was having some doubts and trouble adjusting to all of this, Dr. Daley and I finally got together at a couple of my wife's sessions. I came with a fairly open mind, hoping to gain some greater understanding about my wife and this whole

MPD subject. Keep in mind that I was a strong person as opposed to my wife, who was weak and vulnerable and seemed to shrink down just a little bit more in the doctor's presence. She was overwhelmed by this whole MPD thing by now and she was in such awe of this woman being a doctor. (That really meant a lot to Victoria.) I have taught at the college level for years and have had many other professional dealings, so this was a fairly objective meeting for me.

I got a very strong impression that this doctor was a crackpot and a very eccentric person. She was full of contradictions and not very specific about many details and had a very nonchalant attitude about my wife's treatment. Many times in the conversation she would say to me, "I really do not have an answer to that, but you are just going to have to trust me because I am an expert in this field." Or, "You should be focusing on being supportive and understanding in your wife's illness, not questioning it." Then she would slip back into her nonchalant attitude: "Oh, well, it is no big thing. I've seen many such cases. Besides, it would take me too long to educate you all about MPDs."

Well, the way I felt about it was that this is my wife and I am taking this whole thing rather seriously now. After all, it is her mind we are talking about, not just a strange toe infection that the doctor thought I may not be able to understand. What made the whole session even more frustrating was that Dr. Daley was constantly trying to be humorous. She told a lot of silly jokes and anecdotes which she seemed to revert to when she could not come up with an answer. She did this a lot!

Maybe I just did not believe enough. Maybe I was trying to dig too deep. These personalities just felt false to me.

These different characters my wife was supposed to be or was trying to be just seemed fake. Not real. But I thought, okay, I'll go along with this program some more. Maybe I am missing something. It was suggested that I meet some husbands of her other patients to better understand my situation with my wife and get some support from these other men who have been through it all.

It was a night of one of my wife's MPD support groups. There were usually about six women in the group and three or four husbands would usually drop off their wives. It was arranged for me to meet one of the husbands. He was very gung-ho about talking with me. My wife and Dr. Daley both talked about him like he was the guru of the MPD husbands. So we met and walked down to a little local diner. He proceeded to tell me that this whole multiple personality thing was very big stuff and difficult for most people to understand. But he had been dealing with it for some time now, with his wife, and was there to help me through the hard time I was having with accepting the diagnosis. He told me that he has been so impressed with the doctor that he has even seen her as a therapist/counselor several times. And, in fact, she told him that she believes he may be an MPD himself. H wasn't so sure about that diagnosis, but did think it was a possibility. He told me that I must be "in denial," partly because it was a macho man thing. He was a professional military man for over a decade and is now a truck driver, and quite a big guy. But he was sensitive to *this* issue despite his usual hard outlook on things, because of his love for his wife. He said I didn't need to understand, but just be supportive and nurturing to my wife.

One of the things he suggested, which he had done for his wife, was to buy a gift for each one of the personalities.

For every birthday and Christmas (I don't recall if he included Valentine's day, Mother's day, Easter, etc.) he would give his wife thirty-some gifts. I don't recall the exact number, but my wife says the amount of personalities in his wife was supposedly much higher than 30.

Well, this did sound very sweet, but my wife was still just trying to find *names* for the six to 10 personalities she and her doctor were trying to uncover. All the while the doctor is telling her, "You must work harder, Victoria. Open them up." But his wife had all these names and he said she was discovering more personalities all the time. So the gift list just keeps getting bigger, he said. And with his wife, as with mine, some of the personalities were supposedly men. I do have to say here that Dr. Daley pushed the men personalities on my wife pretty hard. And because my wife had a harder time accepting these male characters, they obviously seemed very real. The stronger the denial, the more valid the personality must be.

After a while, I met almost all of my wife's group members, many times in a social situation or at our home or theirs. I never saw anyone become another person. And almost all of her group members had questioned this diagnosis. They would usually say, "I just don't really feel it, but it must be so because Dr. Daley says so." Almost every woman from Victoria's MPD group who I talked to had one thing in common: They had been searching for a therapist who could give them some answers as to why they had been depressed and full of anxiety.

There was one member of the group who tried so hard to be a multiple. She obviously agreed with the diagnosis. She had been in and out of several psych wards in hospitals around town. Well, now she found a place to belong. She would always announce who she was at any given time.

Or, "Oh, I just switched. Now I'm so and so." And at first I thought she might be a legitimate case. I really tried to believe and understand. And I thought that maybe I could get a better perspective about my wife through this woman. But she became rather embarrassing at times. She was such a bad actress. At times when she was supposed to be one of her many personalities, she would forget who she said she was. She would actually say things like, "Oh, did I say I am Sally? I meant to say I'm Rita. That's who I'm supposed to be now." Her whole presentation of each of these characters was fake, with stiff-sounding dialogue, almost like a bad soap opera, or more like a poorly acted junior high school play.

At different times, before or after a group session, or in a hospital psych ward, I actually observed Dr. Daley playing along with her. She would interact with the patient with total belief in the particular personality. Even when I would think that she must have noticed that she just mixed up her personalities, the doctor would simply say, "Stay focused now. Don't forget who you are supposed to be." And Dr. Daley always used a very little girl type of whining sing-song voice when she was relating to this patient's personalities. It made the whole situation seem all the more unreal.

As time went on my wife seemed to be slipping further away from me and the kids. She was becoming more depressed just thinking that she had been an MPD all these years. Her medications had been changed and then changed again. She was sleeping all the time and becoming more and more housebound, only going out to her therapy sessions or to her MPD groups. Whenever Victoria felt she was in crisis, which was becoming all the time, the doctor would always up her meds. And when this would not do the trick, Dr. Daley would put her into a psych ward for a week or two.

The psych ward became her second home after awhile. I had no wife at home, and the children had no mother. And when she was there, it was like having a stranger in the house. She wore sun glasses all the time, put on extra weight, dyed her hair a different color every few weeks, was always depressed, did most everything from bed (eating, reading, watching TV, using the telephone), had anxiety and breathing attacks, and cried or else became extremely angry and would scream a lot. I would run to her beck and call, as would the kids. She was in some sort of crisis many times during any given day. I would always run her medication to her. And if I forgot, she would not take them many times, and then blame me for her mental state of mind. I did the cooking. My daughter and I did the cleaning and the laundry. Our little boy also contributed. The three of us were constant servants to Victoria's every need. Because she was often absent from the household, due to her hospitalizations, we became a team of sorts. So when mom was home, we had our routines well practiced. It was kind of like a life without her, whether she was in a psych ward or at home.

Things got worse. The routine of the doctor telling me over the phone to "up her meds" became just that – a routine. And when I would say to the doctor, "This routine doesn't seem to be working. How much is going to be too much?" She would then talk of changing to a different medication again. And then every conversation would end with the same frustrated phrase: "Just bring her down to the hospital tonight and I'll see her when I make my rounds tomorrow." During these phone conversations Dr. Daley usually said things like, "I can't deal with this," or "I don't know what to say to her when she is like this." She was not very helpful even though she was on call for times of crisis. She did not even want to talk to Victoria. I would ask her to please say a few calming words to Victoria because it would mean so much to her. Many times she refused to give those words because of my wife's condition. It was a power play. And Victoria would be in the background crying, "I just want to talk to Dr. Daley. Please, Dr. Daley, I need you to talk to me."

Now this doctor knew that after a little talk my wife would be fine for the night. Instead, she would demand: "Bring her in." My wife was becoming totally dependent upon Dr. Daley. Eventually Dr. Daley was telling my wife to leave me. She was also telling Victoria that she was bad for the kids and to have them placed in foster care or give them up for adoption. The diagnosis got even stranger as she told my wife that more male personalities were coming out and she had animal personalities coming to the surface too. On top of this, a whole satanic realm was being suggested also. This went on much further than I care to write about now. But it did go as far as Victoria seeking out different priests to perform an exorcism. The exorcism was never done because one priest finally had the strength to say to my wife that she was *not* possessed and he had the wisdom to see what she needed and give it to her – a little compassionate understanding and soothing conversation.

Eventually Dr. Daley was telling my wife that *I* was an MPD too, but I just didn't know it yet. And one time when Dr. Daley was at our house, our daughter ran in from school and changed her clothes and went back out with friends to a school game. The doctor announced that she thought our daughter had multiple personalities. Dr. Daley could not understand why our daughter had to change her clothes. I said she is just a teenager wanting to get out of school clothes into more hip and casual clothes for the game. The doctor still thought it was odd. She did not have custody of her own teenage daughter nor did she see her very often. But even if she was a little out of touch with kids, it was no reason to make such an absurd statement that our daughter had MPD.

My own stress over my wife, MPD and this doctor led me to find some relief in a men's group. It was a general group where any issues could be discussed. I attended for six months, once a week. It was a great help for me to have some place to go and just vent all of my frustrations and my confusion. And it gave me a scheduled break from the kids, my wife, the whole distorted weekly reality I was a part of. The men and the counselor were as helpful as they could be with advice and support, but they were all usually in shock and disbelief as well. We could all relate to each other's stories in some ways. But when it came to me, everyone had a hard time because it sounded like such a stressful, bizarre movie. In fact, many times some of my group members became overwhelmed and filled with stress and anxiety. So over time I started telling less and less and would candy-coat things a little.

My support system was breaking down. I also had a couple of friends who knew some of the details. But they always let me know that they did not want to know too much and eventually didn't discuss it at all. Family members on her side and mine were not told any details because we were still patching up our marriage after being separated. Family can be very judgmental, you know. So now after about two years of this I was feeling pretty helpless and depressed. I was starting to feel like I had nowhere to turn. Nobody knew or understood the strain I was under. My wife was starting to threaten suicide, the doctor was trying truth serum (sodium amytal) to help her remember more details of the satanic ritual abuse and to find more personalities. I would feel more and more guilty giving my wife increased medication. I felt so sad for her each time I would take her into a lock-up unit, and in my dreams the sounds of my wife crying and the other patients I saw there crying and moaning and babbling and mumbling and gurgling and screaming and whimpering were haunting my sleep.

Dr. Daley would avoid me whenever she saw me at the hospital. And she would never answer the calls from us, even though she was on call. My wife would have another group member put in a call to her because she would answer the calls of the other patients in her group. She would only see Victoria on scheduled appointment times or group nights or while in the hospital psych ward.

Eventually the women of the group formed a group of their own because they were not getting their needs met. This led to most of them finally breaking away from Dr. Daley and finding other therapists and doctors. My wife tried another medication which helped one of her group members and it cleared things up for her enough so she could see the situation she was in. With the new meds and the women forming their own group, she finally had the strength to seek out new counseling.

It was a two-year nightmare. My wife never got the help she sought. And now, for the last two years, she has been doing new therapy. She is trying to help resolve the issues she originally sought therapy for. But she spends most of her therapy time trying to come to grips with the two years she lost. The whole family is still trying to heal. Some of the old patterns with the way we interrelate as a family are still there and are hard to break. When my wife is in a depressed state of mind I feel my insides start to churn with the fear that she may cry out, "Take me to the hospital." It's like I have shell shock.

I know Dr. Daley is out there somewhere with a whole new group of women. I see her ads running in different feminist papers and gay women's papers. Yes, I try to keep track of her.

It is sad to think back to all of the events and family holidays I would attend without my wife; all the excuses I made; the phone calls she never returned but I did; the shopping and the cooking (I still do those and enjoy it); and the emotional drain more than anything. I missed time from work, missed some events and holidays too. Though I had a lot of sadness and frustration and anger, I am glad we stuck it out through the storm. My wife could have taken the doctor's advice and dumped the kids, or I could have left her. We now attend family therapy to help heal the wounds of the Dr. Daley years. But mostly, we help each other with our deep love and commitment.

Victoria's Daughter –
"Mom, Where Are You?"

At 15 years old, most teenagers are looking forward to the next school dance. I was looking forward to the next time my mother would actually get out of bed for a couple hours. As a child I realized that life had its ups and downs, but nothing ever prepared me for the four years of pain and loneliness and being abandoned by my lifelong best friend – my mother.

Just before I turned 15, my parents separated. I thought it was hard for me but I guess it was harder on my mom. She seemed terribly depressed and somewhat withdrawn, even from me, until she and my dad (stepdad) got back together. I thought life would get back to normal again but it was not to be. She slowly began crawling more and more into a shell, withdrawing from everything, not eating. I tried to pay no mind at the time until feelings of suicide brought her into the hospital. There, regrettably, she met Dr. Daley.

Life with my mom had been great for me. She was the ultimate mom. She was a great companion. We even made up our own special songs. She was always there to talk to. I could cry on her shoulder. No matter how old I got she would hold me on her lap and rock me. She cried on my shoulder, too. We talked about our dreams and shared our problems. We were nothing short of lifelong best friends.

After she met Dr. Daley all of that changed. There were "secrets" now. I wasn't even told the truth about her going into the hospital. They said she was having problems with her asthma. But watching my mother leave the house, I knew better. You can't be that close to someone and not know.

The instant she left, my world crumbled. I felt alone, hurt and heartbroken. What did I do to make my mom put so much distance between us, and why wasn't she telling me the truth? In the hospital my mom seemed to be getting help, I hoped. She eventually came home, but nothing was ever the same.

She was on medication now, sleeping more, eating lots and watching TV. She seemed to be becoming handicapped in her own world. I became responsible for watching my little brother. We were constantly fighting for some positive attention. I began slipping in school. Except for one friend, I isolated myself from the rest of the world. Not only did I withdraw, but our whole family had to stop seeing my mom's relatives for Christmas, Easter and other holidays. The few times we saw them over those years, my mom was always wearing these big sunglasses, even inside. My mom seemed to be falling off the deep end.

My mom was filled with hope when she starting seeing Dr. Daley, but I had sensed something eerie from this doctor. I felt deep hatred for this woman. As time went on my mom saw her almost as a god, a savior for herself, and I feel that she took advantage of my mother's naiveness and false hope, to brainwash her.

Dr. Daley soon began telling my mom about a sickness called MPD. The doctor gave my mom books to read about this illness. With constant brainwashing by Dr. Daley my mom began to believe in her. Soon after, so did my dad and so did I. Dr. Daley had a couple of sessions with me. I was scared and confused as she described the illness. She told me to let my mom's "children" come out and play with me.

This was too strange. I was to be the parent. I tried to see if this was true. I looked for subtle hints of different personalities. One minute my mom was childlike and the next angry, she became the Screamer. Believing what was being said was true, I slowly began to think my mom was crazy. I thought she was a real life Sybil and I was living with "IT." I started to have frequent headaches and stomachaches.

My mom began going to a group for women with the same problems. These women became her best friends. I guess they could relate to each other. But I hated them and the doctor for taking my mom away from me!

At 16 I fell in love with a boy from my high school. I strived for his attention, acceptance and praise – all the things I wasn't getting at home anymore. When our relationship ended I fell into a state of depression. I was sad, lonely and devastated. Not just from this boy, but because my mom had emotionally abandoned me too. My sadness soon grew into anger. I started smoking cigarettes, drinking and fighting with my mom.

I was eventually put in a "kid's psych unit" and on medication. I refused the pills that were forced on me. I learned how to "cheek" them so it looked like I had taken them but I would actually spit them out. The fear of ending up like my mom, who was constantly medicated, scared me half to death. After all, now she was on so much medication you could have filled a pharmacy for a year! As months passed I thought my mom was getting better. At least she got up to go to her weekly women's group conducted by Dr. Daley. But she only got sicker. She was getting sucked in even more now, believing everything the doctor said. The next step was satanic ritual abuse and the insanity of those stories. I started thinking she would never get better. Still fighting with my mom, I couldn't wait until I was old enough to move out on my own to be away from her.

One day I came home about the same time as my dad and brother. We came in and saw Mom dressed; she had cleaned the house and was making dinner. I had no idea what happened, but it reminded me so much of my earlier years. We all hugged and cried. I knew then my mother was beginning to doubt her treatment with Dr. Daley. It turned out she had taken herself off the prescribed medicine and for the first time in years she semed like her old self.

Still frustrated with a lot of things in life and still feeling bitter, I dropped out of high school in 11th grade. I was planning to move out on my own. Too much had happened. I would never be a parent like her. Eventually I did move out with a friend's family and then into my own apartment.

On my own, I did a lot of thinking about my life and what I wanted to do. I went back and got my G.E.D. It was the happiest day in my life. That day I knew I could really be someone and do it with no one's help but my own. Also that year, the pain that I had been through began to ease and instead of hating my mother, I tried to understand her better. We both did some growing when we were apart. Even though I know the pain will never go away, I tried to learn from it. It's taken quite a while, but my mother and I are now getting along normally. I'm working and will be going to college soon.

Now that my mother and I are both better after all the "crazy" times, I still think of Dr. Daley and the other families she is hurting with her brainwashing and quackery. I just hope she gets what is rightfully hers: No respect, no new patients, and at least one brain cell for her to realize the pain she put people through. I just turned 20 and even though my teen years were hard, I'm looking forward to the upcoming years.

The Epidemic Grows

Millions of dollars have been spent in psychotherapy to recover what is purported by many psychotherapists to be memories. Most of the women who wrote their stories for *True Stories of False Memories* were hospitalized at one time or another at great cost. While the cost measured in dollars was great, the cost measured in suffering, their own and their families, was even greater.

This epidemic of False Memory Syndrome is widespread. The eight women come from seven different states: Minnesota, Ohio, Illinois, Utah, Nevada, Michigan, and two from Texas. The epidemic is nationwide. As of June 1, 1993, False Memory Syndrome Foundation documented stories from 4,042 families in the United States. Families in Australia, England, France, Germany, Ireland, Israel and New Zealand are now coming forward with similar stories. Eve-

WHERE DO 4042 FAMILIES LIVE? JUNE 1, 1993				
AK(8)	AL(14)	AR(12)	AZ(126)	CA(723)
CO(65)	CT(46)	DE(13)	FL(170)	GA(51)
HI(5)	IA(31)	ID(17)	IL(145)	IN(37)
KS(39)	KY(16)	LA(15)	MA(115)	MD(62)
ME(18)	MI(131)	MN(83)	MO(80)	MS(2)
MT(24)	NC(56)	ND(5)	NE(19)	NH(18)
NJ(102)	NM(32)	NV(19)	NY(165)	OH(129)
OK(38)	OR(102)	PA(234)	RI(10)	SC(17)
SD(10)	TN(27)	TX(149)	UT(148)	VA(58)
VT(19)	WA(204)	WI(131)	WV(7)	WY(6)
		DC(6)	VI(3)	
Canada:	AB(18)	BC(43)	MB(39)	NS(6)
ON(142)	PQ(4)	SK(7)	PE(1)	

ry state has some families affected.

What makes this mental health crisis so different from other epidemics is the fact that many well-meaning people are unwittingly contributing to it. We don't believe that the authors who have written their books which provide the theory behind repressed memory mean to harm people. We don't think that the hospitals are set up to create havoc in the lives of their patients and make them worse rather than better. We don't believe that the state legislators which have extended the statute of limitations on repressed memories want to create a great injustice. And we certainly don't believe that hundreds of thousands of psychotherapists intentionally want to destroy families.

But theories which may have some validity are being carried to the extreme.

Many families may, in fact, be dysfunctional – but 100 percent of them? To us a family is made up of a group of people who care for one another, during good times and bad – they have their crises and often have to adjust to changing circumstances. But to condemn the American family as a place where child abuse is condoned is irresponsible.

Harmful incidents may, in fact, be repressed or suppressed, but to spend months, even years, to dredge up such memories is ludicrous. In the name of healing, does it make sense to employ techniques which are unproven and unscientific such as hypnosis, dream interpretation and body work? Does it make sense to abandon a "family of origin" for a "family of choice" on the basis of such unscientific methods of retrieving memories?

The women who shared their stories with us for this book all suffered untold agony and thousands of others are out there suffering. In every reliable procedure there is room for criticism, consultation and corroboration. Not in this type of therapy. Criticism is labeled as denial, consultation as evasion and corroboration as unnecessary.

Referring to recovered memory therapy, University of California sociologist Richard Ofshe and journalist Ethan Watters wrote in an article entitled "Making Monsters," "This treatment leads clients to see their parents as monsters who sexually abused them as children. Parents have to witness their adult children turn into monsters trying to destroy their reputations and lives. In less than ten years' time this therapy, in its various forms, has devastated thousands of lives. It has become a nation-wide phenomenon — one that is becoming entrenched in our culture and the mental health professions with enormous speed" (Ofshe and Watters:4).

One way or another, these eight women survived the ordeal of abusive therapy. They are all now going on with their lives in productive ways. They wrote their stories in order to help us understand the issue of False Memory Syndrome.

As of June 1992, the False Memory Syndrome Foundation heard from about eighty women and men who recant the accusations they made against their families while under the influence of survivor therapy.

A MOTHER'S STORY

She went through it alone – the agony of seeing her daughter destroy her family by entering into the world of false memories. Guided by a therapist, the daughter recreated a childhood that is so sordid, so horrendous, that the very thought of such a childhood is shocking. It is a childhood the mother doesn't recognize, where sexual abuse occurs and the daughter is shamed and humiliated.

The mother takes us on her journey. Not to be able to help a daughter in distress brings unfathomable pain, and to see yourself and your husband considered perpetrators is too dreadful to imagine. She hasn't found the road to reconciling with her deluded daughter, but she is trying, and she shares those efforts with our readers. Thousands of other parents are on the same journey, looking for a way to regain the trust, respect and love that has been lost as their adult children wander in the maze of repressed memory therapy. All names in the story have been changed.

A Mother's Journey with FMS

After practicing law for 14 years, my husband decided he was ready for a new profession and sold his practice. Then, after almost a year, he established his own company, working as a manufacturer's representative. Our son, Josh, was married and living in another state, and our youngest child, Lori, had just turned 21 and decided to move out on her own with two of her friends. We were officially classified as "empty nesters." We felt as if we were newlyweds again and really enjoyed each other's companionship. I decided to work temporary jobs so I could take time off and travel with my husband when he was called out of town. We felt we had been truly blessed. We had raised two beautiful children we were very proud of and, after 26 years of marriage, we still reveled in each other's love.

We had always been a close family, and although my son lived 800 miles away, Lori was here in town and we invited her for dinner every week. She would come home to wash her clothes, and we would occasionally take her to a movie.

During the last part of 1991, for some reason, Lori had become very upset with one of her roommates, Mary, and had virtually kicked the girl out of her life. This was after being best friends with this girl for five years. She and the second roommate, Joe, got a new apartment that was only five miles from our house. The only thing Lori would say about the breakup was that Mary would act like such a child, never taking any responsibility, that Lori felt as if she was acting the part of a mother and Joe was acting the part of a father. She was tired of it; she felt Mary needed to grow up.

She and Joe found a new apartment after much discussion about how things would be between them. While she had always looked upon Joe as a brother, he felt more for her than that. She told him that she just didn't feel the same way, and she would get angry with him if he acted jealous when she went out on a date. They talked it over and smoothed out their differences, and agreed to live together as friends. I always hoped that she would eventually care more for Joe because he was really a nice person, and he genuinely cared for her.

After they moved into the apartment, she began to use the laundry facilities on the premises, and we hardly saw her. When questioned about saving money by bringing the laundry to the house, she said she liked meeting new friends at the laundromat. We began to see her only about every two weeks when I would call and invite her to dinner and/or a movie. At the time, we took it as a sign of her growing up and breaking the ties with her parents, even though we missed her.

It was the end of January, 1992, and Paul, my husband, had to go to Miami for a week on business. "Tough job," we thought as we dreamed of getting out of the cold. The weekend before we were to go I called Lori to ask her to dinner. She told me she was having dinner with the Whites.

Lydia White was in her late thirties/early forties and worked in the same office with Lori. For some reason, even though Lydia was old enough to be her mother, she had befriended Lori at their office and taken her into her home practically as a family member. For many years I had worked where Lori worked and had gotten her the job there several months before I decided to terminate my employment. There were a lot of wild rumors (that I have since been able to confirm) about Lydia, and I was shocked and somewhat concerned when she became Lori's "best friend." I confronted Lori about this, and she told me that Lydia had changed and that everyone there liked Lydia now.

She began to spend more and more time with Lydia's family. When I saw her, she would show me all these self-help books that Lydia would loan her. Every time I called, she couldn't be with us because she was going to Lydia's house, or taking Lydia's 13-year-old daughter somewhere. Lori told me Lydia's daughter was like a little sister to her and she was having a great time being the big sister. Inside I began to feel terribly jealous, but I said nothing.

We went to Miami and had a very good time. When I came back and invited her out, Lori made an excuse that she already had plans with Lydia's family.

In a couple of weeks, we had to make a week-end trip to nearby Small Town. I called Lori on Thursday to tell her where we would be in case she needed us over the week-end. I got her answering machine and left her a message.

Friday, after work, Paul and I left for Small Town. He had a seminar to give on Saturday morning, and we were coming back Saturday evening. After check-out time at the hotel, I went to the lobby, had lunch, then spent about three hours reading while waiting for Paul to return.

He picked me up about 3:00, and when we were settled in the car for our trip back home, he said he had something to show me that was bad news. I couldn't imagine what it was since he hadn't been anywhere to get any bad news. He pulled a letter out of his pocket and said it was a letter from Lori that had come in the mail on Friday. He had not shown it to me because he knew it would upset me and would have made it very hard to sit in the hotel lobby with this letter on my mind. He was right!

Lori's letter was addressed to Paul and Kathryn. It said we wouldn't be hearing from her for awhile, and she did not want us to contact her. She said she was working through some issues from her childhood, and she needed a total separation from family right now. She said she wasn't blaming anyone, just taking responsibility for her life because only she could "fix" it. If we tried to contact her, she would have her phone number changed. It was signed "sincerely." I cried.

This hit us like a ton of bricks. What had happened? What was she remembering about her childhood? It had been a wonderful childhood. We talked and cried all the way back to Big Town. When we returned, trying to respect her wishes and not call, we wrote her a letter:

February 23, 1992
Dear Lori,

Needless to say, we were shocked to read your letter. You indicate that something is wrong in your life, and the cause is something that happened to you in your childhood, which you are just now beginning to remember. And, since you don't want to have any contact with us while you are working through this problem, we can only assume that we are somehow directly involved.

It is quite devastating to have someone you thought you had a great relationship with all your life drop this kind of bombshell on you with no explanation at all. The worst part is not knowing what is going on and how long this estrangement might last. We don't know if this is temporary or if we have lost our daughter forever. After hours of searching the past, we can't think of anything we did that was bad enough to cause this kind of reaction.

If you are attempting to remember your past, we may be the best people you could talk with since no one was closer to you as you were growing up. Or have we done something so horrible that you can't discuss it with us? It also occurs to us that maybe the best way to work out problems with people close to you is to confront those people openly under the supervision of a trained counselor. With this approach, each person understands the problem, learns how everyone else is feeling and why, and with the help of the counselor, the problem can be resolved in such a way that everyone benefits individually and the relationship can then resume even better than before.

Please give this approach some thought. If you decide to let us help you, naturally we will pay any costs involved. On the other hand, if you want us to stay away for a while, we will respect your wishes. However, if that is the case, please have the heart to at least write and let us know if this situation is permanent or temporary, and please try to give us some idea of what you are remembering and what is wrong. We wouldn't ask this of you if we weren't going nuts over this.

Lori, we both love you very much and have nothing but the very best memories of our relationship from the time you were born to the present. We want you to know that we are here for you and will help you in any way that we can. All you need to do is ask. Looking back over our lives, we both feel that you are the best thing that ever happened to us, and you are certainly our greatest achievement. I guess one of our faults as parents is that we didn't tell you often enough just how much you mean to us, but we are telling you now. I just hope it's not too late.

Please let us hear from you soon

When we didn't hear from her right away, I began to get in touch with everyone I could think of. Lori suffers from lupus, so the first person I contacted was her physician. We went to see Dr. B. and showed him the letter. Lori had spent quite a bit of time in his office lately. She had been suffering from anxiety attacks and depression as well as tiredness, all of which can be caused by lupus. Dr. B. had come to like her because she always appeared "up" in spite of her illness. She had written him a poem and given him a demo tape of her singing. She was a well-liked patient of his and the feeling was mutual.

He said Lori had never mentioned anything wrong in her family relationship. Quite the opposite, in fact; she had expressed only feelings of respect and love for us. Knowing that lupus can attack the central nervous system and cause delusions, he agreed that her disease might at least be a contributing factor to her behavior. He said he would call her and encourage her to come in for a checkup, which he did, but she refused, and still has not been in to see him.

I then got in touch with Mary, Lori's ex-roommate, and her mom, Kay. When I went to visit them, Mary said Lori had felt, for a long time, that someone had sexually abused her, but she didn't know who it was. She had even thought it could have been her brother or father, but she couldn't remember anything — just a feeling. I was shocked, to say the least. Lori had never mentioned this to me. Kay also told me that she had thought it rather odd when Lori had told her that at the time the doctor discovered she had lupus I had cried, and that had made Lori very angry. She told me that Lori had said she hated me for crying. I just couldn't believe what I was hearing!

Then I talked to Joe. He told me virtually the same thing Mary and Kay had. He was able to add some information since he and Lori had originally dated before they had become just friends. He told me that when he would try to kiss her, she always acted a little odd, and he had always wondered if someone had hurt her. I began to put the pieces together. Lori never could sustain a relationship; she always seemed to get more enjoyment out of the chase. When she would catch a guy, she didn't seem to want him anymore. She always told me she didn't want to get serious about anyone because she wanted a music career, and she didn't want a relationship to get in the way. I just thought she had a one-track mind and being a famous singer was her final goal. She always jokingly said she would get serious when she was about 27 or 28, but until then she was just going to have fun, so I took her at her word. Looking back, I guess I wanted to take her at her word because I didn't want to think anything was wrong with her.

I couldn't stand it. I stopped by her apartment one day with the excuse that I was dropping off some mail that had come to our house for her. When she came to the door, I asked her if I could talk to her. With a smile she said, "I can't talk now." "Oh, Lori," I said, "Can't you please explain what is going on?" She said, "I can't talk now." I asked her if she knew when she would be able to talk, and she said, "I can't talk now." She wouldn't say anything else. By this time I started to break down, and I couldn't talk through my tears. I handed her the mail along with a note I had written her about how I was feeling — crying all the time, unable to eat, stomach upset — pleading with her to please talk to us, and then I walked away. That's the last time I saw her. She was smiling and never changed her expression!

Joe called us again and wanted to come by and talk to us. By this time, Lori had kicked him out of the apartment, and he was confused and very hurt. He said Lydia had introduced Lori to a friend of hers who was a "psychic" named Ramona, and that she had been hypnotizing Lori and doing "past life regressions." He said that this Ramona had told Lori that she had been sexually abused in previous lives. He thought that Lori had somehow gotten things turned around in her mind and had come to believe that it had happened in this life. He questioned her about her visits with Ramona, and she said she would lay on a couch in Ramona's office and Ramona would use hypnosis and ask her questions. Joe said she had come home from Ramona's one evening and told him that she had to talk seriously to him. She then told him that Ramona had helped her "remember" her childhood and that her parents were really sick people. She said that we had done all manner of things to her and that they were too sick for her to tell him about. He said she told him that we had invited our friends or family in, and they had all abused her.

I was in shock. I wrote her another letter:

March 15, 1992
My dearest Lori,

I think I have talked to just about every friend that you have had in trying to figure out just what is going on.

The consensus is that you believe that someone has sexually abused you in the past. Lori, if this is true, you certainly have nothing to be ashamed of, nor do you need to feel any guilt. I want you to know I love you very, very much. You were and are one of the best things that has ever happened to me.

My concern now is how to help you get over this, and I want to know who did this to you and when. You know that if I had known about it, I would have taken action against this person immediately no matter who it was, and you also know that Daddy would have killed any-one who harmed you.

Yes, I was also told that you thought it might be Daddy. I want you to know that he is devastated that you would think this, and has said that he would be glad to take a lie detector test or sodium pentothal to prove to you that he had never done this. But, the thing we want most is to know what you are thinking and to be able to address that and take proper action against the offend-ing party. Maybe we could do it with Rebecca [Rebecca Scott was a very good friend of ours, and a psychiatrist] or anyone else whom you might choose and just sit down and talk about this. I have searched my mind trying to remember every place that I have ever left you. I've wondered if anything had happened to you in church or in the day care that you had been in for a two-year period.

But, whatever happened and whenever it did, I have a right to know and do something about it!

There is one thing that Kay told me that I wanted to explain to you. She said that you had told her that when I found out you had lupus that I cried, and you said that you hated me for crying. She thought that maybe you had felt guilty because you were sick. Lori, there was no reason for you to feel guilty because you were sick. You didn't ask to have lupus just like I didn't ask to have headaches. I cried because, when we lived in Small Town, I worked with a teenager in our church who had lupus. She had a severe case and at that time they really didn't have anything to treat it with except cortisone. She was very thin, and when they would treat her, her stomach would swell up to the size of a basketball, and her face would swell all out of propor-tion. Her family was from Mexico and, although I was fairly close to her, one day out of the blue I found out that she had returned to Mexico. She was 16 at the time. Her family told me that she had returned to Mexico because there was a well-to-do family there whose son wanted to marry her. Because of the lupus, she wasn't expected to live much past 20 so they let her go so she could have that experience.

So you can see that in my mind, lupus meant a death sentence, and I was devastated at the thought of losing you. I know now that there are different types of lupus and more advanced medicines for treatment. But that is why I cried.

Lori, I love you dearly, but this is the last letter I will write to you. It's your choice whether you will ever contact me again. I am hurting as much now as if I had already lost you and am devastated at the thought of never hearing from you again. Please, Lori, let's talk this out. I need this so I can get on with my life one way or another. I want to know who might have hurt you to the point that you no longer want me as your mother.

I don't even know how to sign this so I'll just say,

With love

Needless to say, from the start of all this, I was going crazy. I cried hysterically for weeks on end and lost 15 pounds in a month. We finally called Dr. B. back and asked him to recommend a psychiatrist who was familiar with lupus and its effects on the psychological makeup of patients. We wanted to know if the lupus could be causing all this. We also wanted to ask a psychiatrist if there was any possibility that we could have committed such horrendous crimes and then completely put them out of our minds. We didn't think so, but we were looking at all avenues to try to explain this madness.

Dr. B. gave us a referral, and we made an appointment with a psychiatrist, Dr. J., and told him the whole story. He said the lupus could be playing a part, but he was very noncommittal. He said there was no way we could have sexually abused our daughter and forgotten, unless we had a habit of dissociating. We asked him what it meant to dissociate. He said that if we ever felt like we were outside of our bodies or had lost time, we could have been dissociating. Since neither of us had ever experienced situations like this, we knew we were right in assuming that we could not have done this terrible thing and forgotten it.

As time went by, we received a second letter from our daughter. She told us that her memories were of sexual abuse. She stated that although there were some others, primarily her abusers were the two of us. She stated that these were her memories, whether we remembered or not, "I know what I know, and I have to deal with it and heal my life." She told us that she had plenty of support, many new friends and an "excellent" counselor. She stated that she was doing well. I replied to her letter right away:

April 14, 1992
Dear Lori,

Thank you for communicating with us. If you really believe the things you said, then it must have been very difficult for you. You will never know how difficult it was for me to read it.

Lori, I don't know where these memories are coming from. I know right now they seem real to you, but we never, never did anything of a sexual or abusive nature to you.

I only have good memories of you growing up. From the day I brought you home from the hospital you were the most wonderful child in the world. I remember listening to you "sing" to yourself when you went to bed and when you awoke in the morning; sitting on pins and needles the first time you performed at your middle school; and then hearing the first song that you put to music and sang. I recall seeing you off to first grade; watching you graduate from high school. I can picture the mornings over on the street where we used to live, when I would call to you from your bedroom doorway that it was time for you to get up; you would get up sleepily, walk across the room and hug me in the doorway. I would stand there and hug you back, and think to myself, "Just stand here and let her hug you as long as she wants to because someday she'll be grown-up and won't be home to give you hugs." So I would stand there and just feel your love for me until you would break away and start getting ready for school. That is one of my fondest memories.

Lori, I don't quite know how to say this, so I will just say it: It seems to me that if you ever felt anything for us, you would be hoping your memory was somehow wrong. And, you would be doing everything in the world to find out why you remembered something as horrid as you describe. If it were me, and I realize you are not me, I would be wanting to get some professional help to understand if what I was remembering was real or possibly had some other source. It frightens me to think of anyone abusing you, but if it happened we would have to face it. No matter what, we love you very much.

By professional help I mean someone who has had years in school learning to deal with situations like this—a psychologist or psychiatrist. Dr. B. recommended a doctor by the name of Dr. J. We met him last week and will see him again tomorrow. As I expected, since Dr. B.

recommended him, he was very nice. I am enclosing his
card in hopes that you will see him also. We, as well as
Granddaddy, need very much to understand what's go-
ing on. If you can't talk to us directly, maybe you can talk
to us through him. Please try to do that. We'll pay for
anything your insurance doesn't cover or all of it if the
insurance doesn't pay anything.

Please, let us hear from you as soon as you are able. I
miss you so very much I can hardly stand it.

By this time, I had quit my job. At first I had been able to
confine my crying to the car going to and coming from
work. Eventually, however, I would have to get up from
my desk and go to the rest room where I would cry and
then try to get cleaned up so I wouldn't have to go back
with a red and swollen face. I didn't want to have to
answer questions from my co-workers. What do you say?
"My daughter has accused me of sexually abusing her."

As I mentioned in one of my earlier letters, we have a
friend, Rebecca Scott, who has been a practicing psychiatrist for about five years. We have known each other since
the time our husbands were in law school together. When
all this first happened, before I had talked with Lori's
friends and found out that she was accusing us of sexual
abuse, we had given Rebecca a call to see if maybe she
could help us in trying to find out why Lori didn't want to
see us. We were surprised when she said, "That's funny
you should call today. Lori called last night and is bringing
her boyfriend over tonight. She said she wanted to play
some of her new songs for us." This was Saturday, and she
said she would call us back Sunday morning after church,
and we would get together for lunch if she had anything to
tell us. When she called us back Sunday, she said she didn't

have anything to tell us. She said Lori never mentioned anything. She said she took Lori aside before she left and told her that we called and that we were worried about her. Lori told her there was nothing to worry about and that she was trying to work out some things on her own right now.

We left it at that but made plans to meet Rebecca and Don, her husband, for dinner the next week. By the time we met, I had talked with all of Lori's friends and had found out the problem was sexual abuse, even though we had not yet received Lori's letter with her formal accusations. Nothing was said about Lori at our dinner meeting. How do you bring up something like sexual abuse in a crowded upscale restaurant? After dinner, Rebecca and I went to the restroom. No one else was there, so I told her what I had found out and asked if she had ever heard of anything like this before. She acted totally shocked. The look on her face was genuine. She said Lori had not mentioned anything like this to her. I told her if there was any way she could think of that would help, to please let us know. I didn't hear any more from her.

About a month later, still going out of my mind trying to figure out where all of this was coming from, I decided to call one of my former co-workers who had been a friend and still worked with Lori. It was a difficult move, but I had to hear some news about her. This friend was very kind. I had worked with her from the time Lori was 15. She was aware of the friendship that Lori had with Lydia and she told me that she worried about Lori going to lunch with Lydia every day. She told me that everyone at the office still felt the same about Lydia; that there had been no change in her. She said she was aware that something was wrong between Lori and her family, but she hadn't known what. She was very sympathetic and said, "Everyone at the office knew Lori hung the moon as far as you were concerned." I couldn't believe what my friend then told me. The first shocker was when she asked, "Didn't your son come down and spend his spring break with her?" I couldn't believe this! Our son's wife works as a school teacher and he is a student. I knew that they didn't have money to buy airplane tickets. The next surprise was when my friend told me that she thought Lori was living with some of our friends. She described how Lori talked about them—you guessed it, Don and Rebecca Scott!

At this point we had not brought Josh into the situation because we didn't want to alarm him until we could figure out what was going on. I called Josh and asked him about his clandestine trip. He admitted to it and said it was bothering him, but he had promised Lori not to tell he had been here. He said that Lori had wanted him to go see Ramona, the psychic, with her and he did. He cautioned me that this Ramona was a dangerous woman and that she was a fake. He said that when Lori brought up the subject of suing her parents for abuse, Ramona told her not to sue because that would just make Lori feel more like a victim. Ramona said she knew because she had two people suing her!

I had been trying to find this Ramona person for weeks. She wasn't in the phone book. I had gone to every psychic bookstore in Big Town and questioned workers and patrons alike trying to find out who this person was. I pored over new age newspapers and advertisements trying to find her. Finally, although Josh didn't know her last name, he was able to describe where her building was, and from that I was able to locate her office. I walked into her office, and picked up one of her business cards without anyone seeing me.

My husband asked, "Now that you've got her card, what are you going to do with it?" That was a good question. I wanted to go see Ramona and confront her with the things she was telling my daughter; everyone in the family cautioned me against doing this. I was having such a hard time dealing with it, and I didn't know what to do. My family kept telling me to put this behind me and go on with my life, but how could I — this is my daughter!

My husband then called Rebecca to tell her that we understood that Lori was living in her home and that we would like to get together and talk. We wanted to tell Rebecca and Don our side of the story and all the things we had learned about lupus and the effects it can have on its victims. She wouldn't see us! She said she would have to talk to Lori and Don about it and see if Lori would approve of us meeting. Paul and I talked about this for hours. We couldn't understand why she had to have Lori's permission. We couldn't understand why Lori had to know! We just wanted to explain what we were going through and find out how Lori was doing, but they wouldn't talk to us.

As the days went by, I began to think more and more about how Lori was being damaged by Ramona and that the further it went the harder it would be to recover. I began to stew and obsess with these thoughts and had a very difficult time just getting by. I knew we had to try again to talk to Don and Rebecca. I wanted to let them know that Lori was seeing a "psychic" who was using hypnosis to put these ideas into her head.

Paul was so upset with Don and Rebecca that he refused to call again. That left it up to me. For most people it wouldn't be a problem, but I am somewhat shy and have what I call "phoneaphobia," which makes it very difficult for me to call people on the telephone. But whenever I have been concerned for my children, somehow that mother instinct comes out, and I can do anything.

Don and Rebecca are members of a certain church

where we were also members for eight-and-a-half years. Because of a difference in opinion, we left this church about eight years ago to attend a Protestant church. Being aware of the beliefs of this particular denomination, I knew that its families are very patriarchal, with the man making most of the decisions for the family. I decided that if Rebecca wouldn't talk because she felt she had to confer with her husband first, then I would skip Rebecca and go directly to the head patriarch himself, so I called Don at his office. I left a message for Don to please call me at his convenience. (Again, let me reiterate that we have known these people for 17 years.) Don called me back around 11:00 a.m. After I talked with him I was so consumed with rage, I decided to write down our conversation right away so that I would never forget a word of it. Before I repeat that conversation for you, let me say that Don has a beautiful, melodious voice. We always told him he should be on the radio because he has such a lovely voice. When I talked to him, he really turned his "radio voice" on. There was no recognition in his voice that he even knew me; his voice very formal and business-like. It was like he was talking to a complete stranger, like I was a prospective new client whom he had not met yet.

This is what I recorded about that conversation when he returned my call:

Wednesday, May 6, 1992
Me: *Hello.*
Don: *Hello, this is Mr. Don Scott. I'm trying to get in touch with Kathryn Anderson.*
Me: *This is she.*
Don: *Well, Kathryn, how are you doing?*
Me: *I'm just trying to hang in there.*

Don: *That's good, that's always a sign of hope if you are hanging in there.*

Me: *Don, I really need to talk with you about Lori. Could we meet somewhere? (At this point I break down and am starting to cry.)*

Don: *That could be a problem. You see, I'm out of town this weekend, and we have another engagement Friday night.*

Me: *I really need to talk to you.*

Don: *Well what about now? Can we talk over the phone?*

I broke down and was crying hysterically. I told him what I knew of what was happening to Lori and that I really needed to talk to someone who had seen her. He said he saw her now and then but not very often. He told me she was seeing a counselor who he believed was a psychiatrist, but he didn't know who it was, although he thought Rebecca probably did.

I asked him to have Rebecca call me if she knew anything else. I thanked him for talking with me to which he replied, "Well, it's always a pleasure talking with you." I hung up without saying good-bye!

Even though I broke down and was crying throughout the entire conversation, he remained very formal, talking to me as though I were a stranger. He never once said, "I'm sorry this is happening to you; we're your friends; if there is anything we can do;" nothing.

Paul and I just couldn't understand their reaction. Had they really bought Lori's story so completely they didn't even want to hear our side? Were they judging us guilty without even a trial? This left us with feelings of disbelief, betrayal, anger, and great sorrow. We kept thinking how we would be handling the situation differently if it was one of their four children who came to us. It was still so hard to understand.

Some time later I called our son Josh again to talk with him further about what was happening. As I was talking with him his voice suddenly changed and grew very low, almost to a whisper. He said, "I think Daddy abused me, too." I think I stopped breathing!

We had always been very close to Josh until he was 17, and then out of the blue he just decided he didn't like us anymore. I think the problem was a common one in that he was just trying to find his own individuality. He had met his future wife to whom he gave his allegiance, and we just got in the way. He also got upset with us when we refused to pay to send him to a small private college that he wanted to attend. At the time, we told him we would pay all of his tuition if he went to an in-state school. Or, we would give him that amount of money, and he would have to make up the balance if he insisted on going to this private college that cost $14,000 per year. He was very angry with us because he felt we were withholding funds from him because we didn't want him to be near his girlfriend (which, we felt, was the only reason he wanted to go to this small, private school). He didn't understand that just because his dad was a lawyer, it didn't mean we had unlimited supplies of money. Our relationship deteriorated so badly that, at the time, I didn't think we would ever have a chance at putting it back together. During this time, Lori had always been a complete angel – never doing anything wrong–and we treated her accordingly. Because of our reaction, I'm sure Josh felt that we probably cared more for her than we did for him which, I might add, was completely untrue.

Several things happened that worried us during that time. One was that my husband had found one of Josh's darts stuck in the tire of his car. Since it belonged to Josh, we assumed he had done it. We blamed him even though he kept saying he did not do it. We tried to get Josh counseling, but after a few times, he absolutely refused to go back. When we tried to find out what was bothering him, he would just say we'd have to ask Elizabeth (his girlfriend, and now his wife). When he finally decided he was moving out of the house, I was a little relieved. I loved him so much, but I just didn't know how to handle him any longer. I figured we had done the best we could and the psychologist we all saw said he thought it was just a case of Josh always having things so good growing up that it was difficult for him to leave home. The doctor said sometimes kids feel they have to make things difficult so they have a good excuse to leave.

I have to admit, my first thought when Josh said Paul had abused him was, "Why is he saying this?" I wondered if maybe Josh still felt a lot of anger toward us, and this was just his way of getting back. He told me that he was so upset and depressed after seeing Lori that he had been to see someone with an MSW (Master of Social Work) for counseling three times. While working with her, using relaxation techniques, he had regained his "memories." He told me what he "remembered." It was of one-time abuse, supposedly taking place in his bedroom, which was directly across the hall from ours. We were still living in Small Town and Paul was in law school. Josh said he could see the episode in his mind just as if he were watching a television screen, but he couldn't see the perpetrator's face. Nevertheless, he was sure it was his dad. After the attack, he said he went into the backyard for awhile and then came back inside. He kept telling me he was really afraid for me, and he really sounded like he was. He didn't want me to tell his dad because he was "worried about my safety." After listening to him, I couldn't even talk. I had to tell him I would call him back later.

To me, Paul is probably the world's best husband. He is always there for me, he builds my self-esteem, he loves to surprise me, he helps me with anything and everything, he has always been a wonderful father, and never in his life has he ever been violent. Sure, sometimes he gets angry, but it is over as fast as it comes. I hung up and went to our bedroom and cried until Paul found me and wanted to know what was wrong. I told Paul what Josh had said. It was like I had hit him with a brick! He was shocked, angry, hurt. We kept going over and over every point of his story saying there's no way something like that could have happened. The story that Josh told, including a claim that he had a tiny scar from the experience, almost sounded like the stories you read about people who say they have been abducted by space aliens. I kept saying there was no way he could have been sexually abused right across the hall from me with all the doors open, and then gone outside in the middle of the night without being heard. The kids were only five and eight at the time, and if someone had abused them at the house, there would have been telltale signs of it, especially in the laundry. Even realizing that, we kept trying to figure out if the perpetrator could have been a visitor, or maybe Josh spent the night with someone who had abused him. And maybe, because he was still angry, he had assumed Paul was the perpetrator. We tried to look at every possible angle and figure out an answer. We must have talked halfway through the night; we certainly didn't sleep!

The next night I was more composed and had made out a list of questions that I wanted to ask Josh and some things that I wanted to point out to him. He was much calmer the next night, and we both found it easier to talk. We were on the phone for a couple of hours, and I told him many of the things that Paul and I had discussed: how I had been a light sleeper; how his open door had been directly across the hall from our open door in a very small house (about 1100 sq. ft.); and how I had always heard him even when he coughed. I ended by asking him to be open-minded, to give it more thought. I suggested that he talk with a good therapist and that we would help him with the cost. He also made an appointment with a urologist to try to determine where the scar had come from.

I would call and talk with him every few days, and finally he said that whoever had abused him, he was now sure that it wasn't his father. He kept saying he couldn't remember any of his childhood. I began to remind him of a few things that had happened and he kept saying, "Oh yeah, and I did such and such," and he would pick up the story and run with it. It was like he just needed to be reminded. We talked about anyone who had ever spent the night at our house—what they looked like, etc.; about his school and the day care he had attended; how I had taken him to see a psychologist when he was in the second grade because his teacher had thought he was hyperactive and how the doctor's report said he was just a normal boy. I sent him a copy of that report in which the doctors said he was extremely bright and seemed to think highly of himself. They had also commented how they had left me alone in one of their small rooms with Josh and Lori for about two hours and, even though the children had been very active, I had handled them very well, never yelling at them, but turning their attention to other things.

I made up a package to send him. In it, I included a copy

of that report, and a copy of all his drawings and stories I had saved over the years. I also went through scrapbooks and pulled pictures of everyone who had ever come to our house and spent the night. I taped each one to a separate page and wrote down everything I could remember about the people and their visits. I drew a floor plan of the house we lived in when he claimed to have been abused.

After awhile, I spoke to him again. At this time, he was absolutely positive that his dad had never abused him. In fact, he said, he was positive that he had never been abused by anyone! The urologist had told him his scar was a birthmark. He assured me that he was okay now, and he was anxious to see us as soon as we could get together.

* * * * * *

We continued to see the psychiatrist, Dr. J., for about a month. He was very nice — not blaming — but I just didn't feel like I was getting any help, nor did Paul. Dr. J. had told us that four other couples had come to him within the last two years telling him of false accusations and mentioned that maybe it was time to start thinking about a support group. As the months went by, I couldn't seem to do anything. I wanted to sleep most of the time. I got in the habit of going to bed about 3:00 in the morning and sleeping till about noon. I didn't clean. I didn't cook. I only washed an occasional dish when the sink would be overrun. I scoured bookstores, reading about child abuse and trying to find any book I could that might explain what was happening. There were NO books on families falsely accused. When I wasn't reading or sleeping, I was watching every talk show I could since just about every other one is on child abuse. I thought maybe I would find something that would help me.

One night, on a Prime Time Live (ABC) segment, there was a story about unlicensed "therapists" who were treating people and causing them to believe that they had been sexually abused by their parents or by satanic cults. I just knew this was what was happening to Lori! I was going crazy because there just didn't seem to be anything I could do about it. I couldn't even find any information on it to read.

I really needed help, and then I remembered a certified hypnotherapist whom Lori had met and gone to see a couple of years ago. She had liked her so much that, at the time, I decided I would go see if she could help me lose some weight. Jane was a very friendly person, very easy to talk to, and I liked her immediately. I spent a couple of months under her care before I decided she couldn't take me any further. So now, in our time of need, even though she was not a licensed psychologist or psychiatrist, and therefore against Paul's better judgment, he agreed to go with me to see her because he knew I was hanging by a thread. We went together and told her everything that had happened. She volunteered the information that she and Lori had talked about a lot of things, but sexual abuse was never one of them. She told us that Lori kept her feelings bottled up and that maybe she was angry over something and had held it in for so long that it was now coming out in this manner. She didn't feel Lori was doing it on purpose, but rather it was just how her subconscious mind had worked. She said that while she could do nothing for Lori, she thought she could help us work on ourselves so that when Lori did decide to come back we would be able to handle it better. Because of a "boundary" problem, she wanted to work with each of us separately. We both made appointments to come back the next week. Thus began our training in "Co-Dependency and Dysfunctional Families," "trauma therapy" and our misadventures (and education) in modern day "pop" psychology — or how to blame your troubles on someone else!

One of the greatest things about working with Jane was that you really felt like you were participating in improving yourself. She recommended books for us to read, and through talking with her and each other about what we read, we began to make progress getting out of our depression with her guidance. I began to take my mind off of Lori and really concentrate on myself. She first told us to read *Bradshaw On: The Family,* by John Bradshaw (Health Communications, Inc., 1988). I hope all of you Bradshaw fans will forgive me for saying this, since many people talk about Bradshaw being the best communicator on the face of the earth today, but I just can't see it. That was the most difficult book to understand I have ever read, and I read a lot. The man has some good ideas, but he really has a hard time getting his ideas across — of course you have to learn a whole new vocabulary. As Paul said, if you are able to stick with the book long enough, you will eventually understand what he means. Instead of stating his ideas simply, he runs round and round the bush. He repeats himself over and over again saying the same thing in different ways until you finally say, "Oh, so that's what he means!" Paul stuck with the book. I couldn't get through it because I was bored to tears.

Jane kept saying I needed to learn how to feel anger. We talked about my mother, who had been deceased for 15 years. For two days, I sat at home thinking and writing about things my mother had done when I was growing up that made me angry and how those things had affected my life negatively. I got into the real spirit of it — "Yes, I was angry!! It's no wonder I sometimes doubt my self-worth after the way she treated me," I reasoned. When I went to see Jane the next week, I told her that I had really gotten angry at my mother for a couple of days, but I was over it now. I told her I didn't like trying to hold on to that anger when I didn't feel it any more. I told her I had made peace with my mother before she died and, even though I didn't agree with everything my mother had done, I still loved her very much. I could see now, with the eyes of an adult, that the things she had done to make me mad were done because she loved me and had my best interests at heart. Bottom line, I love and respect my mother and her memory very much! "No, no, no," Jane said. It had taken me years to get to where I was. I couldn't just expect to be rid of the anger in a couple of days. It was still there, she said, festering. I had to get it out.

I decided I would try Bradshaw's second book on my list, *Healing the Shame That Binds You* (Health Communications, Inc., 1988). This one was a little easier. Then I read *Home Coming*, also by Bradshaw (Bantam Books, 1992). This book included some questionnaires for the reader to answer so you could see just how badly off you were. The more "yes" answers, the more your "inner child" was supposed to be wounded. Keep in mind our "co-dependent" mind-set at this time. Paul completed the questionnaire first, and out of 16 questions he answered "yes" to eight. Then, I took it and answered 10 with "yes" responses. All sorts of abuse, including sexual, were suggested as ways your inner child could be wounded. Oh my gosh, we both thought, is it possible that someone abused us as children? Here was a man who was supposed to know, writing with authority on this subject, and we both began to question our own memories. Were we remembering everything about our childhood? Could something have happened to us that we had blocked out? What had happened that was so terrible we had repressed it? For days we talked about it but neither one of us could come up with anyone in either of our families who would have done such a thing. We finally began to calm down and come back to earth. We could see the fallacies in Bradshaw's theories and realize that he was just like any other "how-to" author. You have to use common sense when reading. What is good, use it — what is bad, discard it!

I also bought Melody Beattie's audio cassette on "Co-Dependent No More." I decided I was very co-dependent and should release Lori to live her own life. I kept telling Jane I just couldn't turn my back and let go. I said, "What if she were sick with some disease, such as cancer?" I wouldn't turn my back on her then. In fact, if I did, I certainly wouldn't be considered a good mother. To me it was the same thing; whether physical or mental, she was suffering from some disease. How could I just turn my back and abandon her? Jane said, "What if she had cancer and she told you she didn't want you taking care of her?" My answer was, "I'm her mother and she's my daughter. I would want to find out why she did not want me, because there would have to be a reason, and then I would still take care of her." In my mind, all I could think of was, "What kind of mother wouldn't stay with this thing until she had her daughter back?"

* * * * * *

I bought Melody Beattie's book *Codependents' Guide to the Twelve Steps* (Prentice Hall/Parkside Recovery Book, 1990), which at the time I thought was the best book yet. I really liked Ms. Beattie's writing. It was very easy to understand and seemed to speak to me. I began to read it and tried to practice each step, examining myself with a magni-

fying glass. One thing Ms. Beattie said that seemed particularly to touch me became my prayer each night. It went as
follows:

> *I'm willing to let go of preconceived notions*
>   *about what should happen.*
> *I'm willing to let go of my limitations, my*
>   *agenda, my script, and my beliefs.*
> *I'm ready and willing to be open to what You*
>   *have in mind for me.*
> *Now, just show me what that is.*
> *Let me know in a way I can understand.*

I just knew that now I had the right attitude and that
God would step in and make things all right. I prayed and
prayed and prayed. I got no answer. Nothing was changing, and as this self-examination went on, I began to realize
that this "co-dependent therapy" had done nothing to
make me feel better about Lori. It had simply taken my
mind off Lori and caused me to spend all my time thinking
about me, me, me! But, in the meantime, Lori was just
drifting farther and farther away. I don't think she was
picking up on my "psychic vibrations," knowing that I was
sending her unconditional love and thinking about her, as
the therapy said she would.

I began to think more and more about Ramona, the
psychic. I kept thinking I'd like to meet her and give her a
piece of my mind. If I could find out who was suing her
and why, maybe I could jump on that bandwagon. I even
thought if I wrote to her, she would perhaps listen to
reason. This is what I wrote:

June 7, 1992
Dear Ramona:

I have been wanting to meet you for a long time. It took me so long to locate you. By asking questions everywhere I went, I finally met someone who had heard of you. They didn't know your last name or how to get in touch with you but they were able to explain which building your office was in. I walked into your office and looked over the different brochures on a table until I spotted your card. I took it and walked out without anyone noticing me.

I have carried that card around in my wallet for a month now trying to decide what to do with it. As I said, I would like to meet you, but I was afraid if I called and gave my name you would refuse to see me. I thought of calling and making an appointment using a fake name or my maiden name, but I am not the type of person who can present myself under such a falsehood.

Who am I? My name is Kathryn Anderson and my daughter is Lori. I don't know what has gone on in your office or how in the world Lori came up with "memories" that we abused her. I need for you to know that nothing could be further from the truth and to tell you how much I love my daughter.

From the time she was born, she has been everything I ever wanted in a child. As a baby, even before she could talk, she would express herself in such sweet ways. It was as though God planned this little baby just for me! I realized then, as the old saying goes, that the dust could wait, and I just allowed myself to marvel in my daughter. When she was born, and for a long time afterwards, I felt like I was walking on a cloud with her — to have had such a sweet baby girl. That time was so precious!

As she grew, I never got over the wonder of Lori. I was so tickled to have a little girl. I wanted to sew for her so badly, but I put it off until she was about five years old because I was so fearful that I would drop a pin and that she would pick it up and swallow it. When she was old enough and started school I think I made all of her clothes that year, and loved every minute of it.

I would sit for hours and read to both her and Josh, our son, because I loved being with them. No one was more hurt than I when I had to go back to work when Lori started school, because more than anything, I wanted to be a good mother to my children.

When we lived in Small Town, I had to leave them in day care, but I always returned for them as soon as I could get off work, and we would talk about their day on our way home. When we moved back to Big Town, I was fortunate enough to have family members that could stay with them after school, but even then they didn't have to wait long before I was home from work.

We always tried to give both children everything they wanted or asked for, and sometimes that meant asking my parents to give it to them. Whenever they were interested in anything, we always tried to support them or get them lessons, or pay for school trips they wanted to go on. We always tried to plan vacation spots that they would like and kids' activities that they would enjoy, such as water slides, goofy golf, and amusement parks.

We tried to be open with the kids and to let them know how we felt about things. One of Lori's complaints to me a few years back was that our family never got angry, never yelled at each other. My husband and I have always gotten along. We love each other very much, and we never felt like yelling at each other because neither of us thought that would solve anything. Back then we were taught (from books) that parents should not argue in front of their children, so if we did have a disagreement, we discussed it in private. I would always tell the kids "maybe," so I could discuss things with my husband before giving them an answer; when they were about six and nine, they jokingly told me one day that my "maybes" always meant "yes."

As Lori grew, we thrilled with each success she had. I used to help out with her school plays by teaching her schoolmates to dance. I made costumes for her choral performances, and the first time she performed solo in front of an audience I was thrilled. I can remember making her costume and taking some black shoes to work with me and sewing sequins on them during breaks. This wasn't an easy task, my fingers were sore for days. But this was my little girl and if that was what she wanted, then she would have the best costume going! We watched her grow and her talent mature. We read with awe the stories she wrote in school and marveled at her talent. Then she began to write songs and, for the talent show her senior year in high school, she secretly worked to put her first song to music and performed it as a surprise for my husband and me. You just can't imagine how proud we were, and are, of her.

Ramona, what I'm trying to tell you is that both Paul and I love Lori very much. There is no way in this world that we could or would have done anything intentionally to hurt her. She won't even tell us what types of things she remembers, except for one letter she wrote us where she tells us that she believes we, and others, sexually abused her. There is no way either of us would have done this to anyone, much less to our own children. We *have always loved them, nurtured them, and given them the best we had to give. We weren't perfect parents but I don't understand what is behind this accusation.*

It's even worse that she will not communicate with us. I want to know what is going on in her mind so maybe I can understand where this is coming from and help her. I want to know if someone did abuse her, and who that someone might be. If she doesn't feel like she can talk to us, I wish she would at least write us a letter, or communicate with us through a counselor, or better yet, talk to us with the counselor present. If she wants you to be the counselor, that would be fine with us. I told her that I would leave her alone, and that I wouldn't write to her or bother her if that was what she felt she needed, but Ramona, I love her so much I can't just forget her. I don't want to run her life. I just want to solve this and have her know we love her unconditionally and have her love us again.

Ramona, I have been told that you pick up psychic vibes from the things you hold of others. I have tried to tell you how I feel here and I have carried this letter around with me for awhile, so it has been close to me. I urge you to hold it and know that there is only love in my heart for Lori. Neither my husband nor I would be capable of committing such acts.

I don't even know if Lori is seeing you any more. If she is not, then there is nothing you can do; but if she is, please, let her know how very, very much we love her, and how much we wish to be reunited with her.

Sincerely

After careful consideration, I never mailed the letter because I was afraid that Ramona would use it against me. She could use some of the details in the letter to further convince Lori of her psychic powers.

* * * * * *

Finally, one morning a real breakthrough happened. I was still sleeping late, but I would videotape the morning talk shows and listen to them when I got up. I was listening to Sally Jesse Raphael. The guests were two families that had been falsely accused of child abuse and another woman who had falsely accused her father of abuse only to realize later that the psychiatrist had caused her to believe this. The doctor had told her that anything that "popped" into her mind could be accepted as fact. These families could have been us on that stage. The stories were so similar it was incredible. Although they didn't talk about a group dedicated to this syndrome, they flashed the name—False Memory Syndrome Foundation—on the screen with the telephone number. I called.

These people were so helpful. Their foundation gathers facts and prepares studies on this phenomenon, but they are not a support group. I could hardly believe it when I heard this situation was happening all over the country. We definitely were not alone! They sent me a packet of information. It was the end of July, and it was the first relief I felt. Just knowing there were others and that there was someone to talk to who could really understand what we were going through was very comforting.

* * * * * *

It was now the first of August, and it was time to take our vacation where we were meeting some of our oldest and dearest friends. This vacation had been planned before any of this happened, and when we got the note in February from Lori, I kept thinking that by August all of this would have blown over and she would be going on our vacation with us as she usually did. I had really built myself up over this and felt let down when I realized it wasn't going to happen. Paul talked with me for hours, helping me get over this particular bout of depression. I decided to go on this vacation and try to put all of this out of my mind for a week or at least not talk constantly about it and ruin everyone else's vacation.

We met our friends at the beach, and they had one of their daughters and her boyfriend and their son and his friend with them. We really had a wonderful time with them as they are the best friends we have ever had. However, their oldest daughter was planning to get married in October, and a lot of conversation was centered around the wedding plans. I was so excited for them. Their daughter and Josh were only three months apart, and they had spent their first three years together before moves had separated all of us. I remember toward the end of the week taking a walk with Paul on the beach one evening and crying. I told him how much I loved this family but at the same time seeing them together, like our family had been, kept making me think of what we were missing. We had heard from Josh that my daughter had gotten back together with an old boyfriend and that they were planning to get married in a year when they had saved some money. I kept thinking how I would miss that wedding, and she was my only daughter. I had been at my son's wedding, but you don't get involved in all the planning and parties as is the case in a daughter's wedding. It hurt me so to realize that I would miss that.

We had a wonderful week, but when I returned home, I buried myself in all the reading that the FMS Foundation had sent me. They talked about a book called *The Courage to Heal* (Bass and Davis, Harper and Row, 1988) that was doing a lot of damage. The author is a feminist, a writer and teaches English courses. The FMS Foundation mentioned in some of their literature that a lot of parents had found that the letters their daughters had written to them had come straight from the book. I wanted to see if Lori's letters had also, so I bought the book. I read the first chapter, but to me it was pornographic, and I had a hard time continuing because it really was making me sick, not to mention very angry. I began to skim the pages, reading here and there. I'm going to force myself to sit down and read the whole thing one day so I can truly critique it. As far as I'm concerned, these authors have done a terrible injustice to the family – to good families.

This book, *The Courage to Heal*, is referred to as the "Bible of the Incest-Memory Recovery Movement." On page 14 of the book, Bass states *"I am not academically educated as a psychologist . . . But none of what is presented here is based on psychological theories."* On page 22 she teaches, *"If you think you were abused, and your life shows the symptoms, then you were."* On page 81, *"If you don't remember your abuse, you are not alone. Many women don't have memories, and some never get memories. This doesn't mean they weren't abused."* There is even a section in the book for counselors that tells them on page 347, *"If a client is unsure that she was abused but thinks she might have been, work as though she was."* Page 349, *"If sexual abuse isn't the presenting problem but your client has eating disorders, an addiction to drugs or alcohol, suicidal feelings, or sexual problems, these may be symptoms of sexual abuse."* Page 350, *"When you work with someone you think may have been abused, ask outright, 'Were you sexually abused as a child?'"* and

"If your client says she wasn't abused but you suspect that she was, ask again later . . . . 'No, I wasn't' may mean 'No, I don't remember yet.' " This is like Roseanne Arnold's statement on the Oprah Winfrey Show: *"When someone asks you, 'Were you sexually abused as a child?' there are only two answers: One of them is 'Yes,' and one of them is 'I don't know.' You can't say 'No.' "*

This is pure lunacy. I would like these people to know there are some of us out here who put the blame for our personal problems where it belongs—ourselves! I'm overweight because I eat too many sweets, and I also take a drug to prevent headaches that has a weight-gain side-effect. I have headaches because I have allergies as well as a genetic predisposition for such, NOT because I was sexually abused! I don't doubt my memories because I have studied how memory works, and I know that it is NOT normal to remember ANYTHING other than bits and pieces before the age of six. I also don't doubt my parents because I know from their actions over many years how they would, and have, reacted to certain situations. By no means am I trying to play down the horror that a legitimate survivor goes through, but I'm trying to say, DON'T make everyone a victim of child abuse! Don't call me a liar and say that I'm in denial because I can say I know I was not abused. There is not a bogeyman in every closet!

The more I studied, the more I began to understand why some things had happened. For instance, I believe the reason our long-time friend, Rebecca, has not contacted us is the fact that the younger the therapist is or the less time a therapist is in practice, the more likely they are to be true believers or moral crusaders. Schools have taught them that the number of girls who have had sex forced upon them by a relative or other adult is as high as one in three.

For boys the estimate is one in 10. However, those numbers are only "guesstimates." Can you really sit with a group of people and believe that one in three is a child abuser, or can you drive through your neighborhood and believe that every third house holds a child abuser? The actual number ranges anywhere between six percent to 62 percent, a range so wide that it tells us that we don't even have a ball park figure of the actual statistic. The therapists coming out of school are expecting to find childhood sexual abuse. They are looking for it. Since I have been aware of this, I have even heard of two people studying psychology in school who have come down with "memories" after reading some of the books and taking the "test." It's been found that there is a correlation between minimal credentials and maximum discovery of sexual abuse. Therapists with master's degrees find more of it than therapists with doctoral degrees. Psychiatrists find less of it than anybody. ("When Therapists 'Find' Childhood Sexual Abuse," an article by Darrell Sifford, reprinted from the *Philadelphia Inquirer*, March 15, 1992.)

I also learned that most of the people who are experiencing False Memory Syndrome come from upper middle class families and generally have higher educations. The symptoms the "survivors" report are so general they could be attributed to several diseases, and throughout a lifetime, all of us have probably suffered several of them at one time or another. Here are some of the symptoms, taken from The Incest Survivors' Aftereffects Checklist as listed in E. Sue Blume's book, *Secret Survivors* (Ballantine Books, 1991):

Fear of being alone in the dark, of sleeping alone; nightmares, night terrors . . . swallowing and gagging sensitivity; repugnance to water on one's face when bathing or swimming ... alienation from the body ... failure to heed body signals or take care of one's body ... gastrointestinal problems; gynecological disorders; headaches; arthritis or joint pain ... wearing baggy clothes ... eating disorders, drug or alcohol abuse (or total abstinence); other addictions; compulsive behavior ... self-destructiveness ... phobias ... need to be invisible ... suicidal thoughts ... depression (sometimes paralyzing); seemingly baseless crying ... anger issues ... splitting (depersonalization) ... rigid control of one's thought process ... (security-seeking behaviors); adult nervousness over being watched or surprised; feeling watched; startle response ... inability to trust ... high risk taking; inability to take risks ... boundary issues ... guilt, shame; low self-esteem, feeling worthless ... pattern of being a victim ... feeling demand to produce and be loved ... abandonment issues ... blocking out some period of early years ... feeling of carrying an awful secret ... feeling crazy ... denial; no awareness at all; repression of memories ... sex feels "dirty;" aversion to being touched, especially in gynecological exam ... compulsively "seductive" or compulsively asexual ... pattern of ambivalent or intensely conflictive relationships ... avoidance of mirrors ... desire to change one's name ... active withdrawal from happiness ... aversion to making noise; verbal hypervigilance; quiet-voiced ... stealing, and starting fires ... multiple personality.

This is crazy. On some of these, you're damned if you do and damned if you don't! No matter what traits you have, you can be put in the category of probably being sexually abused as a child!

According to Hollida Wakefield, a psychologist and co-director of the Institute of Psychological Therapies in Northfield, Minn., it seems the adult children who "remember" childhood sexual abuse decades later are "not just anybody. They are women who already have problems, such as personality disorder, and they're likely to be unusually suggestible. . . . They see a therapist who believes that sexual abuse is very common and that it could be a factor behind many problems in adulthood. The therapist starts saying things like, 'Do you think you could have been abused? Don't you have some memories?' Under hypnosis, they're even more suggestible . . ."

These therapists believe in the "rightness" of their diagnosis, and this belief, to them, justifies any means. The parents automatically become guilty. There is no "until proven guilty" because the parents aren't allowed to defend themselves. It's a no-win situation. It becomes much like a cult. Therapists tell their patients to abandon their "family of origin," create a "family of choice," and drop any friends who aren't supportive. They're told to join support groups such as SIA (Survivors of Incest Anonymous), and make new friends there. They're encouraged to share their stories and listen to other members' stories as possible triggers for their own repressed memories.

As I continued reading the FMS Foundation material, I realized that two of the doctors who were quoted a lot were in Big Town. Paul had begun to feel that Jane had taken him as far as she was capable of, and I felt that I wasn't getting any help in understanding where Lori was coming from and what I could do about it. We also began to feel that eventually we would work toward getting a law passed in our state whereby a person would have to have at least a Ph.D. in psychology to practice counseling. Therefore, since Jane did not have such credentials, I could not in clear conscience continue to see her. Paul and I talked, and we decided to make an appointment with Dr. A.

Dr. A. is a specialist in psychiatric aberrations of memory. He is also a clinical assistant professor of psychiatry at a local medical school and director of a local psychiatric program for Dissociative Disorders. He has been very helpful in explaining to us how memory works — and doesn't work. He explained that for several years, both professionals and the public believed that memory worked like a recording device such as a VCR or computer that stored everything a person was exposed to, and that through hypnosis or therapy the memory could be accessed. But, current research shows that memory is far from archival. Memory resembles an incoherent or dreamlike world where the past is constantly reinterpreted and reconstructed depending on our current life situation. In other words, on days that you feel bad, you might interpret something from your past differently than on days that you feel good.

He believes that poorly trained therapists working with vulnerable patients are partly responsible for the satanic sexual abuse scare, and may also have led patients to believe they were abused, sexually or otherwise, when they were not. False memories can be planted through tone of voice or the phrasing of a question. Under hypnosis, the therapist may ask, "Was there a group? Were they wearing robes? Were there babies present? Did you do anything to the babies?" The patient's imagination takes over from there.

Dr. A. didn't have any good ideas for ways to make me feel better, but somehow going to see him once a week and hearing of studies and other happenings in the false memory field helped. I guess it made me feel less alone. He made me understand that my not wanting to go to sleep at night was like the situation of the people whose family members had been held hostage in Iran. They felt like they couldn't sleep until the family member was safe and they waited to hear any word. He also likened our situation to parents who have had their child kidnapped. The only difference was we knew who the kidnapper was, where she worked, and where she lived, but we were powerless to do anything about it.

A few weeks after I started seeing Dr. A., we went to visit Josh. Finally, we learned of the specific accusations Lori had made. After all the studying and worrying that maybe we had done something that she simply miscon- strued, we were greeted with the horrendous reality of the situation. Somehow, I had come to believe that if we could just sit down and talk with her we could straighten things out. I was working under the assumption that things would somehow make sense. For instance, Bradshaw and others are teaching that if you make some off hand comment, for example jokingly referring to the size of someone's breasts, you are committing "emotional incest." This emotional incest is looked upon as being just as bad as physical incest. Maybe her "psychic" had taught her things like this, and somehow they had gone in and picked apart our lives to find anything they could label as "incest." But, boy, was I wrong! Her accusations are so bad, there is no way she could have taken any of our actions and twisted them into the horrendous crimes of which she is accusing us. I wouldn't dare write all of the accusations, because they are so filthy I could not stand to put them on paper. Here are a few of the "milder" ones:

- She is saying that her roommate Joe got so mad at one of his friends, he castrated him in a fight.
- She is saying Paul once tried to drown her in the

bathtub to keep her from talking.

- She is saying that my aunt abused me when I was a child, making me a closet lesbian, and that I had affairs with a co-worker and a church friend. I supposedly invited the church friend into my home and the two of us sexually abused her.
- She is saying that Paul had affairs and transmitted a venereal disease to both her and me.
- She is saying that Paul performed a home abortion on her after getting her pregnant, and he laughed at her pain the whole time he was doing it.
- She is saying we used to lock her in a box in the basement of my father's house.
- She is also saying that she is the one (when she was 14 and a perfect angel) who put the dart in the car tire to get "revenge" for the things we had been doing to her.

There are many others but, fortunately for us, these accusations are so bizarre and unbelievable, it would be relatively easy for us to prove our innocence. For instance, Paul and I could readily prove that neither of us had ever had a venereal disease, and I think that if Joe had castrated someone, that person would be in a hospital, and Joe would be in jail! During Josh's secret visit to see her, she kept telling him she had scars from the abortion that Paul supposedly performed. Josh actually talked her into going to a gynecologist for a checkup. Josh went with her, and sat in the reception area. He doesn't remember, and we don't know which doctor she saw, but it was a doctor of her choosing. The doctor told her she had no scarring whatsoever, and her only comment to that was, "The doctor is in a conspiracy to discredit me."

During our visit, Josh told us how ashamed he had felt about accusing Paul. He also confessed that when I had dropped by Lori's apartment with her mail and the note telling her how I felt, he was there and had been in the apartment asleep. When he got up, she showed him the note and then burned it and laughed at the pain she perceived she was causing me. She then took Josh to Don and Rebecca's and again laughed as she told the story. Josh said the meanness of her attitude and the things she said made him so sick he had to go in the bathroom for about 10 minutes so he wouldn't have to listen to her. He said he debated over and over with himself whether to come see us at that time. He said he was sorry he had not. I am too. He saved a piece of the burnt note that he showed me.

He told us after his trip to see Lori, he got so depressed that all he could do was lie around on the sofa all day in his bathrobe. He and Elizabeth decided it was time to seek some help. Elizabeth investigated the difference between an MSW, a psychologist and a psychiatrist. From talking to people, she got the impression that the MSW was a qualified therapist. Since there was a cap on their insurance, the MSW's lower fees would make it possible for them to have more sessions and stretch their insurance dollar further. Elizabeth was very concerned about Josh, so they decided they would go together.

When they arrived at her office, the MSW told them that it would not be a good idea to work with both of them at the same time, so she referred Elizabeth to another MSW in the practice. The MSW whom Josh saw told him that if his sister was saying she was abused, he had to believe her. Then she told him if his sister was abused, the chances were that he was abused, too. Josh told her that he didn't want to be hypnotized, so she told him she could use some relaxation techniques—which he did not realize were the same as hypnosis—to help him "remember" if he was abused.

Then she told him that if he dreamed something, or it "popped" into his mind, he should accept it as "fact."

When he went home he became more depressed than before. His usual 4.0 average dropped to a 1.5 and he would have flunked out of school completely, Elizabeth said, if she had not done his work for him that quarter. Josh said that one morning he was lying in bed floating between sleep and wakefulness, and he began to do what the MSW had instructed him to do. He began to think, "If something did happen to me, what would the situation have been, who could have done it, where would I have been at the time?" He said he then slipped into a dream and saw the whole thing laid out like it was showing on a movie screen. He really got depressed then!

By this time, it was Elizabeth's turn to see the MSW she had been assigned to. Since she was so worried about Josh, she wanted guidance from the MSW on how to cope and what she could do to help him. His attitude was really frightening her and she was concerned for his health. She told all this to the MSW who looked her in the eye and said, "This seems to really have upset you; this information must have struck a nerve. YOU were probably sexually abused as a child too, and you just don't remember."

Elizabeth told the woman her parents were divorced when she was very young, and she only saw her father every Sunday afternoon. Because she had perfect recall, she was certain her father had never abused her. The insistent MSW did not want to take this for an answer, so Elizabeth and Josh both terminated their visits. However, at the same time they thought, if people in authority who are supposed to know about these things tell you this is highly probable, then you have to listen to them, don't you? But they just couldn't believe it. They began talking for hours, trying to figure things out, wondering if this could really have happened.

Fortunately, the group they had seen called and said they would each have to schedule appointments with the psychiatrist who headed the group or the insurance would not pay for their visits. When they saw the psychiatrist, he told them it was not necessarily true that either or both of them had been sexually abused as children. This incident shocked both of them back to reality. It was as if someone else in authority had given them permission to again trust their own thoughts and memories.

* * * * * *

A few days after we arrived back home from Josh's, I received my last letter from Lori. She had written it in August but had not mailed it until October. It said:

August 4, 1992

Dear Kathryn,

I have come to assume that you have made yourself unconscious to a lot of things, which I can certainly understand. But one thing that I want you to know is that I realize that you were probably emotionally taken advantage of and somewhat intimidated into the lives that we led. I don't necessarily blame you for the things that happened to us as children, but my understanding of the situation does not mean that I can excuse it or forgive it, or that I can ever love you in spite of it, because I can't. I hope one day you will find some understanding of that.

One other thing I want to tell you is that I have a family now that I love very much. I understand you must feel some distaste for this, but I want you to be aware of it and respect it. My life is full and rich and very happy, and

I want you to leave me alone to live it. I love someone else as my mother now. I don't want you to contact me any more. This is my life now, and you are never going to be a part of it. I wish you well. Good-bye.

Lori

Needless to say, Paul and I were both very upset. I cried all night long. As time passed I began to get angry over it. I was tired of fighting and I just didn't want to have to handle it any more. I wrote a letter right back to her.

October 9, 1992
Lori—
   You got it — you won't hear from me again unless you initiate the communication!
   I am packing up your things and giving them to friends or Goodwill unless I hear that you want something by Oct. 23. After that, they're outta here!
   Good-bye — Good Luck

The real victim,
your Mother

I also wrote a last letter to Rebecca explaining to her all of the crimes that Josh said that Lori claimed we had committed. I also sent her several articles from the FMS Foundation plus their phone number and address. I gave her Dr. A.'s card and told her that he had said he would be glad to talk with her or refer her to another colleague as a third party if she didn't want to talk with him, since he was talking with us. We still have not heard from her, nor has she made contact with Dr. A. I thought surely after she had read of the ludicrous accusations she would be able to see through them and she would call. Then somehow, together, we would get Lori into treatment.

Lori's last letter seemed to have brought both Paul and me full circle emotionally, back to when all of this first started happening. We both became very depressed again. Finally Paul voiced what was bothering him about the letter, and was eating me too—even though the thoughts had not really formed clearly in my mind yet.

He said he just couldn't believe that after all the years Lori had been with us that she didn't know my personality well enough to realize that before I would have let anyone force me into doing anything harmful to my children I would have committed suicide to keep from doing it. He was right, because he knows me well. At any sign of abuse, the first thing I would have done was take the children and go to my parents' house. If it had been a situation where I would not have had that option, I would have put them in the car and just started driving – anywhere. I'm one of those people who doesn't panic in a tight situation. I think clearly; the energy comes from somewhere, and I do what has to be done. I don't fall apart until it is over.

After this soaked in, I really began to be angry. How dare she insinuate that I had been intimidated into allowing such a thing to happen? I was highly insulted for her to pigeonhole me into the "typical" wife of a child abuser. She made me sound as though I were a wimp totally at the mercy of an overbearing man. I strongly resented it! Had she just forgotten all of the times I stood up for her? Were 21 years of my life wasted while I was mothering her? I became angry all over again at everyone who had anything to do with her beliefs.

* * * * * *

We haven't heard from Lori again. I still haven't thrown

out any of her things. Every time the phone rings, I want it to be her. As angry and hurt as Paul and I both are, we still find it hard to just forget about it and go on with day-to-day life. Neither of us has worked in nine months and our savings are just about gone. We have to remind each other that she is mentally ill and the hurt and pain she is causing us is not really coming from our Lori. We love her so much. If we should ever reunite, I don't think the relationship will ever return to what it was. There would always be an issue of trust between us.

However, if she walked in the door today, I would throw my arms around her and all would be forgiven. There would be a living recreation of the "Prodigal Son." Unfortunately it looks like that celebration will be a long time coming – if ever.

Years ago, Lori wrote a song that was my favorite. She wrote it just as she broke up with the young man that she has now gotten back together with and is planning to marry. At the time, she was devastated. She had sat with her dad in the family room one evening, his arms around her, and just cried. I always felt she had written that song to express her feelings about the break-up and as her farewell to the young man. Now, to me, it seems quite prophetic that the ideas in it are the same ones I would express to her if I could talk to her now. The last words in the song are: *Maybe you'll turn around and I'll be there.*

Lori, somehow, if God is willing, Daddy and I will both be there. And, if it doesn't take too long, so will your granddaddy and your great aunt. Please remember, they are old.

We all love you – Mom

Epilogue

My curiosity finally got the better of me and I made an

appointment with Ramona, the psychic, using my first name and my maiden name. I did not want to deceive her, but desperate situations require desperate actions, and I just had to see her. I was a little nervous but not as much as I thought I would be.

When I got to her office she took me in and asked to see a piece of jewelry that I was wearing. She took it and began to turn it around and around in her fingers. She said she kept getting so many messages she was having a hard time zeroing in on any one. She asked me if I was married, saying usually she could tell but for some reason she was picking up too much confusion. Then she said that she saw some trouble in my marriage, something about me wanting to express myself more, have more freedom, and this was causing trouble with my husband. I told her I had no idea what she was talking about, that our kids were grown and my husband and I were closer and had talked more than we had in years. She made a couple of other guesses but came up with nothing correct.

She finally asked if there was anything specific that I wanted to know, saying that if she looked for something specific maybe she could zero in on one of her voices. I told her that I wanted to know why I couldn't lose any weight, and why I had headaches. She said she felt that the headaches were from tension. She then came over and felt my back and said yes, it was definitely from tension. While she was standing there looking at the back of my head, she could see that my hair is not real thick and asked if my hair had been falling out. I said it was thinner now than it was when I was young but I hadn't been aware of it falling out. She asked if I had ever had my thyroid checked. There was a possibility that I had a problem with my thyroid. I said, "Yes, I had it checked and the doctor said there was no problem." "Well, definitely tension," she said.

She then told me she was going to show me a technique that I could use to obtain my own answers when I was at home. She gave me some paper and a pen, and asked me to choose a colored marker out of several colors she had (a color that my inner child would like). She then instructed me to write down a question that she dictated, using my dominant hand. Then she told me to use my non-dominant hand to write down the answers. I guess your non-dominant hand is supposed to have a mind of its own. I now know that this is a popular writing exercise that the "survivor" movement uses. At any rate, I guess the cat had my non-dominant hand that day because I couldn't come up with any answers to her questions. She decided that my inner child was "blocked" so she decided to move on to something else.

She sat down on the sofa and out of the blue she said, "I feel that your weight problem has something to do with sex." I looked at her kind of funny, and she said she thought I was using my weight to hide from something. She didn't know that I take a certain medication to prevent the migraines that causes weight problems!

Then, without missing a beat, she said she felt that my father had been emotionally distant from me when I was a child. I wish I could have played along at this point, but I was so taken aback that I couldn't. I said that my father had always been a kind man. She said, "Well, didn't he kind of keep to himself?" Then she jumped to another subject.

She said she saw me doing a lot of writing and that it would probably be published after the first of the year. I asked her, "What do you mean — like stories?" She said no, she saw it more as journaling. This may be the only thing she got right!

Then she said, "I see a lot of turmoil in your life. Are you sure there is nothing else bothering you?" I told her, "Yes, my daughter and I had a falling out and I was wondering if there would be any chance for reconciliation?" She said she felt that my daughter was just going through some things right now that she had to accomplish on her own. Then you could see the lights go on and Ramona began putting two and two together. She said, "How long have you and your daughter been separated?" I told her. She asked, "What is your daughter's first name?" I told her. Then she asked if I had a son who lived far away, to which I answered in the affirmative. Her tone then changed and she said, "Well, why don't we just get down to business and talk about what you came here to talk about?"

The scene probably could have turned ugly, but I burst out crying hysterically and she immediately softened. She was very kind to me and told me she had not seen Lori in about four months. She also told me of the visit between her, Josh and Lori. She volunteered the information that Josh was the one who had wanted to sue us and that Lori had talked him out of it. This upset me because the story Josh had told was that Lori was the one who wanted to sue. He said that Ramona had advised her not to because at the time Ramona had two people suing her and "it just made you feel more like a victim." I had spent two days in two different counties, before ever seeing Ramona, trying to find records of who was suing her and why. I had come up empty-handed.

This story left me confused, not knowing who to trust. I cried over it for two days and felt like I wanted to melt into nothingness. I suddenly realized that Josh probably felt so bad about the false accusations that he didn't want to add salt to the wound by telling us that he had wanted to sue us.

Before I left Ramona's office I apologized for deceiving her and she told me that it was all right, she understood. She then put her arms around me and hugged me while I cried. This did not cause my feelings to soften toward what she had probably done to destroy our family, but how ironic that this very needed gesture had to come from this woman. No other woman has said to me, "Talk about it, cry about it, I'm here for you." Some don't want to hear and yet, they would expect us to listen to their problems and give them all the encouragement and good wishes in the world. One person told me if we are depressed, it's because we choose to be depressed. We all make choices and we don't have to choose to be depressed.

I thought about this for a while and then I felt awful and hurt about what she said. I wished I had said, "How do I stop thinking about it when every time I hear a song that Lori has sung, I think about her? Every time I go shopping, I find myself saying, 'Lori would have liked that.' I find myself looking at a picture with her in it; I run across a letter that she wrote, or a card, or a gift that she gave me. Maybe I make a dish that was her favorite, or the phone rings, or a movie that she loved is shown on television. How do I forget? How do I prevent the catch in my throat, the tears in my eyes, and the longing? How could I choose to do this?" I wish someone knew.

EMERGING FROM THE DARKNESS

A father said "I woke up in the morning and the sun was shining. After a phone call from my daughter that afternoon, darkness descended and the sun will never shine for me again."

Accusations against parents become increasingly grotesque. They are reaching outward from parents to grandparents, brothers, sisters, uncles, aunts, teachers, family friends, and neighbors.

There is no mercy shown when a supposed perpetrator is identified. The victim of the alleged abuser has been led to accept the righteousness of disclosure, regardless of the consequences. The parents face an immense dilemma. They turn to one another and to scholars who have studied the mind and memory, looking for solace and solutions. They are seeking ways to emerge from the darkness that has descended on their lives.

The Parent's Dilemma

We are fully aware of the widespread occurrence of child abuse, including incest, and believe it to be abhorrent. It is precisely because of the fact that such crimes are horrific that to be wrongly accused of such behavior is the worst thing that can happen to a person.

We believe that most people in the mental health field are reputable, caring and ethical, but those who believe that a psychotherapeutic setting is a proper place to discover "truth," "guilt" or "innocence" are making a huge impact. And they are often wrong! Therapy is a place to discover feelings, attitudes, interpretations, beliefs, not "historical truth." It is not a proper setting for recreating the past in an accurate version; perhaps in a metaphorical sense, but not with certainty that events actually occurred. Furthermore, when a therapist encourages confrontation by the accuser, without allowing any response from the accused, we consider that absolutely unethical, if not malpractice.

When a parent is accused of child abuse, his or her life is changed forever. No matter how he or she has lived life — with dignity, honesty and esteem — it is all gone in a flash. Family members are pitted against one another and forced to take sides. The seeds of suspicion are sown; divorce sometimes occurs; grandparents are forced to choose one side or the other; siblings, as we have seen, are distraught. Aunts, uncles, cousins, friends are often brought into the fray. When they believe the accuser and don't believe the accused, the hurt is multiplied for the parent. An aunt of an accuser might say, "Well, maybe something happened." Imagine how the sister of that woman feels when her closest lifelong relative expresses doubts.

In-laws are particularly on the spot. Often they support the accuser, grateful they are not being accused. Sometimes they will no longer speak to the accused at all. They must show support for the accuser or all contact will be cut off with them. Sometimes the accuser is very convincing and in-laws are protective of them. We know that the accused are convinced that their claims are true, and they often become proselytizers for trauma therapy and the incest survivor movement.

The family who seeks therapy to aid in this problem often finds it difficult to find a professional who understands the issue. Many therapists, having been exposed to the recent literature on sexual abuse and repressed memory therapy and, having attended seminars, are just as likely as not to be adherents. The parent may find himself or herself in a defensive position when seeking understanding from a professional. We know of parents who went for therapy and were subjected to the same mind-altering techniques to which their adult children succumbed. A mother, whose husband was accused of incest, was asked to sign a contract that she would not commit suicide as she underwent therapy. The assumption was that when confronted with "reality" as she came "out of denial," she would be suicidal.

The Legal Issue

The legal profession has proven to be especially prone to the influence of survivor therapists. Once a lawsuit is started it becomes vicious. Many of the lawsuits against parents are settled out of court. The very threat of a lawsuit on a charge of sexually abusing one's child is horrifying. Here's what happens: Many lawyers are willing to take such a case for the accuser, on a contingency, especially when they know that there's much money involved, or if they are strong believers in the incest survivor movement. After the papers are served, they count on a settlement. Rather than be publicly humiliated and suffer through years of litigation and the accompanying embarrassment, hundreds of parents are paying to stay out of court. Many are paying therapy fees for their adult children rather than face a lawsuit and become adversaries of someone they still care about. There is a case of a father being sued for $600,000, estimated by the daughter's attorney to be for 30 years of therapy to overcome the supposed years of terror inflicted upon the daughter by the father. The accuser claims that her father engaged in satanic rituals, invited friends to rape and photograph her, killed her cat. There is no evidence of any abuse. The daughter's lawyer proposed an out of court settlement for $200,000. The father, president of a large firm, was urged by his board members to settle. They were concerned about the impact that adverse publicity would have on their company. This is extortion, plain and simple, and is happening repeatedly.

The floodgates for lawsuits have been opened, with more than 20 states extending the statute of limitations on repressed memory suits. In 1989, Washington was the first state to change the legislation regarding the statute of limitations. Within three years 18 more states enacted similar legislation. Civil suits for damages do not require the same burden of proof as do criminal charges. However, criminal cases are now being pursued in several states.

Elizabeth Loftus, A Memory Expert

"As a consequence, juries are now hearing cases in which plaintiffs are suing their parents, relatives, neighbors, teachers, church members, and others for acts of childhood sexual abuse that allegedly occurred 10, 20, 30, even 40 years earlier," states Elizabeth Loftus, professor of psychology at the University of Washington, who testifies as an expert witness in many court cases (Loftus:520).

On the accuracy of repressed memories Loftus says, "There are those with extreme positions who would like to deny the authenticity of all repressed memories and those who would accept them all as true" (Loftus:524). If some of the memories are true and others are not, the question arises, where do the untrue memories come from? Loftus cites the research of psychiatrist George Ganaway, a specialist in dissociative disorders. "Ganaway (1989) proposed several hypotheses to explain SRA [satanic ritual abuse] memories, and these same ideas are relevant to memories of a repressed past. If not authentic, the memories could be due to fantasies, illusion, or hallucination-mediated screen memories, internally derived as a defense mechanism. Further paraphrasing Ganaway, the SRA memories combine a mixture of borrowed ideas, characters, myths, and accounts from exogenous sources with idiosyncratic internal beliefs. Once activated, the manufactured memories are indistinguishable from factual memories. Inauthentic memories could also be externally derived as a result of unintentional implantation of suggestion by a therapist or other perceived authority figure with whom the client desires a special relationship, interest, or approval" (Loftus:524).

Besides popular incest survivor books and suggestions made by therapists, "The core material for the false memories can be borrowed from the accounts of others who are either known personally or encountered in literature, movies, and television" (Loftus:525). Loftus is considered one of the nation's leading experts on memory and her experiments indicate how relatively easy it is to implant memories in people's minds.

Loftus believes that it is possible that some therapists are suggesting to their clients that they were sexually abused and repressed the memories. She states, "Whatever the good intentions of therapists, the documented examples of rampant suggestion should force us to at least ponder whether some therapists might be suggesting illusory memories to their clients rather than unlocking authentic distant memories. Or, paraphrasing [Richard] Gardner (1992), what is considered to be present in the client's unconscious mind might actually be present solely in the therapist's conscious mind (p. 689)" (Loftus:530).

During a panel discussion at the annual meeting of the American Psychiatric Association (May 1993), Elizabeth Loftus and Judith Herman met head on. Loftus, whose research on memory spans 25 years, argued for caution regarding repressed memories. She said, "Maybe we ought to be more careful in what we're doing to patients and clients. Perhaps the most serious danger of this collaboration to pursue this bottomless pit of trauma memories, some of which may be completely false, is that these activities are bound to trivialize the genuine proven cases of abuse and to increase the suffering of real victims."

Herman was outraged at this suggestion. She attacked Loftus' research, stating, "Highly contrived studies, such as those of Loftus, are only marginally relevant to our understanding of the psychopathology of traumatic memories. Such studies deflect our attention from the already substantial body of knowledge that we do have and do nothing to further our knowledge."

Loftus and Herman epitomize the split in the mental

health professions. Herman sees a backlash against the "consciousness–raising and organizing of the last 20 years" which have given women access to the legal system and the power to "hold perpetrators accountable." Herman attacks the False Memory Syndrome Foundation as perpetrators organized to defend themselves. Although Pamela Freyd, Executive Director of the FMS Foundation, has invited Herman to discuss the research and documentation of the foundation, Herman refuses. Herman is apparently convinced, without seeing the documentation or speaking to parents, that the members of the FMS Foundation are perpetrators. According to her, only about 10 percent could be innocent. She seemingly disregards that number as being insignificant casualties of the war against patriarchy. If the number of perpetrators is in the millions, as the incest survivor movement would have us believe, even the low number of 10 percent falsely accused is a lot of people. Herman and the other proponents of trauma therapy show no mercy for those who, by their own calculations number hundreds of thousands, are falsely accused on the basis of repressed memories.

NOW Mobilizes Against Patriarchy

The National Organization for Women (NOW) has mobilized its extensive legal resources in the effort to extend the statute of limitations to allow women who have recovered "memories" of incest, decades later during therapy, to sue their families. The position of NOW regarding incest as a political movement is apparent in their "Legal Resource Kit" for adult survivors. In the section called "Incest Injury and Discovery: The Facts," it is stated: "Experts have observed that many incest victims repress the memory of the incest in order to cope with repeated abuse. . . . Because many adult victims have blocked the memory of abuse, they have no idea of what happened to them as children. Recall of the abuse may be triggered in adulthood by therapy or other events."

NOW considers legal action against incest perpetrators a part of the war against patriarchy. The organization's literature claims: "Incest within the family is a direct outgrowth of the traditional patriarchal view that women and children are a man's property and that it is a male prerogative to abuse female family members." Lawsuits against offenders are urged because "allowing incest survivors their 'day in court' will empower them and prove to society at large that violent male tyranny over female family members will *not* be tolerated." It goes on to say how feminist attorneys have worked hard to develop a sophisticated legal argument for extending the statute of limitations on incest to include repressed memory cases. NOW has filed amicus curiae (friend of the court) briefs, drawing on what the organization says is exhaustive legal and psychological research. Attorneys who will take these cases are listed by state, and a "publications resource list," which includes *The Courage to Heal*, is provided.

While the accuser has access to the courts, with child abuse or incest accusations, the accused does not. Even though slander or libel may occur, with unverified accusations, it is not possible to sue. The therapist is protected by patient-therapist confidentiality and it is not possible for the parent, or other injured person to sue, since the adult child makes the accusations and the therapist claims to be merely the facilitator or conduit. A malpractice suit can take place only by the patient against the therapist, not by a third party. So a person's reputation can be ruined with impunity. There have yet to be cases of parents suing their adult children for slander. It would be almost impossible to find a lawyer to take such a case since there is usually no "deep pocket."

False Memory Syndrome Foundation

The False Memory Syndrome Foundation opened its offices in Philadelphia in March 1992. This organization is made up of parents and mental health professionals. It has as its goals collecting data about false memories of adult children that emerged in therapy, informing professionals and the media, and helping parents. Pamela Freyd, a research associate at the University of Pennsylvania is the foundation's director.

The phone rings constantly with family members who thought they were alone with an unbelievable dilemma: How do you answer charges coming from a repressed memory, with no evidence other than the validation of a therapist who uses the power of suggestion to retrieve memories?

A Landmark Meeting

In April 1993, more than 600 people – accused parents, their families and friends, mental health professionals, the press – assembled at the Valley Forge Convention Center, near Philadelphia to share information about their experiences and gain knowledge about the mind and memory from some of the world's most renowned experts in the field.

It was a landmark meeting, and energy and excitement permeated the atmosphere. Parents confronted with grotesque accusations found they were not alone, but rather part of a major social and political movement sweeping the English–speaking world. They discussed how their beloved children are deluded; becoming cruel enough to confront, condemn and crucify their parents. It seemed like a "can you top this" in horror stories: deathbed confrontations outlining stories of rape; public meetings accusing parents of incest; telling grandchildren that their grandparents were evil and denying all visitation privileges; lawsuits for millions of dollars; vicious letters written to friends and relatives; restraining orders against parents.

Parents are stunned. They were at the conference to try to find out what is happening to their adult children. Professionals, including some of the nation's leading psychiatrists and memory experts, were there to try to provide some understanding.

The Crisis in Mental Health

"The most significant mental health error of the twentieth century has resulted in a malpractice epidemic by psychotherapists using techniques of interpersonal persuasion and influence," stated Richard Ofshe, professor of sociology at the University of California at Berkeley. Ofshe explained the suggestive and manipulative techniques used by therapists digging for forgotten memories of childhood sexual abuse. Clients readily believe that what therapists are telling them is true, because of their credentials and aura of professionalism. Therapists make three basic claims, all unfounded, to explain what Ofshe calls "robust repression," that is, repressing the memories of multiple events over a period of years. The three unproven assumptions which lead clients to believe their pseudomemories are real are: (1) This is how the mind works; (2) medical science has established definite symptoms which indicate sexual abuse; (3) there is a proven method of healing. Ofshe said recovered memory therapy is based on pseudoscience because this type of therapy is founded on the erroneous belief that robust repression is a scientific fact. Instead, robust repression is simply a "rumor" which became well established in the psychotherapy community through pop culture paperbacks.

Once convinced that the therapist's diagnosis of robust repression of childhood sexual abuse is correct, the long healing process – Ofshe calls it "ritual magic" – begins. Ofshe said that it is the hypnotic and social influence procedures which create the "memories." A memory re-called in therapy seems real because it is actually the memory of telling the story that becomes the "memory" of the long-forgotten abuse.

Psychologist Margaret Singer, a therapist for 50 years, is concerned with the zealous beliefs of the therapists that help create pseudomemories. Singer said that many thera-pists attend seminars for continuing education credits and learn questionable techniques and beliefs which influence their therapy methods. She believes that the goal of psy-chotherapy has been lost. Rather than help clients work toward the goal of becoming independent, self-confident, responsible and mature, many therapists purposely seek to keep their clients dependent on the therapist. Rather than working toward mental stability, these therapists seek to keep clients in a constant rage. Instead of trying to help patients, it has become common for therapists to try to make clients dependent, long-term customers.

Singer stated, "This is not the proper practice of psycho-therapy in any form. As a trained therapist, I was never taught to be an authoritarian person; to put my political and religious views on others; to bring people's families in and humiliate them in confrontational attacks as part of their daughter's therapy; or to tell people that they can never say no to their therapist. We are now hearing about people who are being made into the politicized agents of their therapist. They are being recycled in therapy to go out as parent abusers. . . . I feel very embarrassed that a healing profession could have strayed so far since Hippocrates declared, 'Do not harm the patient.'"

Social scientist Robyn Dawes also emphasized the role of ideological bias as a key factor in leading therapy clients to believe in memories which are not real. According to Dawes, what happens to a patient in therapy is that she begins to trust the therapist and eventually discards her own beliefs for those of the therapist.

Psychiatrist Martin Orne, one of the nation's leading experts on hypnosis, claimed that the combination of trust in the therapist, the expectation for positive changes resulting from therapy, and the lowering of critical judgement on the part of the patient lead to a belief that memories are real even though they might not be.

Memory Experiments

Psychologist Campbell Perry said, "There has been considerable experimental research on the effects of hypnosis and memory." On the basis of this research, "One can conclude that the three main effects of hypnosis upon memory are: (1) Hypnosis increases productivity, but most of the new material is error (in the language of experimentalists) or confabulation (in the language of clinicians); (2) Hypnosis increases confidence for both correct and incorrect information; (3) These effects are not confined to high hypnotizables; medium and low susceptibles are also vulnerable to increased error and increased confidence when hypnosis is introduced as a method of memory enhancement."

Psychologist Ulric Neisser has conducted memory experiments that demonstrate the many widely held misconceptions about the nature of memory. "It is possible to have vivid recollections of things that never occurred. Once those recollections are established, they become difficult to change." Neisser said, "This can happen without any outside suggestion at all. It is far more likely, I think, in the suggestive context of psychotherapy." On repressed memories, Neisser stated, "Many allegations of abuse are not restricted to single incidents. It is often claimed that certain things happened over and over again, perhaps for years, before being repressed out of consciousness. So far as I know, 'robust' repression of this kind has never been convincingly documented. Everything we know about memory suggests the opposite: the more often something happens, the more likely it is to be remembered. Many women have experienced repeated sexual abuse; my guess is that most of them have neither forgotten nor repressed it. On the contrary, they remember it all too well."

Body Memories

Researcher and author Susan Smith spent 10 years teaching, speaking and writing about the sociological, psychological, political and interpersonal dynamics of random and known assailant violence and rape, family violence, incest, the psychology of the offender and the coping skills and characteristics of survivors. In a presentation titled "Body Memories and Other Pseudoscientific Notions of Survivor Psychology," she reported the results of her survey involving 38 therapists specializing in sexual abuse recovery. Smith said, "One of the most commonly used theories to support the ideology of 'repressed memories' or 'incest and sexual abuse amnesia' is the notion of 'body memories.' Body memories are thought to literally be emotional, kinesthetic or chemical recordings stored at the cellular level and retrievable by returning to or recreating the chemical, emotional or kinesthetic conditions under which the memory recordings are filed. The theory of body memories is a fascinating example of a seemingly logical theory that is not only mistaken, it is dangerously coercive. . . . Misguided and unethical therapists use the 'body memory' theory to manufacture 'evidence' of sexual abuse and traumatic memories where none exists. When the therapist interprets flushing, hives, rashes, headaches, stomachaches and other physiological sensations of stress and emotional arousal as signs or forms of 'memory' during counseling sessions, hypnosis or groups, the notion of 'body memories' becomes a means of indoctrination into 'survivor logic.' " Smith found that many therapists vehemently oppose questioning the legitimacy of techniques used in recovered memory therapy. "Recovery psychologists deflect criticism by projecting that the motives behind reasonable inquiry or outright disagreements are the products of a 'sick' individual or a 'diseased' way of thinking. Survivor psychologists deflect scrutiny, questions and criticisms by chastising the dissenters and claiming that they have 'unresolved issues' or are 'in denial.' It has become so politically incorrect to challenge the cherished (but debunked) psychoanalytical notions or medieval superstitions that have resurfaced in survivor psychology, that questioning the wisdom of exaggerating, over-estimating and simply fabricating 'statistics' of addiction, child abuse, incest, demonic possession and maladjustment makes one a suspected 'supporter' of evil doings or of a 'sick society.' "

Smith stated that this anti-scientific attitude, prevalent in the mental health field, creates an atmosphere where

"Mental health practitioners using invasive, coercive and aggressive practices no longer need to consider the consequences of their actions. Unethical 'educational' programs charging exorbitant fees and peddling urban legends and medieval superstitions proliferate unchecked." According to Smith, this situation has come about because "The crux of the problem seems to be hinged on scientific illiteracy, gullibility and a lack of critical thinking skills and reasoning abilities in the mental health community and in society at large."

Psychiatric Mistakes

Paul McHugh, Chairman of the Department of Psychiatry and Behavioral Sciences at Johns Hopkins University, told of a history of psychiatric mistakes leading to misdiagnoses. When the mistake is eventually discovered a patient needs treatment for the misdiagnosis as well as for the original neurosis. McHugh described the cycle of hysterical epidemics, incorporating the influences of medical diagnostic authority with patient compliance in an atmosphere of prevailing social trends, supported by "proof" provided by a group with the same diagnosis. McHugh is appalled that mental health professionals would determine a diagnosis of repressed memories of incest and begin a therapeutic program based on that diagnosis without any attempt at corroboration. Yet, this has become acceptable among therapists practicing recovered memory therapy. He stated: "To treat for repressed memories without any attempt at external validation is malpractice, pure and simple."

Clinical psychiatrist Fred Frankel discussed how the diagnosis of Multiple Personality Disorder (MPD) has reached epidemic proportions among segments of the mental health community. Frankel claimed that MPD is largely the creation of two sensational stories — *Sybil* and *Three Faces of Eve*. The feminist movement and new interpretations about the lasting effects of childhood trauma helped narrow the gaze of psychiatry since 1980.

Frankel stated that the literature on MPD, which supports the connection between severe childhood trauma and MPD, needs to be reexamined. Claims that the cause of MPD is always some type of traumatic childhood abuse is based solely on accounts from patients who were hypnotized or given sodium amytal. There is no mention in the literature of any attempts to corroborate patients' claims.

Contaminating Memories

George Ganaway, a clinical psychiatrist and director of the Ridgeview Center for Dissociative Disorders in Atlanta, has been working for the past decade with patients who claim to have multiple personalities. Ganaway has treated many female patients who claim to have been abused during satanic rituals. He is critical of the type of psychotherapy which links MPD to satanic ritual abuse and other uncorroborated reports of "repressed" childhood trauma. Ganaway summarized his concerns by quoting from a paper he recently published in the journal *Dissociation*.

"There is a dangerous trend among many psychotherapists to assume that alleged perpetrators are guilty until proven otherwise, and to accept dreams and hypnotically recovered trauma memories *prima facie* as factual accounts, rather than viewing them as the primary process productions that they actually are, subject to condensation, displacement, distortion and elaborative fantasy. If a patient is encouraged to 'go public' with accusations as a soul–cleansing, healing experience, naming his or her parents as high priests and priestesses of a satanic cult (often feeling fully validated by the therapist), only to discover later through further exploration or outside corroborative efforts that these memories are *not* true, irreparable damage will have been done to the accused. Equally as tragic, however, somewhere inside the patient's mind a part of him or her will have known this all along, and eventually will have to deal with the guilt, shame, and rage associated with the realization that he or she has allowed himself or herself to be exploited in the service of seeking acceptance, approval and caretaking from an identified parent surrogate (the therapist).

"Clinicians in this field have a mandate to approach patients cautiously and prudently with respect to the handling of uncorroborated spontaneous trauma memories, and most certainly to avoid contaminating the therapy by introducing any exogenous material that might artificially invoke false memory responses. Anything less than this ignores the sacred dictum, *primum non nocere* (first, do no harm)."

Satanic Cults – A Contemporary Legend

Thousands of psychotherapists believe they have patients who have survived violent sexual abuse at the hands of a secret criminal network of Satan-worshippers. Similar stories of bizarre rituals where babies are murdered and eaten and children are raped and brainwashed have spread across the United States and Canada. Sociologist Jeffrey Victor has investigated the origins of these stories, which are based on the reports of psychotherapy patients. Victor stated, "These testimonials of Satanic ritual abuse cannot be fully understood unless they are placed in their broader social context, because they are not simply products of the personal fantasies of mentally disturbed individuals. These testimonial stories are a product of a collective behavior process, termed a contemporary legend."

Because stories of satanic ritual abuse are "manufactured in the social interaction between believing psychotherapists and their highly suggestible clients," mental health organizations are instrumental in "validating" and marketing these stories. According to Victor, "The main organization which is disseminating claims about ritual abuse to mental health professionals is the International Society for the Study of Multiple Personality and Dissociation." This organization holds regular conferences where training seminars for therapists are offered. "These ritual abuse training seminars present elaborate claims, without any scientifically verifiable evidence and without cross-examining scientific skepticism about the claims. Some of the most prominent psychiatrists specialized in the study of MPD are 'believers' in the Satanic cult conspiracy explanation of the disorder."

Victor said that various child protection organizations also sponsor conferences and seminars to offer social workers special training in the detection of satanic ritual abuse survivors. Victor claimed, "Many of the training workshops on ritual abuse are now co-sponsored by feminist groups concerned with sexual aggression." A number of law enforcement "experts" on satanic crimes also conduct workshops across the country. "Several universities sponsor regularly scheduled law enforcement training programs on Satanic cult ritualistic crimes. Police from around the country can attend these training programs. For the cost of several hundred dollars, they can bring back to their communities, new 'expertise' in the investigation of Satanic cult crime legitimated by university training."

Victor claimed that different professional or ideological groups use the satanic ritual abuse stories for various reasons: to further their careers; to justify their religious beliefs; to make money; to provide sensational entertainment for television talk shows. Unlike many contemporary legends, Victor stated, "The Satanic cult scare and claims about ritual abuse will not soon or suddenly disappear. This contemporary legend has become highly institutionalized and I expect that it will continue for at least another decade. No scientific research; no educational campaign; no political lobby effort will, in itself, bring it to an early end. Yet, all of these things must be done."

Did the Crimes Occur?

Randy Emon is a police officer in southern California. For several years, Emon investigated claims of satanic cults. He appeared in training films to help law enforcement officers identify satanic crimes. Emon, like hundreds of other police officers, believed in a powerful, secret network of Satanists, based on reports of adult survivors who recovered bizarre memories in therapy. He recently came to the conclusion that he had been misled in his beliefs. After years of investigation failed to turn up any evidence of satanic crimes, Emon and two colleagues became convinced that they were wrong and are now speaking out against the hysteria they helped to create.

The Suspension of Common Sense

Professor Henry Gleitman, who has taught general psychology to undergraduates at the University of Pennsylvania for many years, explained that certain notions about memory and childhood are widely believed but are not necessarily true, merely assumptions. "These are assumptions that have crept into our everyday notions as Americans, as citizens and indeed as psychologists, and that I, I am sad to say, as a teacher and writer about general psychology, may well have helped to perpetuate. If for no other reason than by not emphatically and vehemently saying these are assumptions. Many of them are probably wrong and none of them are definite truths. Far, far from it. What I want to now state is that these assumptions are just that — assumptions." The assumptions are:

1. "Memory is permanent and that the only problem about memory is getting to it." Gleitman said this is a widely held belief that is likely false because many events are forgotten, never to be retrieved. This results in memory gaps which everyone at one time has filled in with stories which are not real but become part of memory simply from repetition.

2. "There are special sure-fire ways of getting to that memory. Difficult ones, but sure-fire even so. And the further belief that one of those sure-fire ways is hypnosis." This assumption has been proven to be false.

3. "Memories can be repressed, so to speak, inhibited, pushed down, kicked out of consciousness for various emotional reasons. And that this inhibition, this repression can later be lifted and that once the repression is removed, the memory is there. Beautifully intact in its original form." Gleitman pointed out that this assumption was based on an early theory developed by Sigmund Freud. Freud later discounted this belief. Gleitman wonders "why anyone would accept primitive, early Freud rather than the later one." For repression to work like many people claim goes against everything that is known about memory because even things we "remember" become distorted over time.

4. "If you think you remember something, then it actual-

ly happened." Gleitman said that various external stimuli cause memories to become reconstructed to a point where "the story we tell ourselves will then become a memory. It is a memory of a story rather than a memory of the actual event." When you add the elements of suggestion and leading questions to this confusion, it is extremely improbable that the resulting memory will be a real memory. "Now, suppose that you add not one leading question, but many, plus the tremendous power of a therapist. I mean, after all, therapists are on your side. They are trying to make you better. You are paying them to make you better. And various support groups may support that. We finally add that most powerful device for suggestion yet designed, namely hypnosis. You now put all of these things together and you can create all sorts of supposed memories."

5. "The more confident people are that something happened the more likely it is that it actually happened." This seems reasonable in most cases, but Gleitman warned of an important exception: "Confidence and real memory do go together under most circumstances. But there is one fascinating exception and that is hypnosis. What hypnosis does powerfully is to increase people's confidence in their memories without increasing their actual ability to remember."

6. "The widely accepted belief in this society in the total all-importance of early childhood." This assumption has never been proven but, like many assumptions, is taken on faith. Other stages of life — later childhood, teen-age years, the twenties — might be equally as important. Why believe that one stage of life is more important than any other stage?

Gleitman stated that believers in repressed memories claim that while regular memories may change over time, this is not true of repressed memories. "Repressed memories behave differently, in their own way. Well, what that whole line of arguing amounts to saying is that no matter what evidence you muster, there's always a way out, for these alleged memories, these supposedly repressed memories, are said to be somehow special and behave differently from all other memories. They return in their original form, once the repression is lifted, no matter what laboratory studies say about other memories. No matter what experts on memory or hypnosis conclude on the basis of evidence."

Gleitman provided a fitting summary of this three-day conference: "I would like to say to my students as I would like to say to the American public, for Heavens sakes, go back to one of the things that is most appealing about the American way of looking at the world. Sort of the Yankee way of looking at things, that said: 'Show me!' 'Prove it!'

I would like to combat what I believe has come to pass throughout quite a few years, perhaps decades. What I can only call the *Suspension of Common Sense*."

References

Armstrong, Louise. 1978. *Kiss Daddy Goodnight.* New York: Pocket Books.

Atler, Marilyn Van Derbur. 1991. "A Story of Hope" (videotape).

Bass, Ellen and Davis, Laura. 1988. *The Courage to Heal.* New York: Harper & Row.

Blume, E. Sue. 1990. *Secret Survivors.* New York: Ballantine Books.

Brady, Katherine. 1979. *Father's Day: A True Story of Incest.* New York: Dell.

Britton, A.G. 1992. "The Terrible Truth." *Self,* October: 188-193, 200, 202.

Bradshaw, John. 1992. "Incest: When You Wonder If It Happened to You." *Lear's,* August: 43-44.

Brownmiller, Susan. 1975. *Against Our Will: Men, Women and Rape.* New York: Simon and Schuster.

Butler, Sandra. 1978. *Conspiracy of Silence: The Trauma of Incest.* New York: Bantam Books.

Courtois, Christine. 1992. "The Memory Retrieval Process in Incest Survivor Therapy." *Journal of Child Sexual Abuse,* 1(1): 15-29.

Darnton, Nina. 1991. "The Pain of the Last Taboo." *Newsweek,* October 7: 70-72.

Davis, Laura. 1990. *The Courage to Heal Workbook.* New York: Harper & Row.

Davis, Laura. 1991. *Allies in Healing.* New York: HarperCollins.

Dawes, Robyn. 1992. "Why Believe That for Which There Is No Good Evidence?" *Issues in Child Abuse Accusations,* Fall: 214-218.

Dawes, Robyn. 1993. "Systematic Biases in Retrospective Memory and Judgment." Presented at the False Memory Syndrome Foundation Conference, *Memory and Reality: Emerging Crisis*, April 16.

Emon, Randy. 1993. "Occult Cop: Police Investigation of Ritual Abuse Accusations." Presented at the False Memory Syndrome Foundation Conference, *Memory and Reality: Emerging Crisis*, April 18.

Fennell, Tom. 1992. "The Satan Factor." *Maclean's*, June 22: 29.

Forward, Susan and Buck, Craig. 1978a. "The Family Crime Nobody Talks About." *Ladies' Home Journal*, November: 116, 120, 122, 233.

Forward, Susan and Buck, Craig. 1978b. *Betrayal of Innocence: Incest and its Devastation.* New York: Penguin Books

Forward, Susan. 1989. *Toxic Parents.* New York: Bantam Books.

Frankel, Fred. "Verification of Recall: A Critique of the Literature." Presented at the False Memory Syndrome Foundation Conference, *Memory and Reality: Emerging Crisis*, April 17.

Fredrickson, Renee. 1992. *Repressed Memories: A Journey to Recovery from Sexual Abuse.* New York: Simon and Schuster.

Ganaway, George. 1989. "Historical Versus Narrative Truth: Clarifying the Role of Exogenous Trauma in the Etiology of MPD and Its Variants." *Dissociation*, 2: 205-220.

Ganaway, George. 1992. "On the Nature of Memories: A Reply to 'A Reply to Ganaway.' " *Dissociation*, 5(2): 121-123.

Ganaway, George. 1993. "Dissociative Disorders: Trauma vs. Conflict and Deficit." Presented at the False Memory Syndrome Foundation Conference, *Memory and Reality: Emerging Crisis*, April 17.

Gardner, Richard. 1992. *True and False Accusations of Child Sex Abuse.* Cresskill, NJ: Creative Therapeutics.

Gleitman, Henry. 1993. "Reflections on Memory." Presented at the False Memory Syndrome Foundation Conference, *Memory and Reality: Emerging Crisis*, April 18.

Herman, Judith Lewis. 1981. *Father-Daughter Incest.* Cambridge, MA: Harvard University Press.

Herman, Judith Lewis and Schatzow, Emily. 1987. "Recovery and Verification of Memories of Childhood Sexual Trauma." *Psychoanalytic Psychology,* 4(1): 1-14.

Larry King Live. "Roseanne and Tom Arnold: A Couple of Survivors" (Sept. 25). Transcript from Journal Graphics, Inc. Denver.

Lew, Mike. 1988. *Victims No Longer.* New York: Harper & Row.

Loftus, Elizabeth. 1993. "The Reality of Repressed Memories." *American Psychologist,* May 1993: 518-537.

Masson, Jeffrey Moussaieff. 1984, 1992. *The Assault on Truth: Freud's Suppression of the Seduction Theory.* New York: HarperCollins.

McHugh, Paul. 1993. "Historical Perspectives on Recovered Memories." Presented at the False Memory Syndrome Foundation Conference, *Memory and Reality: Emerging Crisis*, April 17.

Miller, Alice. 1991. *Breaking Down the Wall of Silence.* New York: Penguin Books.

Neisser, Ulric. 1993. "Memory with a Grain of Salt." Presented at the False Memory Syndrome Foundation Conference, *Memory and Reality: Emerging Crisis*, April 16.

Ofshe, Richard. 1993. "Making Monsters: An American Tragedy." Presented at the False Memory Syndrome Foundation Conference, *Memory and Reality: Emerging Crisis*, April 16.

Ofshe, Richard and Watters, Ethan. 1993. "Making Monsters." *Society,* March/April: 4-16.

Oprah. 1991. "Roseanne & Tom Arnold" (Nov. 8). Transcript from Journal Graphics, Inc. Denver.

Perry, Campbell. 1993. "The Problem of Hypnosis as a Time Machine." Presented at the False Memory Syndrome Foundation Conference, *Memory and Reality: Emerging Crisis*, April 16.

Playboy. 1993. "Playboy Interview: Roseanne & Tom Arnold." June: 59-74.

Rose, Elizabeth S. 1993. "Surviving the Unbelievable: A First-Person Account of Cult Ritual Abuse." *Ms.*, January/February: 40-45.

Rush, Florence. 1980. *The Best Kept Secret: Sexual Abuse of Children.* Englewood Cliffs, N.J.: Prentice-Hall.

Sally Jessy Raphael. 1991. "Roseanne Arnold: I Am an Incest Survivor" (Oct. 10). Transcript from Journal Graphics, Inc. Denver.

Singer, Margaret. 1993. "Therapist Zeal and Pseudomemories." Presented at the False Memory Syndrome Foundation Conference, *Memory and Reality: Emerging Crisis*, April 16.

Smith, Susan. 1993. "Body Memories and Other Pseudoscientific Notions of Survivor Psychology." Presented at the False Memory Syndrome Foundation Conference, *Memory and Reality: Emerging Crisis*, April 16.

Steinem, Gloria. 1992. *Revolution From Within: A Book of Self-Esteem.* Boston: Little, Brown and Company.

Tavris, Carol. 1993. "Beware the Incest-Survivor Machine." *New York Times Book Review,* January 3: 1, 16-17

Vanderbilt, Heidi. 1992. "Incest: A Chilling Report." *Lear's,* February: 49-77.

Victor, Jeffrey. 1993. "The Production, Distribution and Marketing of Ritual Abuse Survivor Stories." Presented at the False Memory Syndrome Foundation Conference, *Memory and Reality: Emerging Crisis*, April 16.

Yudkin, Marcia. 1992. "The Nightmare of Childhood Sexual Abuse: Survivors Speak Out." *Cosmopolitan,* May: 246-249.

Suggested Readings

Books

Baker, Robert. *Hidden Memories*. 1992. Buffalo, NY: Prometheus Books.

Eberle, Paul and Shirley. 1986. *The Politics of Child Abuse*. Secaucus, NJ: Lyle Stuart.

Eberle, Paul and Shirley. 1993. *Abuse of Innocence: The McMartin Preschool Trial*. Buffalo, NY: Prometheus Books.

Gardner, Richard. 1991. *Sex Abuse Hysteria: Salem Witch Trials Revisited*. Cresskill, NJ: Creative Therapeutics.

Gardner, Richard. 1992. *True and False Accusations of Child Sex Abuse*. Cresskill, NJ: Creative Therapeutics.

Goldstein, Eleanor with Farmer, Kevin. 1992. *Confabulations: Creating False Memories, Destroying Families*. Boca Raton, FL: SIRS Books.

Hicks, Robert. 1991. *In Pursuit of Satan: The Police and the Occult*. Buffalo, NY: Prometheus Books.

Hughes, Robert. 1993. *Culture of Complaint: The Fraying of America*. New York: Oxford University Press.

Johnson, George. 1991. *In the Palaces of Memory*. New York: Vintage Books.

Kaminer, Wendy. 1992. *I'm Dysfunctional, You're Dysfunctional*. Reading, MA: Addison-Wesley.

Katz, Stan and Lui, Aimee. 1991. *The Codependency Conspiracy*. New York: Warner Books.

Loftus, Elizabeth and Ketcham, Katherine. 1991. *Witness for the Defense*. New York: St. Martin's Press.

MacLean, Harry. 1993. *Once Upon a Time: A True Story of Memory,*

Murder, and the Law. New York: HarperCollins

Peele, Stanton. 1989. *Diseasing of America*. Boston: Houghton Mifflin.

Richardson, James; Best, Joel; Bromley, David, editors. 1991. *The Satanism Scare*. Hawthorne, NY: Aldine De Gruyter.

Tavris, Carol. 1992. *The Mismeasure of Woman*. New York: Simon & Schuster.

Torrey, E. Fuller. 1992. *Freudian Fraud*. New York: HarperCollins.

Victor, Jeffrey. 1993. *Satanic Panic: The Creation of a Contemporary Legend*. Chicago: Open Court.

Articles
Alexander, David. "Giving the Devil More Than His Due." *The Humanist*, March/April 1990.

Brzustowicz, Richard and Csicsery, George Paul. "The Remembrance of Crimes Past." *Heterodoxy*, Jan. 1993.

Coleman, Lee. "Creating 'Memories' of Sexual Abuse." *Issues in Child Abuse Accusations*, Fall 1992.

Csicsery, George Paul. "Repressed Memories, Ruined Lives." *San Jose Mercury News,* Oct. 11, 1992.

Dawes, Robyn. "Why Believe That for Which There Is No Good Evidence?" *Issues in Child Abuse Accusations*, Fall 1992.

Ganaway, George. "Alternative Hypotheses Regarding Ritual Abuse Memories." Presented at the 1991 Convention of the American Psychological Association, August 19, 1991.

Gardner, Martin. "Notes of a Fringe Watcher." *Skeptical Inquirer,* Summer 1993.

Gardner, Richard. "Modern Witch Hunt—Child Abuse Charges." *Wall Street Journal*, Feb. 22, 1993.

Hanson, Gayle. "Malignant Memories: Therapists As Coaches." *Insight*, May 24, 1993.

Hochman, Gloria. "Prisoners of Memory." *Philadelphia Inquirer*, June 6, 1993.

Lief, Harold. "Psychiatry's Challenge: Defining an Appropriate Therapeutic Role When Child Abuse Is Suspected." *Psychiatric News*, Aug. 21, 1992.

Loftus, Elizabeth. "When a Lie Becomes Memory's Truth: Memory Distortion After Exposure to Misinformation." *Current Directions in Psychological Science*, Aug. 1992.

Loftus, Elizabeth. "The Reality of Repressed Memories." *American Psychologist*, May 1993.

Makin, Kirk. "Memories of Abuse: Real or Imagined?" *Globe and Mail*, July 3, 1993.

McHugh, Paul. "Psychiatric Misadventures." *American Scholar*, Autumn 1992.

Meacham, Andrew. "Presumed Guilty." *Changes*, April 1993.

Nathan, Debbie. "The Ritual Abuse Hoax." *Village Voice*, June 12, 1990.

Nathan, Debbie. "Cry Incest." *Playboy*, Oct. 1992.

Ofshe, Richard and Watters, Ethan. "Making Monsters." *Society*, March/April 1993.

Passantino, Bob and Gretchen. "The Hard Facts About Satanic Ritual Abuse." *Christian Research Journal*, Winter 1992.

Rieff, David. "Victims All?" *Harper's*, Oct.1991.

Safran, Claire. "Dangerous Obsession: The Truth About Repressed Memories." *McCall's*, June 1993.

Salter, Stephanie. "Buried Memories, Broken Families." *San Francisco Examiner*, April 4-9, 1993.

Sauer, Mark and Okerblom, Jim. "Haunting Accusations." *San Diego Union-Tribune*, Sept. 13-15, 1992.

Scanlon, Bill. "Skeptics Question Memories of Incest." *Rocky*

Mountain News, Sept. 13–15, 1992.

Siano, Brian. "All the Babies You Can Eat." *The Humanist*, March/April 1993.

Sifford, Darrell. "When Tales of Sex Abuse Aren't True." *Philadelphia Inquirer*, Jan. 5, 1992.

Taylor, Bill. "What If Sexual Abuse Memories Are Wrong?" *Toronto Star*, May 16, 18, 19, 1992.

Whitley, Glenna. "Abuse of Trust." *D Magazine*, Jan. 1992.

Watters, Ethan. "Doors of Memory." *Mother Jones*, Jan./Feb. 1993.

Victor, Jeffrey. "Satanic Cult 'Survivor' Stories." *Skeptical Inquirer*, Spring 1991.

Newsletters

FMS Foundation Newsletter. FMS Foundation, 3401 Market Street, Suite 130, Philadelphia, PA 19104, (215) 387-1865.

The Retractor. Melody Gavigan, P.O. Box 5012, Reno, NV 89513.

Index

Adult Children of Alcoholics
(ACOA). *See* Twelve-step
groups
Adult survivors, 8-9
and anger, 185-186, 191, 241,
245, 247, 338, 355, 360
confronting the accused, 39,
112, 151, 186-188, 191,
196, 259, 371-373
cutting family ties, 2, 6, 58, 67,
154, 182, 188
partners of, 189-190
personality changes, 36, 93,
153
Against Our Will (Brownmiller),
170
Allies in Healing (Davis),
189-190, 217
Armstrong, Louise, 171
Arnold, Roseanne Barr, 169,
209-211, 464
Arnold, Tom, 209
Assault on Truth, The (Masson),
179
Atler, Marilyn Van Derbur, 169,
207-209, 211
Authorities, 166-169

Barr, Roseanne. *See* Arnold,
Roseanne Barr
Bass, Ellen, 169, 184, 202, 203,
283
Best Kept Secret, The (Rush),
170-71
Betrayal of Innocence (Forward),
172
Blume, E. Sue, 169, 199-203,
213, 333, 465
Body memories, 68, 78, 127, 185,
189, 192, 214, 265, 311-312
494-495

Bradshaw, John, 67, 169, 194,
196, 198, 202, 203, 206,
218, 253, 269, 283, 453,
454, 469
Brady, Katherine, 171
*Breaking Down the Wall of
Silence* (Miller), 218
Britton, A.G., 212
Brownmiller, Susan, 170
Butler, Sandra, 172

Changes, 232
Codependents Anonymous. *See*
Twelve-step groups
Computer bulletin boards,
264-265
Confabulations (Goldstein), 6, 7,
87, 112
Conspiracy of Silence (Butler),
172
Cornerstone, 135
Cosmopolitan, 211-212
Courage to Heal, The (Bass and
Davis), 18, 34, 41, 48, 71,
83, 88, 89, 92, 97, 119, 132,
184-188, 191, 195, 207,
208, 211, 217, 220, 229,
235, 244, 245, 246, 247,
248, 249, 260, 262, 264,
383, 322, 339, 345, 375,
388, 389, 462-464, 489
Courage to Heal Workbook, The
(Davis), 189, 217, 229, 244,
245, 322-323, 326
Courtois, Christine, 169, 192

Davis, Laura, 169, 184, 188-190,
202, 203, 211, 213, 283, 323
Dawes, Robyn, 166-167, 493
Denial. *See* In denial

Dream interpretation.
See Therapy, techniques to
recall memories
Dreams, 16, 29, 49, 192, 267,
319, 351, 391, 472

Emon, Randy, 500

False Memory Syndrome, 6, 69,
99, 114, 125, 157, 232, 233,
280, 285, 303, 330, 331,
341, 424, 465
False Memory Syndrome Founda-
tion, 51, 59, 60, 74, 81, 110,
135, 248, 280, 282, 283,
341, 424, 461, 488, 490
False Memory Syndrome Founda-
tion Conference, 491-503
Father-Daughter Incest
(Herman), 175-179, 191
Father's Days (Brady), 171
Feminism, 7, 65, 168-172,
175-183, 214, 216, 304
Fennell, Tom, 215
Finkelhor, David, 132
Finney, Lynne, 305
Flashbacks, 35, 71, 274, 320, 339,
351, 354, 359, 374, 375, 385
Forward, Susan, 169, 172-175,
195-199, 202, 203
Frankel, Fred, 496-497
Fredrickson, Renee, 169,
203-206
Freud, Sigmund, 175-76,
179-180, 182, 501
Freyd, Pamela, 488, 490

Ganaway, George, 486
Gardner, Richard, 487
Gleitman, Henry, 500-503
Grandparents, accusations
against, 16, 37, 72, 131
Group therapy, 20, 51, 55, 67,
89, 132, 173, 175, 181, 193,

199, 210, 214, 225, 227,
241, 248, 255, 266, 307-
315, 340, 354, 355, 364,
373-376, 389-391, 396, 403,
410
Guided imagery. *See* Therapy,
techniques to recall memories

Herman, Judith, 169, 175-179,
181-183, 184, 191, 195, 197,
213, 487-488
Hypnosis. *See* Therapy, techniques to recall memories

In the Palaces of Memory
(Johnson), 272
In denial, 18, 38, 42, 72, 88, 123,
134, 137, 144, 145, 155, 168,
210, 224, 241, 281, 298, 312,
317, 328, 341, 354, 355, 369,
410, 495
Incest
definitions, 170, 174, 177, 197,
201, 469
feminist interpretation of,
168-184, 489
incidence of, 171, 172, 174,
175, 180, 212, 219
offenders, 172, 173, 174, 175,
208
and psychotherapy, 172-175,
178, 198, 207
as a reason for all problems,
29, 38, 81, 267, 289, 334
statistics, 173, 183, 206, 212,
219, 464
symptoms, 2, 173, 174, 177,
179, 185, 193, 198, 200-201,
203, 212, 246, 287, 333
Incest survivor groups. *See* Group
therapy
Incest survivor movement, 169,
195, 198, 207, 209, 273, 484
Incest survivors. *See* Adult
survivors

Inner child, 34, 35, 42, 67, 122, 185, 194, 195, 217-218, 230, 253, 256, 257, 294, 308, 317, 322, 351, 454

Inpatient treatment, 94, 96, 227-228, 230, 242, 244, 253, 255-261, 275-279, 380, 387, 391, 413, 421

In Pursuit of Satan (Hicks), 135

Institute for Psychological Therapies, 110, 111, 135, 467

Insurance, 8, 228, 231, 253, 263, 288, 379, 401

Johnson, George, 272

Ladies' Home Journal, 172

Lanning, Kenneth, 135, 138

Larry King Live, 210

Lear, Frances, 169

Lear's, 206, 213-214

Legal action, 24-25, 31, 90, 91, 186, 214, 265, 362, 365, 484-486, 489-490

Legal system, 7, 364

Lew, Mike, 190-191, 213

Lief, Harold, 73

Loftus, Elizabeth, 485-487

Maclean's, 215

Masson, Jeffrey, 133, 169, 179-181

McHugh, Paul, 496

McMartin Preschool, 132, 142

Meacham, Andy, 232

Medication, 231, 242, 258, 261, 264, 273, 277, 352, 369, 377, 380, 390, 395, 399, 403, 404, 413

Memories. *See* Body memories; Repressed memories

Memory experiments, 493-494

Miller, Alice, 132, 169, 213, 218

Mind control, 7, 20, 40, 45, 60, 129, 130, 132, 225, 242, 257, 273, 283, 331, 342

Ms., 216-217

Multiple Personality Disorder, 8, 50, 77, 213, 271, 354, 370, 384, 388, 390, 395, 399, 408-410, 414-415, 496-497, 498, 499

National Organization for Women (NOW), 488-489

Neisser, Ulric, 493-494

New Age, 7, 53, 65, 87, 121, 195, 204, 217, 343, 345

New York Times, 183

Newsweek, 211

Ofshe, Richard, 425, 491-492

Oprah, 210, 464

Orne, Martin, 493

Parents
    accusations against, 2, 16, 29, 30, 37, 48, 49, 55, 67, 71, 77, 83, 97, 107, 118, 131, 162, 163, 181, 149, 151, 259, 297, 439
    defense denied, 3, 37, 154, 446, 467
    effects of accusations, 9
    lawsuits against, 24-25, 166, 265
    letters from accuser, 58, 89, 90, 162-164, 199, 259, 355, 431
    letters to accuser, 432-433, 436-438, 439-441, 474

People, 211

Perry, Campbell, 493

Philadelphia Inquirer, 110

Playboy, 210

Post-Traumatic Stress Disorder, 227, 245, 265

Psychiatric hospitals. *See* Inpatient treatment
Psychotherapists. *See* Therapists

Rage work, 241, 245, 255-256, 376
Reach for the Rainbow (Finney), 305-306, 322
Recovery books, 253
Recovery movement, 7, 92, 124, 125, 193-195, 283
Repressed Memories (Fredrickson), 203-206
Repressed memories
  accusations based on, 7, 35, 48, 89, 110, 119, 130, 259
  no attempt to corroborate, 131, 155
  recalled in group therapy, 181, 193, 267, 309, 354, 375
  recalled in therapy, 2, 16, 49, 61, 81, 88, 131, 132, 162, 181, 182, 210, 212, 246-247, 259, 267, 270, 273, 287, 289, 306, 310, 353-354, 436, 448, 486-487
  suggested by therapist, 2, 51, 56, 182, 259, 398, 487
  theories of, 2, 84, 119, 127, 141, 176, 180, 181,184-185, 189, 191, 198, 202, 203, 205, 207, 208, 211, 212, 218-219, 225, 294, 298, 313, 318, 322, 336-337, 502-503
Retractors
  dependent relationship with therapist, 226, 301, 315, 340, 350, 358, 368, 378, 413
  inappropriate relationship with therapist, 225, 298-300
  lawsuits against therapists, 282, 362, 365
  realized memories were false, 232, 248, 279, 330, 340,

361, 384, 385-386, 405
  reasons for entering therapy, 223, 240, 253, 285, 333, 348, 387
Revolution From Within (Steinem), 212-220
Ritual abuse. *See* Satanic ritual abuse
Rush, Florence, 169-171, 176

Sally Jessy Raphael, 210-211, 461
Satanic ritual abuse, 24, 49, 50, 55, 59, 61, 77, 131-145, 201, 205, 213, 214-215, 230, 354, 356, 390, 392, 393, 399, 421, 468, 486, 497-500
Secret Survivors (Blume), 199-203, 333, 334, 339, 345, 465-466
Seduction theory, 175-176, 179-180, 182
Self, 212
Sexual abuse
  attempts to corroborate, 6
  public perception, 1, 154
  social history, 171
  See also Incest
Siblings
  accusations against, 29, 47, 116
  letters from accuser, 18, 57, 100
  letters to accuser, 39-43, 79, 101
  letters to therapists, 131-145
Sifford, Darryl, 73, 110, 248-249, 465
Simpson, Skip, 347, 362
Singer, Margaret, 492-493
Smith, Susan, 494-496
Sodium amytal, 399, 402
Steinem, Gloria, 169, 217-220
Summit, Roland, 132
Sybil, 354, 395, 497

Tavris, Carol, 183
Therapists
  controlling family contact, 18,
    35, 104, 151, 155, 371
  credentials, 40-41, 49, 235,
    262, 288, 388, 407, 471, 495
  encouraging cutting off family
    ties, 2, 6, 22, 35, 88, 197,
    199, 338, 355, 357
  ignoring real memories of
    sexual abuse, 224, 292,
    334-335, 363
  no attempt to verify sexual
    abuse, 131, 155, 247
  refusing to communicate with
    family, 164
  and satanic ritual abuse, 25,
    57, 59, 131-145, 217, 393,
    399, 468
  specializing in incest, 16, 57,
    72, 88, 235, 249, 257, 287,
  suggesting sexual abuse,
    44, 55, 56, 59, 67, 109, 153,
    192, 224, 227, 231, 235,
    241, 243, 254, 259, 261,
    287, 290, 305, 334, 393,
    465, 468, 471, 495
Therapy
  cost of, 152, 249, 308
  and incest survivor books, 35,
    208, 220, 229, 274, 294,

    328, 339, 358
  techniques to recall memories,
    1, 6, 61, 89, 119, 136, 176,
    193, 195, 204, 224, 225,
    246, 270-271, 272, 289-
    290, 305, 311, 316, 320,
    321, 350-351, 377, 402-
    403, 424, 436, 448, 471
Three Faces of Eve, 395, 497
Toxic Parents (Forward),
    195-199, 220
Truth serum, *See* Sodium amytal
Twelve-step groups, 13-14, 15,
    16, 21, 23, 25, 26, 85, 193,
    194, 203, 240, 248, 249,
    253, 266, 267, 268, 383

Van Derbur, Marilyn. *See* Atler,
    Marilyn Van Derbur
Vanderbilt, Heidi, 213
Victims No Longer (Lew),
    190-191
Victor, Jeffrey, 498-500
Visualization. *See* Therapy,
    techniques to recall memories.

Wakefield, Hollida, 467
Watters, Ethan, 425
Winfrey, Oprah, 210